ROUTLEDGE LIBRARY EDITIONS:
AGING

Volume 20

SOCIAL AND MEDICAL PROBLEMS OF THE ELDERLY

SOCIAL AND MEDICAL PROBLEMS OF THE ELDERLY

Fourth Edition

Edited by
KENNETH HAZELL

Routledge
Taylor & Francis Group

LONDON AND NEW YORK

First published in 1960 by Hutchinson & Co (Publishers) Ltd
Revised edition 1965, Third edition 1973, Fourth edition 1976

This edition first published in 2024
by Routledge
4 Park Square, Milton Park, Abingdon, Oxon OX14 4RN

and by Routledge
605 Third Avenue, New York, NY 10158

Routledge is an imprint of the Taylor & Francis Group, an informa business

British Library Cataloguing in Publication Data
A catalogue record for this book is available from the British Library

ISBN: 978-1-032-67433-9 (Set)
ISBN: 978-1-032-72717-2 (Volume 20) (hbk)
ISBN: 978-1-032-72722-6 (Volume 20) (pbk)
ISBN: 978-1-003-41015-7 (Volume 20) (ebk)

DOI: 10.4324/9781003410157

Publisher's Note
The publisher has gone to great lengths to ensure the quality of this reprint but points out that some imperfections in the original copies may be apparent.

Disclaimer
The publisher has made every effort to trace copyright holders and would welcome correspondence from those they have been unable to trace.

Social and Medical Problems of the Elderly

KENNETH HAZELL
FRCPE MRCP DPM MRC Psych
Honorary Consultant Physician in Geriatrics, Colchester

CONTRIBUTORS

K. L. G. NOBBS GM MB BS FRCPE
Consultant Physician in Geriatrics
South and East Birmingham Groups of Hospitals

W. A. HURR SRN SCM RMN

SIR WILLIAM FERGUSON ANDERSON
OBE KStJ MD FRCP
Cargill Professor of Geriatric Medicine
University of Glasgow

E. WOODFORD-WILLIAMS BSc MD FRCP
Director of the National Health Hospital Advisory Service

B. J. CLAMPIN AIHM
Chief Housing Officer, Colchester Borough Council

K. P. O'CALLAGHAN
Assistant Principal, Home Help Services
Essex County Council

HUTCHINSON OF LONDON

Hutchinson & Co (Publishers) Ltd
3 Fitzroy Square, London W1

London Melbourne Sydney Auckland
Wellington Johannesburg and agencies
throughout the world

First published 1960
Revised edition 1965
Third edition 1973
Fourth edition 1976

Printed in Great Britain by litho
by The Anchor Press Ltd,
and bound by Wm Brendon & Son Ltd,
both of Tiptree, Essex

ISBN 0 09 126180 5

'I want length of life and you fear giving me
pain which I care not for; I will be
conquered; I will not capitulate.'

SAMUEL JOHNSON

'Inhumanity like charity begins at home'

ANONYMOUS

CONTENTS

PREFACE TO FOURTH EDITION

Errors in the last edition have been corrected and statistics brought up to date as much as possible, though former statistics have been retained where they still make a valid point.

Society is undergoing a rapid change as the result of technical advances. Because machines now replace hand labour, the number of persons employed in positive production of wealth is a not very large minority: the rest of the population, apart from children up to school-leaving age, retired and/or disabled people, are engaged in 'service' industries. One understands that over 13 million are supported in one way or another by social security. This is the present pattern of society and likely to be so in the future.

The care of the elderly depends on a chain of events, with the working together of groups of persons in differing disciplines. The author is of the opinion that each group should know not only its own particular specialty but also how it fits in with what other groups are trying to accomplish. Though particular attention has been given to geriatric medicine, there are sections on retirement, housing, nursing, the elderly at home, preventive medicine, home help services, together with background statistics of a political and sociological nature.

The health of the elderly can be maintained only by attention to both medical and social factors; reliance on hospitalization investigations and the use of drugs has a limited value. Correct diagnosis in geriatric medicine is, of course, as fundamental as in any other branch of medicine, but does not of itself automatically lead to one line of treatment. This is because an individual assessment of the total physical, mental and social state is required, so that a balance can be struck between the possible advantages and the known risks and disadvantages of any particular treatment.

There is some difficulty in the arranging of the sections in a book of this kind. In a personal interview with the late Lord Beveridge, he persistently stressed the necessity of proper housing of the elderly as the vital base on which to build the medical and social care – and how right subsequent experience has proved him to be. Consequently, after a short section on retirement, I have incorporated one on housing.

I am much indebted to the contributors named on the title-page, each of whom is of recognised standing and writes from considerable knowledge and long practical experience of their subject.

The book is intended to give not only factual information on the subject but also, from the state of affairs outlined, to persuade readers that the basic requirement is a warm-hearted, if not welcoming, attitude to the presence of a large elderly population.

PENSIONABLE RETIREMENT

During the course of their lives persons may retire from various hobbies or pursuits, e.g. football, cricket, rowing, boxing, bridge parties, secretary of clubs, and so on. Usually they do this because they find they have become inefficient or have lost interest. Commonly, they then take up alternative interests without any feeling that they have come to the end of a meaningful life – except for a few ambitious enthusiasts.

But retirement at 65 years for men or 60 years for women from perhaps their lifetime employment is of a different character. Society has, as it were, put them aside from the ordinary workaday life, in which they are not expected to intrude unless in some lowly role.

According to the dictionary, the definition of 'to retire' is: to withdraw, go away, retreat, seek seclusion or shelter, recede, go to bed, become a recluse, be uncommunicative or unsociable. I believe this spells out the general attitude of the public to pensionable retirement and one which the retired persons are expected to accept. For the younger age groups, this philosophy suits them very well since they have so much to gain from the vacancies which are left for them to fill. But they can hardly claim to be forming impartial judgements since they are personally affected, albeit beneficially. The wish is so often father to the thought, and many arguments are put forward for the compulsory retirement of older people. The rising generation claim to be modern, progressive, to have drive and initiative and to be 'with it' on the flimsiest of evidence. One of the best ploys is to alter the rules, the office procedure, the customary ways of dressing, speaking and behaving to emphasise how all is different, that the world is new and requires new and younger people to run it. There is no doubt that scientific and industrial development calls for a much greater adaptation to change; but it still requires a certain amount of human experience to make the right adaptations and not the wrong ones, which certainly youth can so easily do.

If elderly people accept the philosophy of 'putting their feet up and taking life easily', of 'growing old gracefully' (but who would care if they did it disgracefully), of taking no sides in the problems of the day and are seen not to do anything effective, they are not likely to be held in high esteem by their family, friends, or society generally and may well attract an amount of patronising familiarity, a little pity or contempt.

There are over 7½ million elderly persons with women at 65 years having a life expectancy of 16·1 years and men at 65 years of 12·2 years, added to which there is a huge number of retired persons under 65 years. Amongst this number there naturally will be those who indeed are lazy, some in poor health and others who have never had much drive or liveliness and are content to do very little; some, indeed, make themselves a little ridiculous by apeing the young in dress and speech as if they were in their twenties. But there are also millions with expert knowledge, skilled training, and a lifetime's experience in many facets of living, all of which is not being put to any purposeful use. What a personal and national waste! One concludes that this situation really arises because there is not enough gainful employment for all and compulsory retirement is one easy solution. Such a procedure with younger age groups would undoubtedly lead to a violent reaction. Of course, the lot of the elderly is ameliorated if a pension is adequate and they now have millions of votes and can have an effect on political issues. But to date there is no change in the philosophy of always having a vast redundant elderly population.

The continuation of today's outlook is bringing about two classes of citizens, the young and working and the unemployed and elderly, the former with a high standard of living, the latter with an impoverished one, helped by free bus tickets, reduced railway fares, by special beef or other food tickets, meals on wheels, with queuing at every post office for all kinds of subsidies, and special entrance to hospital departments on the discrimination of age. One would hardly forecast a class struggle but an 'apartheid' system is developing. In the last century, the great issue was between the poverty-stricken working class and the privileged middle and upper classes, i.e. the evils of the capitalist system. Things are now different. There is a social injustice of a new kind, in its way causing misery to countless people. There appears to be a need for a treatise, not on 'Das Kapital' but on 'Das Apartheid Geriatric'.

Throughout the 1920s and 1930s, unemployment was complained of bitterly but nevertheless accepted as part of the times, and with what dire results! Similarly, today a pensionable population of millions, many of whom are quite fit, is also tolerated. Each week thousands are added to the list of pensioners; many are experiencing just age prejudice and are by no means the least skilled or more inefficient at their work.

One would like to establish a central theme for pensionable retirement:

(1) It is often a social injustice masking true unemployment and affecting a special class of people.

(2) It is a system very wasteful of human resources.

(3) If pensions were really adequate, would those in work be prepared to forgo a sufficient amount of their wages to pay for them?

(4) 'Sit back and take life easy' is a very bad philosophy both for the individual and the country; it can lead to great apathy by a large section of the community on public affairs of vital importance.

(5) It removes from discussion at 'factory' level the steadying influence of persons with skill, humanity and a lifetime of experience.

Of course a time must come when persons are unfit for full-time employment. Such unfitness can occur suddenly but it is usually of gradual onset. The hope is, therefore, that the structure of employment can be changed so that the older person is offered part-time work according to his capabilities and not automatically paid off when there is overmanning. One thinks of a Rota System where there are alternating periods of employment and unemployment without any being wholly unemployed. This should be less expensive to the community and more acceptable to older people.

RETIREMENT AT A PERSONAL LEVEL

A person naturally knows when he or she is likely to be retired, so preparation for a change in life style should be started many years beforehand. Retired people show enormous variations in the way they live and there is no one procedure that will suit all. However, the aim should be to retain as much freedom as possible, and one of the most important aspects of freedom is freedom of movement, and especially the ability to change house or travel freely so as to keep in touch with relatives, friends and, perhaps, places of interest. Retired persons seem to fall into two main groups:

A. A minority who have sufficient money to drive their own car and own their house; this gives them the ability to move to another neighbourhood if they wish by selling their own house. This group of retired persons can keep in touch with their families and interests, do not become isolated and can make the most of their time, provided they have no infirmity that precludes them from driving.

B. A great majority who have only their social security pension on which to live and have no car. Their freedom of movement is limited to where they can walk, or take buses or trains, both of which are expensive. Further, travel by bus at an older age means hanging about in all weathers, queueing up, fitting in with a time-table, and even so a lot of walking. If, in addition, they are in a council house or are tenants in some other way, their chance of moving house to be near their family or friends is almost nil. On their modest means, they are, therefore, forced to live a very restricted and somewhat isolated life. Thus one sees them queueing at the post office, the bus stops and making tedious journeys on winter days shopping around for the cheapest buys. If, in addition, they have some infirmity, e.g. arthritis or heart failure, getting about is too much and they become house-fast.

Clearly the aim is to belong to Group A if possible so as to have a choice as regards where to live and independence at moving about. It must not be thought that the driver of advanced age is a menace on the road – quite the reverse; most of the accidents arise from youthful drivers and, in any case, the elderly have as much right to the Queen's Highway as anyone else.

ADJUSTMENTS

Retirement implies a new way of life and the making of many adjustments to altered circumstances which are basically of two kinds:

(1) Adjustments of a physical nature, e.g. financial matters as regards the maintenance of the house and family, matters of clothing, diet, smoking, drinking, maintenance of club memberships, voluntary work, etc.

(2) Adjustments as regards relationships to people resulting from a change of status likely to affect not only the pensioner directly but the family indirectly, relatives, acquaintances and friends. This adjustment requires both some change in outlook and approach from the pensioner and a helpful and understanding adjustment from other people.

In short, a successful retirement will depend not only on the pensioner but also on the attitude of those who come into contact with him. Thus, apart from the pensioner being informed about some of the problems of retirement, e.g. at a pre-retirement training course, his family and friends should be made aware that they also have a part to play.

FINANCE

During his working life, the person should try to establish a fair level of pension, and not be solely concerned with weekly earnings: further, a pension which takes account of the cost of living and cannot be completely eroded by inflation. At last the social security pension is somewhat protected by being 'indexed' to the cost of living. At least 5 years before retirement age, or 10 years in case there is a lowering of retirement age, he should ascertain (and be supplied with) just what is likely to be his entitlement on retirement. On retirement, in some instances he may find it better to register as unemployed for the first 6 months. Since inflation is likely to be a continuous process, there is the problem of balancing the advantage of buying in advance what is considered necessary against investment for an extra income. It is useful to live for a trial period of a few weeks on what is likely to be the pensionable income.

WHERE TO LIVE

Many have no option in this matter. For those who plan to move house on retirement, plans should be made several years in advance. To move from a large house to a smaller one seems sensible but if the small house does not feel like home, it could be a mistake. A few points should be kept in mind:

(1) Saying goodbye to old friends and acquaintances or to familiar places, sights and sounds, can create a loss never quite replaced. Making new friends at an older age is more difficult.
(2) Relationships are better when those around you have some knowledge of yourself, your occupation and background, and vice versa.
(3) Moving to the seaside only suits some people; travel is restricted to along the coast or inland, and the surrounding society is so often based on retirement or tourism.
(4) Some decide to reside abroad in a sunny climate. The passage of time has shown the advisability of keeping some kind of base in Britain.
(5) If it is decided to live near relatives, it should not be so near as to be 'in each other's pockets'.
(6) It will be important to be able to visit readily the post office, the bank, libraries, shops, etc., and have perhaps deliveries of milk, newspapers, and so on.

LONELINESS

Some of the adjustments required arise not so much from retirement as from advancing age – and thus become apparent on retirement. Nature has so arranged matters that young men and women have a mutual attraction towards each other; society and the coming together of people is largely based on this fact, fundamentally a matter of sex in its broadest sense. A person 15 years older than the group does not naturally fit in. At pensionable age, the woman has long since passed the childbearing age, and the man rarely retains a great amount of masculine attraction. Thus it is that the old and the young do not easily form part of one social group. Unfortunately, many elderly men do not enjoy the company of elderly women and vice versa; at advanced ages there seems a tendency for men and women to keep to groups of their own sex. Some, indeed, are quite content with their own company or that of a dog, a cat, or reading a book or looking at television. Not all elderly couples end up as mutually affectionate Darbys and Joans. Some develop into the images of Alf Garnett and Moo as seen on television. A person can be lonely in the midst of company because in a way he is isolated from it.

COMPETITIVENESS

At work people usually form part of a team with a common object in view; it is this type of companionship that can be missed on retirement. Mankind is essentially competitive either at work or sport, with the wish to be first rather than last and commonly with the desire that there is some gain or recognition for success. This attitude to life, though perhaps more common in men, continues and should be encouraged to continue into pensionable age. One would therefore suggest that the retired should positively try to form companionship in some common endeavour which will continue to bring out an active approach to life.

CHANGE OF EMPLOYMENT OR INTEREST

Long before retirement, preparation can be made to undertake actively some different form of employment or interest. It is unlikely that the older person can compete physically with the younger, but in the realm of art, music, painting, drawing, writing, photography, crafts, politics, inventiveness and many other subjects, he or she may find a hidden talent. It is not so much as a duty to contribute to society – this has already been done over a lifetime – but to have as full a life as possible. Further places for adult education would no doubt help in these endeavours. At the same time, it should be possible to take more interest in the family, the grand-children, friends and neighbours.

It is not possible to touch on all the facets of retirement but, to sum up, it should be approached as challenging and not a situation to be accepted passively. This attitude is better for the individual in particular and for society in general. If decisions involving some risks or discomfort are not taken, the alternative is a flat apathetic kind of life.

HOUSING FOR ELDERLY PERSONS

B. J. CLAMPIN, A.I.H.M.
Chief Housing Officer
Colchester Borough Council

Although Local Authorities have been building houses since the end of World War I, only a small amount of accommodation for elderly people was provided in the inter-war years. This consisted largely of flats or bungalows which simply provided smaller accommodation than the ordinary dwelling house.

The housing programme after the end of World War II obviously again concentrated on building family houses but, in the nineteen fifties, considerable thought was given to the sort of dwellings which ought to be provided for elderly persons to enable them to live independently without being left entirely on their own. In 1958, the then Ministry of Housing & Local Government published the first of their booklets on this matter, entitled 'Flatlets for Old People', which encouraged Local Authorities to build specifically designed blocks of flats which would have a warden either resident in the block, or living close at hand, on whom the tenants could call in case of need. A few Local Authorities had already experimented with this form of housing for the elderly and, as a result of their representations to the Government, certain relaxations had been granted regarding the standards laid down for the provisions of bathrooms and W.C.s which made the planning of the blocks simpler and more economic.

At the time the booklet was published, it was estimated that nearly one-eighth of the population was over 65 years old. Since that time the proportion has increased to one-sixth. It is also a fact that a large proportion of this number are widows or widowers, i.e. single persons and not couples living together under one roof, and no doubt for this reason the booklet concentrated on the building of bed-sitter flats for the single elderly, with only a small provision for the self-contained 1 bedroom flats for couples. Experience had, in fact, already shown that there is a marked reluctance among couples to move into sheltered accommodation – while they have each other, they appear to manage reasonably well. However, the recommendations went much further than the simple provision of independent accommodation. The desire of elderly people to remain independent is well known, but at the same time, especially following a bereavement, or when the children have moved away from the district, there is an awareness of loneliness, an increasing difficulty of coping with a house and garden as one grows older, and a fear of illness. In some cases, friends, neighbours or relatives provide the answer, but in many instances, often it is admitted due to the attitude of the individual, no such help is available.

These proposed new blocks were designed to provide an attractive alternative, without the loss of independence, for the persons who take up residence. They were not to be hostels and were certainly not to be regarded as a 'home'. With regard to this latter point, residential homes in the nineteen fifties were still regarded as 'infirmaries' or even 'work-houses' by many of the elderly people, doubtless due to the bad reputation which such places had acquired in their day and which lingered in the memories of the old people, from tales told them in their childhood.

Independence was achieved by building self contained bed-sitter flats, with an area of not less than 140 sq. ft. for living and sleeping, and an additional 30–40 sq. ft. for cooking. Some flats were built with cupboard kitchens, but those with a separate small kitchenette were generally preferred and were certainly more popular with the tenants. At that time, it was suggested that both bathrooms and W.C.s should be shared in the ratio of 1 W.C. to two flats and 1 bath to four flats, but most Local Authorities now prefer to provide a W.C. to each bed-sitter, and this can only be considered a very essential necessity. Access to the flat was from a common corridor, and the tenant would normally be provided with a key to the outer door, so that there was no restriction whatsoever on his or her movements. Included in the layout of the block were goods delivery rooms, common rooms, a guest room, laundry rooms and a warden's flat, which was linked to each flat in the block by a bell or speech communication system. The warden would 'live in' and would generally keep a neighbourly eye on the residents, without interfering in their private lives. The tenants would have as much independence as in any other Council dwelling, but would have in addition a common room where they could meet informally or for organised social occasions, the facility to accommodate a guest, but, above all, a point of contact with sources of help, i.e. the warden.

Local Authorities recognised the advantages which such schemes offered, and the financial arrangements were not unattractive. The term sheltered accommodation is now generally used to cover dwellings which are built on these lines and, during the nineteen sixties, most Authorities developed the principles set out in their own way, according to the wishes of their local Councillors and the ideas of their own Architects and Housing Officers.

It is now proposed to consider individual aspects of sheltered accommodation schemes, which are perhaps of prime importance to the success of the scheme.

HEATING

Much attention has been directed in recent years to the adverse effect of cold on the health of elderly people, which, in the case of severe winters, means their very survival. A fact which is often overlooked, however, is that the mere provision of heating facilities is not enough. All too often, where a fatality due to cold has occurred, the means of heating were available but the victim has, for reasons best known to himself, failed to use the coal or light the gas fire, or to use whatever heat was available. With some people, there appears to be a misplaced pride in their ability to withstand the cold, while in others a lifelong regard for economy appears to increase with age.

The 1958 booklet referred to the preference of old people for an open fire. Experience has shown that this supposed preference is a myth. With few exceptions, elderly people are happy to be rid of the daily chores and dirt which an open fire creates. They rapidly learn the benefits which central heating has to offer, and it may well be true to say that watching the television screen, with the all round warmth of central heating, is more beneficial than reliving the past in the glow of the living fire. The increase in the safety factor hardly needs emphasising.

The construction of a block of sheltered accommodation offers the perfect opportunity to install a central heating scheme for the whole building which can be run at a moderate cost. The use of gas or oil-fired boilers, which will run with little attention, enables continuous heat to be provided in all parts of the building and, because it is not under the tenants' control, one can rest assured that they have adequate warmth. Because of the vagaries of the English climate, the heating systems are often kept going at a low rate during the greater part of the summer. This discourages the use of portable electric fires which are a considerable hazard where elderly people are concerned, and are now forbidden in many units for this reason.

A practice adopted by many Local Authorities in blocks of sheltered accommodation is to charge a weekly fixed amount for heating and lighting, which is paid in one sum with the rent and rates. This relieves the tenant of the anxiety of receiving a large bill for fuel and power at the end of each quarter, and also enables the Local Authority to negotiate a more favourable tariff with the Electricity Board.

The most recent blocks are often provided with an emergency generator driven by a petrol engine to provide emergency supplies of electricity in case of power cuts. This enables emergency lighting to be used and for hot water to be pumped round the heating circuit, thus maintaining warmth until the mains supply is restored.

LOCALITY AND ASPECT

The term sheltered accommodation should not be interpreted as meaning that the outside world should be excluded as far as possible. In fact, the reverse is probably nearer the truth. It would, of course, be unthinkable to locate such accommodation overlooking a noisy and busy highway, but a quiet cul-de-sac would be equally objectionable. The ideal site, which of course is rarely available, would be off a moderately busy thoroughfare or village street, near to shops for local needs – post office, grocers, chemist – close to a bus stop, a Church within walking distance, and with the living room windows facing South East or South and towards the area of activity. The last mentioned is probably of prime importance, since many of the tenants will be old, or will become old, and the sight of an active area will help to keep an active mind.

Where possible, large housing estates should be avoided. These tend to attract that modern miscreant, the young vandal, to whom sheltered accommodation is a fair target and can drive both the warden and tenants to a point of despair.

Often, of course, a compromise has to be reached but care must be taken to avoid a completely secluded location.

COMMUNICATION SYSTEMS

In recent years, there have been tremendous advances in the field of electronics which can be utilised to make communication between the tenant and the warden so much easier. Yet, even today, some bell systems are being installed which, to say the least, are archaic in conception. For only a comparatively small amount of extra expenditure, a two-way speech communication system can be provided; the terminal box at the warden's end can be such that it may be carried about by the warden, and plugged in at pre-selected points in the building so that she is capable of being contacted wherever she happens to be in the building.

The advantages of two-way speech over the bell system are overwhelming. The warden can ascertain the reason for the call, whether she need visit the tenant or, if necessary, adjust the apparatus so that she can listen in to a sick tenant. The system can be abused, of course, with unnecessary calls such as to ask the correct time, or calls by visiting inquisitive children, but a good warden will soon establish with her tenants the right way to use the system so that both parties may benefit.

THE ROLE OF THE WARDEN

When sheltered schemes were first introduced, no one was quite sure exactly what the warden was expected to do. Certainly she would keep a neighbourly eye on the tenants, she would ensure that the heating and lighting worked, she would keep records of tenants' next of kin and of the names of the doctors with whom they were registered. She would see that the communal rooms were kept clean, sometimes with assistance, sometimes without, and she would take bookings for the guest room. She was not required to do any domestic work for tenants, nor to cook for them or to nurse them in case of illness, but she would summon help from the Social Services, from Doctors or relatives when needed. Generally speaking, she was given a rent free flat and often free lighting and heating, and paid a wage which took those 'perks' into account.

I think it was sometimes forgotten that the warden would be a normal human being and that, however dedicated, she would like some life of her own. She would have her own shopping to do, would wish to visit her own friends and them to visit her; often, indeed, would have her own family to look after for, in practice, wardens were drawn from all walks of life, and from age groups varying from the mid-twenties to the late fifties or early sixties.

Gradually, however, a pattern has evolved over the years and each Local Authority made its own rules and concessions, so that in most cases a pleasant atmosphere prevailed. The reorganisation of Local Government in April 1974, and the merging of several Authorities into one administrative machine, produced problems which at the time of writing are still being sorted out. Standardisation of wages, rates and service conditions has proved no simple matter when the units concerned had run for years according to the desires of the individual Authority, and the individual wardens took a great pride in the way they ran their units. However, reorganisation necessitated change in the interest of efficiency and the patterns will have to be redrawn.

The main role of the warden will, however, remain – that of being the contact point between the tenants and the various services which are available. How, then, does she maintain contact with the tenants under her charge? She is not a hospital matron and the atmosphere of independence is most important to maintain. Some Authorities insist on the warden making a daily round to chat for a few minutes with each tenant, others call up the tenants on the intercom, while some leave it to the warden to keep discreetly in the background but alert to their activities. Tenants really don't seem to mind very much how the warden works. They soon settle into the adopted routine and accept it in the same way as they accept a news bulletin on the radio. It is important, however, that a relationship should be established, that she should know the tenants' eccentricities, their worries and their requirements. I think it is at this point that a warden runs into difficulties. How far should she get involved, how far can she avoid getting involved, and how far will the involvement with one tenant affect her relationship with the other tenants? It must be remembered that the warden lives in, usually in the same block as the tenants, she does not in practice come on and off duty as does a hospital nurse, and she has had no specific training in the job. A warden who gets too involved with tenants will find this disastrous within a few weeks, but the path between maintaining an interest and becoming involved is a very tricky one to negotiate.

Tenants, too, can become very demanding and unreasonable, and those who tend to treat the warden as an unpaid personal servant must be dealt with firmly and quickly. Generally, though, tenants appreciate the service offered but, with increasing age and gradual decline in their own abilities, wardens can not only find that their work load is building up to impossible proportions, but that it can only be reduced by discontinuing a number of small but very essential services upon which tenants have come to depend. Many wardens will build up within their units a system of voluntary help between the less active and the more active tenants, and the importance of trying to maintain a balance between such types cannot be over-emphasised. A warden who finds that she has a preponderance of tenants who can only just look after themselves is in an impossible position, which can only worsen as the tenants age and become less active.

The support which a warden obtains from the Medical Authorities, Social Services, Voluntary Services and tenants' relatives, can vary to an alarming degree. Furthermore, and this is not meant to be a criticism of the Social Services Department, it appears that, owing to the heavy demands on their time, priority is often given to persons not in sheltered accommodation on the grounds that the latter have a warden.

Wardens often express the opinion that their tenants obtain less priority for removal to hospital, or are discharged from hospital too quickly simply because it is felt that the warden can provide support services.

The new Area Health Authorities can do much to dispel the idea that seems to exist in certain quarters that sheltered accommodation is a form of Local Authority Nursing Home, that the Social Services Department can respond to any call from the warden for nursing or other assistance, or that medical assistance is part of the wardens' duties.

So far as relatives of tenants are concerned, most wardens find these to be a most unpredictable source of assistance. The hearty, once every six months' visit, with a bunch of flowers for both tenant and warden, a shower of compliments about 'the wonderful place you've got here, keep up the good work, she'll live to be a hundred, thanks to you', will often produce complete indifference when the warden calls for help in between visits. 'You are paid to look after her' is a reaction which is not unknown. Local Authorities can help here by ensuring that both tenants and relatives are made aware of the responsibilities of the warden, but even where this is done, it is not unknown for tenants or relatives completely to ignore the true facts. Many relatives, of course, appreciate the real position and are only too pleased to co-operate with the warden in every possible way.

TENANT REACTIONS

During the first few weeks of occupation, there exists a holiday, even a honeymoon, atmosphere. Everything is bright and new, the majority of tenants have been waiting for months, or even years, for such a move, and there is the excitement of setting up a new home, meeting new people, making new friends. It is often found that tenants vie with one another in making their flatlets attractive and, if one has a fitted carpet, others will rapidly follow! Furniture, of course, is a problem. A Local Authority who has the staff and the time to do some pre-tenancy work with their applicants, will be able to attempt to sell the idea that a bed-sitter flatlet is not suitable for three piece suites, dining room suites and large wardrobes. However heartrending it is to get rid of furniture which has been tended with loving care for years, it simply is not practical to move the contents of a three bedroom house to a 140 sq. ft. flatlet. Once the move has been made and only essential furniture retained, or even new furniture purchased, the tenant is usually delighted. It is a new start and a new interest.

Most tenants enjoy the company available and find the privacy adequate. Petty feuds and acts of unfriendliness will develop in spite of all the wardens' efforts to maintain an overall pleasant atmosphere. Not all tenants have the ability to grow old gracefully and appear to be continually on the lookout to find fault with the accommodation, the warden, or other tenants. This has got to be accepted, and, providing it is kept within bounds, it is bearable and can be amusing. It happens in all walks of life. If a tenant simply cannot adapt to the life, the Local Authority will usually arrange a transfer to an unsupervised flat. Sheltered accommodation was likened by one tenant to going on an indefinite coach tour. While it may be possible for coach parties to tolerate each other for a couple of weeks, such tolerance could never last if it was not known when the tour would end.

Tenants undoubtedly like the sense of security of being able to contact help without difficulty. Relatives, especially if at a distance, appreciate being able to telephone the unit to obtain news and the tenant is relieved of the burden of having her own telephone. (Many still do, of course.)

THE DIFFICULT TENANT

Most wardens will have the occasional difficult tenant, and probably the most difficult of all is where the mind begins to wander, lapses of memory occur or the tenant appears to be affected by hallucinations. Often the tenant's actions do not seem, when reported, to be very serious. It may be, for example, that she retired to bed early and gets up shortly after midnight to make breakfast. Well, why not, if it suits her that way. But the noise created by one old lady in the still of the night, when everything else is quiet, can be intolerable and, if she starts to wander about the block, her activities not only disturb the other residents but are a source of constant worry to the warden. Often too, when seen by the Doctors or Social Workers, the tenant appears perfectly normal, and it is not unknown for it to be thought that the warden is exaggerating, or that she has a down on Mrs. So and So.

The more unco-operative the tenant, the harder is the solution. Most Doctors would be reluctant to move her to hospital, at least until she has become an intolerable nuisance, and short spells away in holiday homes give only temporary relief. Local Authorities will mostly be unwilling to take action to obtain possession, and again this would be only as a last resort. It does seem that considerable help is required from the specialist medical authorities for tenants of this type.

LIFTS

Government Departments tend to be penny wise and pound foolish where lifts are concerned. One would have thought that even in a two-storey block for elderly people, a lift would make the whole block viable for all types of tenant and, with the current cost of building land, nothing like the cost of land for building another block for cases which must have ground floor accommodation. Local Authorities can provide lifts for two-storey blocks but entirely at their own expense, with no grant or subsidy. The argument that old people would not use a lift has been proved false on many occasions, and in any case tenants of the next generation will have had experience of lifts over many years.

Many tenants, especially after experiencing it, prefer to live upstairs; they feel safer, they can have windows open without fear of cats or other invaders, they get a better view and it is often quieter.

FURTHER DEVELOPMENT OF SHELTERED ACCOMMODATION

Desirable or not, modern techniques appear to have the ability to extend the span of life well beyond three score years and ten, for more and more people. It therefore seems that further thought must urgently be given as to how this increasing number of elderly persons should be accommodated, and whether medical and social requirements should be available to them within their own homes. God forbid that we should ever revert to the pre-war institution type of home where all old people were regarded as ill and treated accordingly. But can we cope with a situation where numbers of elderly people are passed as not ill enough to be in hospital but who are really becoming incapable of living on their own, and who exercise a prescriptive right to refuse to move from their flat and go into residential accommodation. Even now, financial restrictions are holding up the development of residential homes, and the longer this is delayed the more urgent is the case for being able to cope both from a medical angle and a nursing point of view, with some of the elderly in their declining and terminal years in their own homes.

It may well be that some form of mobile nursing auxiliary will have to be formed, that the present meals on wheels service will have to be developed beyond its reliance on voluntary help, that the warden will have to give way to a fully manned 24-hour day supervisory service, which will take into account many more elderly people than those in the present sheltered blocks. There has recently been an interesting development at Luton where tenants in five sheltered blocks on a large estate are connected by two-way speech to a central office, from which help can be sent to any elderly person who requires it. This operates on a full 24-hour day, every day of the year. Such development will need great care if the elderly person is not to lose his individuality as a person, it will mean even greater and closer co-operation between the Housing, Social Services and Medical Authorities, it will need more money and resources than appear to be available at present, and it will need continuous research to ensure the real purpose of proper housing for the elderly is not lost in a surfeit of ideology and technical efficiency.

1

SOCIAL CONSIDERATIONS

SOCIAL CHANGES

It is interesting to reflect on some of the social changes that have taken place since about 1900 and contrast them with conditions today. Then, the number of persons 65 and over were approximately a million and a quarter, now there are over 7½ million. The total numbers in 1900 were not great and of them about two-thirds were married couples and one third spinsters or widows. It must not be thought that the elderly people only came from the richer class since they were very small in numbers, the large majority were quite poor and without any pension. One would perhaps imagine that life expectation at 65 in 1900 was consequently poor, but in point of fact, today for men it is only increased by about a year and for women a little less than three years. Thus there has been some improvement in expectation of life at 65 but bearing in mind all the social and medical advances, for example: pensions, social security, special housing, home helps, free general practitioner, free hospital service, the advent of antibiotics, modern anaesthesia and surgery, blood transfusions and so on – the improvement is not very great. A point can be made very quickly, namely that the vast increase in the number of elderly has arisen because more people are living to the age of 65 not that those at 65 are living very much longer. It also raises the disturbing thought that a lot of very stressing and expensive medicine and surgery could perhaps be more of a luxury than a need. To take one matter as an example; retention of urine and an enlarged prostate gland has always been a common illness of elderly men and today numerous operations are done to relieve the situation. Why didn't these men die in the early 1900's, because evidently they did not. It is then probably true that 'cabbies' kept a catheter in their hats and used them in the public convenience at times of difficulty – I certainly have been told that this was a common custom.

It is not practical to list all the social changes but perhaps one could consider some of the changes resulting from a horse-drawn to a motor car society. Today the horse is rarely seen except at riding schools, but in the early 1900's and for centuries up to that time people had to either walk to and fro to work or to shop or go by horse-drawn vehicles, such as cabs, gigs, traps, governess carts and the like. This limited the distance people travelled (except for the unusual train journey) to a few miles from their homes.

The stable yard often adjoining an hotel was a common meeting place and there were to be found a series of stables, horses being fed and groomed plus an occasional donkey – a friend in every stall! About the yard it was common to see pigeons, chickens, geese; quite often an egg could be found in a manger or a nearby nest and almost invariably there were dogs, puppies, cats and kittens about. The whole atmosphere was lively and friendly and one half expected Mr Pickwick and Sam Weller to drive in at any moment. The whole activity was that of a warm human society suited to the way of life of young and old, rich and poor, all jostling together. This was the kind of society that had been going on for very many centuries. Around and about the vicinity there may well have been and indeed there was poverty and neglect, but it was not pointedly for those over 65 years as a special class, neither was there loneliness.

Contrast this with the advent of the motor car in the early twenties, the fragmentation of town life by road traffic and the growth of the car park. At the latter it is just a mass of vehicles, difficult to get in, often cold and wet, no friendly shelter like a bar or a stable yard, hardly any exchange of greeting between the people, a general dehumanising scene. Around there are no obvious signs of poverty or neglect in the vicinity of the car park, but for those who care to look within a few hundred yards there are often to be found numbers of old people alone and solitary sometimes housebound from infirmity and devoid of family and friends. How has this all come about? In the unplanned society there was always much unemployment and too big a difference between the rich and poor; with the poor doing menial tasks of all sorts. But unemployment was not limited to the old, a great number of them had their own little businesses, for example: shops, shoe repairing, ironmongery, blacksmiths, tailors and so on and they never really retired. Others worked for small family concerns and were kept until advanced ages. The worst features of unemployment affected all equally. A good deal of employment came about through family and friends from whom there was also help during an illness or phase of being out of work; thus people tended to keep together as families and not to disperse to other areas where they had no such family influence. This may have been happening in a whole series of *Coronation Streets* but from the elderly folks' point of view their sons, daughters and grandchildren were all around and about them. Pensioning off and compulsory idleness did not occur. At first changes in work pattern took place slowly, but with the advent of quick travel by car and the replacement of men by machines followed by little mergers of local firms, then bigger mergers and finally nationalisation the work pattern changed very rapidly. With each phase of change, just as today, the work force needed became less and less and many workers became redundant – how very easy and convenient to pension off those at 65. The very fact that a national pension exists is sufficient to select the elderly employee for retirement even though he may be a better worker than the younger man.

The planned society, by the statistician, computers and 'campus' minded, appears to take away a lot of individuality from society and ironically depresses millions of people into special sub-standard kind of citizens – the people who really benefit are the young.

The number of elderly women far exceeds those of elderly men. The latter also usually has a wife living, but since the women live so much longer they become widows. The social changes affecting women are therefore worth considering.

The emancipation of women has its drawbacks. It is very fine to give up the tie, and drudgery, of staying at home, looking after mum and dad, and/or the children, but it is not so wonderful to be tired out with buses and tube journeys, to work all day in a shop or in a factory or office; it can get a bit uninteresting and boring. It is even more so when to pay off the mortgage and keep up with the 'Jones's' one *must* go out to work and perhaps see little of the children or because of difficulties have very few children. Certainly whereas in former times it was possible financially for a daughter to care for an aged parent, it is becoming less possible today. The latter must live on her own and look to home helps and neighbours for personal company and help, but as time passes the daughter herself is likely to become widowed and to spend many of the later years of her life also lonely and isolated – this is how the system works.

The motor car society has only been with us about fifty years and the planned society even less; how long will it take to make it all satisfactory. The welfare state owes much to the late Lord Beveridge but the planning was done in the 1930's for a population harassed by unemployment and dole queues. The maintenance of good health was considered in terms of people being kept fit for work even though there was insufficient work then and this is partly true now. The problem of the care of the huge elderly population was not in their minds; yet the same old principles and ideologies of planning for an impoverished unemployed working class continues; only the phrases like 'technical revolution', the 'compassionate society', the 'civilised or humane society' and the like have been added to the ideological soup.

The point being laboured is that social change has brought about isolation and loneliness for a large number of elderly people.

Loneliness is the cause of much misery and also the root cause of much ill health and disease in the elderly. It leads to depression, a disinterest in what is going on around and, coupled with a poor memory, presents many of the features of mild dementia. Commonly it results in lack of interest in meals with dietary restriction and imbalance leading to loss of weight and malnutrition. To this may be added bowel disorders (especially chronic constipation), with restlessness, insomnia and chronic mental confusion. Then again care of the house is neglected as also is that of the person and the patient is apt to become resentful, anti-social and a recluse. In the winter minor illnesses become major ones, falls may occur and the patient confined to bed without attention or she may suffer from hypothermia and so on, or the patient is constantly worrying the doctor for tablets and pills of various sorts; frequently getting muddled and overdosing herself.

Enough, I hope, has been said to establish a direct link between loneliness and ill-health. The causes are complex and the condition will not fully respond just to higher pensions, indoor sanitation and hot water supply; these may help. It is also very doubtful if hospitalisation even in new district general hospitals will meet the problem. The latter so often deal with necessary operations and perhaps a lot of unnecessary investigations and treatments keeping doctors and nurses very busy, but not always making life that much better for old people and, in many instances, sometimes worse!

In the first instance elderly people should plan as best they can not to become lonely and isolated from their accustomed neighbours, friends and acquaintances and should attempt to make new friends and keep up activities. The family should give more thought when moving or setting up home elsewhere, as perhaps also should close friends. No one can live their own life without it affecting others. One hears about the 200 000 to 300 000 people who emigrate from Britain with the accent on the cost of their education and upbringing and the loss of their skills to the country; little is said of the sadness to so many people at these partings and its general effect on the happiness of the community, though this is surely a more important matter.

The social services appear to be designed to meet the bodily requirements of elderly people, as if this were all that was necessary, but unless at the same time the services deal with loneliness they are unlikely to prevent deterioration in physical and mental health or maintain good health which should be the central theme for the health service.

PENSIONS AND SOCIAL SECURITY

Some figures on pensions are given in a later chapter. In 1963 the basic pension was £3.7s.6d. for a single person and £5.9s.6d. for a married couple. In 1970 the pension was £5.0.0. and £8.2s.0d. respectively. There have been various analyses and surveys about what can be done with an old age pension, and perhaps one might name Rowntree's 'Survey of the City of York', as set out in his book *Poverty in the Welfare State.* There is, however, no need to go into sordid details in the matter; most people would agree existence is possible, but life is not worth while on such an income.

Lots of ordinary people spend 75p a week on tobacco, or £1 on drink, cinemas, football matches, going to dances, and so on. For elderly people, luxuries are not possible, a bus fare can be a hardship, an ounce of tobacco ruinous, a cold day and a coal crisis a calamity. Rents and rates have to be paid, clothes repaired and renewed, washing done or paid for, soap is for them the most fashionable detergent, and their company is often a cat or two. The highlights in their week are chats with the butcher, baker or milkman. Carpets become worn out or non-existent, and their clothes threadbare; they go to bed early or sit in the gloom to save electric light, and favour cups of tea and bread and butter and jam rather than the trouble and expense of a cooked dinner.

They can, of course, apply for Social Security and without it many would die very quickly; but with it many still die, but rather slowly. I think many pensioners feel they have earned a pension which should be adequate for their needs and are affronted by the idea of having to apply for assistance. Others are so aged, bemused and beyond even thinking about the matter that they may be quite incapable of asking for and filling up the necessary forms or putting their case properly. Theoretically, since there are pensions, and for those in need there is Social Security no one can starve in Britain. This claim looks well on paper, but in point of fact, as is well known to any doctor in touch with the problem, large numbers of the elderly have all the signs manifest of malnutrition and slow starvation.

Social Security is, of course, an excellent and necessary thing, and one can make no criticism of its use, or of the people who carry out the work, but the assistance is very limited and is not sufficient to allow elderly people to live properly and maintain good health. In many instances, Social Security allows an old age pensioner to pay for some help in the home. Usually, this means rewarding a nearby neighbour for her services, though in other cases it pays towards the employment of a home help from the public health department. Unfortunately well over 2 681 000 people in 1973 over the age of 75 implies the need for a great number of home helps. Of course many frail pensioners have sons and daughters, and in the main they do the housework that is needed. Nevertheless, there are a large number of debilitated pensioners who have no help from their relatives, and cannot afford a home help. Sons and daughters have no legal responsibility for the care of their parents, and some, for one reason or another, do not help and often refuse to look after them. The pensioner, as a result, may have to apply for Social Security and he quickly finds out that the Board has laid down criteria for assistance. The pensioner's income and commitments are taken into account, but also whether there are near relatives. Should there be relatives living with the pensioner, or in the vicinity, commonly no assistance would be given towards a home help; that is to say, the Board takes the view that the relatives have some responsibility, which is the reverse of the legal position.

The above is a statement in general terms, since there are varying interpretations from time to time, and from place to place throughout the country. Nevertheless, it throws a greater hardship at times on the pensioner with relatives than the one without. At first sight, it may seem reasonable to expect the relatives to cope with the situation, but though a daughter may live with, or near her mother, all too often she goes out to work all day; should she give up employment to look after her mother, it could mean that both her mother and herself would require Social Security. In short, in these days of almost full employment, it is well nigh impossible for all relatives to look after their parents.

EFFECT OF FULL EMPLOYMENT

The great social evil of thirty years ago was that of unemployment, which was world-wide. Today, it is an axiom of good government that there should be full employment. Admittedly, there are small pockets of unemployment, but in general more work has been created than there are people to do it, and immigrants have been welcomed into many industries. Some industries survive because they are subsidised out of taxation, which in effect seems to mean a benefit to those who are employed at the expense of those pensioned off. Presumably, there are also phases of over-employment and relative under-production.

The most apparent serious consequence of full employment is that the mass of people from 15 to 60 and 65 years are out working and away from home from morning until night. This is in strong contrast to former generations when there was usually a daughter or grand-daughter at home looking after the old folk. Nowadays even when the home conditions are comfortable, and the income satisfactory, there is still no one to look after the old. This may be of no great consequence if they are independent as regards the activities of daily living (ADL), namely, they are fully ambulant, can climb stairs, go to the toilet by themselves, make their beds, dress and undress on their own, cook a meal and open the door to callers; but if they are 75 years or older, they may become bedridden as a matter of convenience. Should they have even a minor illness, lasting only a few weeks, where there is no one to give them food and drink, medical attention is of little avail and the results may be unnecessarily disastrous. Therefore, while the benefits of full employment as regards income are very great, it weakens the stability of the home in an era marked by the vast number of elderly people in retirement.

HOUSING

In regard to the housing of old people an important point to bear in mind is whether the planning is for elderly people to live in some isolation in localised groups or in some other manner. And how much priority is to be given to the housing of old people as compared to the young. Again there is a difficult decision as to whether to improve old properties or demolish perhaps whole neighbourhoods and build new houses. As regards actual housing the value of the number of new ones built can only be assessed against the number of houses that have been demolished or been allowed to fall into disrepair. There are undoubtedly good and bad housing developments but the pity of it is that the poorer elderly and there are millions of them, cannot themselves take part in the planning. Because of rent control freedom of movement from one house to another has been lost; the elderly cannot get a life assurance policy or mortgage and have to accept what is before them. This loss of freedom to move house I would place as a big factor in the isolation and loneliness of old people. The rent control act designed to prevent people becoming homeless seems to lead to dilapidated houses, lack of movement and many other unpleasant features. Is rent control really a good thing for old people?

An increase in population naturally implies a need for more houses. In former times an increase in the population of a nation was always considered a very good thing implying that it was prospering and in time of war was stronger and more secure. It is very doubtful if this is true today and particularly for an island like Britain with insufficient home food production. The task ahead of suitable housing for some $7\frac{1}{2}$ million or so elderly people is obviously a very great one, and likely to take decades, so presumably for some time to come the elderly will have to be cared for though they are not well housed.

One has dealt rather cursorily with the matters of housing and rent control; there is no quick easy solution, but there does appear to be a need for more radical thinking, for new outlooks and philosophies over a wide range of subjects.

The following is an impression gained after visiting innumerable homes to see elderly patients. Of course, some live in well-furnished, attractive houses, but this number seems very small as compared with those who are otherwise placed.

All too often the house is in a slum area of the city rather than in a pleasant suburb, in a back alley rather than a main street. The house may have been built a hundred years ago; many are the workmen's dwellings commonly erected in industrial parts of Britain. If so, the whole street will be built in a similar manner, lacking in architectural beauty. If there is some difficulty in finding the number, it often turns out to be the most drab house in the street. This can be easily accounted for because the tenants are unlikely to have been able to afford any repairs or paintwork for some years. If there is a small garden, as likely as not it will be untidy, because the work is beyond the capacity of the patient. The workman's dwelling is usually two rooms on the ground floor and two bedrooms upstairs, with an outside lavatory, a cold water tap in the scullery and no bathroom. The staircase usually is not lighted, neither has it a handrail, though this may be remedied by a rope from top to bottom. The stairs themselves are very steep; some lead straight up to the bedrooms, others are a sharp spiral. The outlook from the bedrooms is usually on to back streets; there is often a fireplace which is never lit, and the furnishings may be 30, 40 or more years old. Quite a number of elderly people retain a Victorian outlook; light is obscured by heavy curtains or by an aspidistra in the window, pictures about the house are perhaps of a wedding group sixty years ago when they first became tenants, or of father as a young man in the First World War. The kitchen usually has an open fire of the old-fashioned cook and heat type, there is no fireguard. The front door is likely to open straight into the front room where the better furniture is kept. In some instances, the room has been used, in the past, as a shop. The occupiers may have given the business up many years before and the remnants of the shop have been merely pushed to one side.

The very elderly in such circumstances undoubtedly feel the cold a lot. As a result, most old people wear layer upon layer of clothing. The elderly man is given to long pants and vest, a thick flannel shirt, thick waistcoat, a sleeved pullover and a thick jacket, but seems to like a neat tie and collar. The women likewise seem to wear lots of clothes and finally a large apron. One would hesitate to suggest that they do not wash often, but one remembers there is no bath, no hot water, not many clean towels, and it must take a long time to dress and undress. The bedrooms are particularly cold in the winter. There may be no hot water bottle in use, but this is overcome by warming a brick in the oven and wrapping it in cloth. Army blankets are commonly used, and an old overcoat.

Some houses have only gas lighting and many old people still use candles to go to bed. Should an old person be ill for a long time in such a bedroom, it must be dreariness itself. These old houses have no dampcourse and the walls can be seen to be damp. The most favourite household pet appears to be the cat, or cats, and they seem to find it difficult to keep clean. The next pet is, of course, a dog, who may well be the only friend a patient has. Needless to say, they have complete freedom of the house and frequently sleep in the bedroom or on the foot of the bed.

Many old people do not leave the house for weeks, or months, and in some cases for years, on end, and become cut off from the world outside. Many are deaf, so that conversation is difficult or impossible. A large number have defective eyesight and rarely do any reading. The majority persist in going up to bed, but a few live downstairs in the kitchen. In the latter case, the bed is likely to be by the fire, and one is a bit alarmed to see how close to the fire the bedclothes are. Some dislike a bed downstairs and make-do by sleeping on a couch, and I have met quite a few people living alone who never go to bed, but sleep in an arm-chair. On the other hand, there are a great number of elderly persons who are bedridden and spend weeks, months, or even years, in a cold bedroom, with a relative giving them food in the morning, a neighbour at midday, and a relative again in the evening. This kind of isolation is particularly pathetic and inexcusable where there is room downstairs, with a little company.

OLD PEOPLE'S BUNGALOWS

Supplying suitable houses for the elderly has always been a problem. Originally, the Church gave a great deal of attention to this, and from the Middle Ages has established almshouses. The Church has also established religious homes, and at times the elderly have been allowed to enter monasteries. In many parts of the world, this is still the main way of caring for and housing the elderly. In addition, both private organisations and councils have set aside homes for the elderly, and in particular have built groups of bungalows. The old-fashioned bungalow usually consists of a kitchen, scullery, bedroom and sitting-room. Some have an indoor toilet, and again some have a bath and others not. Very few have any hot water system. Heating is usually limited to the kitchen, which has an open fire with a range.

There are many disadvantages to this old-type bungalow. First, coal in 1960 cost £10 to £12 a ton, in 1970 it cost 40% more and then only one room can be heated. The bedrooms and other rooms in the winter can be very cold and damp. An open fire is unsuitable for very old people, since it carries the risk of setting fire to their clothes, or their bedclothes, or of burning them should they become giddy and fall on the fire. Then again, the work of cleaning out the grate, taking out the ashes, bringing in the coal and sticks and relighting the fire, all of which means a great deal of stooping, may be just the kind of work they are unable to do with safety.

When the person is confined to bed with a short illness, as so often happens with the elderly, the fire goes out and the whole bungalow becomes very cold. At such times, the pensioner has to depend on help given by his neighbours, but since they also are of an advanced age, this may not be forthcoming. Thus, a short illness like bronchitis may prove fatal.

The most useful addition to these groups of bungalows would be a young couple to act as wardens and to carry out simple home help duties. There would then be no need for elderly patients to go into hospital unless they were seriously ill. The hospitals are already over-worked and the cost to the public for a patient may be £80 in some hospitals and up to £160 a week in a London teaching hospital.

Bungalows of the type described are still being built but there is need for greater thought and planning in their construction. Particular attention should be paid to the medical care of the elderly at home. Until various improvements and adjustments have been made, the bungalows would appear to be suitable for the younger pensioner, who is fully ambulant, others are better cared for in a welfare institution. But this involves the close co-operation of the welfare services department, the hospital, and the local public health authority, and points to a need for greater liaison between these authorities – this subject is dealt with more fully later on in the book.

There are many ideas as to how old people should be housed. First there is the bungalow as outlined above, then there is the block of flats with small self-contained flats for an elderly couple, fitted with central heating. Much of the housing problems revolve around the question of economical and safe heating, the absence of stairs, and ready availability of cooking facilities and toilet. Some countries have built flats or rows of houses which are heated by waste steam or hot water from the electricity power station, and this should be possible in many parts of Britain. Then there is heating by electrical means: the electric fire, which for old people would seem to be unsuitable, the Dimplex which is safe, or electrical heating of either the floor or the skirting boards. The latter is admirable and I am surprised that it is not installed more often in the new flats and bungalows designed for the elderly.

The following account of a domiciliary visit to one of the above bungalows will perhaps bring out some of the points which have been considered.

Consultation was requested on a very cold evening in January. On arrival at the bungalow, it was getting dark. With the help of an aged neighbour, the family doctor and myself were advised to try the back door, since there was no sign of life at the front of the bungalow. The former was found to be open, there was no one about and the patient was discovered in bed. He was 81 and he had been living in the bungalow for a few years. Apparently he had caught a chill some two days previously and had taken to his bed. At that time, the family doctor did not find him to be very ill and a neighbour was coming in to give him food and drink. However, on our arrival, the bronchitis was very much worse and he had a wheezy cough, bronchospasm and a little cyanosis. The bedroom was cold and damp and he was very cold in bed, tucked underneath some army blankets and a greatcoat. His tongue was rather dry, indicating he was not having sufficient to drink, and he was in no condition to get one for himself. At this point his sister, aged 85, and another neighbour, came in to see what they could do. By all accounts they were in an almost similar plight and could not be expected to light a fire, cook a meal, or produce a hot water bottle. The patient's bowels had not been opened for three days and he evidently required a great deal of nursing care. Though a district nurse might have been able to come daily, this clearly would not have been sufficient.

The problem was how to find a bed in a hospital, and quickly. A wait of a few days would be too late. On inquiry, no vacancy could be found in the area, but fortunately for the patient, within the next two hours a vacant bed was found because of a death in the hospital. Admission to hospital was quickly arranged by ambulance, and treatment and nursing care started immediately. Within a week the patient was up in his chair again and could walk with assistance. Later on, he was able to walk about the ward, though rather weak and unsteady on his legs. The weather was still cold and bleak and any return to his bungalow seemed to be plain suicide, yet he did not require further hospital treatment. Had his bungalow been nicely warm, and had a home help been available near at hand, he would probably have been alright, but of course this was not so. Inquiries were then made as to a place in a welfare home, though the old gentleman was very loth to part with his bungalow. Two months later the patient was still in hospital awaiting disposal and his bungalow was empty.

CONTROLLED RENTS

The question of the control or de-control of rents is the subject of great political controversy, into which I do not wish to intrude. There have been controlled rents for many, many years, presumably on the assumption that if the houses were de-controlled the rents would rise beyond the capacity for the tenant to pay, and this would be followed by an incredible number of orders for eviction. I think it is clear that any raising of the rent for pensioners would only mean passing the burden on to the Social Security, and thence back to the ratepayer.

Be that as it may, as regards the elderly, the benefit of the controlled rent is rather dubious. So often they continue to live in a house which becomes a hovel and should have been pulled down years ago. The owner, whether it be the Council or a private person, has not been able, or thought fit, to keep up any repairs. The signs of neglect are all too obvious; the house is damp, the roof may leak, plumbing is non-existent, ceilings are cracked and the plaster falling, wallpaper peeling off the walls. It is clear that a great number of houses are deteriorating to a point when they will become uninhabitable. Most of them are those in which the elderly live.

Some elderly people living alone offer part of their house to a young couple, either to supplement their income or in return for some help, but though this is occasionally successful, the younger age group generally refuse such accommodation, or if they do accept are very anxious to get away from it as soon as possible. The problem for the elderly seems insoluble: either they should be rehoused just as much as the younger age group or their houses should be repaired and put into good order as a matter of urgency.

COOKING AND DIET

There is a great deal of malnutrition among the elderly, due not so much to disease as to inadequate or wrongly balanced diet, or wrongly cooked meals. There is a need for a much bigger emphasis on diet in old age, such as there is already for children.

First there is the problem of cooking with an old-fashioned range. The making of cups of tea, coffee or cocoa is relatively easy. The next easy method of cooking is by frying, i.e. bacon and eggs. By a great deal of thought and a good deal of arithmetic, it is possible to plan some kind of balanced diet out of the money available. However, there is a great difference between a theoretical diet and the actual way of living an elderly person may choose. There is always a tendency to produce a simple meal, and not one which involves stoking up the fire, scouring out pots and pans, and a great deal of washing-up. In a good number of cases it is physically impossible for the elderly to produce an oven-cooked meal. This problem of the feeding of the elderly is of course recognised in most parts of the country. In many areas there is a 'Meals on Wheels' service, whereby an elderly person receives a hot meal once or twice a week, at a moderately low cost per meal.

Apart from the actual diet chosen and the cooking, the elderly frequently have some difficulty in masticating their food and in its proper digestion. Natural teeth may be few and dentures may be taken out for meals. There may be an associated history of old gastric ulcers or of gall bladder trouble, or of a poor appetite or inability to take large meals. Again, the elderly often take very little outdoor exercise such as would stimulate the appetite, neither do they get into the sun or benefit from sun-bathing.

From a medical point of view, the malnutrition appears to be due to a total insufficiency of food, that is to say, the total number of calories are too few, to a lack of first-class proteins, and to a lack of fresh fruit and vegetables, leading so often to avitaminosis and iron deficiency anaemia. Osteoporosis is very common in the elderly and while its cause is still very obscure, in far too many instances there is an obvious lack of calcium and protein in the diet and an insufficient intake of milk. A poor diet leads to malnutrition, to muscular weakness and debility, to anaemia, to polyneuritis with impairment of balance and co-ordination, to cardiac weakness and a lowered resistance to infection. In addition, it causes local alimentary tract disorders such as soreness of the tongue, dyspepsia, and perhaps most common of all, obstinate constipation, or even faecal impaction.

One can well imagine the difficulties of the elderly in cooking and providing a suitable diet when they are well, but how much more difficult it must be in cases such as a wife who has to cook for an aged husband, or a widower quite unused to preparing his own meals, or someone ill with a cold or fever, and in any way confined to bed. While every effort should be made to produce a properly balanced diet for the elderly, this may be difficult to carry out; therefore in practice it is as well to supplement their diet as a matter of routine by vitamin capsules, by medicines containing iron and by a liberal allowance of milk. I am confirmed in this opinion because so many patients admitted to hospital put on weight and respond remarkably well to normal hospital diet, plus the above supplements, and this improvement occurs despite the fact that hospital diet is not particularly attractive or digestible.

LAUNDRY

The washing and laundering of clothes, towels, blankets, sheets, pillow cases and table cloths, can be an impossible burden on the elderly and quite beyond their economic means. Apart from the normal soiling, occasional incontinence of urine is not uncommon and presents a very special problem. The soiling of bed clothes may be the last straw in the burden of looking after an aged person, and the main reason for removal to an institution, though frequently it can be remedied by proper attention to the bowels or control of a minor infection of the bladder. In some areas, institutions with a large laundry department give a free service to the elderly, but so far these are few and far between. There is a need for organising help on a much greater scale. More recently there has been an issue of incontinence pads on a large scale and this has eased considerably the matter of washing soiled clothes, so much so that the necessity for a free laundry service to the elderly is not so great. In addition urinary catheters and bags have come into use for the very incontinent patient and have additionally reduced the soiling of clothes and diminished the risk of bedsores.

HABITS OF THE ELDERLY

It should be remembered that the very old, born some 75 years ago, particularly in slum areas, grew accustomed to poor home conditions and working conditions, when there was no great accent on hygiene. Added to this, there is the absence of hot water, a bath or an indoor toilet, plus physical debility and mental lethargy. Sometimes their old-fashioned ways and habits cause a good deal of domestic stress, and often they are complete misfits if residing in a new council house with their in-laws.

Men suffer commonly from bronchitis and are apt to spit a lot, sometimes into sputum mugs, sometimes into bits of newspaper, sometimes into the fire, sometimes anywhere. As a result of bad working conditions they may have been accustomed to eating their meals with grimy hands or dirty finger nails. They may ignore dental hygiene and be content with carious, discoloured and offensive teeth. Shaving may be neglected and they may have unkempt beards. To this may be added noisy, demanding and sometimes offensive language. In general, the women are much more hygienic, though as age advances there may be a similar deterioration and lack of interest in personal hygiene. It is particularly distressing to a young family to live with somebody whose hair is all over the place, hands are grubby and food is hastily gulped at the table. Conversation with some old people may be wearisome because of the frequent repetition, misunderstandings and age-long reminiscences.

I hasten to add that the habits of the elderly are related particularly to their upbringing and education, and there are of course the majority whose conversation is mature and personal hygiene beyond reproach. In passing, one would like to add that it is a great hardship for a person who has been well brought up to have to live in an institution surrounded by those who have mentally deteriorated. Clearly it is important to sustain the self-respect of older people though this is difficult on a meagre pension, Social Security and impoverished home conditions.

CHIROPODY

The feet are particularly neglected and toe nails allowed to grow and sometimes curl under the toes like rams' horns. The nails may be too thick to be cut with ordinary scissors and require special chiropody shears. Neglect of the feet is especially deleterious because it prevents the person walking about and taking the exercise he or she should. This in its turn leads to confinement to the house, physical debility and mental vegetation, since the mind is not stimulated by contact with the world outside. It is advisable that a qualified chiropodist should carry out the treatment since old people are more subject to nail infections and local gangrene. There is consequently a great need for a chiropody service for the elderly. Throughout the country there are various voluntary bodies who provide it, and so do the hospitals in some areas, but there are grave deficiencies everywhere and there is a need to organise chiropody on an extensive scale in the hospitals and welfare homes, as well as in the homes of the people. In 1973 the Community Chiropody Service treated 993 000 persons aged 65 years and over. (Ref. Health and Personal Social Services Statistics 1974).

OLD AGE CLUBS

When elderly people leave their homes they have quite a problem to know how to spend their time, particularly as they often have little money. Throughout Britain, the Continent, Canada or America, a familiar pattern is apparent. The public library is a favourite place, since it is warm and has a comfortable chair, and the daily newspapers can be read freely. Some also manage to eat a few sandwiches there. Then there is the museum and the art gallery which serve a similar purpose. The railway station is still a favourite place as there is a bustle of activity, a coming and going, and perhaps a warm waiting room. In the summer there is the bench in the park, the street corner and, in warmer climates, a sleep on the pavement or doorstep. The market hall and market place are favourite resorts, and with a few coppers a warm café is attractive. Some prefer a glass of beer and the company in a bar rather than a meal, but nowadays the old and friendly cadger is rarely seen. Living out and tramping round the countryside is frowned upon by the authorities, although a few still do this. Men, rather than women, spend their spare time in the manner just described. Women stay in more and spend more time chatting to neighbours or doing their shopping. Occasionally, a pensioner spends his time in an unusual manner and one has noticed from time to time the odd person searching through the litter bins and putting his or her findings in an old bag.

Voluntary bodies in particular try to meet this problem by establishing old age clubs, and most towns today have several. They tend to have sentimental names like the 'Darby and Joan' or 'Golden Age' Clubs. They are often organised by churchgoers and their club uses the church hall at a low rent. They are for men and women and usually have someone in charge, a small kitchen to serve tea, coffee, sandwiches or cakes, comfortable chairs, a fire, tables on which to play cards, dominoes, cribbage, draughts, etc., a room for knitting and sewing, a radio, and a piano for community singing. The clubs meet the needs of the ambulant elderly pensioner, though naturally it does not suit all of them. Though there are hundreds and hundreds of clubs in Britain, the numbers are probably inadequate. At this stage it is perhaps appropriate to make the point that it is *voluntary* effort which pioneers and initiates new aids to the elderly, rather than the statutory authorities, who always seem to be lagging behind.

The old age clubs are commonly part of a greater social organisation for voluntary service.

MEALS ON WHEELS

We still have flag days and door to door collections to provide money for voluntary service, though it was imagined this would be a thing of the past when the National Health Service was inaugurated. One useful service is the provision of hot meals to elderly pensioners in their homes. This is quite a difficult undertaking, what with finding the personnel, the cooking and other facilities and maintenance of hot meals, and the provision of them to the homes. There has to be a good deal of improvisation, and as a result the numbers dealt with in any locality are very small. Nevertheless, the service is a popular one, except that strangely enough some pensioners do not seem to be able to pay for two meals a week, moderately priced. In certain areas this work is subsidised by local authorities.

HOME VISITING

Voluntary bodies have also organised home visiting of the elderly. Many elderly persons are very lonely at home and welcome the interest shown by a visitor. The latter aims to give the pensioner a little extra interest in life and to help with the pension book, Social Security forms, advice about local social services, arranging for neighbours to call in and assisting in some of the problems of running a house. Home visiting can be a very valuable service but appears to be very difficult to carry out. Sometimes the pensioner resents any interference or intrusion into his home, or takes a dislike to the visitor, or is out, or does not answer the door when the visitor calls, and may even accuse her of stealing things out of the house. Consequently, home visiting is fraught with difficulties, it can be a very unpleasant job, and it has one great disadvantage; when once started it is difficult to give up. It looks as if the home visitor requires a thorough knowledge of what assistance can be got from social services and how to bring these benefits to the elderly without causing any irritation. Though the 'Englishman's home is his castle' may be a good idea for the well-to-do, it is not so good for the elderly pensioner with a home which may be more or less a prison.

OUTINGS

Most voluntary organisations arrange outings for members of their old age clubs and it is really surprising how they manage to carry it off with so few accidents and collapses. Frail old ladies and gentlemen are taken by bus to the seaside where they spend the day, returning in the evening or sometimes next day. One can well imagine the worries and anxieties the organisers must have transporting some 50 or 60 persons in this kind of enterprise. Fortunately for their peace of mind, they are not aware of the medical dangers. I doubt if many a doctor would be prepared to pass these elderly people as fit for the journey, though I am convinced the risks run are small in comparison with the gain obtained. Some of the more enterprising organisations even take the old people to the Continent; one person who took a party to Paris for the weekend tells me that they all enjoyed it and there was no flagging of the spirits at all. Holiday parties are also arranged for the elderly, usually at the off-season times. As far as one can judge, the numbers taking holidays in this way are increasing year by year and there is scope for a greater effort.

2

HOSPITAL SERVICE AND THE ELDERLY

It will be appreciated that there is at present a division in responsibility for the care of the elderly. Pensions and national assistance are controlled nationally and paid from the national exchequer. Housing, home helps, district nurses, health visitors and welfare services are the responsibility of the local authority and paid for by local taxation, though it may be subsidised from the national exchequer. Despite all the goodwill, such divisions of authority and responsibility impair smooth co-ordination.

It is now perhaps useful to consider the care of the elderly before the advent of the free National Health Service, that is to say, before 1948. In those days the problem was not quite so acute. In any locality there was likely to be a voluntary hospital which dealt almost entirely with acute medical and surgical illnesses. As soon as a person was considered fit for discharge from the voluntary hospital, either they were sent home, or the local authority was informed. The local authority had under its control not only welfare homes but also hospitals. Many of these hospitals were built almost a century ago and were originally designed as workhouses. Some had cells for the difficult inmate. By and large, these institutions were large rambling structures with the accent on care and accommodation rather than modern medical treatment.

As time went by, the institutions took on a new look and became the poor law infirmaries, and later the infirmaries. Generally speaking, the institution had little medical attention. Sometimes it consisted of one medical superintendent, with or without assistant. Sometimes there was no resident doctor and patients were attended by doctors on call. It is almost unbelievable, but true, that at one time in 1959 one hospital of over one thousand beds had no resident doctor. Such institutions rarely had a pathological department, an out-patient department, paediatric wards, maternity wards, eye departments, operating theatres, or any of the other wards and departments commonly found in a hospital. All the beds in the institution, often too close together, could be devoted to the care of the so-called chronic sick. I think at any one time the local authority was likely to have at its disposal three beds, or if the welfare homes were included, perhaps four beds, for every bed available to the voluntary hospital.

While treatment in the voluntary hospital was virtually free, it was not so in the local authority institution. A means test was applied to the patient or inmate, and to the relatives, who were under legal obligation to make some contribution towards the cost of maintenance. The position may have been unsatisfactory, and in many ways discreditable, but in practice there was little difficulty in finding a bed when one was required, and there was virtually no geriatric problem. From the voluntary hospital's point of view, the beds in the local institution were used as an escape route for those they classified as chronic sick, and the voluntary hospital had no particular discharge difficulties. The death rate in the chronic hospital was rather high, there was much confinement to bed, and the use of the cot bed. One can remember the atmosphere of death and despair that pervaded the wards and institutions.

The advent of the National Health Service has changed everything.

Whereas the voluntary hospital service dealt with the serious illnesses that occurred in about a fifth or so of the population, the Health Service has made the hospitals responsible for the investigation and treatment of all illnesses of the whole population. Even before the Health Service, the voluntary hospitals were overburdened, out of date, and too few in number to cope with their responsibilities. How then were they to take on the tremendous new task? Obviously it was beyond their capacity and of course the local authority hospitals were taken over and included in the national programme. In certain cities, notably in London, the local authority institution had been brought up to a standard approaching that of the voluntary hospital before the Health Service, but this cannot be claimed for the country as a whole before the Health Service.

Gradually, the older function of the local authority hospital has been changed. Wards have been set aside in them for maternity work, as children's wards, for acute medical cases and surgical cases, portions have been altered to serve as a pathological department, or out-patient department, operating theatre, eye department, etc., and today such a hospital has become to all intents and purposes an acute general hospital.

But unfortunately, with this change, the number of beds set aside for chronic sick patients has become less and less, while the needs of the elderly person with a chronic illness, that is to say, the geriatric patient, have become more and more. Adverse home conditions are causing a pressure on the geriatric patients to go into any hospital where they can gain admission. Many of the beds in the formerly voluntary hospital, and in the modernised local authority hospital, are being blocked by the presence in the wards of elderly patients who do not require hospital treatment, but cannot return home because of poor home conditions and lack of a home care programme. The National Health Service has spent enormous sums of money to give adequate treatment to the people, and every hospital is very expensive to run, but it is being overloaded by having to care for long stay patients who could be more properly dealt with by the local welfare authorities.

Statistically, the health of the people in Britain is no better than that in Canada or America, despite the National Health Service, and one wonders whether the real key to good health is not primarily good social conditions. At any rate it appears that, for the elderly, better social conditions are a prerequisite to better health. The use of the National Health Service to ameliorate conditions caused by insufficient income, bad housing, poor diet, lack of help in the home, must be one of the most expensive methods and one very detrimental to the Service itself.

The present problem may be viewed from several aspects.

THE GENERAL PRACTITIONER

At the outset it is worthwhile considering the changed relationship between a patient and doctor under the previous payment for services rendered and the present free at the time, at any time, service via the National Health. Under the payment for service except in a country district the patient personally selected the doctor of his choice and was inclined to choose one who gave the necessary care and attention in the manner the patient wished, i.e. visits to the surgery or visits to his home, more expensive, or visits at night, even more expensive. Since everything had to be paid for only the rich indulged in calling the doctor in for trivial reasons or at inappropriate times. Again the contract was solely between the patient and doctor, the confidence had to be mutual; considerations of the efficiency of the health service, example: use of beds, of equipment, cost of this or that drug or appliance, priority of cases for treatment, etc., was a very secondary matter. Only in teaching hospitals was the patient a subject for teaching or research which at present has now spread to other hospitals. The fees charged and method of payment were also mutually agreed. The method certainly was not perfect, the poorer patient received less time and care or even felt he could not come forward for treatment; hospitals were for the indigent poor supported by charity – not a very pleasant feeling for the patient. Anything above the minimum treatments could be expensive and with the advent of modern anaesthesia, surgery, antibiotics, chemotherapeutic drugs, costly radiology and pathology the total cost could be catastrophic. Notwithstanding these drawbacks one likes to think the poorer patient was medically and therapeutically dealt with in a standard equal to the rich patient.

Under the present system the doctor–patient relationship has changed In practice the liberty of a patient to make a personal choice of doctor has been lost in hospitals and almost of little value when choosing a general practitioner since so much depends on who is the nearest doctor who has not already too many patients. There is no financial incentive for the doctor to undertake many items of service within his capability, it being more convenient to refer the patient to hospital though this may be an additional cost to the health service. On the one hand the patient has practically a 'blank cheque' to ask for almost any investigation or the latest drug or fashionable treatment without any sense of personal responsibility that he is making the service more expensive and using personnel and facilities which are in such short supply as to be on the verge of being rationed.

On the other hand the medical profession feels it should have the basic right for a doctor to investigate and treat a patient according to his personal inclination and that everything should be supplied free by the state. This seems to be another 'blank cheque'. The author does not think either party can be given such freedom unless the state has a bottomless purse and an endless supply of skilled personnel. Some limitation must be set on both freedoms to ensure a sensible expenditure of money and use of staff, otherwise the whole health service will suffer and be pitted with instances of substandard medical care and attention. Some extent of the wastage can be gained from the very high percentage of normal results from radiological and pathological investigation. There is no villain in the piece; it is rather that the ideology and excellence of free medical care for all and complete clinical freedom is the enemy of a *good* sound health service. Most things have to be paid for. It might appear that clinical decisions have nothing to do with management and administration, but on reflection clinical decisions to press ahead with new operations, investigations or treatments or an advocacy of certain routines. Example: every patient to have chest X-ray or pelvic X-ray, or all persons with winter bronchitis to be given a vaccine and a prolonged course of antibiotic; will as a result take up part of the available resources leaving less for something else. This can be very important to old people since almost invariably they have to do with what is left over. With the above thought in mind one may now consider the work of the general practitioner.

The general practitioner may be responsible for the medical care of up to three thousand patients of all ages. He is asked to attend and advise and treat all the minor ailments, to be patient with the number of hypochondriacs in his practice, to be on call night and day, to issue certificates and arrange admission to hospitals. As the number of aged in the population increases, he finds a greater demand on his time in looking after the elderly. Frequently, it is clear to him that the patient requires nursing and home care and that, without this, his visits are fruitless, and active therapeutic measures impossible to apply. He may request admission to hospital for the patient, but as likely as not, particularly in the winter, no bed may be available for some time. Sometimes relatives or neighbours reach the end of their tether in caring for some old person, and are insistent that they be taken to hospital, though they may not, on medical grounds, require hospital treatment. The persistence on the part of the relatives might take the form of frequent night calls.

The general practitioner is now placed in a very invidious position. Failure to attend is fraught with serious complications; the patient may have developed a more serious illness and there is always the possibility of the doctor being called to account by the executive committee. Should the patient gain admission to hospital and improve sufficiently to be fit for discharge, unless there has been an improvement in home conditions, he is likely to lapse into the previous state of ill-health, and the general practitioner is faced with the same old problem all over again. From his point of view, the return of a frail ambulant to bad home circumstances can be most unsatisfactory.

In a practice of a little over 3000 patients, a general practitioner may have, say, 400 elderly patients. If it were thought reasonable to visit an elderly patient once in three months, this would mean 400 visits in 13 weeks, or about 30 visits a week to the elderly. This is not really possible, especially in the winter. Whilst it is true a number of elderly patients would not want visiting as frequently as this, others require very much more frequent visiting. Elderly persons may find it difficult to attend a doctor's surgery, or may be unwilling to call in a doctor because they fear being put into a hospital. Since it is still the practice to await a call from the patient, many elderly persons, therefore, do not receive attention until *in extremis*. It looks as if a home nurse should be attached to a practice, with the duty of visiting elderly people regularly, under the guidance of the general practitioner.

THE RELATIVES

There are some relatives whose first thought is to send the patient to hospital as soon as he or she becomes a burden, but most sons or daughters undertake the task of looking after their parents; 95 per cent of old people live outside institutions. Basically this means that there is only institutional accommodation for a small percentage and it must not be thought that all those at home are being properly cared for or that they would not enter a welfare home if they had the opportunity. It simply means that 95 per cent of elderly people have to fend for themselves as best they can, and a large number are living alone.

However, as time goes on, the burden of looking after a bedridden or incontinent patient becomes a tremendous ordeal; sometimes this state may continue for months, or years, without any hope of respite by admission to hospital. During this time holidays are impossible and normal home life is disrupted. It is little wonder, therefore, that should the lucky day come when the patient is admitted to hospital, there is a natural disinclination to accept the patient back unless she is fully ambulant and requires no personal help. Unfortunately, for persons aged 75 and over, it is often impossible to restore them to such a state of health. They are still likely to require a little help with dressing and undressing, with meals, or getting to the toilet, but even this lesser burden is still a heavy one.

Nevertheless in 1973 there were 7 591 000 persons aged 65 years and over in the United Kingdom with a total population of 56 021 000 (Ref. Population Projections No. 4, 1973–2013, Office of Population, Censuses and Surveys), and since there are still only about 69 000 beds for the geriatric and chronic sick the burden of looking after the elderly must fall on the family. As may be expected there are still thousands of people on the waiting list for a bed in a geriatric ward.

Views of relatives regarding the care of the elderly are often expressed in letters, and the following, though not extracts from real letters, are the sort of letters that have been received:

'I have living here a Miss X, aged 89. She is quite helpless, cannot move hand or foot. There is no one else but myself in the house and I am a 63 year old bachelor. She is almost too heavy for me to lift and I am forced by common humanity to perform tasks which I ought not to do. I cannot go to work and the whole trouble is breaking me down. I cannot go on any longer and something will have to be done about this matter.'

'But my husband is worse again. His colostomy is working very bad. It has been on now since Saturday, night and day. It is getting beyond me, as the smell is terrible when it is like it is.'

'Conditions are such that I could not have my mother at home. I am on my own and out at work daily, also the daily help I had was a lady of 74 years, who unfortunately fell sick herself and is unlikely to return. Very little help is forthcoming from other directions and I should find great difficulty in caring for my mother in her present state.'

'Then again in the downstairs room where we have to put mother, the fireplace smokes so badly that we have ceased using it. My sister uses an electric fire, but it is too cold for an elderly person to sit in a chair all day. Consequently my sister has kept her in bed. If there is any query about my mother's details, these are as follows: sees only with one eye, very deaf since her twenties, aged 80 next October, mind very confused at times, loss of power to control legs.'

'You will realise that if my father is sent home, I shall hold you responsible for all that happens to my mother, because I shall not stay home to receive him, and naturally if I am not there, my mother will have to go away as she is not able to look after herself.'

'I regret that it is impossible for me to accommodate my mother at this address, as I am disposing of the property and leaving the district. There will be no one in the house on Tuesday, as my duties take me away for 14 hours each day.'

THE NEIGHBOURS

Very often the care of elderly patients is undertaken by neighbours who look in and do what they can. However, though at first they act as the good neighbour, as times goes on they are likely to be saddled with their new responsibility, which becomes more and more onerous, until their whole life is involved. They realise that if they do not give the patient any drink, no one else will, and that if they do not take in some food or light a fire, the patient must go hungry and cold. If the patient is old, forgetful and unsteady at walking, the neighbours' sleep is disturbed by imaginings of what may go wrong. The following story by a neighbour may perhaps be of interest.

She lived in a semi-detached house, the other half of which was occupied by a lady of 85, who lived alone, had never married and had no living relatives. They had been neighbours for some fifteen years. At 75 years of age, the old lady began to become forgetful, sustained a few falls about the house and took to the habit of getting up at night.

At this stage, the neighbour, whom we shall call Mrs X, began to look in when the old lady had a day or so in bed with a cold, or when the milk was not taken in for a day. Then there were little shopping errands to be done for the old lady, a little work with the pension book and posting letters, then on cold mornings it became a habit to go in and stoke up the fire, or light it. Several years ago, Mrs X became a widow, with the responsibility of bringing up two children, and took a job outside her home, but still managed to look in next door in the morning and evening.

For the last few years, the old lady's mental state has deteriorated and she had developed rather grubby habits, not washing, undressing or tidying her house, and at the same time has become very much more feeble and unsteady. The habit of getting up at night has continued and Mrs X has glimpses of her wandering round the house with a lighted candle, with all its attendant risks. Despite the old lady's mental state, she refuses to go into a home and so Mrs X suffers the strain and anxiety of such a neighbour, week in and week out, presumably until something dreadful happens.

THE CASUALTY DEPARTMENT

The original intention of a casualty department was to deal with injuries, particularly at work or on the roads, or falls in the home, cuts, bruises, etc., or collapses in the street. The casualty officer today may have to receive a very elderly person who has fainted or had a slight fall and who has been brought up by a taxi or private car by a neighbour or relative. If the patient is of great age, it may seem necessary to admit him for observation for a few days. If at the end of this time it is known that the home conditions are bad with the patient living alone, etc., discharging them is a grave responsibility.

Other cases brought to the casualty department may be serious accidents like a fractured femur, which may necessitate a stay in hospital for six months and longer, because there is no one to nurse the patient at home. This kind of fracture is very common and if all had to be dealt with in hospital, many more beds would be required. All too often, an elderly person may be sent up to the casualty department by relatives, a neighbour or a doctor, because conditions at home have reached a crisis, rather than that there has been any recent injury or illness. The patient may have been suffering from a stroke for several months or years, or may have been mildly confused or incontinent for weeks, or months, or have been given to wandering away from home at night, and so on, and at last the relatives have refused to carry on. The patient is now taken to the casualty department and literally dumped there. Naturally, it creates a very harassing time for all concerned.

THE BED BUREAU

In towns where there are two or more hospitals, a bed bureau has usually been set up. The bureau is manned day and night by clerks who receive telephone calls from doctors for urgent admissions. The idea is to save the doctor the trouble of telephoning round all the hospitals and to gain admission for the patient as quickly as possible. In the bureau, the bed state of all the hospitals in the area is recorded and any vacancies shown. It is a most valuable service, both to the patient and the doctor, and one wonders how any hospital service could be run without it. However, in the same way as the casualty departments may have to deal with patients who are not really *medically* urgent, so the bed bureau may have numerous requests for beds for elderly patients who have been ill for a long time, or who have illnesses normally treatable at home. The urgent need for admission may be basically on social grounds and so again hospital beds become filled with social cases.

THE MEDICAL OR SURGICAL CONSULTANT

The consultant physician, or surgeon, is beset with the problem of having patients staying on in the ward, usually those of advanced age, who do not require further hospital treatment. Yet they continue to occupy beds for weeks and sometimes months at a time. The physician or surgeon is being constantly reminded of the very important matter of the cost of maintaining a patient in hospital.

It can therefore be well appreciated that the use of hospital beds as a substitute for domiciliary care or care in a welfare hostel is a very extravagant procedure.

The admission of every elderly patient is fraught with the danger of long stay. It may be particularly awkward because the patient cannot be transferred to a chronic sick ward or hospital, as was formerly possible, or because there is so much delay in this transfer. The alternative of sending the patient home may entail a long argument with the relatives, or the discovery that home conditions are impossible. Sometimes the patient may still have to be sent home, but this is attended with grave risks in the elderly; the patient may collapse in the ambulance, or suddenly deteriorate within a few days or sustain a fatal fall. The responsibility for all these untoward events may be placed on the consultant and he may be found answerable publicly in the Coroner's Court. Alternatively, the hospital may be charged with some form of neglect.

The idea of convalescent or 'cold' wards partly meets this problem, but in so far as the social conditions are unlikely to change, convalescence in the elderly is likely to be lifelong. Consequently, at a later stage, another doctor will have to bear the onerous responsibility of discharging the patient home, or the cold wards, in turn, will become quite static. In general, there has been a diminution of chronic sick or convalescent wards, because of the modernisation of the old public local authority hospital, so that today there is often a need to increase the number of these wards. If this was done they would become filled up rapidly and the problem goes back once again to its root cause, namely the large number of old people living in adverse home conditions.

THE DULY AUTHORISED OFFICER

Before the National Health Service, the duly authorised officer (DAO) acted as the relieving officer. In that capacity he was usually able, at the request of the consultant in charge, to remove a patient from the ward to the local authority hospital or institution. Usually there was little difficulty in finding a bed somewhere. Today, he can rarely do this and a good deal of his work is limited to dealing with the certified patient. If an elderly patient has considerable mental confusion (about 15 per cent of them have some confusion on admission), then the condition may warrant certification for compulsory admission to an observation ward for three days on a Three Day Order, or fourteen days on a Fourteen Day Order. By the time the order has elapsed in the majority of incidences the patient has responded to treatment, and the use of a tranquilliser, and is not certifiable. The public frown upon the idea of sending old people to mental hospitals, and in any case there is rarely any room in them. Already, over 30 per cent of patients in mental hospitals are 65 years or over, and the majority of them are women. As a result, border-line cases, who perhaps are just certifiable, are not so certified.

The observation ward is commonly located in a general hospital and has a small number of beds. When the patient comes off the certificate, and is free to return home, all the difficulties of discharge home, previously mentioned, at once become evident. The patient may now have to be transferred to one of the ordinary wards, again not because she requires hospital treatment, but solely on account of social considerations. A stream of elderly patients therefore gain admission to hospital in this kind of way.

THE MAGISTRATE'S ORDER

Legal provision has been made to compel an elderly person, who is living in a state of neglect, to enter a hospital. There are a number of old people living alone whose homes have degenerated into a filthy state. All the linen may be soiled, dirty and offensive, the bed bug-ridden, the patient infested with fleas and everything in a mess. Surprisingly enough, some of these patients are fairly reasonable and rational on interview, and can hardly be certified as being of unsound mind. Yet the patient may refuse to leave home or accept admission to hospital. Under these circumstances, the magistrate may sign an order, compelling the patient to be admitted.

It should be remembered that the ordinary hospital does not have locked doors, or persons on the look-out for someone trying to escape. Consequently, the magistrate's order is not suitable for a patient who is fully ambulant and is likely to attempt to leave the hospital. The order is very rarely used, but is applicable to the patient who is debilitated, in very bad home conditions, and yet refuses hospital treatment.

WELFARE DEPARTMENT HOMES

The welfare homes, which originally dealt with persons of all ages, are also experiencing the necessity of admitting the elderly. The homes are often not designed to accommodate the very elderly, who may require a good deal of personal assistance and some nursing. Nevertheless, the majority of persons living in these homes are of pensionable age. They are often ill and need to be admitted to hospital. Again, today this may be a matter of considerable difficulty, owing to the shortage of beds, and can sometimes only be accomplished by accepting patients from the geriatric ward in exchange. But such patients are usually the very frail ambulant, with the result that the welfare homes are gradually being filled with persons who require a great deal more personal attention, and are a much greater responsibility in every way. This change is bringing in its wake very serious problems of staffing, nursing attention and the reconstruction of old buildings.

THE MENTAL HOSPITAL

The old age problem is also a matter of great concern to the mental hospitals, who have a large percentage of patients of pensionable age. About one-third of them, the majority being women, are 65 years or older and one-fifth of the hospital admissions are in this age group. It has been estimated that there are many patients of pensionable age, who though legally certified in mental hospitals, could be more suitably cared for elsewhere. Under present difficult circumstances, it is well nigh impossible to accept patients from mental hospitals into geriatric wards or old people's homes, since their rehabilitation and return home is so extremely difficult after their being institutionalised for so long.

In former times mental hospitals received elderly patients from their homes which could be within a radius of 30 miles or more from the mental hospital. The mental hospital was used so often to dispose of unwanted or troublesome old people. Not surprisingly old people in a mental hospital were living in overcrowded wards and slum like conditions. The advent of the welfare state, free hospital admission and the build-up of geriatric departments has meant that many of the elderly people formerly going to mental hospitals now gain admission to acute medical wards, the geriatric department and perhaps welfare homes or to special housing. In short the numbers of old people in mental hospitals should be going down and indeed are doing so, but unfortunately the result is a great overcrowding of the ordinary hospitals. It is very convenient for the mental hospital personnel to feel they are gaining success with their elderly patients, to claim that community care programmes have been built up and all is going well. But unfortunately in many areas of the country old people are denied admission to a mental hospital and there is insufficient community care, or sufficient ordinary hospital beds; consequently numerous elderly emotionally disturbed patients are living miserably at home.

THE COMMUNITY PHYSICIAN

The Community Physician still has a measure of responsibility to see that persons living within his area are able to obtain medical treatment or social help, when either is considered necessary. He has, of course, a responsibility to persons of all ages in the community. Generally, he has under his control the ambulances, district nurses, health visitors and home helps. In some areas he also controls admission to the welfare homes and other similar accommodation. I think the old age problem is imposing a considerable strain on the local health department. There are likely to be innumerable requests for health visiting, for the use of ambulances, for district nurses, and particularly for home helps. If the Medical Officer of Health has control over admissions to the welfare homes, he is, of course, in a position to relieve an acute crisis in the home, but if he has no such authority he may be forced to deal with a home situation by overburdening the services of the district nurses and home helps at his disposal.

Before the National Health Service, it can now be appreciated, the care of the chronic sick, which included a much smaller geriatric problem, was dealt with almost completely by one authority, that is the local authority, whereas today the responsibility is divided between the Health Service and the welfare services. Further, there are divisions within the Health Service and welfare services themselves. These divisions carry with them the risks of trying to solve a problem in bits and pieces; there is the possibility of duplication in certain instances, and of deficiencies through lack of co-ordination and integration in other instances. Under new administrative arrangements the Home Help Service comes under the Social Services.

TEA TROLLEYS AND LIBRARY

Practically all the organisation for taking tea trolleys round the wards in hospitals and other institutions, together with the library facilities, is undertaken by voluntary effort. The trolleys sell tea and coffee in the out-patients department, and such things as buns and sandwiches, chocolate, sweets, cigarettes, tobacco, etc. Pensioners in hospitals and institutions have about 50p a week to buy personal comforts, and the trolleys give them an easy way of making their small purchases.

Voluntary organisations undertake various kinds of work relating to hospitals and the care of the elderly. Sometimes they supply wheel chairs on loan, night commodes, toilet requisites, back rests, rubber bed pans, etc., and in some hospitals and homes they have seen to the hanging of pictures in the institution and wards. I think one of the much appreciated services is the hanging of copies of the oil paintings from the

National Gallery and other collections. These are changed from time to time. The pictures take some of the bleakness away from institutional living. Very often the radio or television is supplied to the hospital and maintained there in good order by voluntary funds.

Despite all the voluntary work that is being done, there is a great deal of goodwill still untapped and great numbers of people quite willing to undertake voluntary work if they could be suitably approached.

THE CONSULTANT GERIATRIC PHYSICIAN

Of recent years the problem of the elderly has become more and more acute, with the result that geriatric physicians have been appointed in charge of the old 'chronic wards' in many parts of the country. Previously these wards were attended by local general practitioners, or served as convalescent wards to consultant physicians or surgeons. At times, it appears, there was no clear indication as to who held responsibility for the patients in such wards.

A good deal has been said about the home conditions of the elderly and how the problem affects various interested parties. However, there appears to have been a great reluctance on the part of the Ministry of Health, and particularly of the medical profession, in accepting geriatrics as a special branch of medicine and in appreciating the necessity of appointing a physician to take a special interest in the old age problem. Most people like progress but only a few like change, and yet the former is hardly possible without the latter. Old habits of thought remain when everything else has changed. It is a fact that there are now millions of elderly persons and that they create a particularly difficult medico-social problem. It is a problem that has come to stay and one which is unlikely to be solved by juggling with old ideas, or patching here and there. There appears to be the need for someone who is actively engaged in the treatment of the elderly to survey and restate what the problem is in a prescribed area, with a view to bringing about closer co-operation and integration of all those concerned, and to make every turn of events grow to a common aim and purpose.

The reluctance of many consultant surgeons and physicians to have a geriatric physician placed in charge of these chronic wards is quite understandable. The chronic wards in the past have served as an escape valve from congestion in the acute wards, and the appointment of a geriatric physician carries the implication that the wards will have other functions. However, if the annual number of cases admitted over several years to the chronic wards be carefully considered, in most instances it will be apparent that the chronic wards have already failed to fulfil their original function. This is mainly because the acute general hospital has been overloaded with geriatric patients, who have been transferred to the chronic wards, so reducing these wards to a static condition. The correct relationship between the geriatric wards and the general hospital wards has yet to be worked out, but clearly some way must be found to allow the acute general hospital to carry out its proper functions. It may be that a greater emphasis on the rehabilitation of the elderly in the geriatric wards, plus an improved home care programme, will bring fruitful results.

There are still large areas of the country without a geriatric physician or geriatric unit, and it may be that these are being planned in the near future. The following chapters deal with the work of a geriatric unit and give some account of its organisation and the medical problems commonly seen in the wards.

3

THE GERIATRIC UNIT

Commonly these days a geriatric department consists of about 400 beds together with hospital, day and other clinics. Whilst the whole department is the responsibility of the hospital management committee and its various sub-committees the clinical responsibility is usually placed on the consultant physicians whose duty it is to concern themselves with everything that touches on the care of patients. In practice this means the consultant is concerned with junior doctors, nurses, auxiliary nurses, physiotherapists, occupational therapists and medical social workers in addition to his direct responsibility for the diagnosis and treatment of patients.

Since every clinical decision in practice carries with it some aspect of management it is clear that the consultant should have some understanding and skill in management and administration. The latter undoubtedly is a vast subject in itself, but it is useful to consider a few aspects of it. One would expect that everyone at work in a hospital, doctors, nurses, auxiliary nurses, etc., should know just what their duties are and the limits of their responsibility. But the hospital service is a vast training area with frequent arrivals and departures of people from all points of the compass and of many nationalities – somewhat like a railway station. This in itself makes it more difficult to maintain a stable team of skilled persons, so that as much effort as possible has always to be made to retain at least a framework of skilled doctors and nurses and make adjustments towards this end. There is probably a case to be made for actually itemising the duties of each person and of the lines of communication and responsibility. Certainly each person should be given some clear guidance, not just brought into a ward and left to adapt herself. As a prelude to all this some form of 'job analysis' should be carried out.

DELEGATION AND RESPONSIBILITY

The relation of responsibility amongst hospital professional staff is not just of one person to another in a simple hierarchical system. For instance a *Ward Sister*

(a) has to accept some guidance and disciplined behaviour from the general nursing council

(b) be answerable to the matron for some of her duties

(c) co-operate and follow the requests of consultant physicians or hospital doctors

(d) take the major responsibility for how nurses under her control attend to the patients

(e) be expected to assist the sister tutor in the training and supervision of nursing staff

(f) co-operate with the physiotherapists in the timing of nursing care and physiotherapy treatment

(g) assist the medico social worker when possible

(h) feel personally responsibility for each patient and so on

Whilst attempting to clarify the duties of each person it is almost equally important to indicate when such a one is going out of position. *Example*: A medical social worker should not advise a ward sister how to nurse and care for a patient, neither should a ward sister take upon herself the work of a medical social worker when the latter is present and has responsibility in the matter. Each new delegation of duties depends on the ability of the person to learn to carry out such duties and this may take some time. It is not a good thing to have a rather raw recruit suddenly left in charge of a ward as can happen when there is shortage of staff.

Other matters of management constantly require attention as the skills of interviewing, committee work, a constant attempt to maintain channels of communication by proper consultation and co-ordination when the measure of control is largely informal and when the total result cannot be easily expressed on a production or output chart.

In the health service the doctor is not simply a clinician, his decisions greatly affect the balance of the service, and the author is of the opinion that at all levels the doctor should have some understanding of his link with management and administration.

The treatment of the elderly can be undertaken in many ways. They are subject to many of the illnesses, both acute and chronic, common to younger age groups, but in addition have illnesses peculiar to their age. Perhaps one of the best ways to start a unit is by having an acute medical ward complete with properly trained staff and all facilities, together with the aid of the pathological and radiological departments, set aside for the care of those of pensionable age. This kind of approach has rarely been adopted, though one notes that in Dundee some £45 000 has been spent in building a special geriatric unit.

However, such a ward is not altogether suitable. Perhaps the most fundamental principle in treating the elderly is that they should be confined to bed as little as possible. Rest in bed for them has the attendant risks of muscular wasting, foot drop, stiffness of the joints, pressure and bed sores, obstinate constipation, congestion of the lungs, difficulty in passing urine (especially in men with enlarged prostates) and impairment of free respiration. The elderly also easily become mentally withdrawn, apathetic and inclined to sleep most of the day. They therefore lose their mental alertness and will to recover unless they can maintain conversation with others and be mentally stimulated. This fundamental principle of having the patient up in a chair, rather than in bed, runs counter to many of the accepted medical procedures for younger people. For the latter, rest in bed carries very few hazards and a great number of advantages. Hemiplegia is a very common illness among the elderly, and this in particular should be treated by early activation of movements and ambulation. Though there is undoubtedly a need for the acute geriatric ward, it does differ in many essentials from that of the ordinary medical ward.

The task of taking over an acute medical ward rarely arises because the geriatric physician is usually put in charge of the chronic sick wards. He is likely to become responsible for several hundreds of beds.

TAKING OVER THE CHRONIC SICK WARD

The average chronic sick ward seems to have the following features at first inspection. There are far too many beds in the ward, there is no room between the beds for a comfortable chair, there is no sister's administrative office; toilet and bathrooms may be inadequate, sometimes no sluice, no steriliser, no clinical room for testing urines, etc. The case history sheets are very scanty in character, pulse and temperature charts are not in use. A ward stethoscope and blood pressure apparatus is unlikely to be present, and such things as a drip stand, intravenous set, lumbar puncture set, needles and syringes have never been considered necessary. Most of the patients are confined to bed, some have bed sores and loaded bowels. A few are always in a dying state.

THE COT BED

The more backward the ward, the more the cot bed seems to be in evidence. Some patients have been confined to the cot bed for months, or even years. Such patients are usually considered to be incontinent and demented. Incontinent they must be of necessity, but they are not always demented and many can be got up, rehabilitated and sent home, even though they have spent several years in a cot bed.

The idea of the cot bed is that when the sides are up, the patient cannot fall out of bed and injure himself, neither can he wander to some other part of the ward out of observation. If a patient is sufficiently strong, he can of course climb over the cot sides, consequently the cot bed is of particular value in restraining the weak and debilitated patient. No doubt, for short periods of restlessness, and properly used, the cot bed has a place in medical care, but it is fraught with all kinds of abuses and means towards medical neglect. It is a cheap replacement for inadequate nursing staff and it follows that after a few days the patient must resign himself to urinary incontinence. Faecal incontinence can only be avoided by the supply of the bed pan at the right time; otherwise a loaded bowel may be preferable.

It is perhaps worth considering two types of case that might be placed in a cot bed. First there is the patient with a cerebral thrombosis, some mental confusion, perhaps some aphasia and paralysis. Such a patient may be considered as a senile dement, though if properly treated the mental confusion subsides and much of the aphasia and paralysis can be improved, and the patient rehabilitated. Should he, however, be placed in a cot bed, the muscles waste, paralysis is followed by contractures, little attempt is likely to be made to treat the aphasia, which therefore persists, and since the patient's life is spent gazing vacantly at the ceiling there is no stimulus to reawaken the mind. Should he come to a realisation of the position in which he is, the forced incontinence thrusts him back into gloom and despair, in which condition he may survive for many years. A similar sequence of events can happen to any very debilitated patient placed in a cot bed.

The next type of case may be an elderly lady with a fractured femur, which is considered inoperable. A number of these patients develop bed sores and bronchial pneumonia and do not live long in bed. Those who do not suffer complications in this way may become extremely weak and are apt to curl up in bed with flexure of the body and limbs, and to go into a twilight kind of existence. The cot bed can have all the features of a prison to the elderly patient, as did the Château D'If to the Count of Monte Cristo.

The nursing staff It is unlikely there will be a sister to each ward, and the staff are mainly composed of state enrolled auxiliary nurses and ward orderlies. One is immediately impressed by the immense amount of work the staff are doing under such trying conditions, and with such little appreciation. All too often they are few in number and hopelessly overworked. Since so many of the patients are in bed, most of their time is taken in supplying food and drink, cleaning backs, changing wet sheets, supplying bottles, giving enemas, washing the patients, combing their hair and so on. Then the very debilitated patient has to be turned frequently in bed, to avoid bed sores. Urines are unlikely to be tested on the wards, since the staff are so fully occupied and untrained. The staff also have the unpleasant task of laying out the dead. It is little wonder that there is some difficulty in recruiting and maintaining nursing staff in chronic wards of this type.

The patients These are a mixture of a few young and many old persons, suffering from all kinds of medical and surgical conditions. A few are uncertified mental defectives and may have been in the ward for twenty years, a few controlled epileptics, again of some ten years or more duration; then there is the young paralysed patient with disseminated sclerosis, or the very crippled person with rheumatoid arthritis. In the same ward, there may be one or two fractured femurs, or a colostomy, or a person with a suprapubic catheter. There are also likely to be a few with inoperable cancer. In the ward, too, there are likely to be a few walking about, or comfortably sitting up in bed, complete with all their personal belongings, worrying what to do with their empty houses or other property.

Uncertified mental defectives are also cared for in the local authority hospital, and with the increasing demand for beds, the chronic sick patient may be put into the ward for mental defectives. Thus, one or other of the chronic wards may be adjacent to, or intermingled with, a mental defective ward, and the nursing staff originally engaged to look after the mental defectives also supervise the chronic sick. The immediate problem is how to use the beds, staff and facilities available in the best interests of the community in general and of the elderly population in particular.

INITIAL MEDICAL AND SOCIAL EXAMINATION

Because of the great number of beds, the shortage of staff and their lack of training, it is necessary to introduce streamlined methods in order to control the situation. The first thing is to examine each patient as thoroughly as possible and make a diagnosis. A written down diagnosis is not only the end result of a proper examination, it is also a considered opinion as to the cause of the illness, its main clinical features, likely prognosis, and an indication of the treatment that should be given. The diagnosis cannot in every instance be very precise, it may only be tentative, subsequent events may prove it to be wrong. The written diagnosis may not have great value to the physician in charge, since he may have an open mind as to alternative possibilities, but it is of great assistance to all those who have contact with, nurse, or give treatments to the patient; this is particularly so with an untrained staff, since for them it opens up the possibility of reading up, and getting to know more about, the patient's condition.

It is rare for a geriatric patient to have only one illness; the wearing out process usually affects the heart, the lungs, kidneys and central nervous system, and all may require special mention. All vague kinds of diagnosis should be avoided, as they only serve to fog the mind of those concerned. Chronic cough has very little therapeutic meaning, whereas bronchitis with bronchiectasis is a reasonably precise diagnosis. Senile dementia is so frequently a blunderbuss name for endless sins of omission, so is senility, and also incontinence, etc. An examination of all the urines is likely to show up one or two missed diabetics; blood haemoglobin estimations are likely to reveal a minority of patients with anaemia. Further examination will show that most cases of the anaemia are due to nutritional deficiency, and the rest to intestinal bleeding, or to malignancy. Perhaps there will also be an untreated case of pernicious anaemia. Cerebral thrombosis is common and it will be found that many so-called bedridden patients can be got up and will respond to treatment. A few will have positive Wasserman reactions, but it is rare to find the completely untreated case. The patient with blindness and cataracts can at times be successfully referred to the ophthalmic surgeon. A surgical re-examination of the patient with suprapubic catheter may show that the full operation may now be safely performed, or that the catheter is no longer necessary. The epileptic whose fits have been controlled by drugs may be discharged, or the burnt-out schizophrenic taken over by the psychiatrist.

It is, of course, impossible to discharge a patient who is bedridden, but as the examination of the patients continues it will become clear that an effort must be made to get them up in chairs. The next thing is to meet as many relatives as possible, with a view to discharging some of the patients to their care. Successes along these lines may be few, but one can always remember the relative who says: 'Of course I will be happy to have so-and-so out' (who may have been in many years) 'but you are the first person who has ever asked me.'

CASE NOTES

Remember that the geriatric patient is likely to be in hospital for a long time, that he is particularly subject to illnesses which are of a degenerative nature, and that further illness is apt to recur. Therefore, even after discharge he is likely to be seen some time in the future for one condition or another. It is therefore essential that the case notes should be orderly, full and easily readable, and that all investigations and happenings should be placed in a chronological order. By this means, expensive re-examinations and investigations can be obviated, and any omissions in examination can be easily checked. Further, since the number of doctors in the geriatric unit are very few in comparison with the number of beds, perhaps one or two residents to 400 beds, it is necessary to save time in writing medical notes. The following is a simple system and consists of a folder, a punch to make holes in the folder and history sheets, and two tags to keep the notes together.

On the front of the folder is kept the temperature chart; immediately inside the folder a prescription sheet followed by the history sheet. The history sheet sets out a few points about the patient's home and is then devoted to the medical examination; it should be specially prepared for geriatric illnesses. This in turn is followed by an investigation sheet. When there are ample numbers of fully trained staff, an investigation sheet may be unnecessary, but it has been found to be of great use in the geriatric ward. As each investigation is requested, the date of the request and the type of investigation is noted. When the result is at hand, a brief synopsis is jotted down. On doing a ward round, it is possible to check any delay in the investigations, and to avoid over-looking a result that has gone astray in some way or other. At the same time, it initiates some method which the nurse in charge can follow and begin to build on. The investigation sheet is followed by an ordinary continuation history sheet, which records the patient's progress, and after that comes the doctor's letter which should accompany the patient on admission to hospital. At the back of the folder are placed the actual investigation results as they appear in chronological order. The case history can now be read like a book, starting with page one. The sheets cannot become in a muddled order because they are all firmly fixed by means of the tag, and any new sheet can be readily attached.

ROUTINE INVESTIGATIONS

In selecting what investigations should be made the physician should be guided by the nature of the illness. It is a mistake to omit a necessary investigation, for example: haemoglobin if anaemia is suspected, and equally a mistake to request an investigation for which there is no indication and which will not help in the diagnosis. However, in the elderly many complaints occur so frequently that a routine of *basic* investigations is almost necessary. If a routine test gives a positive find-ing in about 10% or more of instances it should probably be retained; if the positive result is customarily less than 5% the test should only be used selectively. Amongst the tests that give 10% and over helpful results are blood haemoglobin, blood film, white blood count and differential, alkaline phosphatase, the thrombo-test, blood urea, and the acid phos-phatase in men with enlarged prostates. The chest X-ray and pelvic X-ray are also usually necessary as also electro-cardiogram and occult blood tests of the faeces. Even routine tests should not be slavishly followed and one or two may be omitted if they are unlikely to give a positive result.

HISTORY SHEET
GERIATRIC UNIT

NAME

AGE

Former Occupation
Address (home)
Diagnosis
Admitted
Referred by
Discharged
Home background
Neighbour's address

Type of accommodation
 Bedroom
 Toilet
 Remarks

COMPLAINT
DURATION
FAMILY HISTORY

PREVIOUS ILLNESSES AND PERSONAL HISTORY
 Fractures
 Falls
 Drug History

GENERAL CONDITION

Height	Temperature
Weight	Former Weight
Nutrition	Respirations
Pallor	Clubbed Fingers
Cyanosis	Exophthalmos
Jaundice	Puffiness under Eyes
Oedema	Night Sweats
Petechiae	Lassitude
Varicose Veins	Teeth
Enlarged glands	Tongue

CARDIOVASCULAR SYSTEM
 Dyspnoea
 Precordial Pain
 Palpitations
 Giddiness

Pulse	Arteries	Right	Left
Rate	Radial		
Regularity	Brachial		
Vessel Wall	Carotids		
Visible Pulsation	Temporal		
Blood Pressure	Femoral		

Heart
  Apex Position
  Character
  Force
  Extent
  Pulsation
Distension of Veins during inspiration
Thrills
Cardiac Dullness
Sounds
Murmurs

ALIMENTARY SYSTEM

Pain:	Hernia
Bowels: Constipation	Abdominal Aorta
Diarrhoea	Distended Bladder
Haemorrhoids	
Rectal Exam.	
Stools	
Benzidine	
Liver	
Spleen	
Palpable Mass	
X-ray	

RESPIRATORY SYSTEM

Cough (Morning   Day   Night)
Expectoration
Haemoptysis (Streaks   Mixed   Free)
Dyspnoea

Pain in Chest	Evidence of Emphysema
Voice	Broncho Spasm
Larynx	Effusion
Nose	Lung Collapse
Nasopharynx	Pneumonia
Tonsils	
Percussion	
Auscultation	

RENAL SYSTEM

Pain on Micturition
Increased Frequency (Day   Night   )
Urine

Colour	
Reaction	Chlorides
Spec. Gr.	Urobilin
Albumin	Sediment
Sugar	Casts
Acetone	Pus
	R.B.Cs.
	Bacilli

REPRODUCTION SYSTEM
Uterus
Prostate
Gonads
Breasts

INTEGUMENTARY SYSTEM

Colour	Rashes
Elasticity	Pruritis
Nails	Ulcers

BONES AND JOINTS

| (Skull and Spine) | Hips | Shoulders |
| Kyphosis | Nodules | |

CNS

Memory	Noisy
Intelligence	Agressive
Attention	Wandering
Emotions	Drowsiness
Hallucinations	Apathy
Delusions	Delirium
Confusion	Coma

Fits or Abnormal Movements
Chorea
Athetosis
Tics
Fits
Tremors
Speech

Motor Functions	Neck Rigidity
Wasting	Fasciculation
Tonicity	
Power	
Gait	
Co-ordination	Evidence of a Cerebellar Lesion

Sensory Functions	
Pain	Joint
Headache	Kinaesthetic
Vertigo	Deep Pressure
Tingling	Stereognosis
'Pins and Needles'	Vibration
Touch	Skin traction
Pain	Localisation
Temperature	Discrimination

Reflexes	
Corneal	Jaw
Pharangeal	Biceps
Upper Abdominal	Triceps
Lower Abdominal	Radial
Cremasteric	Patella
Plantar	Ankle
	Clonus

Cranial Nerves
  (1) Smell
  (2) Visual Acuity   Ophthalmoscopic Exam.
      Fields of Vision   Colour Vision
  (3) Pupil – size   Shape   React. to Light   Accomm.   Conv.
  (4)
  (5) Eyes – external movements   Squint   Diplopia
      Nystagmus
  (6) Sensory
      Motor
  (7) Sensory
      Motor
  (8) Hearing   R.   L.   Tinnitus
      Vestibular Sensation
  (9) Taste: Post 1/3   Pharynx anaes.
 (10) Palate   Heart
                         Respiration
 (11) Stermastoid
      Trapezius   Digestion
 (12) Tongue – Motor
Features of a 'Stroke'   Paralysis
                         Hemianopia
                         Sensory Loss
                         Postural Loss
                         Aphasia
                         Dysarthria

Investigation sheet....................
Unit No. ....

INVESTIGATIONS

Patient's Name...

Date	Investigations	Result	Performed by

THE DOCTOR'S LETTER

On the initial examination of patients in the ward, certain difficulties become apparent. There may be no family doctor's letter and it may be not at all clear what reason brought the patient into hospital. The patient himself may be too deaf, or have too poor a memory, to give a rational account; sometimes it is unknown whether he or she is married or single, or what relatives and family there may be. The doctor's letter, which is so often a matter of courtesy with the younger patients, is a vital omission. He may have previous notes about a patient and a record of various investigations made, all of which may be difficult to recollect. Relatives may visit only infrequently and it may be some time before they can be interviewed and a coherent history compiled – even this may be difficult if the relative is also a very aged person. Sometimes a geriatric patient comes for admission without any accompanying relative and without a doctor's letter; his name may have been picked out from a waiting list, and though originally there may have been a telephone conversation between a family doctor and a reception clerk, or resident, this may have all been forgotten.

Clearly, therefore, a request for admission should be accompanied by, or followed by, a letter from the family doctor, giving as much information as possible. However, there are still some practical difficulties over this; the doctor may be very busy and have a large number of patients to see. On his rounds, he foresees that one patient perhaps should be admitted, and when he gets back to his surgery he is able to telephone the hospital, though he may be unable to contact the resident and have to leave his request with the medical clerk. If the patient is admitted by ambulance, there will be no accompanying letter unless the doctor has made special provision. He must then either revisit the patient to leave a letter (which is expecting rather a lot) or post one off the same, or the next, day. Human nature being what it is, such a letter may never get posted. This is but one of the minor difficulties of geriatrics.

THE HISTORY SHEET

Not only should a social medical history be taken from the patient on admission, but the relatives should always be interviewed, with a view to completing the medical history, ascertaining the home conditions, finding out what co-operation can be expected and to confirm that if the patient can be got better he may be discharged home. Otherwise, some relatives assume that the patient is coming in for life and do not keep up the tenancy, or make moves that will make the ultimate discharge of the patient impossible. This kind of interview is equally essential if the patient goes to an ordinary general, medical or surgical ward, so as to avoid discharge difficulties in advance.

Not all the points listed in the history sheet will be referable to the patient's illness; thus it may be of no consequence that he once suffered from measles if the presenting features are those of cancer of the stomach, though it might have some bearing if the patient had a chronic lung condition. According to the presenting symptoms, emphasis will be placed on varying parts of the history sheet. Negative answers can be recorded by means of a nought, positive ones by underlining the feature with a small accompanying note.

Residents at first are a little put out at the idea of such an extensive history sheet, but after a while they find they can record a history and physical signs very quickly and accurately, make their examination more methodically, and learn to highlight significant findings or significant omissions. They find they make a habit of noting any and everything about the patient and relating the physical findings with the clinical symptoms.

A rectal examination is usually done to diagnose enlargement of the prostate gland and faecal impaction, two common conditions in the elderly, and the senses of smell, sight and hearing, so important to an elderly person, are always checked. Coronary thrombosis is a very likely occurrence in the elderly, who so often have arterial degenerative changes, and it does not always give the classical acute symptoms described in younger persons; or because of mental confusion no clear history can be obtained from the patient. A careful record of the cardiovascular system is therefore desirable so that any change in the physical signs can be readily checked.

The history sheet has been considered in some detail, but it is the numerous details that are so important in the efficient running of a geriatric unit, and it is considered that the history sheet is the core of the medical care. For this reason, it is difficult to exaggerate the importance of the properly recorded medical history and examination of the patient.

URINARY EXAMINATION

Illnesses affecting many organs in the body cause clinical features that can be brought to light on physical examination, for example, pleural effusion, pneumonia, congestive heart failure, high blood pressure, enlarged liver, etc., but failure of renal function is not so apparent. It is therefore very easy to overlook assessing the function of the kidneys. But the kidneys deal with some 1–2 litres of blood a minute and are vital to life. Their failure is reflected in disorders of the electrolyte balance and in the chemical state of the body. The kidneys in the elderly are subject to the same vascular and other degenerative changes that are affecting the heart, lungs, skin and other organs, and there is likely to be some impairment of function in all elderly persons. But the renal failure does not commonly take the form of glomerular tubular nephritis with casts and albumen in the urine which may be expected in a younger person, so much as failure in urinary concentration. A simple examination of the urine which records sugar absent, albumen absent, is not really very helpful as it gives no indication of the functioning of the kidneys. A full urinary examination is considered necessary with every patient, and particularly a record of the specific gravity and the amount of chlorides present, in addition to examination for sugar and albumen.

Elderly persons, though not diabetics, may show acetone in the urine, especially in states of malnutrition and dehydration. Cystitis is a common illness and bacteriological examination of the urine is frequently necessary. The importance of the specific gravity and the chloride content is dealt with in a later chapter, but for convenience the chloride estimation is done as follows:

Ten drops of urine are measured into a test tube with a pipette. The same pipette is rinsed and one drop of 20% of potassium chromate solution is added. The pipette is again rinsed and 2.9% silver nitrate solution is added drop by drop. When the colour of the urine changes suddenly to brown, the number of drops of silver nitrate used will express in grammes per litre the amount of sodium chloride in the urine. To test the freshness of the solutions, a control test may be done either with distilled water or with a salt solution of known amount, for example, normal saline.

UROBILINOGEN AND UROBILIN IN THE URINE

Jaundice is commonly seen in the elderly, and is often caused by cholecystitis, biliary calculi, hepatitis, carcinoma of the head of the pancreas, and of more recent years by largactil poisoning. The test for urobilinogen in the urine is fairly simple to perform and throws considerable light on the patency or otherwise of the bile duct. This information may be of key significance in the clinical picture and on it may turn diagnosis of an inoperable growth, or a condition amenable to medical or surgical treatment, which would otherwise be neglected. For the above reasons, the test is carried out whenever indicated and, for the convenience of the reader, the test procedure is set down as follows:

Take 10 cm^3 of fresh urine, add to the urine 1 cm^3 of Ehrlich's aldehyde reagent; this is made up of para-dimenthylamino-benzaldehyde dissolved in 5% hydrochloric acid. After 3 to 5 minutes, normal urine should show a reddish tinge intensified on heating. If this colour is not seen, then urobilinogen is not present in the urine. An excess of urobilinogen in the urine may be estimated by finding out the highest degree of dilution of the urine which will give a red colour.

ELECTROCARDIOGRAPH EXAMINATION

It is the aim of rehabilitation in the elderly to encourage them to be as active as reasonably possible. The idea is to add 'life to the years' and not the prolongation of chronic invalidism, of suffering, or of a mere negative existence. Reactivation of the bedridden carries several attendant risks. Though these may be minimised by careful handling, and by use of suitable geriatric chairs and other equipment, there is still the risk of the patient feeling faint and sustaining a fall, or of collapsing because she has exceeded her cardiac reserve. To avoid catastrophe, it is important to know as much about the state of the heart as possible. A recent coronary thrombosis, or an old thrombosis, may be surmised from the history and clinical features, but the latter are not always sufficiently reliable, and an electrocardiographic examination ought to be made, so that no unreasonable risks are taken in getting the patient up and about the ward. An electrocardiograph is just as important for the elderly as for younger persons in making an accurate diagnosis and prognosis on which to base treatment, and should be available to all geriatric units. Electrocardiographic records in the very elderly are rarely completely normal, and a different standard has to be accepted from that customary in younger people.

RADIOLOGY AND X-RAY SCREEN

Old people suffer from illnesses which require radiology, just the same as the younger age groups, and radiological examination should be available to old people as well as to young. But this is not so if the elderly are nursed in chronic wards or in a block of buildings where there is no X-ray apparatus. Under the latter circumstances, there are some difficulties in X-raying the geriatric patient. He may be too debilitated to walk to the X-ray department, or to wait in a queue; this may mean he has to be taken by a nurse in a wheel chair. This can be very time-consuming, a little risky if long draughty corridors have to be negotiated and almost impossible if there are stairs to mount or descend between the ward and the X-ray department. X-ray screening may make a good deal of chest radiology unnecessary. A small screening set is not very expensive, and is an invaluable adjunct to any geriatric unit. It not only allows of a better examination of the patient, but saves much of the expense of producing X-ray films. The X-ray screen is dealt with later on when considering the out-patient department.

OCCULT BLOOD IN THE FAECES

Both anaemia and malignant conditions of the bowel are all too common in the elderly, so much so that a test for occult blood in the faeces is a matter of routine, and usually immediately follows a rectum examination. The ward staff quickly learn how to test urines and with very little effort they can also carry out the test for occult blood in the faeces. The test is performed in the following manner:

A small amount of faeces is smeared on a little thin blotting paper. An occult-test tablet is now placed on the smeared area and a few drops of water are pipetted on to the tablet. If occult blood is present (the test is sensitive as to thirty red corpuscles per cubic millimetre) a blue colour will develop around the tablet in about a minute. If negative, blue colour may still develop, but after a much greater lapse of time. The test is not positive unless haemoglobin is present in the faeces, and it is not too sensitive. It is not positive even if iron is being taken by mouth. It is, of course, likely to be positive if much meat has been taken, and it is usually positive when there is obstinate constipation, though there has been no intestinal bleeding. Repeated occult blood tests are more significant than one result and in any case the test should only be interpreted in relation to the clinical features. A consistently positive test strongly indicates intestinal bleeding and suggests common conditions such as peptic ulcer, neoplasm of the bowel, diverticulitis, etc. If the patient is anaemic, and the test is persistently negative, then intestinal bleeding is unlikely to be the cause of the anaemia. The test should obviously be included in the investigation of any patient with anaemia.

PATHOLOGICAL EXAMINATION

A shortage of resident medical staff in the geriatric unit may mean the nurses have to assist in the collection of specimens for the laboratory, and they will need to know how the specimens should be collected and prepared for the pathologist. In most hospitals the consultant pathologist has already issued simple instructions that should be followed in the ward. If the geriatric wards have not been covered in this way, it may become the geriatric physician's responsibility to train the ward staff in collecting specimens. The following are the instructions commonly issued by the pathologists and, if carefully followed out, will prevent a lot of waste of time and material.

The request card should always be fully completed and a christian name as well as the surname of the patient filled in in block letters, since it frequently happens that the hospital has several patients with the same surname. Specimens should be clearly labelled and any name should be on the specimen tube rather than on the container.

Collection of blood A dry syringe and dry needle will be required to take an intravenous specimen. 5 cm³ of blood in a Wintrobe's anti-coagulant tube is commonly used for haemoglobin estimation, leucocyte or reticulocyte counts. If Erythrocyte Sedimentation Rate is requested, the Wintrobe's anticoagulant tube is again used but it is important that there should be no delay in sending off the specimen. Blood grouping and Rh. grouping is usually done on 5 cm³ of clotted blood in an ordinary test tube. For a Plasma Prothrombin Level, usually 4·5 cm³ of blood exactly in a fluid sodium oxalate is required. The tube should also contain 4·5 cm³ of anticoagulant. Any haemolysis in the sample, or too much or too little blood, causes inaccuracy.

KIDNEY FUNCTION TESTS

Urea concentration test For this the patient should receive restricted bland fluids after 4 p.m. on the previous day, and should have nothing to eat or drink after 7.30 p.m. Next morning the bladder is emptied and the whole sample is sent to the laboratory. The patient now drinks 15 gm ($\frac{1}{2}$ oz) of urea in 100 cm³ of water (3 oz) which is flavoured with lemon or orange. At the first, second and third hours, the patient empties his bladder and the samples are sent to the laboratory. No food or drink is given until the test is completed. The test is rarely used.

Urea clearance test The patient should be in bed on ordinary meals and fluid. After a breakfast of tea and toast, the patient empties his bladder, the time is noted and a specimen sent to the laboratory. The patient then drinks $\frac{1}{2}$ to 1 pint of water or tea. After 1 hour, the bladder is again emptied and the specimen sent off, together with 1 cm³ of intravenous blood. After 2 hours, the bladder is again emptied completely and the whole specimen sent to the laboratory. This test is rarely used.

Glucose tolerance test in diabetes mellitus On the previous evening, no fluid or food is allowed after 9 p.m. and only a cup of tea without milk or sugar in the morning. At 0 hours the patient empties his bladder and a specimen of urine is sent to the laboratory, and at the same time 0·5 cm³ of venous blood is collected. The patient now drinks 50 gm of glucose in 5 oz of water flavoured with lemon or citric acid. All the fluid must be swallowed, followed if necessary by water. At $\frac{1}{2}$, 1, 1$\frac{1}{2}$ and 2 hours further blood specimens are repeated, and at 1 and 2 hours the bladder must again be emptied completely and the urine sent for examination.

Urine For ordinary examination a clean 3 oz specimen passed in the morning on awakening is required. For a 24 hour specimen the patient empties his bladder at a noted time and this specimen is discarded, after which all urine passed up to and including the same hour on the following day is collected and stored in a Winchester bottle. At this stage, it is perhaps important to point out that in elderly patients with incontinence or mental confusion it is difficult to obtain clean and accurate specimens.

Gastric analysis for suspected achlorhydria On the day previous to the test, no aperient should be given. On the following morning, at 7 or 8 a.m. the complete gastric juice is removed by aspirating the stomach while the patient is turned into varying positions. At one hour, 0·5 mg of histamine is injected, and at 1 hour and 2 hours further samples of gastric juice are aspirated. All three samples are then sent to the laboratory. This test is now rarely needed.

The above is the kind of information that has to be passed on to the nursing staff, if they have not already been trained. Naturally, if there is a sister in charge this will be done by her. There are of course many other points about the collection of specimens which the geriatric ward staff will learn as time progresses. It is useful to keep a typewritten account of the instructions in every ward so that the staff can readily refresh their minds on the matter.

When the pathological results are reported back, it can be very important that the doctor be informed of its contents quickly. This, in effect, means that one or more of the nurses must be able to appreciate what report is significant. It is therefore invaluable to have in the ward a typewritten statement of the normal pathological results. When the pathological report is received, the nurse on duty is able to note any significant abnormality. For example, a blood examination may be requested and a haemoglobin of only 35% reported. Clearly the question of a transfusion may have to be considered and the doctor ought to be informed of the result at once. Or there might be an abnormally high blood glucose or blood urea that should receive immediate attention; or a high acid phosphatase may indicate an immediate change in the treatment of the patient. A copy of the following normal findings can be usefully pinned up in each ward: these values have been taken from the *Physician's Handbook*.[1]

NORMAL HAEMATOLOGICAL VALUES

Whiteblood cells 5000–10 000 per mm³

Myelocytes	0%	Lymphocytes	20–40%
Juvenile Neutrophils	0%	Eosinophils	1–3%
Bank Neutrophils	0–5%	Basophils	0–1%
Segmented Neutrophils	40–60%	Monocytes	4–8%

Platelets: 200 000 to 500 000 per mm³
Red blood cells, in million per mm³
  Men: 5·0 (4·5 to 6·0)   Women: 4·5 (4·3 to 5·5)
Reticulocytes: Less than 1%
Haemoglobin in gm/100 cm³
  Men: 15–16 gm (13·5–18)   Women: 13–15 (12·5–16·5)

Haematocrit (packed cell volume)
  Men: 45·47% (38–54%)   Women: 40–42% (36–47%)
Cellular measurements of r.b.c.; Average diameter: 7·3 u (5·5–8·8 u)
  Mean corpuscular volume   87 c.u. (80–94c.u.)
  Mean corpuscular hgb   30 yy (28·32 yy)
  Mean corpuscular hgb conc   35% (33–38%)
  Colour, saturation, and volume indices, each: 1·0 (0·9–1·1)
Bleeding time: Duke, 1–4 minutes. Ivy, less than 4 minutes
Coagulation time: Lee and White, 5–15 minutes

Normal renal function and urine values

Phenol red test (P.S.P.): 15 minutes, over 25%; 2 hours, over 55%
Urea clearance: 75–120% of A.N.F. or 40–100 cm^3/minutes
Addis urine sediment count (values for 24 hour period):
  pH: acid   Specific Gravity: 1025–1030   Protein: 0–30 mg
  r.b.c.: 0–1 000 000   Casts, hyaline: 0–100 000
  w.b.c. and small epithelial cells: 1–2 000 000

Normal blood chemistry values

Constituent	Value/100 cm^3	mEQ/litre
Sodium	310–335 mg	136–145
Chloride (as Cl–)	350–375 mg	100–106
Total Chlorides (as NaCl)	580–620 mg	100–106
Potassium	14–20 mg	3·5–5·0
Phosphorus	3–4·5 mg	0·9–1·5 (mM)
Magnesium	1–3 mg	1–2
Calcium, total	9–11 mg	4·5–5·5
CO$_2$ content	55–75 vol %	24–28
Cholesterol	150–240 mg	
Cholesterol, esters	65% of the total cholesterol	
Amylase	80–180 units	
Phosphatase, alkaline	2·0–4·5 units (Bodansky)	
Phosphatase, acid	0·5–2 units (Bodansky)	
Protein bound iodine	4–8 micrograms	
Serum albumin	4·5–5·5 gm	Total:
Serum globulin	1·5–3·0 g	6·0–8·0 gm
Fibrinogen (plasma)	0·2–0·6 mg	per 100 cm^3
Bilirubin, direct 1 minute	0·1–0·4 mg	
indirect 30 minutes	0·2–0·7 mg	
Glucose 60–100 mg (true):	80–120 mg (Folin-Wu)	
Total non-protein nitrogen	15–35 mg	
Urea nitrogen	10–20 mg	
Uric acid	3–6 mg	
Creatinine	1–2 mg	

DIET SHEETS

Patients may require special diets, such as a diabetic diet, an obesity
diet, a salt-free diet, a low-fat diet or a high protein diet, and again it
is very useful to have diet sheets already prepared and available to the

nurses, or to be given to a patient so that he can continue on the same diet after discharge. Attached are some specimen diet sheets which may prove of value.

DIETS FOR CONVALESCENT

High CH. Low fat High protein diet
Approximately: Prot. 120. Fat 45. CHO. 400. Calories 2500

Early morning	Glass of water, hot or cold
Breakfast	Porridge, or average serving corn flakes or other breakfast cereal with syrup, or Fruit, e.g. stewed prunes or mashed banana, average serving Fish, small serving, or egg, boiled or poached Bread, as crisp toast, butter Jelly, marmalade or honey Weak tea with milk and sugar
Forenoon	Juice 1 orange Glass hot water Juice ½ lemon Sugar
Lunch	Small serving steamed white fish, tripe, chicken or rabbit Coating sauce without butter, using cornflour and milk Potato, boiled or baked Average serving vegetable Average serving stewed, or raw, ripe fruit Few boiled sweets
Mid-afternoon	Fruit drink as above
Tea	Bread – may be toasted Jelly, honey or syrup Weak tea with milk and sugar
Dinner	Average serving lean meat, liver, fish, chicken or rabbit – not fried Crisp toast Small serving vegetable Average serving fruit, stewed or raw Biscuit (sweet) Weak coffee with milk and sugar
Bed-time	Fruit drink as above
DAILY RATIONS	Milk, whole, ½ pint Milk, skim, 2 pints or 1 pint special milk (double strength 'household' milk) Butter (or vitaminised margarine) piece size of walnut

GENERAL INSTRUCTIONS
Eat slowly and chew thoroughly

AVOID
Large meals and indigestible articles of food
All fried foods, all foods made with fat and oils, cream, egg yolks
Duck, goose, salmon, bacon, herring
All pastries, Yorkshire and suet puddings

Chocolate, cocoa, strong tea and coffee
Condiments, spices and alcoholic beverages

TAKE FREELY
Fresh fruit and vegetables which should be sieved
Honey, jam and sugar
Water and fruit drinks

DIABETIC DIET NO. 2

2000 calories. C.198: P.68: F.107 gm

Breakfast Tea or coffee, milk ¼ pint
Bacon, 1 oz (1 good rasher) or 1 egg with ¼ oz extra butter or margarine, or 2 oz fish with ½ oz extra butter or margarine
Bread, 4 oz (4–½ inch slices)
Butter or margarine, ½ oz (size of a walnut)
1 small apple or pear, or ½ oz extra bread

Lunch Lean meat or cheese, 2 oz (a fair portion), or 4 oz fish (a good portion) with ½ oz extra butter or margarine
Meat, fat, butter or margarine, ½ oz (piece size of walnut)
Cabbage (a good helping)
Potatoes, 4 oz (a good-sized potato)
Junket of ¼ pint milk (or you may drink the milk)
1 small apple or pear, or ½ oz extra bread

Tea Tea, milk ¼ pint
Bread, 1 oz (1–½ inch slice)
Butter, ½ oz (piece size of a walnut)

Supper Meat, 2 oz (a fair portion), or cheese, 2 oz, or fish, 4 oz with ½ oz extra butter or margarine
Bread 3 oz (3–½ inch slices)
Butter or margarine, ½ oz (size of walnut)
Cabbage (a good serving)
Potatoes, 4 oz (a good-sized potato)
Milk, ¼ pint

Summary

Glucose value	248 grammes
Calories	2027
C	198 grammes
P	68 grammes
F	107 grammes

Alternative breakfast Tea or coffee, milk ½ pint
Oatmeal, weighed dry, or cornflakes, 1 oz
Bread, 3 oz (3–½ inch slices)
Butter or margarine, ¾ oz

Summary

C	72 grammes
P	22 grammes
F	29 grammes

DIABETIC DIET – ALTERNATIVES

X

Any of these biscuits (approximately 6 grammes CH in each)

Cream cracker
Breakfast
Thin captain
Water biscuit
Rye-vita
Vita-weat

Y

A good helping of any of the following vegetables (approximates 5 grammes carbohydrate)

Beetroot
Broad beans
Carrots
Onions
Parsnips
Turnips

1 oz of any of the dried fruits (approximates 20 grammes of carbohydrate): or any of those fruits weighed raw (approximates 10 grammes carbohydrate)

Apples	3 oz
Apricots	6 oz
Blackberries (raw)	6 oz
Gooseberries (ripe)	4 oz
Blackcurrants	6 oz
Oranges	6 oz
Peaches	4 oz
Pears	3 oz
Plums	4 oz
Raspberries	6 oz
Redcurrants	9 oz
Strawberries	6 oz

Z

Or the following, in any amount desired:

Asparagus
Brussels sprouts
Celery
Cucumber
Grapefruit
Leeks
Lettuce
Marrow
Melon

Cabbage
Cauliflower
Mushrooms
Radishes
Rhubarb
Scarlet Runners
Seakale
Spinach
Tomatoes

One egg may be replaced by any of the following:

$\frac{3}{4}$ oz cheese
1 oz bacon and $\frac{1}{4}$ oz. less butter
1 oz sardines
1 oz lean meat or corned beef and $\frac{1}{4}$ oz more butter
1 oz tinned salmon and $\frac{1}{8}$ oz more butter

Milk – When fresh milk is not available it may be replaced by evaporated, condensed full cream, sweetened, condensed full cream, or dried 'household' milk, but the fat deficiency in the dried milk should be made up with an extra ¾ oz of butter or margarine for each pint. 3½ oz of *fresh* milk contains 5 gm of carbohydrate.

Meat – may be replaced by offal, fish, eggs, cheese: 2½ oz of lean meat is equivalent to:

3½ oz white fish and ¼ oz extra butter
2½ oz rabbit and ¼ oz extra butter
2½ oz kidney and ¼ oz extra butter
3½ oz liver and ¼ oz extra butter

Bread – 1 oz National Bread – 1 thin slice – approx: 15 gm of carbohydrate. Where weight is given, exchange *must* be weighed accurately.

Macaroni (boiled)	2½ oz
Shredded wheatflakes	¾ oz
Biscuits:	
3 cream crackers	
2 rich tea biscuits	
3 water biscuits	
Prunes, stewed without sugar	3¾ oz
Apple, eating	6 oz
Banana, raw	5 oz
Potato, cooked	3 oz
Rice (dry weight)	¾ oz
Bengers Food (dry weight)	¾ oz
Oatmeal	¾ oz

WARD STATISTICS

Very often the nursing staff in a chronic ward have become discouraged because their work apparently has led to so little success. All too often the same group of patients have remained in the ward for months, or years, very few have been discharged home and new patients only come when there have been deaths in the ward. It has been found that they are encouraged by keeping, on a graph, a monthly account of the admissions, the discharges and deaths. They are thus able to mark any improvement and relate it to any change in their nursing procedure or additional efforts.

WARD REQUIREMENTS

No ward can be operated satisfactorily without a ward stethoscope, blood pressure apparatus, lumbar puncture set, intravenous set, drip bottles and drip stand, needles, syringes, sterilising apparatus and a small clinical room for examination of the urine. The ward will also require cupboards where these articles can be stored, as well as a drug cupboard and a poison cupboard. The geriatric ward will also need numerous arm-chairs, walking chairs, wheel chairs, sufficient room for ambulation and a *day room* for patients in a convalescent stage awaiting discharge.

The stethoscope Cardiac failure is a frequent occurrence in the elderly and commonly takes the form of congestive heart failure with auricular fibrillation. The patient usually responds to the digitalis groups of drugs, but during this therapy it is necessary to have a stethoscope to record not only the pulse rate but also the cardiac rate. The patient can then be properly digitalised without poisonous effects.

Lumbar puncture set Hardly a week passes without the admission to the ward of a few patients in a coma, and a lumbar puncture is a diagnostic necessity. The confirmation of a cerebral haemorrhage by this means carries a grave prognosis and requires a line of treatment which is much simpler and less arduous to the nursing staff than would be the case if the patient only had a cerebral thrombosis. There are of course many other instances where the lumbar puncture findings, for example, meningoccocal meningitis, indicate life-saving procedures.

Intravenous set Dehydration is very common and it is a constant battle to maintain correct fluid balance in an elderly person no matter what illness he or she may have. Intravenous therapy may be not only life-saving, but in many instances easier and more successfully carried out than other methods of restoring fluid balance. Blood loss from haematemesis is also a not uncommon condition, and for this and very severe anaemias, blood transfusion may be the best therapeutic procedure.

Dehydration bottle It has been found that the elderly patient in dehydration is often confused and frequently adopts a supine position in bed. It is difficult to give fluids to this kind of patient in this posture even when using a feeding cup; the fluid is apt to fall to the back of the mouth and enter the larynx, or the patient will only just take a sip. For this reason wards can be issued with dehydration bottles and in practice these have been found to be very useful. The bottle is made of polythene and holds a pint of fluid; it is fitted with a rubber stopper – a cork stopper becomes soiled too readily. Passing through the stopper to the bottom of the flask is a polythene tube extruding about 3 or 4 inches, and the flask is filled to within a fifth of the top. The polythene tube is fitted tightly into the stopper so that the fluid will not ooze alongside the tube: prepared chewing gum can be used for this.

The flask, being made of polythene, is quite safe, since it has no sharp edges and does not break on falling. Fluid can be fed to the patient by a gentle squeezing action, but the patient usually learns to suck up fluid in a short while. The flask can be turned upside down without loss of fluid and can be left in the patient's hand in the bed without fear of soiling the bedclothes. The flask is transparent and consequently it is easy to see how much fluid the patient is getting. The bottle can be thoroughly cleaned when necessary.

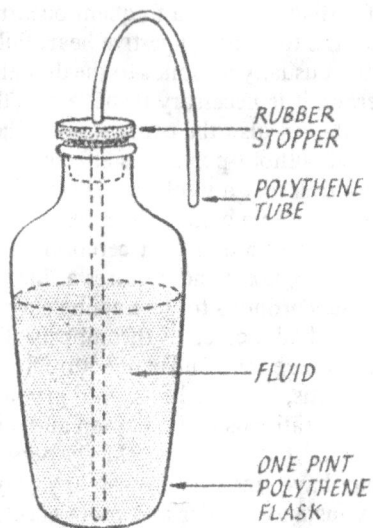

RUBBER
STOPPER

POLYTHENE
TUBE

FLUID

ONE PINT
POLYTHENE
FLASK

Dehydration bottle, devised by the author

The geriatric chair

The use of this bottle reduces the amount of nursing attention required and more readily ensures that the patient gets sufficient fluids.

The geriatric chair The dangers of undue rest in bed have already been pointed out and one of the first steps in rehabilitation is to get the patient up in a chair. By this means, the danger of pressure sores is lessened, basal congestion of the lungs is avoided, as also weakness of the muscles and stiffness of the joints, and the patient is able to have a more normal action of the bladder and bowels by use of the chair commode. There should therefore be room near each bed for a geriatric chair into which the patient can be slipped for a short while every day. The beds therefore must not be too close together, but if there are ample wheel chairs and a suitable day room, the patient can of course be wheeled there.

The elderly patient requires certain features in the geriatric chair. The seat should be soft and neither too high nor too low. The back should allow the patient's head to rest comfortably and should have wings to prevent him slipping sideways. There should also be arms to the chair. Because of the risk of incontinence, the seat of the chair, at least, should be covered with waterproof material. On the front of the chair there should be a removable table. The patient can then use this for meals, or for reading, or for resting in a forward position. It is also useful for the confused patient who has to be left unobserved for a short while. It is difficult for the height of the seat to suit all patients so that some geriatric chairs have a small footstool which pulls out from underneath the seat. The value of a really good geriatric chair can hardly be exaggerated in the treatment of the geriatric patient. Unfortunately the geriatric chair can be misused, and the patient just allowed to sit there from morning to bed-time. In other words 'aids' do not replace the need for proper nursing attention.

The sanitary chair It is of course not only nicer for the patient, but much less work for the nursing staff, if the patient can go to the toilet on his own. This may be accomplished by a wheel sanitation chair which can be hand-propelled by the patient. The chair is designed to fit over the lavatory and is fitted with a false bottom. One or two of these chairs in a ward can save a great deal of nursing work.

The wheel chair There are many varieties of the wheel chair, but they fall naturally into two groups. In the first group, the patient has to be pushed about by someone else, and in the second group the patient can propel the chair himself. The former group are generally cheaper and can serve a useful purpose when it is anticipated either that the patient will be able to walk shortly or that he will never be able to use a self-propelling chair. Self-propelling chairs are more expensive, but allow the patient a great deal of freedom of movement and independence, so much so that an intelligent patient can run a home with very little personal assistance. The most mobile of the self-propelling wheel chairs has a light metal construction and is more commonly supplied to the patient who has had poliomyelitis. This type of chair is fairly suitable for elderly patients, if a few modifications are made. The chair tends to tip up backwards and so may require two runners at the back, and of course it is not suitable for an elderly person to sit in for too long because it is not comfortable enough. When a geriatric patient has lost a leg, the self-propelling wheel chair may be a better solution than the supply of an artificial limb and the long tedium of re-training which may be unsuccessful.

Electric Wheel Chair Where indicated a battery operated propelling wheel chair is available, which has very simple and safe control switches. This is particularly valuable to the paralysed patient who cannot walk and who cannot use the self propelled chair because of weakness in his arms.

The walking aids A patient who has been bedridden for some time, or who has been partially paralysed from a stroke, may require a great deal of re-training in the art of walking. At first this is undertaken by the personal assistance of a nurse, physiotherapist or other person, but since there are not enough staff for this work, the patient is encouraged to make use of a walking chair. In its simplest form this consists of obtaining support from the back of another chair, but specially designed walking chairs are now available. One such is in the form of a pulpit on wheels so that when the patient is supporting himself on the front there is also support on both sides as he moves along. With the use of such a walking chair many a patient is able to go to the toilet on his own, and the chair can be used in conjunction with walking exercises on a gangway with parallel rails. Other aids are of course crutches, sticks and appropriately sited handrails.

Day room and room for ambulation It is important not to overcrowd the ward with extra beds; otherwise there will be no room for walking exercises, so vital to the elderly. A day room adjoining the ward can be most useful. The patients can be collected there in wheel chairs and have their meals together, enter into conversation, knit or sew or undertake some occupational therapy. The day room is, of course, suited more to the patients who have got over the acute phase of an illness and are gaining strength preparatory to discharge. But even if a patient cannot be discharged, it adds a fullness to his way of living.

STAFF REQUIREMENTS

The idea that elderly patients cannot benefit from modern medicine is quite wrong, and it seems unfair, especially when there is a National

Health Service, that they should have to be cared for by an untrained staff. The shortage of nursing staff is of course by no means easy to solve since there is so much competition for the employment of women in industry and many other occupations.

There are also difficulties in the training of student nurses. Though the nursing councils, for Scotland, England and Wales, allow student nurses to spend a proportion of their training in a geriatric ward, naturally the wards in question must be suitably staffed and with adequate facilities. But bringing even the admission geriatric wards to the required standards is difficult because there is an objection to having student nurses and assistant nurses in the same ward. Since there is a general shortage of nursing staff, it is hardly possible to empty the admission wards completely of assistant nurses so that student nurses can work in the wards. When the admission wards can be brought to the required standards, there could be a break in what at present appears to be a vicious circle in recruitment for geriatric nursing.

It is perhaps appropriate at this stage to draw attention to the dangers of inadequate nursing staff or untrained nurses. Elderly patients require feeding, to be given drinks frequently, to be turned in bed often, to have their backs kept clean, to be assisted to the toilet and, in addition, dangerous drugs have to be administered, pulses and temperatures have to be recorded, etc. Further, in the acute wards there are enemas to be given, catheterisation, blood and other transfusions; and for the sister, interviews with relatives who wish to enquire about the patients. Inadequate staff means thirsty patients and dehydration, loaded bowels, wet beds, bed sores, falls by the patients attempting to go to the toilet alone, and lack of reasonable control of the giving of dangerous drugs. One can well imagine the anxiety of both the physician and the sister in charge of a ward where staff are insufficient or unsatisfactory.

It is perhaps of interest to read what a student nurse thinks of her work in a geriatric ward. The following are some extracts taken from an essay written by Mrs Moira Storrier of Sunderland (personal communication):

'It is an unhappy fact, but unfortunately a true one, that the dignified old patriarch revered by children and respected by grandchildren, seldom penetrates the hospital ward. The geriatric is usually unwanted, a cumbersome burden handed from one member of his family to the other to be received with reluctance by each in his turn, then thankfully passed along, until the family as a whole admit defeat and he is received in the hospital ward. He may arrive both dirty and underfed. This is when a true nurse comes into her own. A warm bed, clean clothes, adequate food and a few kind words can do wonders for the average geriatric. He can be transformed in a matter of days from a defeated species of humanity to a companionable and even lovable individual. For this transformation, he relies entirely upon his nurse.

To the geriatric a nurse becomes a personification of that which he has wanted and never had, or once possessed and then lost – a loving wife, a consoling sister or a devoted child; she is his 'bonnie Nellie', his 'canny Meg', or his 'wee Dolly'. If letters arrive, she reads them to him, and the wishes for recovery come from her voice. Often she will find herself called upon to listen to strange reminiscences of a past era, coal strikes, soup kitchens, dole queues, bare-footed children and vague rambling accounts of long-forgotten wars. It is she who is the first to note signs of progress and offer encouragement. Her arm steers the patient in his first adventurous journey up the hospital ward, to a seat by the fire.

Now the battle has just begun. During the weeks of convalescence, treacherous floors and projecting furniture may cause a stumble, which will undo the good of months of care. Geriatric convalescents can be very venturesome and the nurse must be constantly on the alert for pitfalls. The fire fascinates him. Hitherto it has just been a distant glow seen from the ward bed, now it is near at hand to be poked and explored. He is intrigued by enticing smells of food coming from the ward kitchen, and sometimes rises unsteadily from his chair and makes off, with the kitchen as his goal. The final reward comes eventually, however, when the nurse assists her patient through the ward doors, and out to the waiting ambulance which is to take him home.'

TYPES OF GERIATRIC WARD

The clinical problems of the elderly make it desirable to divide the geriatric wards into three classes.

The acute geriatric ward deals with new admissions and all the acute illnesses met with in geriatric patients. It is likely to be full of patients suffering from haematemesis, pneumonia, acute bronchitis, congestive heart failure, acute dehydration, diabetic coma, recent hemiplegia, pernicious anaemia, gangrene of the feet, carcinoma of the lung and so on. A ward sister, staff nurse and other trained nurses are clearly essential. Even if theoretically it is planned that acute emergencies in the elderly go to ordinary medical wards, in practice it is found continually that the geriatric ward has to admit a patient with an acute treatable illness. Thus the need for an acute geriatric ward is forced on the geriatric unit by circumstances. It therefore becomes essential it should have a fully trained, adequate nursing staff.

In the acute male ward, because of the high incidence of bladder conditions it may be helpful to have a trained male nurse.

Short stay ward The next class of ward is the short stay ward where patients may stay for a few months. To this ward will be transferred the hemiplegia cases who have made a little progress, the recovering patients from bronchitis, heart failure, malnutrition, mental confusion, anaemia, diabetics, arthritics, and so on. The accent in this kind of ward is on restoration of function by ambulation and physiotherapy, but there is still a fair amount of sub-acute illness and there should be a sister and staff nurse in charge with suitable nursing help. In this ward, of course, physiotherapy should be actively pursued.

Long stay ward Despite all treatment, there are still a number of patients who remain demented or bedridden for one reason or another, and while a few of these may be nursed in the acute or short stay wards, the bulk of them may be better cared for in the long stay ward, or annexe. In this ward the patients are unable to respond to medical treatment, but require nursing care and accommodation. The long stay wards should have a sister in charge, but it cannot be claimed that they require the trained staff so vital to the acute wards, and much of the work can be done by untrained staff.

A geriatric unit usually requires beds to be divided in the following proportions. One-fifth for the acute geriatric wards, one-fifth for the short stay wards, and three-fifths again for the long stay annexe.

REHABILITATION

There is a great difference between the person who can carry out the activities of daily living, and the one who is dependent on assistance for dressing, undressing, the toilet and so on. The former has a great measure of freedom and independence and is a burden to no one, whereas the latter must be a burden to someone. If at home, he must be a burden to the relatives or neighbours, and if in hospital, to the ward staff. Success in the rehabilitation of a person to a point of personal independence not only gives the patient a new lease of life, but brings relief to all those concerned in the patient's welfare. Some elderly persons become dependent on account of gross cardiac weakness, or the ravages of paralysis, but a vast number of them have no such illness, and their dependence has been brought on by an impoverished diet, malnutrition, debility and neglect. Many of the bedridden patients admitted to hospital need never have become so weak and debilitated. It is frequently possible to improve their health by a good diet, the correction of avitaminosis or anaemia and adequate attention to the bowels, but this alone is insufficient; they now require physiotherapy.

The physiotherapist can by active and passive movements free the stiff joints and build up the strength in the muscles, and re-educate the patient in walking, in dressing, undressing and going to the toilet. At the same time, the physiotherapist may bring hope and initiate psychological improvement. There is undoubtedly great scope for physiotherapy in the aged. In fact, physiotherapy may be *the* therapeutic agent responsible for returning the patient to active life. In the past, orthopaedic conditions have monopolised the physiotherapy department, but there is every reason to think that in the future the physiotherapist's most successful work will be in treating the hemiplegic or debilitated geriatric patient. Needless to say, physiotherapy is an integral part of geriatric medicine and of a geriatric unit.

However, there is also a considerable shortage of physiotherapists, so much so that in parts of the country ward physiotherapeutic aids have been taken on to do the more simple forms of therapy under the instruction of the physiotherapist.

Many elderly people benefit considerably by being taken for short walks up and down the ward, an exercise which does not require the services of a highly qualified physiotherapist; a ward physiotherapist can be taught this kind of work. In certain areas, such ward physiotherapists are recruited through the local newspaper.

It must not be thought that a request for physiotherapy is sufficient to bring about successful rehabilitation of an elderly patient. The physiotherapist may only be able to visit the patient for a short period once or twice a day and this would be insufficient for most patients. The whole ward plan needs to be evolved along the following lines so that a whole system of movement can be formulated. The ward should have low beds so that a patient can be taught how to get out of bed into a suitable chair – only high beds are needed when the patient is actually nursed in bed. The chair should be of a geriatric type and of a height which will allow the patient's feet to touch the floor comfortably. The bed should also have an overhead pulley and the patient when up should wear heeled shoes or heel pads. There should now be a separate dining room or lounge or failing this very considerable ward space in which can be placed tables for about four persons. All steps should be ramped and there should be wall bars leading to the lounge and to the toilet and walking aids should be freely available. Each day the patient should then be got out of bed into a chair, dressed as much as reasonably possible, escorted from the chair to the table for all meals and back again and likewise escorted to the toilet, or to some exercise frame. She should not just be sat in a chair with a tray in front of her and really left there until she goes to bed again. Until some such arrangement as outlined above is in being it is most unlikely – apart from bed exercises – that the physiotherapist can be employed in a specialist capacity. A planned system of movement implies that there is a chain of events with interlocking activities of nurses, auxiliary nurses, physiotherapists and occupational physiotherapists.

At the beginning of the rehabilitation procedure the patient should be carefully assessed not only as to pathological diagnosis but also as to muscle tone and movement, features of paralysis, of sensory loss, of postural loss or hemianopia, any evidence of mental confusion or depression so that both the physiotherapists and the nursing staff should understand what the problem is and what measures should be undertaken. Certain illnesses, such as strokes, Parkinsonism, rheumatoid arthritis, osteoarthritis and fractured neck of femur, will require special regimes. To assist a physiotherapist it will also be necessary not to give the patient a sedative or a large dose of a diuretic or undertake dressings before she is about to start treating the patient. If the patient has an indwelling catheter the bag should be fixed to the thigh by vulcro bandaging so that the arms are free for walking perhaps in a walking frame. Clearly nurses and physiotherapists must work together.

After a period of physiotherapy the patient should be re-assessed. Sometimes a patient makes little progress because they feel their relatives have abandoned them, or they are comfortable in the ward and are not keen to get better and go home or they are too confused, too paralysed or too infirm to benefit from treatment. Regrettably some patients show no progress and reluctantly the staff accept that they are chair-fast. If a ward is crowded with beds and there is no space elderly patients easily become chair-fast, lose their sense of balance, their ability to walk and develop contractures of the knees and ankles, finally requiring catheterisation for persistent incontinence. It is common to find that the so-called acute wards both medical and surgical are so overcrowded and quite unsuitable for elderly people except for a very short stay – the longer they are there the more likely it is they will develop bed sores, bowel troubles and chair-fastness.

It is important not to overclaim the value of physiotherapy in the paralysed patient since it cannot actually repair neurones which have been destroyed from lack of a blood supply, or to underestimate its value for the infirm patient recovering from an illness.

Naturally physiotherapy can best be undertaken in the physical medicine department, but all too often it takes too much time to escort the patient to and from the department to make it a common practice.

MEDICAL SOCIAL WORK

A geriatric unit places a great load of work on the medical social worker. From what has already been said, it will be appreciated that any return of a geriatric patient to his home is encompassed with numerous probblems and difficulties, so much so that practically every geriatric admission requires some medical social service. The medical social worker usually has to interview each patient and the relatives, to acquaint herself with the home situation, and the attitude of the relatives and neighbours. There may be the problem of the patient's pension book. Recently a leaflet has been issued by the Department of Health and Social Security which explains the way in which patients' benefits are affected by a stay in hospital. Thus, after eight weeks' stay in hospital, the benefit may be reduced by £1 a week – and after two years the benefit may be lowered to 50p a week. If a patient is discharged from hospital for 28 days, full benefits may be restored.

The medical social worker will need to be well informed about pension benefits, so as to be able to give advice when required. She may also have to deal with the problem of who will pay the rent when the patient is in hospital, see to the gas and electricity bills and prevent the house getting damp. Or there may be the need to arrange a health visitor to the home, or to have some repairs done. When the time for the patient's discharge approaches, it will be necessary to give the relatives warning, ensure that there is somebody at home to open the door and receive the patient and have the house warmed. It may be necessary to arrange that there is sufficient food in the house and see that the bedclothes are aired. The question of a home help for the patient is likely to crop up, and on this account the medical social worker will have to apply to the public health department, or for likely relatives or neighbours to undertake the work. There may be a large correspondence relating to the supply of wheel chairs, commodes, bed pans and so on for the patients' use.

The medical social worker may also have to deal with requests for admission that have come from the local public health authorities or from other hospitals, and likewise may have to ascertain whether other hospitals or institutions can accept a patient when the geriatric ward is unsuitable. The medical social worker is usually well versed in all the minute details relating to the social services, including the running of the ambulances, and she is commonly in personal contact with numerous people concerned with the care of the elderly. A great deal of the medical social work is visiting the patients in the wards and being present on visiting days to see relatives. There is some advantage if regular meetings are arranged between the physician and the medical social worker, either in the wards or during the ward round and in any case the social information gained by the medical social worker should be included in the medical history folder. Again, when domiciliary visits have to be made, it can be mutually beneficial if the medical social worker accompanies the physician, since the medical social worker can then start immediately to deal with the social problems.

Clearly the whole efficiency of a geriatric unit is gravely impaired if there is no active medical social worker.

It takes many years of hard work and study to become a medical social worker and the work is not always well enough paid. There is a shortage of medical social workers and geriatric units often make do with an unqualified person. In some instances it has been found necessary and advantageous to train some other person to undertake some of the duty of social work. Such a person is in close contact with the consultant physician, deals with the correspondence relating to the patients, as also with numerous telephone calls from doctors, welfare authorities, the M.O.H. department, ambulance department, relatives and so on. She usually knows about the patient's illness and comes to understand many of the medical problems involved. It is of course essential that she has a personality acceptable to relatives, doctors and social workers generally, and if she can gain the co-operation and help of any qualified medical social worker in the district she is likely to be more successful. An auxiliary social worker has been employed in this way to deal solely with geriatric problems, and so far it has been very successful and reasonably economical. It allows the physician to make a greater emphasis on the social care of the patient than is possible when a medical social worker to a large hospital only does part-time duties in the geriatric department.

SECRETARIAL WORK

There is a good deal of secretarial work to be done in any hospital, and the geriatric unit is no exception. Patients have to be admitted in an orderly manner, case notes prepared, a waiting list has to be kept, patients sent for as vacancies occur, and for each outgoing patient a résumé has to be made of the case history and treatment, and a copy sent to the family doctor. This is an important letter and can be lengthy. Absence of good secretarial work is detrimental to the patient's future medical care and may result in needless and expensive readmission or investigations. It may also cause unnecessary delay in discharge or admission, all of which wastes the hospital's efforts.

BED UTILISATION POLICY

The great number of elderly people requiring hospital attention makes it advisable to adopt some kind of policy on the question of which types of illness should take priority over others. There are of course a great number of elderly patients seeking treatment; the problem is how to use the staff and facilities for all concerned. Naturally, every young 'chronic sick' patient admitted excludes the admission of an elderly person, and though this is necessary in certain instances, if any large number of young patients was admitted, particularly of the long-staying type, e.g.

disseminated sclerosis, it would seriously interfere with the service to the elderly.

A large number of people die annually and it does not seem to be a good policy, either for the patient or the hospital, that patients should be admitted merely because they are about to die. Nevertheless, where social conditions are very bad, it is necessary to admit such patients, but it should be remembered that the social conditions of the elderly are most unsatisfactory and it would be impossible to admit every ill patient because of the adverse social conditions. All too often, doctors request admission for an ambulant person solely on the ground of social conditions, but the recent memorandum on geriatric care[2] places the responsibility of the 'care of the infirm (including the senile) in dressing, toilet, etc., who may need to live on the ground floor because they cannot manage stairs and may spend most of the day in bed (or longer in bad weather)' on the local welfare authorities.

Accordingly, the 'social problem' who requires simple home care is unsuitable for admission to hospital, but unless the patient is seen before admission, either at home or as an out-patient, it often happens that the new admission walks into the ward with a suitcase and personal belongings to take up permanent residence; meanwhile the family burn the bedding, terminate the tenancy of the house and make return impossible.

In order to treat as many patients as possible it is necessary to ask relatives to share the burden of caring for patients on discharge, and this can often only be accomplished by agreeing to readmit the patient if the illness recurs, or difficulties arise in home care. On an agreement of this kind it has been possible to send quite a number of patients home, but it is, of course, essential that requests for readmission be honoured meticulously. Sometimes patients have to be admitted because the family doctor is being pestered day and night by relatives or neighbours who have grown tired of the nursing burden. Many patients are accepted as transfers from other wards or hospitals and it is felt that this is an important part of the geriatric work, but it is perhaps necessary to remember that if the transfer has been on account of bad home conditions or refusal by the relatives to take the patient, the battle is half lost as regards returning the patient home from a chronic ward, or securing admission to a welfare home.

Hemiplegia is one of the commonest of the illnesses in the elderly, and a frequent reason for admission, but the condition is so very common that if all the hemiplegias were admitted the wards would be full of them alone. Consequently, the co-operation of the general practitioner has to be sought so that only those patients who require, and are likely to benefit from, hospital care are treated as urgent admissions. Congestive heart failure and respiratory infections, so often fatal at home, especially under poor conditions, respond very well to hospital care and form a common reason for admission.

FRACTURED FEMURS

Fractured femurs in the elderly, if of recent origin, are not suited to chronic wards where the whole emphasis is on medical attention, whereas the patient requires expert surgical treatment and supervision. But such fractures are so frequent and numerous that, again, no hospital could admit every case without seriously affecting its other work, and clearly there is a special problem and the need for a particular policy. One would suggest that a prescribed number of beds be set aside for fractured femurs in the elderly, under the care of an orthopaedic surgeon, as regards admission, treatment and discharge, with geriatric medical coverage available on request. But in this respect it is quite clear that *surgical* conditions do not come within the chief principal causes of death and that the first priority as regards beds is still, and overwhelmingly so, *medical*.

Gangrene of a foot is frequently seen and amputation may be the only method of saving the patient's life, but then one is left with a non-ambulant elderly person. The purchase of a wheel chair is sometimes a more suitable form of rehabilitation than attempting the fitting of an artificial limb and re-education of the patient. Unfortunately, it can take a long time to obtain a wheel chair, by which time the home may have disintegrated. It would therefore be more economical if the Ministry of Pensions could supply wheel chairs on loan to the patient rapidly, i.e. within one week.

About 15% of admissions are mentally confused and restless; the bulk of them return to a rational state of mind after treatment, but a few remain demented and incontinent, though perhaps fully ambulant. So far it has been possible to cope with the problem by the use of tranquillisers. Many of these patients have been left over in the hospital after the lapse of 'three day orders', but it is felt that a proportion of them would be more rightly disposed of in a mental hospital. The admission policy can be summarised as follows:

(1) Admissions are primarily designed for those of pensionable age.
(2) For patients with medical illnesses who will benefit from hospital treatment.
(3) For patients who are temporarily beyond the care of the relatives.
(4) For patients with a fatal illness who cannot possibly be nursed at home.
(5) Admission from other hospitals or wards.

(6) Admission while relatives take a holiday or when there is a crisis at home.

(7) Admission of young disabled patients.

DISCHARGE PROCEDURES

Difficulties over discharge are innumerable and include the great age of these patients, their infirmities and poor home conditions, the reluctance of relatives to take responsibility, the lack of home helps and the problems of admission to welfare. Every discharged patient has the attendant risk of sudden deterioration of health, or fatal home accident. As a result of numerous home visits, it is possible to state that there are a large number of very debilitated persons living alone. The risk of falls and other accidents in the home is very great. Fifty-seven per cent of fatal home accidents affect persons aged 75 years and over. Further, the pension plus supplementary pension is frequently insufficient to pay the rent, cost of food, cooking and heating in the house. Quite a number of elderly people have not left their houses for several years, some are confined for months to cold, desolate bedrooms and many lie on bare boards covered with army blankets and an old overcoat. It is little wonder that on admission it is common to find patients thin, emaciated, with dry tongues, sunken eyes, loaded bowels, unclean and in all ways uncared for. Clearly, the benefits of home medical attention are ineffective when there is no one to give the patients food and drink. Further, the good done in hospital is soon lost under adverse home conditions.

With the above difficulties of discharge in mind, it is important that the physician in charge be responsible for the discharge of every patient. Before a patient is considered fit for discharge, it is as well therefore to conduct a brief examination of his fitness. In particular, inquiries should be made as to whether he can carry out all the activities of daily living, that he is not incontinent or mentally confused, and that he cannot be expected to benefit from further treatment in hospital. Sometimes it is necessary to make the patient walk about, or up and down steps, to make sure he is reasonably ambulant. The home situation as outlined by the medical social worker forms part of the medical notes, and should be reviewed before discharge; the patient should also be examined for bruises and abrasions, because if these become apparent at home it may be wrongly surmised that he has been sent out incorrectly. If the patient is on some special medicines, it is customary to give him a few days' supply pending the attendance of his family doctor. If it is in any way a dangerous drug, it is unwise to give a large supply, because a poor memory may allow him to take an overdose. With the co-operation of the medical social worker, everything should have been done to receive the patient in his home. He certainly cannot be discharged, as can a younger patient, without some assurance that as much has been done as possible to make his home satisfactory. Yet with all these precautions, and sometimes with the knowledge that home conditions are unsatisfactory, the necessity to admit some other patient may cause a patient to be discharged against the physician's better judgment.

The patient is usually discharged by ambulance, and a discharge note is sent to the family doctor, or given to the patient for transmission, outlining the diagnosis and suggesting the treatment the patient should receive.

NOTICE OF DISCHARGE OF PATIENT FROM HOSPITAL

Tel. No.................... Date....................

Dear Sir,

I have to notify you that

Name...

Adress...

....Age............

Diagnosis...

who was admitted ....19....

will be discharged on ....19....

Will the $\left\{ \begin{array}{l} \text{Medical Practitioner} \\ \text{Medical Officer} \end{array} \right\}$ of Health kindly arrange for the appropriate after-care.

Special remarks including recommendations as to treatment:

....

....

....

....

Yours faithfully,

....
Medical Officer

If the patient should also receive help from the local health department, this is noted on the discharge note and a copy is sent to the M.O.H. for his information. A typewritten résumé is now made of the case history sheet and medical notes. This can be a little tedious, but since the notes are always kept in a set order, most of the significant facts can be quickly recapitulated.

At one time, consultants' letters to general practitioners were of a very friendly and almost intimate nature. They usually contained some personal references such as 'Did your daughter enjoy her birthday party?' or 'How is little George getting on at school?' or 'Have you heard about so and so . . .?' and so on. Letters today tend to become very stereotyped and formal, and much less interesting. It is hardly possible, because of the large number of patients dealt with, to write the old-fashioned personal type of letter, but as far as one can gather, the more formal the letter the less it is read by the G.P. so this fault should be avoided. A copy of the résumé of the case is therefore sent to the G.P., together with such informal remarks as seem appropriate. A good résumé of the case history makes it unnecessary at a later date to thumb through the case history, and when the patient is seen at a follow-up clinic the doctor taking the clinic need only refer to the résumé to obtain all the information he requires.

REFERENCES

1 KRUPP Marcus A, SWEET Norman J, JAWETZ Ernest, ARMSTRONG Charles D *Physician's Handbook* Long's Medical Publications California 9th Edition 1956

2 Memorandum HM (57) 86 *National Health Service* paragraph II (ii) and Circular 14/57 7 October 1957 *Local Authority Services for the Chronic Sick and Infirm* paragraph 2 (ii)

4

THE OUT-PATIENT DEPARTMENT AND HOSPITAL DAY CENTRE

A brief outline has been given of the work in the wards and the need for a methodical approach there, in diagnosing and treating the patients, but the number of patients that can be dealt with in the wards is very small in comparison with the number of elderly people in the area who may have indifferent health. Throughout the country out-patient attendances by the chronic sick and geriatric patients are counted in thousands, whereas the attendances for general surgery, to take an example, are counted in millions. Brief statistics indicating this are as follows (Report of Ministry of Health[1]):

In-patients department	Medicine	Chronic sick	General surgery
Staffed beds allocated	33 669	57 641	34 059
Average daily bed occupation	32 842	56 254	33 198
Discharges and deaths	519 448	118 457	807 863
Average duration of stay	20·8	164·4	13·2
Waiting list at 31 December	8 553	10 626	131 215
Out-patients			
Annual number of clinical sessions	127 456	3881	115 681
New out-patients	633 212	7676	885 146
Total attendances	2 683 822	39 200	2 901 347
More recently on December 31 1969 the beds available were	31 299	47 637	31 171

In 1973 (Ref. Health and Personal Social Service Statistics 1974, page 2), the total Out-patient attendances in thousands were:

Medical	10 961
Geriatric	187
Surgical	20 714

The above statistics[2] give some indication of the medical activity devoted to the chronic sick compared with that devoted to general surgery and general medicine and there has been little change in the pattern over the last ten years.

There is every reason to think, and it is strongly advised by the Ministry of Health, that an out-patient department is vitally necessary in the medical care of the elderly. Out-patient treatment may prevent, especially when it is undertaken in close co-operation with the family doctor, the high incidence of malnutrition, anaemia, debility and untreated 'strokes', chest infections and cardiac illnesses, which might otherwise continue until the patient is *in extremis*. In this way, an out-patient department may obviate the necessity for many admissions. By including out-patient rehabilitation therapy, many patients can be maintained in a fair state of health, who would otherwise deteriorate at home, so becoming a burden on their relatives. The out-patient department should, of course, not be designed to replace the family doctor, but only to supplement his efforts.

The elderly experience many difficulties in attending an out-patient department. They may be frail ambulants and so cannot be expected to walk across busy streets, to board 'tubes' and buses, and then perhaps walk a considerable distance to the hospital. At the hospital, there may still be far too many steps and corridors and doors to negotiate; neither does their physical health allow them to wait a long time in a waiting room. Filling up forms and going to and from the out-patient clinic, pathological laboratory, radiological department, or the dispensary, is usually beyond them. Because of deafness, a case history taken by the doctor may become a public performance, and because of slowness in dressing and undressing the patient may occupy the examining room for a period three or four times longer than that normally given to a younger patient. All these difficulties point to the need for an out-patient department specially designed for the elderly.

AMBULANCES

Most geriatric patients will have to come to hospital by ambulance, usually as sitting cases. Not all ambulances are warm and comfortable, so that the ambulance journey should be brief. It does not suit the geriatric patient to be picked up by an ambulance which then roves round picking up other patients a great distance off and dropping them at various hospitals before bringing the original patient to his hospital. The most desirable method is that a little group of geriatric patients be collected in a small locality and brought straight to the hospital. The ambulance drivers may experience many difficulties; the geriatric patient may forget that the ambulance is due to call, or take a terrifically long time to dress and get into the ambulance, or if the ambulance is late, may have given up waiting and started on some domestic chore. When the day for attendance at hospital arrives, it might be a very cold or wet day, and the patient is reluctant to attend. The opening of a geriatric out-patient department throws an extra load on the ambulance service and brings with it numerous problems as to how the ambulances should be used.

AMBULANCE APPROACH

The approach to the geriatric out-patient department should allow the patient to get straight out of the ambulance and enter the waiting room. This is most important, otherwise there is a great waste of the time of the ambulance or nursing staff. The out-patient department will also be the normal place for admission, and should be so arranged that the patient can be brought in on a stretcher and immediately transferred to a warm examination couch.

THE WAITING ROOM

The waiting room should be warm, well lit, with comfortable chairs and should be large enough to accommodate not only the patients but accompanying relatives. A public toilet should be near at hand. Canteen facilities should be available.

THE INTERVIEW ROOM

Adjacent to the waiting room, there should be a room which is reasonably soundproof, because the relatives may be very deaf too, where a medical and social history can be obtained from the patients and the relatives.

THE EXAMINATION ROOM

Here there should be two or more cubicles, curtained off, where the physical examination of the patient can take place. It is important that the examining couch be of a similar height to that of a stretcher on wheels so that if immediate admission is required the patient can readily be transferred to the stretcher and taken to the ward.

THE CLINICAL ROOM

Adjacent to the examination room there should be a small room where the patient's height and weight can be recorded and urinary, faecal and other examinations readily done. A steriliser and hand washbasins will also be required. After clinical examination, if there are pathological investigations to be made, the specimens, for example, blood, urine or faeces, should be taken and sent to the laboratory.

X-RAY SCREENING ROOM

Near to the examination room should be a small X-ray screening room, so that when indicated the patient's chest can be screened without any further ado. This is likely to lead to a more accurate diagnosis and prognosis, and if the patient is admitted to a ward it will, in the majority of instances, make it unnecessary to request a chest X-ray, an expensive and time-consuming feature for the elderly patient.

ELECTROCARDIOGRAPH INVESTIGATION

While the patient is on the examining couch, by the use of a portable electrocardiograph apparatus an electrocardiogram can conveniently be done when this is clinically indicated.

PHYSIOTHERAPY

Often physiotherapy can be carried on in the out-patient department, and for this reason, where possible, the waiting room should lead naturally to a physiotherapy room, where individual and group therapy can be given.

STAFF

The department should, of course, have a sister in charge of out-patients, though she may combine this with being in charge of a ward, if the latter is close to the out-patient department.

GENERAL FUNCTIONS

The department is used for examination of new patients, the re-examination of discharged patients, i.e. as a follow-up clinic for out-patient physiotherapy, for minor treatments, for example, the giving of an enema, checking the function of a colostomy, dressing large varicose ulcers, or rodent ulcers, etc. Specimens for pathological investigation can be collected in the out-patient departments which have now developed into day hospital centres. In addition to the usual requirements for out-patient diagnosis of illnesses which basically required medical or nursing attention, experience has uncovered a whole host of conditions in the elderly requiring a mixture of social and medical care. One of the most common conditions is the combination of loneliness, depression, bowel disorders, malnutrition, infirmity to the point where the patient is house-fast. This class of patient is medically ill, but they also require attendance at a clinic to combat loneliness and to give them a chance of making friends, of having a well balanced mid-day meal and having attention to such matters as anaemia, blindness, deafness, care of the feet and to receive physiotherapy and occupational therapy so as to strengthen muscles and joints and assist the patient to greater mobility and activities of daily living. At the same time via the medical social worker at the clinic the patient may be helped at home by the provision of a home help or a home nurse and the installation of various aids in the home. For example the provision of a home help three times a week for a patient with heart failure is more logical and usually more effective

SUGGESTED LAYOUT OF GERIATRIC CLINIC

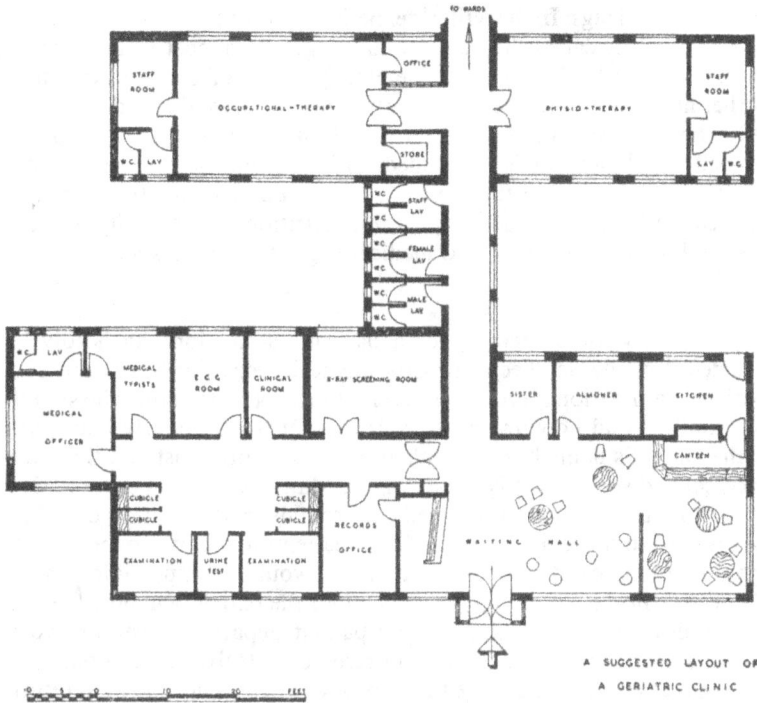

A SUGGESTED LAYOUT OF A GERIATRIC CLINIC

The suggested layout allows of the following requirements:

1. An easy ambulance approach.

2. A waiting hall which can be used for new patients for follow-up clinics and for out-patient physiotherapy. Thus the ambulance can bring patients of several categories, and physiotherapy clinics and medical clinics can be run at the same time.

3. A kitchen and canteen service, so important to elderly patients and elderly relatives who may have to spend a considerable time in hospital.

4. A medical social worker's office which will allow the social worker to interview relatives straight away and to give all necessary advice and to make arrangements about home care.

5. Medical examination section which will allow of very full medical assessments. Because of the high incidence of chest conditions in the elderly, electrocardiographic examination of the heart and X-ray screening of the chest will add considerably to the accuracy of diagnosis and obviate the usage of nursing staff to take the patient to some other part of the hospital, or the inconvenience of having the patient up again for some ancillary investigation.

6. The physiotherapy and occupational-therapy rooms are set apart from the medical examination section but adjacent to each other and with a free entrance from the waiting-hall.

The basic principle of the layout is to ensure an orderly flow of patients within the department and the wards.

(Layout prepared by N. E. J. Goldfinch, BSc, AMICE)

than cardiac drugs. In the writer's experience the out-patient department or more rightly called the hospital day centre does most valuable work in *maintaining* health amongst the elderly group of patients. It is also rather noticeable that where day centres have been established they have often been too small to meet the demands made upon them. It might be argued that loneliness is not a medical illness and such people should look to the local authorities to provide clubs. But in reality the loneliness so frequently results in self-neglect, malnutrition and infirmity that the distinction between social and medical neglect is unrealistic.

NEW PATIENTS

The necessity, or otherwise, for a patient's admission can hardly be decided until he has been properly medically examined, and the out-patient examination serves a very useful function in deciding who should be admitted and how urgent the matter is. It is particularly important if the patient's name has been taken from the waiting list and the exact medical and social state is rather vague. Many patients on examination do not require admission on medical grounds, and attention can then be diverted to the social problem. Other patients may come to the department in an almost dying condition, and it would be impossible to send them back home without grave risks. Since the patient will now have to be admitted it follows that an out-patient department cannot work unless some empty beds are kept in reserve to deal with such patients. It is wise to ensure in advance that any out-patient is not too ill to return home after examination. The stretcher cases are generally unsuitable for out-patient attendance, unless it be with a view to admission. Without an out-patient department, 'blind' admissions have to be made from the waiting list and this may mean taking in social rather than medical problems, otherwise a great number of domiciliary visits would have to be made to ensure a proper selection.

FOLLOW-UP CLINIC

On discharge, many elderly patients are not restored to full health. They may have recovered from congestive heart failure, but still require digitalisation and a modern diuretic; they may be diabetics or persons with anaemia, peptic ulcer, etc., who require periodic clinical survey and pathological or radiological investigations; or they may have new social problems which require attention. For many reasons, the progress of an illness should be observed so that action can be taken promptly and in time to avoid unnecessary complications.

For many pensioners, the follow-up clinic serves not only for a medical examination but also as a psychological stimulation. For many of them it is something to look forward to as a change from a rather boring life at home; it allows them to meet friends they have made in the wards and to have a cup of tea or coffee in congenial surroundings. The usual practice is to see a discharged patient about a month later and then gradually lengthen the period to three months or six months. Six months is quite a long time in the life of somebody over 75; since prevention is always better than cure, a half-yearly medical check cannot be considered unreasonable. There are a large number of elderly people who do not bother to call in a doctor, and some have not seen a doctor for several years. Perhaps one of the reasons why an elderly patient does not call in the family doctor is because he fears he may be sent into hospital or away into an institution. By linking the follow-up clinic with the activity of voluntary workers and old age clubs, much of this reluctance of old people to attend hospital can be overcome.

OUT-PATIENTS' PHYSIOTHERAPY

Many of the patients who have received physiotherapy in the wards require such treatment to be continued as an out-patient. This is especially so for the rehabilitation of the patient with hemiplegia, and for the partially ambulant patient with arthritis or muscular wasting. There is always a shortage of physiotherapists, and to minimise this patients are given treatment in small groups or classes. The physiotherapist will, of course, require all the necessary equipment to bring about restoration of function, but basically the apparatus required is relatively simple and inexpensive.

In the minds of the relatives, sometimes the physiotherapists are too successful. I can recall a bedridden patient who was rather a burden at home, but did not cause any undue anxiety, being restored to full ambulation by physiotherapy. The relatives' next complaint was that whereas previously they knew exactly where the old lady was, namely in bed, they were now concerned because she preferred to get up and go for trips into the town.

DOMICILIARY VISITS

It often happens that a family doctor wishes to have a second opinion on the treatment and management of a patient. Where there is a geriatric out-patient department running, this second opinion can be obtained by referring the patient to the hospital, but often the patient is not willing to go to hospital, or there are some good reasons why the patient should be seen at home in his ordinary surroundings. A domiciliary consultation is accordingly arranged. The proper working of a geriatric unit does depend on the goodwill and co-operation of others concerned in the welfare of the elderly, and in particular that of the general practitioner.

The family doctor is more fully conversant with the patient's home, social conditions, past medical history and present state of health than anyone else. Further, in his practice he has many elderly patients under observation and knows which patient should take priority of admission to hospital, and which could be effectively treated at home. It is important, therefore, to work with the family doctor and take advantage of every possibility to gain his co-operation and understanding of the old age problem.

Domiciliary visits are one of the most important links between the family doctor and the consultant, and too often the only link. This is because under the National Health Service most general practitioners have been excluded from hospital practice and practically all hospital doctors from the medical care of patients in their homes. There are many disadvantages in this strict division of work and responsibility, particularly in the way it affects the care of the elderly. So often the doctor in hospital has no true understanding of the home and social environment of the patient, while the family doctor tends to become out of date with recent advances in medical diagnosis and treatment. Domiciliary consultation may give not only necessary advice about the patient's treatment but also serve to restore the confidence of the relatives in their doctor, lessen the reluctance of the patient to go to hospital for a fuller examination, and usually serves as a meeting-point for the exchange of much medical knowledge. Domiciliary consultations can be very time-consuming, but without them a geriatric unit might develop along lines which are unhelpful to the family doctor, and therefore out of step with reality.

Domiciliary visits can also be made by a junior resident physician, the more fully to assess a patient's need for admission. But such a doctor is commonly very junior to the family doctor himself, and can hardly on a short visit be expected to know much about the patient and the patient's home, and the procedure can be irritating to the family doctor and devoid of many of the advantages of the proper consultation mentioned above. This second type of visit should only be necessary when there is a long waiting list; if there is a long waiting list the needs of the elderly patients are not being properly met and the situation is not likely to be corrected in this way.

The following are some personal reminiscences regarding domiciliary visits.

One visit was to an elderly woman who had her leg in plaster after a Potts fracture. She was found to be confined to a bedroom at the top of a steep flight of stairs. Apparently she could not descend the stairs without great trouble. She lodged with people who had been her friends, and one of them was practically blind. The friends were all comfortably seated round the fire, and they claimed, including the blind person, that there was no room downstairs for the patient and it was too much trouble to assist her up and down the stairs every day. The patient had thus been confined to her bleak bedroom for almost six weeks. She complained of headache, pains in the stomach, giddiness and cough, but examination revealed that she was very tearful and in a state of considerable depression, there being no organic illness discoverable. The problem was discussed with the orthopaedic surgeon who was dealing with the fracture, and the plaster was removed as soon as the surgical condition allowed. A daughter was also interviewed, who agreed to take her mother home with her until the patient had recovered. The patient was also asked to attend hospital once a week as a psychological boost and for physiotherapy. By these means, and the administration of an appropriate tranquilliser, all went well. This happens to be a success story, but in another home a patient similarly placed managed to get downstairs and put her head in the gas oven.

Another visit concerned a lady of 84, who had fallen down at home. She lived as a lodger with another woman of 79, and also in the house was the tenant's brother, over 80 years old. There was no bed for the patient downstairs, so many cushions had been collected and she was found to be lying on these on the floor in a bay window. She had broken no bones, but had bruised her hip and had severe arthritis of both knees with inability to straighten her legs. She also had mild anaemia, emphysema, auricular fibrillation, and a little cardiac oedema. A proper bed was obtained, and for a short while she was treated at home, but she could not get the personal help she needed there, and at a later date was admitted to hospital, where she responded quite well to treatment. She managed to return home but likes to come to the follow-up clinic from time to time.

Another visit was to an elderly woman who had received mercurial diuretics for cardiac oedema. She was comfortably in bed downstairs near a fire and had a son and daughter to look after her. Examination indicated that salt depletion and diuresis had been carried too far and she was mentally confused, with moderate dehydration. She responded very favourably to extra fluids, the restoration of a little salt in her diet and a greater measure of digitilisation. The case illustrates that the control of cardiac oedema, which is a relatively easy matter in hospital, is by no means so easy to carry out in a person's home.

One memorable visit took place at night to a large house with stables adjoining. Sixty years ago, the house apparently was surrounded by fields, but today it was an oddity in the middle of a street of houses. It was approached through the stable yard, now turned into garages, and inside the entrance door was an old-fashioned pump. The kitchen had a huge fireplace, and there were curtains, knick-knacks and bric-àbrac everywhere. Round the walls were old-fashioned pictures of 'Gleaning' and 'Harvesting' and one of Redcoats capturing a deserter at the bedside of his dying mother – all this in the middle of an industrial slum. Lighting was by candle. The relative was a bachelor son and it was soon apparent that he was of poor mental calibre but could just read and write. The patient, who was an elderly lady of 85, was in an upstairs bedroom. This was approached by a sharp spiral staircase. When we struck a match and lit a candle we could see an iron four-poster bed with the bed-springs coming through a worn mattress. The old lady was lying in a dishevelled heap. She was clearly in a state of extreme mental confusion and dementia, with gross incontinence. Apparently she had been in this kind of way for a week or two, but the son was not sufficiently intelligent to have called in the doctor. The patient was removed to hospital at once, against the wishes of the son. As we left the house, the last view was that of a large aspidistra in the window silhouetted by the light of the candle in the room.

Many and varied are the kind of patients which have been seen. Some have been suffering from acute corpulmonale and have rallied after home oxygen therapy, others had acute bronchitis requiring a new antibiotic in place of one to which they had become resistant, and others with severe broncho-spasm have responded to aminophylin.

One patient seen with acute corpulmonale was a man of 65. Until a day or so previously he had been fully ambulant, but had to take to his bed because of a cold. The day following this, when he was examined, he was almost unconscious, very cyanosed and dyspnoeic. Though he was clearly in a very critical condition and might die at any moment, one of his sons, who seemed to be quite devoted to him, nevertheless proposed to go off to work as usual, and was very put out when he had to drop this idea and hurry off for any oxygen bottle. Luckily the patient recovered from the acute phase and was found to be of a most cheerful disposition, had spent many years in Australia and was full of some very interesting reminiscences. The further care of this patient has been particularly difficult, since he is always trying to exceed his cardiac reserve.

GERIATRIC UNIT RECORDS

Many doctors think records are a tedious waste of time. But any ordinary business firm in which there is an expenditure of either money or effort invariably finds it important to keep some statistics. How otherwise is it possible to assess what channels of effort are successful and worthwhile, and what are time-wasting and fruitless? In fact, even from early times, the medical advantage of keeping and collecting case histories has been clearly demonstrated. It is by such means that the essential signs, symptoms diagnosis, and prognosis of the various diseases have been delineated. The keeping of proper records should be looked upon in the same way as an accountant's report; the report makes no difference as to the actual profits or losses that may have occurred, but it affords critical and decisive information as to how the future should be planned. Geriatric unit records should be useful in a similar kind of way.

The simplest record to keep is a monthly graph, showing the number of admissions, discharges and deaths. Information should also be kept on the source of admissions. The hospital authorities themselves customarily keep statistics as regards bed occupancy, length of stay, new out-patients, old out-patients, etc., but it is often advisable to keep some statistical analysis of the kind of cases seen. If the case histories are filed under diagnostic headings, it will then of course be possible to select fifty cases of hemiplegia, fifty cases of peripheral gangrene, or so many cases of carcinoma of the lung, etc., and study them in more detail whenever it is required.

Perhaps one of the most important things is to find out accurately details of the population in the area served. This can usually be obtained from the last census figures. The census may give the actual age groups, or these can be estimated from the national average. It will then be possible to state how many males and females there are of pensionable age, and how many are over 70 years, 75 years, 80 years and so on. Nowadays since the capitation rate for persons 65 years and over, to the general practitioner is higher than for the younger population, it is possible to obtain from the Executive Committee a statement of the numbers of old people in a given area – and this is the most accurate statistic available. Today it is estimated that out of every thousand in the population in Britain, forty persons are 75 years or older. Other figures which should be of value are the number of hospital beds and the number of beds in welfare homes and private homes within the area, together with some account as to how many home helps and district nurses there are. The following is a sample of statistics that may be recorded for a six-month period.

IN-PATIENT STATISTICS FOR A SIX-MONTH PERIOD

The figures shown below are the basic factors to describe the work done in each in-patient department separately, for the above period. These figures are as follows:

(1) *Turnover* is the average number of patients treated per bed during the period.
(2) *Length of stay* is the average number of days a patient occupies a bed.

(3) *Turnover interval* is the average number of days a bed lies vacant between successive patients.

(4) *Percentage occupancy* shows the percentage of beds occupied during the period.

(5) *Waiting list figures* are the number of patients waiting admission at the end of the six-month period.

Example	Medicine	Geriatrics
Turnover per bed	8	7
Length of stay in days	19	87
Turnover intervals in days	2	5
Percentage occupancy	90	83
Waiting list	2	0
Bed allocation at end of six month period	39	226

If some statistics, as indicated above, are kept, they will serve as a very useful guide on the work of the unit. Statistics have a further value when the work of the unit has to be discussed with boards and committees. The latter are more likely to be impressed by data which can be placed before them on a table than by any amount of clinical work, no matter how brilliant, that may have been done at the bedside. This is particularly so when the committee holds its meetings miles away from the hospital concerned.

REFERENCES

1   MINISTRY OF HEALTH   *Report*   ending 31 December 1957   part 1   pages 164 and 166

2   Department of Health and Social Security Annual Report 1970   pages 252 and 256

5

SPECIAL MEDICAL PROBLEMS IN THE ELDERLY

Laymen have recognised for some time that there are problems peculiar to the elderly. But the medical profession, despite the great number of specialities already recognised, and equal number of diplomas that are issued, are reluctant to accept the fact that the elderly have special medical problems calling for special experience and knowledge. Those doctors who have worked for a few months in acute geriatric wards are very soon enlightened, but there are still a large number of physicians who have had no such experience. The latter are inclined to base their outlook on geriatric medicine on the few elderly persons they see in the general ward, where perhaps the average age of the ward can be up to 65 years. This is a vastly different background from the acute geriatric ward, where the average age is likely to be over 75 years. In the following chapters an account is given of some of the special problems in the elderly, with a view to enlightening the general physician on the common pathological changes that occur, leading to clinical features peculiar to the elderly.

Senile Changes

Whereas the tempo of metabolism in the young is geared to growth and development, in the elderly a slow deterioration of all the organs is going on. In the young the various functions of the body are carried out fully, and usually the organs concerned have considerable function in reserve. Thus the heart can maintain an efficient circulation at rest, walking or during the most violent exercise. In a similar way, the lungs have adequate reserves, and so do the kidneys and other organs throughout the body. In the young, any damage done to the body by injury or infection is rapidly repaired by normal physiological processes and if there is slight loss of function in the process, this is adequately covered by normal reserve. But in the elderly, any such damage or infection is repaired very slowly, often inadequately, and the loss of function in the process may be a most serious matter, since there is no great normal reserve. In youth there is a development of the body and a functioning of vital organs which reaches a peak performance at certain ages. The age may vary from individual to individual, but there is a common pattern. In the realm of athletics, even in young men, age begins to tell in the twenties, and for most people, though they may be in excellent health, they are beyond first-class athletics in their thirties.

As time continues, there is a decline in the performance of vital bodily functions which may be considered as the normal process of ageing. In this process there is a large hereditary factor, but in addition there is the factor caused by injury and disease, malnutrition, etc. 'The child is father of the man', and many of the conditions that occur in childhood have a bearing on the state of health in old age. Old age should be defined, therefore not in terms of so many years of life, so much as in terms of the degree and extent of the impoverishment of vital functions. The elderly person is rather like someone who has a banking account, but no reserves or securities, and can be overdrawn at any time; from a medical point of view, he has a hand-to-mouth kind of existence.

SKIN

In the elderly, the skin tends to be drier, rougher, more lined, the hair turns grey, baldness makes its appearance, the face becomes lined and the patient looks older. At the same time, there is decay of the teeth, and losses have to be replaced by artificial dentures. There is also some atrophy of the jaw, adding to the difficulty of fitting suitable dentures.

HEARING

As age continues, there is likely to be a loss in the sense of hearing. In fact, in younger persons round the age of forty, careful audiometric testing may show some loss of hearing in the higher frequencies. Deafness is a great sensory loss, since it cuts off the patient from normal conversation and contact with other people. As time goes on, the patient lives in a world of his own and may develop all sorts of queer ideas. He may be given to muttering and mumbling and will frequently misunderstand a conversation and take umbrage at some remark which he thinks is slighting.

VISUAL DISTURBANCES

One of the first changes is the inability to focus properly for reading. This condition commonly comes on before the age of 50, when people find they require reading glasses. Though the condition is easily correctable by glasses, if there are no glasses available the patient cannot read the newspaper, the letters he receives, small notices, or write his own letters. Some elderly people with mental lethargy take on new life when they are supplied with proper reading glasses. Sorsby[45] has carried out a Survey of Blindness in England, and draws attention to some very pertinent facts, namely: 66·3% of new registrations of blind persons during 1951 were persons of 70 years and over; and that blindness in this age group was caused by:

	percentage
Cataract	33·7
Senile macular lesions	30·4
Glaucoma	14·9
Myopia	5·8
Diabetes	3·6
Cardiovascular affections	3·2

As regards cataract,[46] he states that 'some 50%, and possibly more, of those registered as blind from cataract might well benefit from an operation'. He contrasts the 8·22% of cataract patients that had had no surgical treatment against the 60% of those registered as blind from glaucoma who had undergone such treatment. He also comes to the conclusion[47] that if surgical treatment is to become feasible on a substantial scale, geriatric care is also likely to be needed. At the time of registration for blindness due to cataract, many patients are very old and frail, but it would appear that in many cases an operation would have been successful had it been undertaken many years previously.

The blind population has increased from some 67 000 persons in 1935 to 94 000 in 1954.[48] In England 1973 the registered blind aged 65 years and over was 69 900 (Ref. Health and Personal Social Services Statistics 1974, page 121). The number of elderly blind is creating grave problems for institutional care. Many such persons are, in welfare homes, intermingled with the ordinary patients, but in many parts of the country the building of new homes is under consideration, and in some places special homes for the blind. In the planning of such homes, it is evidently important that those concerned should bear in mind that the blind persons in the population will be greater in number, and in addition will be frail ambulants, unlikely to negotiate stairs or steps on account of the latter disability; a problem that does not seriously arise in the blind at younger ages.

SMELL

Many elderly people suffer loss in the sense of smell; also appreciated as a loss of taste. Some are unaware of this sensory loss and are oblivious to offensive smells about the house, or to the smell of escaping gas. The inability to sense escaping gas is of course dangerous, and annually results in a few old people being accidentally gassed to death.

LUNGS

Emphysema is common in the elderly, of either the atrophic or hypertrophic variety, and is often accompanied by a mild chronic bronchitis and a shortness of breath on exertion. Because of this impairment of respiration and diminished respiratory reserve, the elderly prefer to sleep with their backs raised by either a pillow or back-rest.

CARDIOVASCULAR SYSTEM

Widespread degeneration affecting the heart and arteries is perhaps the most important change that occurs in old age. In all probability it is the key change which leads to the atrophy and degeneration in other organs. Essentially the change in the cardiovascular system is one of fibrosis affecting the heart and arterial walls, and atheroma of the arteries roughening the surface of the lumen and impeding the free flow of blood. If the condition is advanced, then the blood supply is correspondingly diminished to every part of the body. Such supply may be sufficient to keep the part functioning only if the patient lives a very quiet, very sedentary life. If any extra respiration, heart action, kidney function, etc., there may be a complete breakdown with a fatal termination. Thus it is that an injury or illness, or exertion, that would be considered as a minor one in a young person, may carry a risk of death in a very old person.

The pulse rate in the elderly at rest is usually round about 72 but it may be a little slower and a little irregularity due to presystole is quite common. In some elderly people the pulse rate is more rapid than normal, and this may point to myocardial weakness, though occasionally it is due to nervousness. The arteries as felt at the wrist, the elbow and temple regions are frequently thickened and tortuous. Peripheral circulation may be impaired, with some coldness of the fingers and toes, and perhaps a little cyanosis. The actual size of the heart may be obscured by accompanying emphysema. Blood vessels may be seen in the retina on ophthalmoscope examination and the arteries may be thickened and tortuous. Mild exercise will confirm that there is very little cardiac reserve.

Systolic blood pressure is commonly raised and it is difficult to lay down a normal figure for each age, but 100 plus the age of the patient, expressed in millimetres of mercury, is an approximate figure, e.g. a person of 70 has a systolic blood pressure of 170. But in many patients systolic pressures far above this are recorded, without carrying any significant implications. The diastolic blood pressure is of much more importance. Figures up to 100 are very common, and it is only when this figure is exceeded that the problem of high blood pressure is more seriously considered. Many elderly persons have systolic pressures of 120 mm of mercury, which for their age may be pathologically low. Such a figure, taken with a relatively low diastolic pressure, for example

80 mm of mercury or below, is more likely to point to cardiac weakness than a healthy state of affairs.

ALIMENTARY SYSTEM

Apart from the decay of teeth, there may be many atrophic changes throughout the alimentary tract. Thus, there may be atrophy of the papilli and taste buds on the tongue; there may be atrophy of the wall of the oesophagus, some difficulty in swallowing, atrophy of the gastric mucosa, with diminished gastric secretion and general diminution of the secretory activity of the whole bowel, together with weakening of the bowel wall. Elderly people tend to suffer from colonic stasis and obstinate constipation. Some disorder of gall bladder function is likely and gall-stones are a common feature of old age.

BONES AND JOINTS

Generally, there is a degree of atrophy and osteoporosis of the bones. This may result in varying deformities, of which flexural kyphosis of the spine is common and joint deformities, especially in the knees. The joints themselves tend to become stiff because of the atrophy of the synovial tissue and surrounding fibrosis. At the same time, there is muscular atrophy and consequently a general impairment of joint movement. The atrophy of bone may be so marked that spontaneous fractures can take place. Alternatively, a minor injury may cause a serious fracture. In particular, the neck of a femur fractures very easily and heals very poorly, or even not at all. The bone marrow may be affected in the atrophic process, with an impairment of blood regeneration, a defect more readily brought to light by a small haemorrhage or systemic infection.

Renal function is dealt with more fully later on in relation to fluid balance, but some loss of function is very common in the aged.

CENTRAL NERVOUS SYSTEM

The neurones of the central nervous system have a distinctive feature which sets them apart from the cells of other organs in the body. Namely, when a neurone dies, or is destroyed, it is never replaced and its function can only be carried on by any pre-existing neurone that happens to be present.

The other cells in the body, for example, connective tissue cells, red blood cells, leucocytes, are immediately replaced by others when they die. In other instances, when a cell dies, though it may not be replaced its function may be continued, or partly so, by cells of a different order, for example fibrosis in place of muscle.

There are also certain other differences, thus the functioning of the brain may be greatly improved by training, and from experience gained, so that a person even in advanced age may have a much more active and efficient mind than he did as a young man, despite the natural process of physical deterioration. In the aged, therefore, there are very great individual differences as regards mental activity, though presumably in two persons the number of functioning neurones might be roughly the same.

Commonly, however, elderly persons are apt to be forgetful, to reminisce unduly, to find it difficult to adjust themselves to new ideas and to have lost a certain amount of initiative, drive and ambition. There are also changes in sleeping habits. They seem to prefer short periods of sleep during the day and for this reason may get up during the night to make a cup of tea, write a letter, or just fidget about. There may be some shakiness of the hands, some incoordination of muscular movement and impairment of balance and a slight faltering of the voice. These latter symptoms may seem to imply advanced senility but the patient may still have complete mental clarity, so that the physical signs are misleading.

An outline has been given of the ordinary senile changes that commonly occur and it will be appreciated that the addition of a special illness is likely to produce clinical symptoms and signs of a pattern unlike that seen in younger persons.

Before considering the various illnesses in the elderly, it is perhaps of interest to note the death rates for the various age groups, which are as follows: [29, 30, 31]

England and Wales. Death (All Causes, 1962 and 1972)

	Death rates per 1,000 living				No. of deaths	
	1972*		1962		1962	
	M	F	M	F	M	F
Under 1 year			24·50	18·70	10 573	7614
1			0·94	0·77	1435	1115
5	0·4	0·3	0·44	0·32	753	518
10	0·4	0·2	0·43	0·25	759	424
15	0·9	0·4	0·92	0·36	1648	609
20	1·0	0·4	1·10	0·49	1614	711
25	1·0	0·6	1·07	0·76	3184	2193
35	2·4	1·6	2·40	1·78	7588	5651
45	7·5	4·6	7·25	4·39	22 708	14 226
55	21·0	10·7	22·20	10·80	56 957	31 714
65	53·8	27·8	54·30	30·10	79 139	64 297
75	119·8	78·2	123·90	86·20	74 201	95 319
85 and over	248·0	197·3	267·00	227·00	24 595	48 091
All ages	12·6	11·5	12·60	11·30	285 154	272 482

*(Ref. Annual Abstract of Statistics 1974, page 45.)

It will be noted that there is a great increase in the number of deaths with the peak in males at the age of 65, and females at 75, though there is a noticeable fall in death rates at this age for females in 1972 compared with 1962. As is naturally expected, high incidence of death does not start until after 45 years of age. From the above figures, it would appear that the medical care of the middle-aged and the elderly is now the major problem rather than the care of younger age groups.

The accompanying table indicates the change in medicine. For instance, deaths from rheumatic fever show a decrease of 71·6%, those for deliveries and complications of pregnancies a decrease of 67%, while that of hypertensive heart disease shows an increase of 59% and so on.

The calculations in the following tables as to per cent 65 years and over, and the percentage increase or decrease have been made personally from the *Statistical Review*.[38] In 1973 deaths in the United Kingdom from diseases of the circulatory system were 347 251, that is to say the death rate for this condition is still going up, whereas deaths from acute rheumatic fever were only 51, i.e. a considerable fall. (Ref. Annual Abstract of Statistics 1974, page 39.)

It is also of interest to compare the death rates in England and Wales with those of other European countries as set out later on.

In the younger age groups we compare very favourably, not so favourably at middle age and are almost at the bottom of the 'league' for the 65 years and over. One, of course, cannot blame the Health Service for this; there are many possible reasons, e.g. perhaps we are more industrialised, or over crowded, or badly housed, or have a shortage of doctors, or just simply we are English and they are a lot of foreigners and so on. Nevertheless the comparison is disappointing as we, of all the countries, have large, organised Health and Welfare Services. In the United Kingdom, even the death rates in 1962 are slightly worse than in 1956, and there is an increase in morbidity in men 60 to 64.

It is felt these unpleasant comparisons should incline us to clarify in our minds just what the Health Service is trying to accomplish; whether it is proceeding on the right lines. Is it successful, being not only socially convenient but also actually improving the health of the people, including elderly people?

Pathological Conditions in the Elderly

INFECTIONS

In the young the usual accompaniments of infection are of feeling ill, headaches, either sweating or shivering, a rapid pulse and a rise of temperature above the normal of 98·4 °F. A rise of temperature is almost a constant finding, so much so that if the temperature is not raised it is usually and correctly assumed there is no infection taking place. This is not so in the elderly; frequently there is bronchial pneumonia or acute bronchitis, cystitis, mild pyelitis, influenza and so on without a rise in temperature. The pulse may be rapid or even irregular, but this is no

Deaths by cause and sex at all ages 1946–56

Cause		1946	1956	% 65 and over	% increase	% decrease
Infective and parasitic diseases	M	16 583	5508	34		66
	F	11 724	2767	33		89
Neoplasms	M	39 244	49 675	54	32	
	F	40 420	44 679	56	10	
Allergic, endocrine system, metabolic	M	3248	2663	52·8		18
and nutritional disease	F	4899	4388	63		10
(a) Avitaminoses	M	123	192	37·5	56	
	F	122	238	52	95	
Diseases of the blood and blood-	M	908	697	68·5		32
forming organs	F	1646	1352	86·8		18
Mental, psychoneurotic and personality	M	543	374	73·7		31
disorders	F	799	764	74·4		4
Diseases of the nervous system and	M	26 734	33 716	78	26	
sense organs	F	34 942	46 339	81·8	33	
Diseases of the circulatory system	M	76 715	98 097	71·4	27	
	F	78 470	95 810	86	20	
(a) Rheumatic fever	M	360	102	13·7		71·6
	F	415	106	17		74·7
(b) Chronic rheumatic heart disease	M	3868	3049	37		21
	F	5989	5161	41		13·8
(c) Arteriosclerotic and degenerative	M	57 697	74 004	72	28	
heart disease	F	56 401	65 935	90	16·9	
(d) Hypertensive disease	M	6486	9298	74	59	
	F	6436	11 100	84	72	
Diseases of the respiratory system	M	31 642	35 732	66·7	12	
	F	23 951	24 047	80	0·4	
(a) Influenza	M	2460	1272	33		48
	F	2812	1354	19		51
(b) Pneumonia	M	10 326	11 144	30	17	
	F	8806	9799	19	27	
(c) Bronchitis	M	16 132	19 852	32	23	
	F	10 917	9818	16·6		10
Diseases of the digestive system	M	11 229	8549	56		22
	F	8443	7174	67·8		15
Diseases of the genito-urinary system	M	10 445	7858	73		24
	F	5197	3845	58·7		26
Deliveries and complications of pregnancy	F	1209	399	—		76
Diseases of the skin	M	392	183	49·7		52
	F	362	292	60		19
Diseases of the bones	M	758	624	60·7		17
	F	1356	1236	76·6		8
Congenital malformations	M	2956	2442	3·7		17
	F	2383	2133	3·8		10
Senility and ill-defined conditions†	M	6640	3208	97		50·8
	F	9840	5537	99		43
Accidents, poisoning and violence	M	11 624	12 992	30	11·8	
	F	7152	8878	58	24	
(a) Fractured neck of femur	†		M 432	94	*	*
	†		F 1176	97	*	*
(b) Fracture of other parts of femur	†		M 521	90·9	*	*
	†		F 1208	97·9	*	*

* % 65 and over was taken from Table 17.[38]
† Not registered for 1946.

International comparison of death rates per 1000 population

Males

	Year	Under 1 year*	1–4	5–14	15–24	25–44	45–64	65 and over	All Ages
England and Wales	1962	24·5	0·9	0·4	1·0	1·8	14·0	82·8	12·6
Federal German Republic	1959	38·0	1·6	0·6	1·6	2·2	13·0	75·7	12·0
Belgium	1959	34·4	1·4	0·6	1·2	2·0	13·4	72·6	12·4
Switzerland	1959	25·6	1·4	0·5	1·5	2·1	11·4	69·0	10·3
Sweden	1959	19·2	1·0	0·5	1·1	1·6	8·7	64·0	10·0
Netherlands	1960	18·5	1·3	0·5	0·8	1·5	9·8	62·1	8·3
Austria	1959	43·5	1·9	0·6	1·9	2·6	15·1	78·1	13·7
France	1960	26·3	1·3	0·4	1·1	2·4	14·5	77·1	11·9
Denmark	1959	25·7	1·0	0·4	1·0	1·8	9·9	64·8	9·8
Norway	1959	21·2	1·1	0·6	1·2	1·8	9·3	62·1	9·4
Italy (p)	1959	48·9	12·4†	0·7	1·2	2·1	11·4	67·2	9·7
Irish Republic	1961	33·5	1·5	0·5	0·7	2·2	12·5	87·0	13·2
Portugal	1960	83·4	7·0	1·0	1·3	2·8	12·6	77·1	11·0

Females

	Year	Under 1 year*	1–4	5–14	15–24	25–44	45–64	65 and over	All Ages
England and Wales	1962	18·7	0·8	0·3	0·4	1·3	7·4	60·1	11·3
Federal German Republic	1959	30·3	1·2	0·4	0·6	1·5	7·2	57·9	9·8
Belgium	1959	26·0	1·2	0·4	0·5	1·3	7·3	56·6	10·5
Switzerland	1959	18·5	1·2	0·4	0·5	1·1	6·8	56·1	8·9
Sweden	1959	13·8	0·7	0·3	0·4	1·2	6·0	55·0	9·0
Netherlands	1960	14·5	1·0	0·3	0·4	1·0	5·8	52·6	7·0
Austria	1959	35·9	1·4	0·5	0·7	1·6	7·7	59·5	11·4
France	1960	20·0	1·1	0·3	0·6	1·4	7·1	55·8	10·1
Denmark	1959	19·0	0·9	0·3	0·4	1·4	6·9	56·9	8·8
Norway	1959	16·0	0·8	0·4	0·4	1·1	5·6	54·3	8·5
Italy (p)	1959	41·7	10·6†	0·5	0·6	1·4	6·7	53·5	8·3
Irish Republic	1961	27·4	1·3	0·4	0·5	1·7	8·4	72·7	11·4
Portugal	1960	71·2	6·4	0·8	0·8	1·7	6·9	64·7	9·9

* Rates per thousand live births
† This figure is for age group 0–4 years.

Men aged 60–64 and 55–59 incapacitated at a date in each year from 1954 to 1962, expressed as a proportion of the population at risk at the same date in the relevant age group*

	Age 60–64		Age 55–59	
	All men incapacitated	*Men incapacitated for over 3 months*	*All men incapacitated*	*Men incapacitated for over 3 months*
5 June 1954	11·6	8·6	7·1	5·3
4 June 1955	12·0	8·7	8·0	5·1
2 June 1956	12·0	8·8	7·8	5·0
1 June 1957	11·9	8·7	7·8	4·9
31 May 1958	12·6	9·3	7·5	4·7
30 May 1959	12·8	9·7	7·5	4·9
4 June 1961	12·7	9·4	7·4	4·6
3 June 1962	12·7	9·4	7·4	4·6

* Estimated from samples of persons recording incapacity for work and persons insured for sickness benefit.

rarity in old people. They may feel poorly, have a poor appetite or a headache, all of which are common complaints. Since the temperature is not raised the patient may still be considered as ill, perhaps to have had a mild cerebral attack or become more apathetic and more senile. Sometimes in a diabetic the patient requires more insulin or diabetic tablets or if the patient is on sedatives or other drugs she does not seem to respond in the usual way. It is difficult to diagnose infection in the absence of fever. For this reason it is commonly necessary to examine the blood for an increased number of white cells, either in total numbers or a rise of polymorphs relative to the number of lymphocytes together with a raised erythrocyte sedimentation rate and all too commonly this is found to be so in the patient who is not doing very well. It is usually considered that a total white cell count of up to 10 000 is within normal limits. It can be, but in older patients the more normal limit is nearer 6000 with polymorphs at about 70%. If a raised white count is found greater attention must be focused on the possibility of lung or urinary infection. Even with good clinical skill and thoroughness it may still be impossible to find an accurate cause of the infection. One of the great difficulties is with a virus infection, example influenza, where in addition to no appreciable rise in temperature there is also no leucocytosis, yet the patient is ill with embarrassment of the heart and pulmonary functions. If there is a leucocytosis considered to be due to infection it is an indication for antibiotic treatment and one cannot really wait until every diagnostic investigation has been done. Very commonly there is a response to treatment, the patient feels better and the white count falls to normal – at which point the antibiotic should be discontinued. The account given above is to emphasise the importance of *non febrile* infection in the elderly; it is not intended that treatment with an antibiotic can replace proper diagnosis and indeed such a procedure would be ineffective and cause dangerous delay in for example a perforated peptic ulcer, appendicitis, diverticulitis and many other conditions. Yet non febrile infection is common in the elderly, can be diagnosed by a white cell count, responds well to treatment which however will not be given unless such infection is borne in mind.

FLUID BALANCE

In the young who are strong and ambulant, there is no difficulty under ordinary circumstances in maintaining fluid balance. If they are short of fluids, they experience a natural thirst and have the mental clarity and physical strength to take some drink or other. If their diet is deficient in salt, their kidneys can normally conserve the salt in the body, and this, in turn, will lead to intense thirst. In the young, fluid requirements can commonly be met by about three pints of fluid a day.

In the elderly, all is very different. There is likely to be a deterioration in the functioning of the kidneys, consequent upon such conditions as poor blood supply due to cardiovascular degeneration, poor blood supply due to anaemia, and possibly impaired oxygenation of the blood due to emphysema, bronchitis and like conditions. The specific renal cells may undergo primary senile decay. Cystitis is common in females and perhaps more common in males with enlarged prostates. There is therefore the possibility of backward pressure and infection affecting the renal tubules.

In the young, the kidneys are able to excrete the waste products of metabolism (notably urea) and various body acids, by the passage of about a litre and a half of urine; but in the elderly the power of concentration of the urine declines. Thus to bring about the same excretion of waste products, a greater amount of urine must be passed daily, i.e. there is a resulting polyurea.

The kidney may not be able to fulfil its function during waking hours and continues to act during sleep, so causing a nocturea. The kidneys not only lose the function of passing a concentrated urine, but also many of the powers of retention of electrolytes with the consequent inability to pass a very dilute urine. In its last stages of failure, it is generally conceded by physiologists that the kidneys can only pass a urine which has a specific gravity of approximately 1010. The elderly commonly pass large quantities of urine round about this figure, though it may vary five points or so either way, since by the time a really fixed specific gravity urine is passed the patient is likely to be in uraemia. The passage of urine of this character requires consideration in more detail.

SALT DEPLETION

The maintenance of the normal salt balance in the body after an adequate intake depends on salt loss which takes place mainly in the urine but also occurs in sweat, or under abnormal conditions by the act of vomiting. The excretion of the salt in urine is effected by the capillaries of the glomeruli and tubules under control of pituitary hormone and the normal functioning of the suprarenal cortex.

In the elderly, without the occurrence of any specific attack of nephritis there is an impairment of renal function mainly as a result of arteriosclerosis and impaired circulation which results in the inability of the kidneys to pass either a concentrated or a diluted urine.

The assessment of renal function has been carried out by O. Olbrich[35] and his associates. They showed in patients over 60 with a normal diastolic pressure a mean decrease of about 30% in diodine clearance, inulin clearance and tubular excretory capacity, and about 25% in urea clearance; and in a second group where the diastolic blood pressure was raised a decrease of 50% of diodine clearance and tubular excretory capacity, 40% in inulin clearance and 35% in urea clearance. They suggested the results reflected changes in renal plasma flow and associated vascular changes rather than glomeruli filtration capacity.

N. W. Shock[44] also did an evaluation of renal function and concluded that there was reduced plasma flow in aged subjects due in part to functional vaso-constriction and in part to a loss of nephrones.

Edward J. Steiglitz[50] has drawn attention to extra lowered renal reserve in the elderly. He states the kidneys cannot clear the blood of metabolic debris unless the circulation is adequate. He draws attention to the close association of hypertensive arterial disease and renal impairment.

Davis and Shock[14] came to the conclusion that there was a steady decline in the effective renal plasma flow per unit of tubular excretory capacity beyond the fourth decade.

Shock,[44] in a further series of experiments, again came to the conclusion that there was an impairment in the renal function of the elderly. 'In aged subjects, inulin clearance was reduced on the average to 60% of the average values observed in young adults.'

Cowdry[13] also came to the conclusion that the available evidence indicates that in the elderly the primary factor involved in the reduction of renal function is based on vascular changes.

Now it is generally conceded that the specific gravity of the urine essentially depends on the amount of salt and urea present; other normal constituents playing a negligible part.

As far as can be made out by studying the literature and by experiment, the specific gravity of a urea solution is as follows:

4%	Specific gravity	1010
3%		1007–5
2%		1005
1%		1002·5

and of salt solution, this:

0·9%	1009
0·45%	1004·5

Further, the mixture of urea and salt in one solution is additive in its effect on the specific gravity.

Example:	Urea	2%	Specific gravity	1009·5
	Salt	0·45%		
			or	
	Urea	1%	Specific gravity	1009·25
	Salt	0·7%		

Though by experiment the measurements are rarely dead accurate, they are sufficiently so to confirm the logical conclusion that a patient with a fixed specific gravity urine has a failure in function to concentrate urea – it is likely to be nearer 1% than 2% in the urine, and as a result the salt content is relatively fixed near a figure of 0·7%.

Thus to keep the blood urea at a normal level the patient has to pass large quantities of urine than normal and is continually and of necessity suffering salt depletion. The situation is shown below.

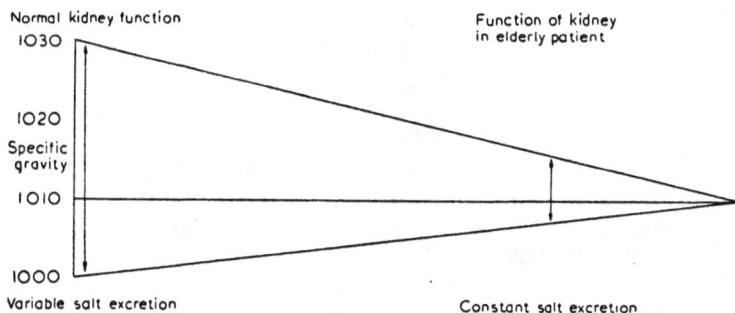

Normal kidney function compared with that of an elderly patient

As will be seen by the above diagram the normal kidney may be considered to be able to excrete urine varying in concentration, i.e. from a specific gravity of 1000 to 1030, and when functioning in this manner the kidney may excrete either a large quantity of salt or practically none at all; this normal kidney has also the ability to concentrate urea in the urine at a level over 3% as required. Conversely, with the elderly the specific gravity of the urine gradually approaches that of 1010 and the urine is likely to contain less than 2% of urea and always to contain salt, usually in the region of 6–7 grammes per litre.

In the elderly, abnormal loss of sodium chloride is commonly considered to be due to vomiting, diarrhoea, suction drainage of the stomach or intestine or excessive therapeutic diuretics, but it also occurs in two fairly common diseases, namely diabetic acidosis and, as outlined previously, in chronic renal failure. In the elderly, acid base balance is impaired by depreciation in renal function and the ammonia-forming power of the kidney is reduced so that fixed base has to be used to neutralise the end products of metabolism with the consequent loss of sodium chloride.

The syndrome presents the following features – as described by D. M. Dunlop,[16] There is an increase of lassitude and apathy which may be followed by mental confusion, progressing to stupor. Muscular weakness and cramps are common, also nausea and even vomiting, not relating to food. The patient becomes dehydrated with dry, elastic skin, especially noted over the eyelids, reduced eyeball tension, sunken cheeks and a pinched appearance. The pulse becomes quick and of small volume with a falling blood pressure, while peripheral cyanosis is apt to develop. The patient may become acidotic and have acidotic breathing. While in a young patient with normal kidneys the urine would show a very low sodium chloride content or its absence, in the elderly with chronic renal failure there is an inability to conserve sodium chloride which will therefore be present in its usual amounts. Thus the progress towards salt depletion is very much more rapid in the elderly and only the onset of anurea will prevent this salt loss and, of course, anurea must inevitably lead to uraemia.

Wright,[57] by experiment, showed the consequences of excess salt and deficient salt on renal function. For instance, an ingestion of 28 grammes of sodium chloride increased the urinary flow from 20 cc to 120 cc per minute, thus showing the importance of salt as a diuretic. On the other hand, sodium chloride deprivation decreased glomeruli filtration by 30% and urea clearance by 40% to 80% of a controlled value. Considerable urea retention occurred with a resulting rise in plasma urea from 30 mg% to 80 mg%.

From a clinical and practical point of view when one is considering the matter of salt depletion or even a mixture of salt and water depletion, it is important to ascertain certain conditions in the patient:

(1) Whether or not the patient is thirsty. If so, any dehydration is likely to be a matter of water depletion rather than salt depletion and, conversely, if the patient appears to be dehydrated but has no thirst there is likely to be salt depletion.

(2) Whether or not there is dryness of the tongue, suggesting dehydration.

(3) The specific gravity and salt content of the urine. If an elderly patient has dry, elastic skin, a dry tongue or a history of a deficient fluid intake, then if the kidneys are functioning normally, the urine should have a high specific gravity. If, however, the urine is at this stage still about a specific gravity of 1010 it points to a degree of renal failure, and if the urine has less than 2% urea and contains salt, over 5 grammes per litre, then it is very possible that the patient is in salt depletion.

(4) A blood examination may now be most significant. No serious salt depletion can occur without a raised blood urea and if this be so, plus some haemo-concentration as evidenced by an unduly high haemoglobin percentage or raised haematocrit reading, then it is almost certain that the patient is going into salt depletion uraemia. If in addition there is a low sodium and chloride content in the blood, this will confirm the matter, but all too often this only occurs *in extremis*.

(5) In the more severe cases a patient with salt depletion is likely to be drowsy and to have acidotic breathing.

Clinical application From what has been said, it is important to examine every elderly patient and assess the renal function, especially as regards their ability to conserve salt. It is as well to assume that elderly patients suffer from salt depletion until it has been shown they can pass either a very dilute or a very highly concentrated urine, and as a routine to do serial specific gravity examination of the urine, their salt content (Fantus method) and a blood urea. A patient may be precipitated into uraemia by the following conditions:

(1) The patient may take insufficient fluid because he is in salt depletion and is not thirsty; this is particularly likely if he is also mentally confused. The causes of mental confusion are dealt with more fully under the heading of 'Organic Mental Syndrome' but common causes are cerebral thrombosis, bronchitis, broncho-pneumonia, cystitis, retention of urine, faecal impaction. Relatives who are looking after the patient may be content to leave a glass of water

by the bedside and fail to observe that he is not drinking properly, or that his tongue is getting dry. Or the patient may only like to take sips of fluids and is insufficiently attended. When the patient is living alone, and perhaps too weak to get out of bed, he may actually thirst to death. Even in hospital there may be insufficient nurses, or insufficient understanding of the problem, so that the patient still receives inadequate fluids. Or the patient may be drowsy, semi-comatosed or comatosed and therefore unable to take fluids.

(2) In younger patients, a bout of diarrhoea or vomiting is relatively common and rarely of serious significance. In the aged, however, the symptoms must be treated energetically and fluid balance restored lest the patient collapses with dehydration and salt depletion.

(3) Patients whose kidney function normally is moderately good but is impaired on account of anaemia, lowered diastolic blood pressure, myocardial infarction, heart failure, shock, loss of blood and so on. Blood loss as by haematemesis, or gross melaenae, not only causes fluid loss but also shock and anaemia, all of which particularly affects the functioning of the kidneys. It is important, therefore, to consider the treatment, not only of the focal point of bleeding, but also the fluid balance of the patient. Elderly persons respond very unfavourably to any restriction of fluid subsequent to a haematemesis.

(4) Body metabolism customarily results in acid end-products. The lungs secrete acid in a form of carbon dioxide and the kidneys secrete acid in the urine, very commonly in combination with a base radical, for example, chlorides are linked to sodium and excreted as sodium chloride. In certain instances, as in fever or excessive protein ingestion, there is likewise a greater need to excrete acids. Again, if on account of disease the excretion of carbon dioxide by the lungs is diminished, then an extra load is placed on the kidneys to maintain the normal pH of the blood. Elderly patients commonly suffer from emphysema and chronic bronchitis with an impairment of respiratory function, and it may be this puts an extra strain on the kidneys. If in such patients there is also a renal lesion such as pyelonephritis or pyelitis or a pressure on the kidneys due to distension of the bladder or urinary obstructions as occurs in prostatic hypertrophy, then the possibility of acidosis developing is greatly enhanced. It would therefore appear that an exacerbation of a respiratory condition in an elderly person, for example acute bronchitis, or broncho-pneumonia, may result in acidosis, which an impaired renal function is unable to correct.

This raises debatable issues since it is not customary to link together respiratory and renal failure, though both organs have a common function in preventing acidosis. Blood ureas are frequently taken in the elderly and it has been found that the outcome of respiratory infections often turns on the functioning of the kidneys. A raised, or rising, blood urea worsens the picture, and in practice it has been found valuable whenever a patient has an acute bronchitis to consider means whereby the kidney function can be improved. Provided fluid balance is maintained, a diuretic can be administered which will bring about a greater excretion not only of base but also of acid radicals.

(5) Patients who have been given diuretics such as mercurials, diamox or saluric tablets.
(6) Patients with diabetes mellitus.
(7) Patients with polyurea, so commonly associated with chronic nephritis.
(8) Patients who suffer fluid loss from extensive ulcers, bed sores, ileostomy.
(9) Patients with Addison's disease.
(10) Patients who are subject to excessive sweating which may be present in fevers, especially influenza.
(11) Patients who take excessive amounts of fluid relative to their salt intake.

CASE HISTORIES

The following are case histories which illustrate some of the points mentioned:

Mrs L. P. aged 78 years Mild organic syndrome: C.N.S. nil focal B/P 150/100; retinopathy grade 11; lungs mild emphysema; urine 24-hour collection – specific gravity 1011, salt 0·7% serum sodium 126 meq (normal 135–150); blood urea 31 mg%.

There was a past history of high blood pressure and a chest X-ray showed an enlarged left ventricle not clinically ascertained because of emphysema. She was treated with fluids and salt 5 grammes daily plus a light diet. After a few days a great return of mental clarity was seen but urine specific gravity was still only 1010, salt 0·7%, but serum sodium rose to 134 meq.

Mr J. G. aged 74 years Gastric ulcer; recently suffering from pains in the abdomen and vomiting. Tongue dry and coated. Pulse 108; B/P 120/60. Urine specific gravity 1014. Albumin, acetone, sugar nil. Chloride 6 grammes. Serum plasma electrolytes – sodium 122 meq, Cl. 97 meq, urea 64 mg%, Hb. 101%.

The patient was given intragastric drip of milk, fluids and saline. The dehydration and mild uraemia cleared up. Later a large ulcer crater was seen on barium examination which also gradually healed. It would appear the vomiting plus some chronic renal failure brought about the salt depletion.

Mrs B. H. aged 79 years Nine serial examinations of the urine gave specific gravities varying from 1006 to 1014. Urea percentage up to a maximum of 1·6 and sodium chloride was constantly present with an average figure of 6 grammes per litre in the urine. The patient has considerable osteoarthritis but otherwise keeps well on adequate fluids and salt.

Mrs A. B. aged 90 years Seven serial urine examinations gave specific gravities ranging from 1007 to 1010 but one outstanding specimen had one specific gravity of 1018. The highest urea percentage attained was 1·7%, but the average was 1·5%. The average chlorides were 5 grammes per litre. This patient was bedridden on account of arthritis and blindness but keeps reasonably well on a very routine light diet.

Mr W. W. aged 80 years This patient was under treatment for congestive heart failure and had been taking diuretics. On admission he had respirations 32; marked oedema of the legs. Pulse 108. B/P 170/80 with an enlarged heart. Abdomen showed some enlargement of the liver. One of his main complaints was pain in the abdomen. His urine had a specific gravity of 1010 with a trace of acetone. Chlorides were 7 grammes per litre. His tongue was dry. Serum electrolytes showed a low sodium 128 meq Chlorides 106. Blood urea 83 mg. Hb. 78% but red cells were hypochromic. He was treated with fluids, small amount of salt and Fergon for the anaemia. He made a good recovery. It would appear the treatment for congestive heart failure had been too extensive. He had been on diuretics.

CONCLUSION

Experimental work already done on renal function in the elderly indicates the likelihood of renal impairment mainly related to changes in renal plasma flow and associated vascular degeneration. Innumerable examinations of patients – and one deals with 1600 admissions a year – fully supports this, so attention has been drawn to the very grave hazard that the elderly person has of running into salt depletion. It is felt that this hazard has not been sufficiently high-lighted as a complication of so many disorders in the elderly. Since salt depletion is a condition which responds very favourably to treatment it is clearly one which should not pass unrecognised, and is unlikely to do so if the hazard is kept constantly in mind.

POTASSIUM DEPLETION

In the foregoing account of salt depletion the problem of potassium depletion was not considered in order to avoid over-complicating the problem of electrolyte imbalance. However, potassium depletion may occur independently of, or commonly, associated with, sodium depletion. Potassium depletion or hypokalaemia is a well-known complication of diarrhoea. The condition is likely to produce the complaint of weakness, anorexia, nausea and vomiting. In particular one should stress the symptoms of muscular weakness. The serum potassium, instead of being of a normal value, i.e. 3·5–5·0 meq litres, is likely to be well below this figure and if an electrocardiograph is taken characteristically there will be a sagged *St* segment, wide inverted *T* waves, *U* waves and a prolonged *Q–T* interval. The condition should respond to intravenous therapy of 4 grammes of potassium chloride in each litre of 5% dextrose. Houghton[26] gives a very detailed account of severe potassium depletion in a middle-aged woman subject to full pathological balanced studies, and the reader is referred to his article for a fuller description.

The problem of electrolyte balance is more fully discussed under the heading of 'Operations in the Elderly'.

CYSTITIS AND PYELONEPHRITIS

Whereas young patients react to infection by a bout of fever, this is not always so in the aged. Many of them have a phase of mental confusion instead, and are likely to complain of discomfort when passing urine. If the latter be examined it may be opalescent to the naked eye and show pus cells and numerous bacteria under the microscope. The condition can be overlooked unless urines are carefully examined and the condition may be the final cause in bringing about an enhanced measure of renal failure.

RENAL FUNCTION TESTS

An outline has been given of the renal function tests that can be performed and it will be understood that there are many variable factors affecting renal function. Consequently, a renal function test is unlikely to give an accurate result while the patient is ill, or in poor health. There are also difficulties in the actual carrying out of the tests, collecting specimens, etc., when the patient is ill, and the water concentration and dilution tests in particular may be inadvisable if the patient is already not in healthy fluid balance. If the kidney is actually in failure, there is likely to be a raised, or rising, blood urea (though renal failure may take place without this phenomenon). One high blood urea of itself may not mean renal failure, but if it is persistently high it usually does so.

A relatively easy method of assessing renal function is by examining successive specimens of urine passed during the night, or in the morning. The specific gravity should be taken at 60°C, and the salt content estimated. The specimens will show the maximum concentrating powers of the kidneys, and the more the specific gravity approximates to 1010, the more the renal failure. If in such a specimen there is a high salt content, i.e. 0·6% or more, then the urea content must be correspondingly less, i.e. less than 2% if the specific gravity is 1010. From this it may be inferred there is a failure in urea concentration and urea clearance.

It is perhaps worth stating that in the elderly adverse pre-renal factors play a much greater part in precipitating renal failure than they do in the young. Since many of these pre-renal factors respond to treatment it follows that much more can be done for renal failure in the elderly than is commonly considered to be the case, and renal concentration can be improved by attention to anaemia, cardiac disorders, infections, diet and so on.

DEHYDRATION (WATER DEPLETION)

In elderly patients with impaired renal function and polyurea, water depletion may come on with alarming suddenness, and its possibility is a constant anxiety. The syndrome is marked by the following features.

There has been a gross deficiency in fluid intake, as compared to fluid loss, and there may be considerable loss in the weight of the patient. There may be *no* accompanying thirst if there has been an associated salt loss. The tongue is dry, the skin is dry, the eyes are sunken, and if the skin is pinched, especially over the upper eyelid, it takes an undue time to return to normal. The patient feels very weak and is feeble, there is coldness of the extremities, with perhaps some peripheral cyanosis of the fingers, toes, nose and ears. There is likely to be a fall in both systolic and diastolic blood pressure – this should be related not to a normal but to pre-existing blood pressure records. There is also likely to be a weak and rapid pulse. In the later stages there may be circulatory failure with moist crepitations at the base of the lungs. At times, because of electrolyte disturbances, there may be distension of the abdomen or paralytic ileus. The amount of urine passed rapidly falls. It may still contain a good deal of sodium chloride, but this does not mean that salt depletion can be ruled out. Examination of the blood will reveal concentration of its constituents to a degree higher than normal. Thus, there may be a relatively high haemoglobin percentage and a high blood urea, and a haematocrit will reveal packed cell volumes of higher than usual, uraemia is likely to ensue with sighing acidotic breathing, and the patient may lapse into coma. A survey of the fluid intake and output, the clinical features and the pathological findings should allow a diagnosis to be made with reasonable accuracy.

Treatment The condition should be prevented as much as possible by ensuring that all elderly patients have a sufficient intake relative to the polyurea. A rise in blood urea should be taken as a danger signal and point to the consideration of further fluids and probably salt. A dry tongue may be the earliest symptom, and again an indication for more fluids. Sometimes the failure to take fluids is because the patient cannot keep up his usual habits of diet; he may be accustomed to take a bottle of beer in the evenings, or a woman may be used to several cups of tea at varying intervals during the day. Some patients with difficulty in micturition deliberately take less to drink. Nursing staff should be well versed in the dangers of dehydration and not rely on the patient to ask for drinks.

In its early stages, the patient can be given a large quantity of fluid – he will usually require several pints. Water, soft drinks, tea, coffee, cocoa, soup, beer, etc., may be given, but milk and water is particularly useful, since milk contains salts and minerals most suited to the body requirements. If it is difficult to give drinks in the ordinary way – and some nurses seem to be better at this than others – provided the patient is conscious, fluids may be given as an intragastric drip, using diluted milk. This latter method is often the most successful, but a watch should be kept for any distension of the stomach. If the patient is unconscious, the gastric drip method cannot be used, because of the risk of regurgitation into the lungs. It is then best to give intravenous therapy.

It may now be necessary to consider the question of salt depletion. Unfortunately, neither electrolyte records nor the amount of salt in the urine may be of value, and the administration of saline may be a matter of guesswork. If too much salt is given intravenously, it may exceed the secretory capacity of the kidneys and there is the risk of causing oedema, especially pulmonary oedema. Generally, a pint of normal saline can be given safely and this may be followed by 5% glucose. While the fluid is being given intravenously, the condition of the patient should be observed, the blood pressure taken from time to time and the bases of the lungs auscultated for the advent of moist sounds. Observation should also be made on the output of urine and its specific gravity and salt content. If there is no increase in urinary excretion, it may be advisable to slow up the intravenous transfusion, but if there is an increase of urinary excretion then things are going the right way. This is all the more confirmed if there is an accompanying fall in the blood urea. In a successful case, and many patients in coma can be treated successfully, the breathing becomes easier, the pinched appearance of the patient passes off, the pulse becomes more full and bounding, and the peripheral cyanosis clears up. Dehydration is an acute medical emergency, is quite common in the elderly and may require some change in therapy from hour to hour. Intravenous treatment may be continued for twenty-four hours, or even repeated next day. It should be discontinued as soon as the patient can drink of his own accord. The amount of fluid given intravenously may vary considerably upwards from a minimum of about three pints.

The giving of fluid by rectal intubation is rarely successful and often leads to a very wet bed. Fluid may be given subcutaneously but in elderly people with poor nutrition there is a considerable risk of local gangrene. The acute phase of dehydration may be over within a day or so, after which it will be necessary to build up the patient's general health and correct any anaemia or malnutrition that may be present.

Complications of dehydration Because of impaired renal function, the elderly patient may suffer from phases of dehydration, from which he may recover by dietetic chance. However, in a phase of dehydration, from which he may be subject, symptoms of mild uraemia accompanied by mental confusion, and dehydration is also a serious precipitating cause of arterial thrombosis. The elderly are prone to atheroma, cardiovascular degeneration and high blood pressure, and particularly subject to cerebral thrombosis, coronary thrombosis and peripheral vascular thrombosis. Patients with recent cerebral thrombosis and peripheral vascular thrombosis are frequently found to have accompanying features of some dehydration. In the wards, dehydration has been observed to precede these two conditions in many instances, and it is a matter of conjecture whether dehydration is not in fact a precipitating cause of cerebral thrombosis and peripheral gangrene in many elderly persons. So far no close association has been observed between coronary thrombosis and dehydration, and the former seems to be in a category of its own. Continued dryness of the tongue and mouth does of course have the attendant risk of ascending parotitis, a condition not uncommon in the elderly.

EXCESS OF BODY FLUID
Excessive body fluid is also met with in the elderly. The most common cause results from congestive heart failure, but it is also met with when there is too little albumin in the blood.

CONGESTIVE HEART FAILURE
Congestive heart failure may come on fairly suddenly in relation to an acute illness, a coronary infarction, etc., or it may follow hypertensive heart failure, but usually it comes on gradually because of increasing cardiac weakness. It is not proposed to go into the physiology and pathology of cardiac oedema, which is dealt with so admirably in the ordinary medical text-books, but to give a simple account of how it affects the elderly person.

The first signs that may be noticed are puffiness of the feet and ankles in the evenings, which is not present in the mornings, accompanied by an increase in breathlessness on exertion. The significance of the puffiness may be obscured by the accompanying presence of varicose veins. The oedema of the feet may continue in this way for many months, or even years, without further deterioration, but gradually the oedema becomes more marked and the legs more oedematous.

There may be other factors worsening the cardiac condition, which are well worth considering, since they may be more amenable to treatment. Blood examination may show there is an iron-deficiency anaemia, or there may be anaemia due to blood loss as evidenced by persistent occult blood in the stools, or the patient may have some other cause for anaemia. It is still not uncommon to find patients with really very advanced pernicious anaemia, e.g. with haemoglobin levels below 30 %, so it would appear there are quite a number of mild cases of pernicious anaemia which are missed. Haemoglobin and blood film can therefore be a very useful preliminary investigation of what may otherwise be considered as the simple congestive heart failure.

It is perhaps relevant at this stage to point out that, whereas the young suffer from one condition only at a time (or usually so), it is a principle in geriatric medicine to assess the function of other organs since two or more pathological conditions are likely to be present. The patient may have an accompanying cystitis, or suffer from recurrent attacks of bronchitis, both of which might respond to treatment, or the diet may be grossly deficient, and were it not for the cardiac oedema the patient would be in a state of malnutrition. An amount of cardiac oedema may escape notice if the patient is lying in bed, so it is important to inquire as to oedema of the legs and look for pitting over the sacral region. The matter of cardiac oedema may be complicated, not only by the presence of other conditions, but also by the loss of considerable quantities of albumin in the urine, with a consequent deficiency of albumin in the blood. In the young, as the congestive heart failure comes under control, natural recuperation soon makes good the albumin deficiency in the blood, but this may be more difficult to achieve in the elderly; they may require an easily digestible diet of high protein content – eggs are especially valuable.

Despite the fact that the treatment of congestive heart failure is dealt with very fully in the medical text-books, numerous patients at home are not digitalised sufficiently or their oedema relieved by suitable diuretics. The cause of this, I believe, lies in the difficulty in controlling the giving of dangerous drugs without adequate nursing supervision. The family doctor naturally feels obliged to avoid the dangers of overdosage. For this reason, it is generally advisable that patients with congestive heart failure be admitted periodically to hospital. There the drugs can be given under close medical and nursing supervision and fluid intake and output kept in a proper balance. Even in hospital it is dangerous to promote a massive diuresis in elderly people, because it can so easily lead to distension of the bladder or acute retention of urine, and if the patient is a little confused this may not be discovered early enough. Generally speaking, it is better to use an oral diuretic, but if an injection of Mersalyl (B.P.) is given, it should be a small dose, e.g. 0.5 cm^3. Since there are a large number of elderly patients with varying stages of congestive heart failure, part of the work of a geriatric unit should therefore be devoted to the periodic admission of these patients.

NEPHROTIC OEDEMA

In some patients there is widespread oedema and the features of the nephrotic syndrome. Sometimes the deficiency of albumin in the blood and a reversal of the albumin/globulin ratio is corrected by an ordinary well-balanced diet. These patients would appear to be suffering from malnutrition. There are many causes of the nephrotic syndrome which are dealt with fully in the standard text-books, but quite a number of cases have been seen in elderly patients who have had diabetes mellitus for many years. In some, the renal pathology has been confirmed by post mortem and the finding has been that of intercapillary glomerulosclerosis of the kidneys as first described by Kimmelstiel and Wilson in 1936. This condition, though uncommon in the geriatric unit, is not exactly rare, which is apparently so in younger age groups. The treatment of nephrotic oedema follows on the lines laid down for younger people.

DEATHS FROM PRINCIPAL CAUSES

It will be seen from the table opposite that the first three main causes of death are Diseases of the Circulatory System, Neoplasms and Vascular Lesions affecting the Central Nervous System.

CLASSIFICATION OF CEREBRO-VASCULAR DISEASES

Adams[1] sets out a very elaborate classification of cerebro-vascular diseases and the following are its main headings:

(1) Cerebral Infarction
    (a) Thrombosis
    (b) Embolism
    (c) Other conditions causing cerebral infarction
    (d) Cerebral infarction of undetermined cause
(2) Transient Cerebral Ischaemia without Infarction
(3) Intracranial Haemorrhage

Deaths by cause and sex at all ages 1967 and 1970. Ref. Registrar General, Statistical Review, England and Wales 1970, Part I, Tables. Medical Table 7

Cause of death		1967	1970
All Causes	M	277 178	293 053
	F	265 338	282 141
Pulmonary Tuberculosis	M	1444	1126
	F	622	480
Syphilis and other venereal disease	M	152	117
	F	117	79
Neoplasms	M	60 404	63 236
	F	51 267	53 840
Stomach neoplasm	M	7445	7263
	F	5495	5473
Malignant neoplasm of respiratory system	M	24 307	25 841
	F	4977	5657
Bronchus and lung	M	23 510	24 913
	F	4679	5371
Neoplasm of breast	M	85	73
	F	10 230	10 677
of prostate	M	3903	3906
of bladder	M	2513	2689
	F	1038	1139
Diabetes mellitus	M	1509	1713
	F	2730	2970
Avitaminoses and other nutritional deficiency	M	61	77
	F	104	143
Cerebro vascular disease	M	30 614	30 849
	F	46 380	48 442
Diseases of the circulatory system	M	135 556	141 363
	F	144 671	149 707
Diseases of the respiratory system	M	39 727	48 367
	F	28 402	37 782
Appendicitis	M	220	165
	F	187	162
Hyperplasia of prostate	M	1804	1276
Accidents, Poisoning and violence	M	13 255	12 677
	F	10 148	10 024

(4) Vascular Malformations and Developmental Abnormalities
(5) Inflammatory Disease of Arteries
(6) Vascular Diseases without Changes in the Brain
(7) Hypertensive Encephalopathy
(8) Dural Sinus and Cerebral Vein Thrombus
(9) Strokes of Undetermined Origin

In all, there are about forty diseases that affect the vascular system of the brain. The subject is consequently very complex and worthy of an extensive study in its own right. Nevertheless, pathological studies have revealed that thrombosis and embolism account for approximately 65% of the vascular lesions.[2] As a result, the whole thinking towards the stroke case is changing; it is no longer concerned so much with the plugging or vasospasm of vessels as with a full general and medical examination and an early and accurate diagnosis.

The present feeling about the word 'stroke' appears to be that the word can be fairly applied to cover all the clinical manifestations arising from a localised and sudden loss of function of a part of the central nervous system.

The term can be used for a sudden monoplegia, hemiplegia, a sudden phase of confusion, or aphasia or loss of balance (drop attack), inco-ordination, blindness, deafness and so on, according to the part of the central nervous system affected. An area of cerebral ischaemic necrosis, commonly referred to as an infarct, will occur if localised hypoxia is long continuing and will almost certainly take place if there is arterial occlusion unless there is a good collateral supply. At one time it was thought that the arteries to various parts of the brain were essentially end arteries and much of the view of the pathology of strokes was based on this conception. It has now been abundantly proved that there are numerous anastomotic channels between the anterior and middle cerebral arteries, middle and posterior cerebral, anterior and posterior cerebral and between the cerebellar arteries as well as numerous collateral channels connecting the internal and external carotid arteries. Experimental evidence has emphasised the importance of general circulatory failure to the brain as a cause of cerebral infarction rather than a pathological change limited to one particular branch of a vessel. Thompson, R. K. and Smith, G. W.[54] occluded the middle cerebral arteries in monkeys and found that if the systemic blood pressure was maintained at normal level no change in cerebral function occurred. This clearly underlines the importance of the general supply of blood to the brain and its anastomotic channels.

The main arterial supply of the brain as illustrated in the accompanying diagram arises from the arch of the Aorta as follows:

On the right side the Innominate Artery coming off the Aorta after a short course divides into the Right Common Carotid and Right Subclavian.

On the left side the Left Common Carotid and Left Subclavian come off separately.

From each subclavian artery is given off a Vertebral Artery which runs up the neck, entering the Costo-transverse foramen in the sixth Cervical Vertebra and passing upwards in successive foramina and between the Axis and Atalas, piercing the Dura Mata and Arachnoid and ultimately joining the other to form the Basilar Artery. This in turn

CIRCLE OF WILLIS

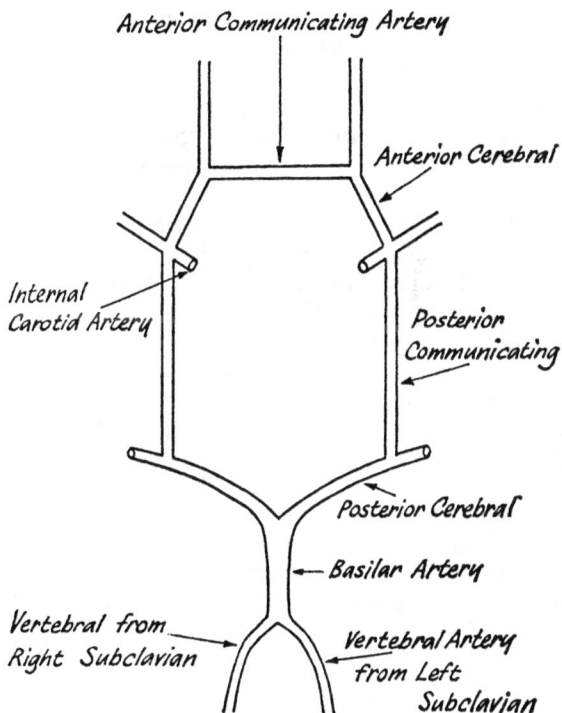

Anterior Communicating Artery

Anterior Cerebral

Internal Carotid Artery

Posterior Communicating

Posterior Cerebral

Basilar Artery

Vertebral from Right Subclavian

Vertebral Artery from Left Subclavian

divides to form the Posterior Cerebral Arteries which link up with posterior communicating branches from the Internal Carotid.

The Internal Carotid Artery is derived from the Common Carotid on each side and at the base of the brain divided into Anterior and Middle Cerebral Arteries. The Anterior Cerebral Arteries are connected by anterior communicating branches whilst communicating branches are given off from the Internal Carotid to link up with the Posterior Cerebral Arteries, the whole thus forming the Circle of Willis.

It will therefore be seen that the blood supply of the brain depends in the first instance on an efficient Circle of Willis mechanism and that most fortunately this Circle is supported not by one artery but by four, namely, two Vertebral Arteries and two Internal Carotid Arteries. There are many variations in the size of vessels about the Circle of Willis – sometimes the same Internal Carotid Artery appears to give the main supply of blood to both sides of the brain and a moderately satisfactory cerebral circulation can be maintained even if one of the four main supply routes is obstructed. It is fortunate indeed that there are four supply routes to the brain, for when the arteries of old people are examined it is common to find gross narrowing of the Innominate Artery, Internal Carotid Arteries and other important vessels associated with distortion and obvious atheroma. The presence of such a state of affairs in the Vertebral Arteries indicates that head movement should be carried out gently during operation and that hyper-extension of the neck might impede circulation through these arteries or initiate an embolus.

In many subjects the extent of arteriosclerosis and atheroma affecting the cerebral-vascular supply is so considerable that it is evident that any fall in blood pressure or cardiac output would lead to cerebral-vascular insufficiency precipitating an attack of cerebral ischemia or even infarction; because the intra-cerebral arteries may be narrowed more on one side than the other, the vascular insufficiency and phase of ischemia may give rise to solely unilateral or focal symptoms. The cerebral-vascular supply has been dealt with rather fully because, of course, cerebral thrombosis is one of the more disastrous complications of operations on the elderly.

The pathological findings of a hundred patients dying with a clinical picture suggesting cerebral infarction have been detailed by Yates, P. O. and Hutchinson, E. C.[58] The patients were hospital admissions and therefore there may be a bias as the type of cases selected. On post mortem examination they found the following conditions:

Cerebral infarction	35
Cerebral haemorrhage	28
Circulatory failure	26
Cerebral tumour	6
Trauma	7
Carbon Monoxide poisoning	4
Hepatic coma	1
Uraemic coma	1
Epilepsy	1

The group with circulatory failure comprised:

Post-operative shock	11
Recent myocardial infarction	6
Left or right ventricular cardiac failure	6
Dissecting aortic aneurism	2
Anaemia due to duodenal ulcer	1

It is, therefore, apparent that circulatory failure can cause the symptoms of a stroke without any accompanying infarction. The symptoms would therefore appear to be due to localised hypoxia and cerebral anaemia.

No case was included where there was evidence of intercranial hae-morrhage during life as ascertained by finding blood in C.S.F. or by angiographic demonstration of an aneurism, so that the twenty-eight cases of haemorrhage were clinically undiagnosable. These findings at once imply that it is almost impossible to rule out cerebral haemorrhage when there are symptoms of a stroke and that anticoagulated therapy would be extremely dangerous.

With regard to the thirty-five subjects with cerebral infarction, in twenty-three of them there were two or more infarctions.

Other conclusions were that in all but three of the thirty-five cases of infarction there was significant stenosis or occlusion of an *extra* cranial cerebral artery, whilst out of the total hundred cases only twenty-two of those with infarctions and nineteen others showed any significant stenosis of *intra* cranial arteries.

VASOSPASM

Their examination of the cerebral arteries also supported previous recorded findings; namely, that the walls of the smaller cerebral arteries were virtually devoid of elastic or muscle tissue and consisted of hyalin-ised collagon, degenerated elastic fibres with calcium deposit. These findings suggest that vasospasm or any tonic contraction of the small cerebral vessels is not possible. Larger vessels could go into spasm but this would almost certainly require a significant local stimulus. The authors also stated that cerebral infarction rarely has a single cause, and even when cerebral arteries, extra or intra cranial, are stenosed, the blood supply from the brain may continue well enough until the balance is upset by hypotension or anaemia.

With the above pathological findings in mind, one may approach the problem of the patient with a 'stroke' in the following manner:

Localised hypoxia The brain requires not only an excellent blood supply but that the blood has ample haemoglobin and is properly oxy-genated. To maintain a satisfactory supply of oxygen to the brain there must therefore be:

(1) proper oxygenation of the blood in the lungs
(2) a sufficiency of haemoglobin, i.e. no anaemia
(3) an adequate cardiac output as regards volume and pressure
(4) a good circulation through the arteries supplying the brain, i.e. both carotid and internal carotid arteries, both vertebral arteries, the basilar arteries and intact 'Circle of Willis' and finally the smaller arteries to various parts of the brain

In a young or middle-aged patient all may be well but it is rather unlikely to be so in the elderly patient.

Lungs One must therefore examine the lungs, consider the possibility of pulmonary insufficiency; bronchopneumonia, bronchitis, broncho-spasm, chronic emphysema, hypoxia after anaesthesia, etc. If there is clinical cynosis or non-acidotic dyspnoea, one can assume there is a measure of hypoxia – but these symptoms may be slight so examination must be careful. If there is evidence of hypoxia then it is logical to give oxygen. Obviously this would not help the oxygenation of a part of the brain which has been deprived of its blood supply by an artery being blocked by a thrombus or embolism. But in the early stages of a 'stroke' one cannot assume an artery is blocked and of course the longer hypoxia continues the greater will be the cerebral damage, and if prolonged it will cause death of the neurones, i.e. cerebral necrosis. Continued hypoxia also damages the intima of the arteries and can dispose throm-bus formation. Though the majority of patients who have suffered from a 'stroke' show evidence of thrombosis or haemorrhage in the supplying artery, a number on post mortem do not show this, i.e. they may have an area of necrosis but no active occlusion. The explanations for this kind of finding can be various; for instance the lumen of the arteries to the left internal capsule may be unduly narrowed due to atherosclerosis, or in addition to this there may be narrowing of the lumen of the left middle cerebral or left internal carotid. The cerebral circulation is to the left internal capsule, therefore impoverished locally so that the addition of a prolonged period of hypoxia could lead to localised necrosis with-out any actual occlusion of a blood vessel.

The blood supply to the brain is so involved that any interference of the flow through one or more supplying vessels would be a nightmare to a plumber faced with like problems of circulation but the latter is lucky compared to the doctor who has to consider the possible added complications of hypoxia and lower cardiac output.

The matter of hypoxia is important because, if present, oxygen therapy can be effective in the treatment of a recent 'stroke', and it may prevent the onset of cerebral necrosis.

Transient strokes from which the patient readily recovers are quite common and one would think a fall in blood pressure or/and a phase of hypoxia is a more likely explanation than spasm of a local artery or hypertensive attacks.

Anaemia As regards the blood haemoglobin one must routinely con-sider whether the patient is anaemic and if in doubt estimate the blood haemoglobin. Anaemia is unfortunately fairly common amongst the elderly and can be an additive factor in the causation of a 'stroke'.

Heart The likely causes for lowering a cardiac output include such conditions as hypertensive cardiac failure, myocardial infarction, shock, over-dosage with hypotensive drugs, blood loss, hypoxia, etc., and in the clinical examination all these causes could be kept in mind.

Arteries Finally the clinical examination should include palpation of the common carotid arteries for any diminution in pulsation – though only occasionally is this clinically evident. Other arteries about the body should also be palpated, though thickening and rigidity of the arteries, i.e. arteriosclerosis, does not necessarily mean the lumen of the vessels is affected as it would be by atherosclerosis.

Non-occlusive cerebral thrombosis has been dealt with at some length because it opens up new thinking as to the pathogenesis of 'strokes'. If there is no arterial obstruction then the prevention and treatment of localised cerebral hypoxia is concerned more with oxygenation of the patient, treating lung conditions, anaemia, cardiac disorders, hypotension, etc., than with the use of anticoagulants, cortisone and like measures.

Arterial occlusion The more orthodox accounts of 'strokes' are usually concerned with the details of cerebral infarction and the neurological signs and symptoms. For full accounts of these the reader is referred to standard textbooks of medicine or neurology. The following account is merely, therefore, a simple approach to the common problem of cerebral thrombosis.

CEREBRAL THROMBOSIS

Cerebral thrombosis appears to be the commonest of all vascular lesions of the brain and its incidence appears to be so high that it may well be greater than the sum total of all other lesions of the central nervous system. It is met with monotonous regularity in the geriatric wards and its treatment forms a large part of geriatric medicine. Though the condition has been fully described in the ordinary medical textbooks, there appears to be a large number of patients who for one reason or another have not been adequately treated, and the condition is therefore worthy of more emphasis.

Lesion of internal capsule There are many possible vascular lesions that may occur, but one of the commonest is that of thrombosis of vessels supplying the internal capsule of the brain and surrounding structures. The condition rarely occurs with a healthy cardiovascular state. In elderly persons, it is sometimes due to an embolus. The embolus is derived in all probability from some atheromatous lesion of the intima of an artery, but sometimes, though uncommonly in the elderly, it may come from the heart. This latter possibility is more likely where there is mitral valvular stenosis, or there has been auricular fibrillation which has returned to normal rhythm. Mitral valvular stenosis of rheumatic origin is not commonly met with in old age, presumably because the condition has proved fatal earlier on.

In many instances of cerebral thrombosis, post mortem examination reveals that there is widespread arteriosclerotic degeneration, with lesions not only in the cerebral arteries but also in the aorta and main blood vessels in the kidneys. Frequently the lenticulostriate arteries to the unaffected internal capsule have a greatly reduced lumen and it would appear that before the thrombosis the lumen of the arteries on the affected side were in a like condition. In assessing the significance of the various clinical features that may be met with in cerebral thrombosis, it is worth bearing in mind that the survival of certain parts of the brain depends on an adequate amount of blood coming through arteries that are being gradually obliterated by disease. Thus the onset of cerebral symptoms may appear in different ways:

(1) The onset will be gradual if the obliterative process is also gradual, or if the cardiac output is gradually reduced.
(2) The cerebral symptoms will be sudden, but of a temporary nature, if for some reason the flow of blood is diminished temporarily by such conditions as shock, blood loss, temporarily lowered cardiac output.
(3) Cerebral thrombosis will be sudden and of a permanent nature if the vessel is blocked by embolism or thrombosis.

In the first type of case, treatment aims at delaying the onset of more grave and widespread cerebral thrombosis, and this may be difficult, perhaps impossible. In the second type, theoretically the patient can recover completely from the 'stroke' symptoms, and clearly every effort should be made to improve the circulation and to prevent the condition going on to one of thrombosis. In the third type, full recovery is hardly possible and treatment again is aimed at improving the cerebral circulation, with a view to limiting the disease process as much as possible.

BULBAR PALSY

Though commonly 'strokes' affect the cerebral cortex or internal capsule many patients suffer from lesions about the crus cerebrae, pons and medulla resulting in a variable picture of paralysis of articulation, swallowing, coughing and speaking. The important point when a patient has difficulty in speaking is to distinguish between the dysarthria of a bulbar lesion and the dysphasia of a cortical lesion since the former is associated with difficulty in swallowing and there may be a risk of inhalation bronchial pneumonia.

In many instances, the patient has other conditions as well as a cere-

Dexion wall frame in use

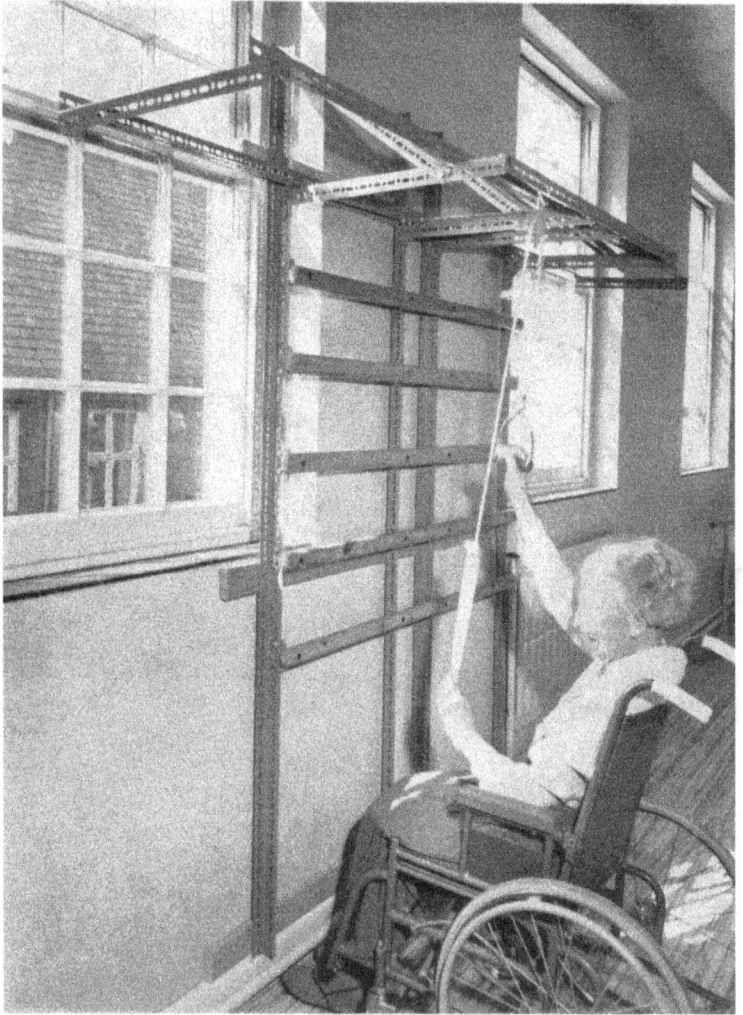

Dexion wall frame in use

bral thrombosis. As indicated previously, renal function is commonly impaired in the elderly and some mental symptoms may be uraemic manifestations, or there may be some region of infection, or anaemia, or some of the mental symptoms are more referable to high blood pressure. The treatment of cerebral thrombosis may now be considered under the following headings:

Prevention The aetiology of arterial sclerotic degeneration is most obscure and therefore there is no clear preventive treatment. Many consider it is related to an over-sedentary life and general lack of physical exercise. Others consider a continued high carbohydrate diet or excessive lipoids in the blood have some bearing on the matter. There is a high incidence of hyperglycaemia in elderly people, which so far has received very little attention, though it could very possibly be a cause of atherosclerosis and so predispose to cerebral thrombosis. High blood pressure also is associated with cerebral thrombosis but this condition is equally baffling with regard to its aetiology. It would appear advisable that the middle-aged and elderly should take a reasonable amount of out-door exercise and receive an adequate diet, in both of which they may be deficient. Acute and chronic infections should be adequately treated, and any anaemia should be investigated and dealt with. Dehydration should be particularly avoided. The treatment of high blood pressure requires special consideration and is dealt with later on in this book.

Treatment of the stroke The symptoms from an embolus come on within a matter of seconds, and that of a stroke within a matter of minutes. Both may, or may not, be accompanied by loss of consciousness. The symptoms vary considerably from minor lapses of memory to mental confusion, and from transient weakness in the face, arm, leg or in speech, to complete paralysis of these parts. The stroke often takes place in bed, or commonly when the patient gets out of bed in the morning (or becomes apparent then). If the patient is living alone, especially if he or she suffers from aphasia, then he or she cannot attract the attention of neighbours and all too often the police or neighbours have to break in and discover the patient unconscious and helpless on the floor.

The first thing to do is to get the patient to bed and carry out a thorough clinical examination. If the patient is deeply unconscious, this will also include a lumbar puncture investigation. There is still an idea prevalent that if the patient is unconscious the physician should wait upon events and let nature take its natural course, on the assumption that if she has a cerebral haemorrhage, death is inevitable; this appears to be true, but of course should be confirmed by finding blood in the cerebro-spinal fluid. If the patient has a cerebral thrombosis, and is unconscious for a long time, then the thrombosis is very extensive, and a fatal outcome is most likely. Even if the patient should recover he is likely to be paralysed and demented, and such an end result is most undesirable.

While a long period of unconsciousness does carry with it a poorer prognosis, it does not invariably do so. In general the therapy of masterly inactivity is quite wrong. Clinical examination may reveal that the patient has a distended bladder, or fever, acute bronchitis, broncho-pneumonia, or a rapid auricular filbrillation, or there may be an associated head injury, or considerable dehydration, etc.

The unconscious patient The patient should be put to bed and a free airway should be assured. This can be a very difficult matter especially when the patient is edentulous and has respiratory distress to the point of requiring to breathe not only through the nose but also the mouth. First the head should be slightly extended and turned to one side; so as to keep the tongue from falling back over the epiglottis. Next if the respiration is still impaired, a nasal airway should be inserted. If this also is unsuccessful, and it is well to remember the patient may well be unconscious for many hours, and there is no anaesthetist to attend to the airway, then a more stable method must be adopted. The difficulty with the elderly and edentulous patient is that the lips and tongue block inspiration. Unfortunately, both the ordinary mouth gag or mouth airway slip out of position after a while, leaving the patient in danger of asphyxia. Trachial intubation is not really practicable for every unconscious patient with a stroke. To overcome these difficulties M. Frost (Dental Department, Colchester) has devised a Geriatric Mouth Gag and Airway. This consists of dummy upper and lower dental plates, bridged together at the sides, and designed to keep the mouth half open. The dental plates are inserted in position – and then a mouth airway is passed from the front between the plates and over the tongue and fixed in front. This gag and airway does not slip out – keeps the tongue from obstructing inspiration – and there is no object that can be swallowed. It has proved most successful in ensuring a free airway in the unconscious patient. Incidentally many elderly unconscious patients have to travel by ambulance and, of course, it is essential that the ambulance has the equipment to ensure a free airway and that the attendant is trained to arrange it when necessary.

The patient's position should be changed from time to time, so as to prevent pressure sores. Incontinence of urine is likely and the back should be kept as clean and dry as possible. Often it will be advisable to put in a Portex catheter since the risk of a cystitis is a much less serious one than that of a bed sore. If there is a loaded rectum, this may be relieved by an enema. There is a risk of lung infection supervening in the unconscious patient, so an antibiotic should be given for a few days.

The mouth should be cleaned with glycerine and borax and moistened from time to time with teaspoonfuls of fluid; a little brandy may be used in this way.

Normally there will be no dehydration, and the patient can do without fluids for a while. Should the unconsciousness continue to a point where there is evident dehydration, and a rising blood urea, intravenous transfusion should be considered. Its value is still somewhat debatable, but since a continuation of dehydration is likely to be fatal, it should be attempted. A great number of cases of cerebral thrombosis have been seen and some have received intravenous fluids with excellent results.

Anti-coagulant therapy Since in fact there is a high incidence of cerebral haemorrhage – not diagnosable clinically – anti-coagulant therapy would appear to be too dangerous for any recent 'stroke' and probably not of great value in a 'stroke' of long standing.

Cortisone therapy This again is a debatable therapy for cerebral thrombosis. But in every thrombosis there is likely to be an accompanying local oedema. The cortisone preparations have a marked anti-inflammatory action, and presumably will lessen this oedema. It is difficult to estimate the value of cortisone therapy without massive clinical trial. Provided the patient is on an antibiotic, the treatment can, however, be given without risk for a short period of time, which is all that is necessary for a cerebral thrombosis. Cortisone acetate has a sodium-retaining effect, whereas prednisone has no such significant action. Either drug may be used; the cortisone acetate may be the one of choice if there is some dehydration, since it tends to retain body fluids; otherwise prednisone is much more potent. Cortisone acetate may be given intramuscularly – an aqueous suspension contains 25 mg cm^3. Dose 25 to 100 mg a day. Prednisone is given by mouth. Dose approximately 5 mg three times daily. Many cases of cerebral thrombosis have been given cortisone therapy. No untoward symptoms or complications have been met with, and the clinical impression is that the treatment is beneficial.

The conscious patient As soon as the patient is conscious, he should adopt a sitting position in bed and receive adequate fluid and diet. A definite regimen should now be followed to aid recovery. If the patient is restless and confused, a tranquilliser such as chlorpromazine hydrochloride should be given in doses of about 25 mg three times daily, or double this amount if necessary. The drug may take a few days to have its full effect.

Some patients have an idiosyncrasy to the drug and there is an attendant risk of hepatitis or leucopenia. If hepatitis occurs, it is likely to develop within a month of administering the drug. Hepatitis is marked by a large, firm liver and severe jaundice. When the drug is discontinued, the hepatitis subsides without further complication in almost all instances. Hepatitis only occurs in a few cases out of many thousands that have had chloropromazine therapy, and its risk is very slight indeed.

Restlessness and confusion in an elderly patient are attended by serious risks, against which the toxic hazards of chloropromazine can only be considered as negligible. If the drug should cause leucopenia, this complication is frequently fatal, but fortunately such a toxic effect is very rare. Some physicians consider that periodic white blood counts will give adequate warning against overdosage, but the amount of chloropromazine used is so considerable that this is not always practicable. There is also considerable evidence that when leucopenia has become evident the patient is beyond successful treatment. A much better guide appears to be the general clinical condition of the patient. Most drugs used to control restlessness and confusion in the elderly carry some attendant risks. Failure to use some drug more often than not means the patient will die from exhaustion. Drugs which cause sleep are usually not indicated, since they interfere with the taking of adequate fluids, and of the tranquillising drugs, chloropromazine seems to be a very safe one indeed. My personal impression is that the risks of a tranquillising drug have been exaggerated, and the risks of restlessness and confusion under-emphasised, to the detriment of the patient.

The patient's bed should have an overhanging arm and should be of chair height. The overhanging arm allows the patient to assist himself in sitting up and turning over in bed. At home it may be impossible to fit an overhanging arm, and then a rope tied to the end of the bed may be used for a similar purpose. Commonly the patient is found to have a hemiplegia, and the following regimen is particularly intended for this kind of patient. On the second day of the illness, or as soon as he is co-operative, the patient should start exercises.

Bed exercises Every few hours the patient should, for ten or fifteen minutes, turn first to the left-hand side, then on the back, then to the right-hand side, and repeat in opposite directions. He should then pull himself into a sitting position with the aid of the overhanging bed arm, and repeat this many times. Next he should move about in bed in a sideways motion, and then he should sit on the edge of the bed with his legs dangling and move along the edge with the aid of his good arm and leg, and perhaps some personal assistance.

It is of the utmost importance to have a bed fairly low, i.e. 19 inches to 20 inches high. If the patient is on a high bed he can hardly begin his exercises. Further it is important that he should be able to sit on the bed and place his feet on the floor, since this latter action initiates the necessary postural reflexes.

While in bed, and during the process of rehabilitation, he should use his good hand to the full, to feed himself, wash, comb his hair, shave, and so on.

A little after the third day of the illness, the patient should have a sling applied to the paralysed arm, to prevent it pulling on the shoulder and causing pain and arthritis. The sling should not be the usual triangular bandage but consist of a supporting brace over the shoulder and a supporting handcuff, as used in the physiotherapy department, Colchester.

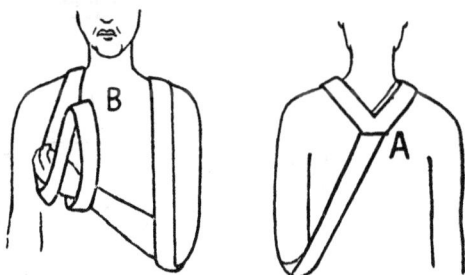

A loop, which should be secured, is made in a length of braid – this is positioned in the centre back (A). One end is brought over the flaccid shoulder down round the elbow and back up to the twist (A) and secured. The other end is folded to form a long loop which lies over the good shoulder. The end is then doubled to make two loops at the required height and secured at (B), the two loops being spread so that one supports the wrist, the other the palm of the hand, the thumb emerging between the two loops. When the sling is correctly placed, i.e. (A) being centred and well down the back, and the two front loops carefully adjusted, the sling should not rub on the back of the neck or slip in use. It can easily be adjusted either at (A) or (B). At the same time, a flat wooden or plastic splint should be bandaged to the affected arm from just below the elbow to beyond the tips of the fingers. The patient should now be got out of bed into an adjacent chair (geriatric chair) and start further exercises. He should be placed underneath an overhead beam and every two hours should exercise himself by pulling himself to a standing position with the aid of his good arm. Next, with his good hand on a horizontal bar, he should try slight knee bending and repeat this from time to time, gradually increasing the extent of the bending. When he can do this fairly well, he should try going up and down on his toes with the support of the horizontal beam. With the aid of a pulley attached to the overhead beam, and by using his good arm, he should now pull the paralysed arm up and down, so producing movements at the elbow and shoulder joints.

A very useful apparatus which can be fixed to a ward wall or the wall of a wide corridor between wards, can be made out of Dexion, as indi-

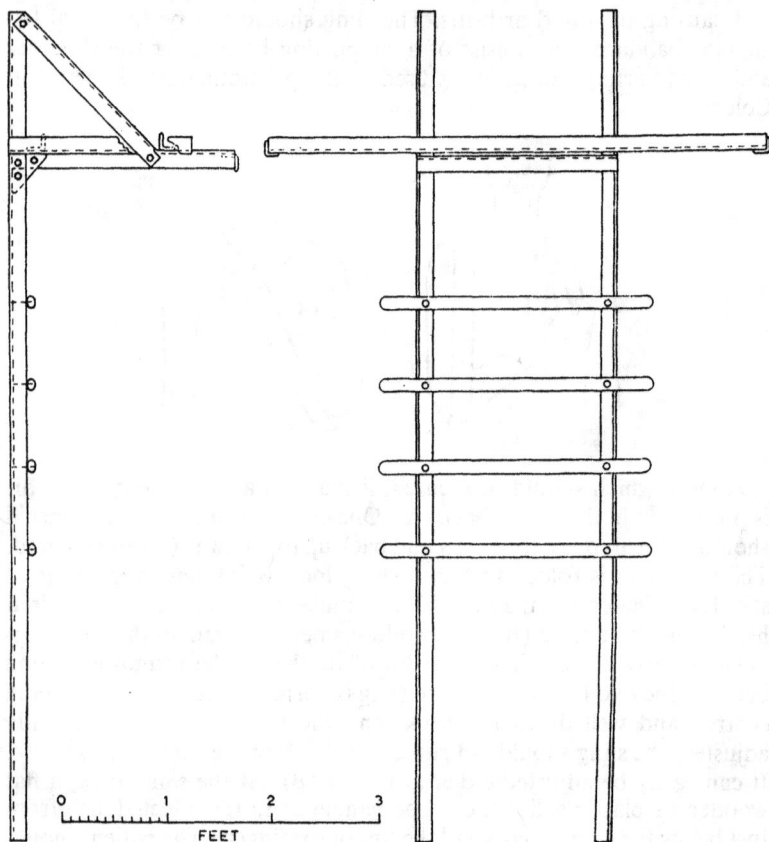

FEET

Wall frame

cated in the diagram above. The apparatus is very suitable for a patient who has to exercise a paralysed arm or leg by using a pulley with the good arm.

As regards a paralysed leg, if this can be lifted in the horizontal position a few inches above the bed, then it is likely that the patient will be eventually able to walk. If after a couple of weeks the paralysed leg still swings limply at the knee joint, then a long leg brace will be required.

The rehabilitation procedure should be initiated by a physiotherapist, but because of the shortage of physiotherapists it may be necessary to teach the ward staff what exercises the patient should carry out, so that they can assist when required.

Walking phase As soon as the patient is able to stand with some success, he should be encouraged to take a few walking steps. For this he will require personal aid, but as he improves he may be able to go alone with the aid of a walking chair. During this time it may be necessary to have the paralysed leg in a long leg brace.

If walking proceeds satisfactorily, then stair-climbing exercises should be attempted. With the patient in the standing position, and holding on to the banister with the good arm, he goes up one step with his good leg and then pulls up his paralysed leg. This is continued for several steps. To descend the stairs, he should step backwards with the paralysed leg and then bring the good leg down to it. This should likewise be continued for several steps. When this has been accomplished, the patient learns to turn round on the stairs. This he does by turning forwards and reaching over to the opposite banister. He then comes down the stairs by descending first with the paralysed leg and bringing the good leg next to it.

To train patients in this way, the physiotherapy department may require a dummy staircase. If during stair climbing the patient is found to have a foot drop, then a short leg brace should be applied with a 90-degree posterior stop at the ankle, and should he show weakness of inversion or eversion of the foot, he should have a short leg brace with a T-strap. When function has returned to the paralysed arm, the arm splints should be discarded, or only worn from time to time.

Cane walking exercises When the patient appears to be able to walk with a walking chair, he should start walking with the help only of a walking-stick. One of two methods may be adopted. First, a cane may be moved forward followed by the good leg and then the paralysed leg is dragged up to the good one, or the patient may stand on the good leg and place the walking-stick and paralysed leg forward simultaneously, putting weight on them both and then swinging the good leg forwards. During these exercises, the walking-stick is held in the good hand.

For a paralysed arm, a sling should be worn until there is return of function, but the arm should be moved periodically by the patient to prevent stiffness and contracture. If only partial function returns, the arm should be used only to the extent to which it is helpful, and the patient's efforts should be concentrated upon training his other arm to the greatest possible extent.

Aphasia The physical rehabilitation procedure implies a good deal of psychological attention and the making of various requests for his co-operation. If he has aphasia, every day an attempt should be made to encourage him to speak. Speech therapists are rarely available; nevertheless, the patient may be shown a common object, for example, knife, fork, spoon, water, apples, oranges, etc., and the name can be repeated over and over again until he is able to repeat the word. The function of speech is located in one hemisphere of the brain, but there is every reason to believe that by re-education the other hemisphere can take over this function, but it may require a great effort on the part of the patient, which he may not be able to do without much encouragement. In a similar way, left-handed writing can be taught to replace right-handed writing.

Unfortunately it is not only loss of power, i.e. motor paralysis, that may prevent a patient using a limb. Some may be so mentally confused as not to understand what they are attempting to do. Others have a lesion of the sensory part of the internal capsule, i.e. the posterior third of the posterior limb or a cortical sensory loss. The patient then, without loss of crude touch, pain or temperature, has insufficient sensory information from the affected limb and as a consequence cannot co-ordinate his muscular efforts. With this there may be associated the loss of power to recognise the shape and consistency of objects touched by the paralysed limb, i.e. astereognosis. Again a few patients continue with a flaccid paralysis and do not develop the usual spastic tone from the paralysed limb. The explanation for this may be a matter of general shock to the central nervous system or a special area of the cortex which reinforces motor tone has been damaged.

Whatever the actual cause the patient with a flaccid limb or with apraxia or astereognosis may be unable to re-learn correlated muscular movements, and the limb may be useless, though there is no extensive loss of power.

Incontinence Many hemiplegic patients are incontinent in the early stages. If incontinence continues it is likely to be due not so much to actual paralysis of control but to psychological indifference. At first the patient should be requested to empty his bladder at stated intervals, so avoiding a wet bed. Psychological encouragement and early ambulation seem to be the best methods of restoring control of the sphincters.

Mental confusion Mental confusion implies interference with the cortical functions of the brain, and is more likely to be present where there is widespread cerebral thrombosis. It is more likely to occur after the repetition of several strokes. Even so, the patient's mental condition may be remarkably improved by the physical rehabilitation.

Rather surprisingly, the walking hemiplegic rarely falls and injures himself. Presumably this is due to the fact that he is aware of the danger and proceeds with caution.

Exercises at home When the patient is discharged from hospital, he should keep up his exercises. Naturally the rehabilitation of the patient at home should follow the lines indicated. In effect this means the patient should be on the ground floor, his bed should be equipped with an overhanging arm. This is a matter of considerable difficulty, but Adams, McQuitty and Flint,[3] devised a portable Dexion frame and clamp which could be attached to the bed-head of the average bed in an elderly person's home. The patient should also have available a

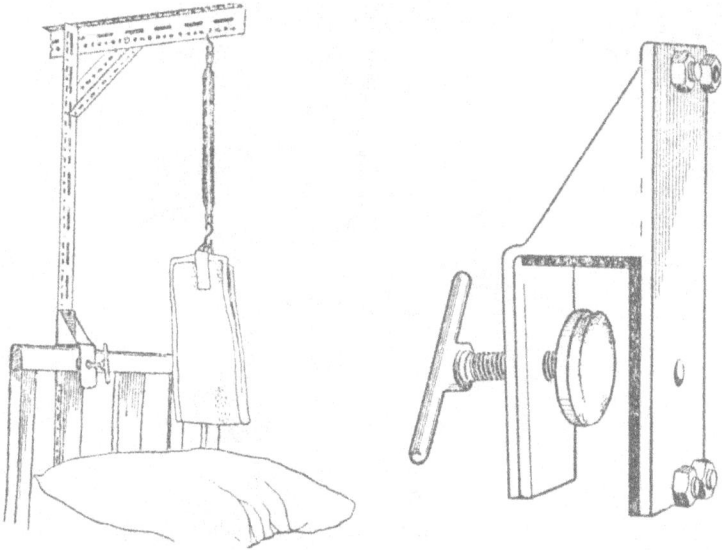

Exercise frame and clamp, devised by G. F. Adams, F. M. McQuitty and M. Y. Flint

geriatric chair and the convenience of a commode. Domiciliary physiotherapy is also advisable, but in practice this is rarely possible. Unfortunately, at times after returning home, he is put in a chair all day long or even to bed; thus, it is necessary that he should continue out-patient physiotherapy for some considerable time.

During hospital treatment, some patients reach a certain stage and then make no further progress. Sometimes this is due to the fact that the patient does not wish to return home; sometimes because he has become dissatisfied, and a little despondent, in hospital. Under these circumstances, it may be advisable to discharge the patient sooner than planned.

There are, of course, a number of patients who have neither the mental clarity nor the will to respond to treatments but a failure should not be accepted until an attempt has been made for three or four weeks. Rehabilitation of the hemiplegic is often a tedious, long-drawn out affair, but it is eminently worth while when it is contrasted with the burden of nursing a bedridden incontinent patient.

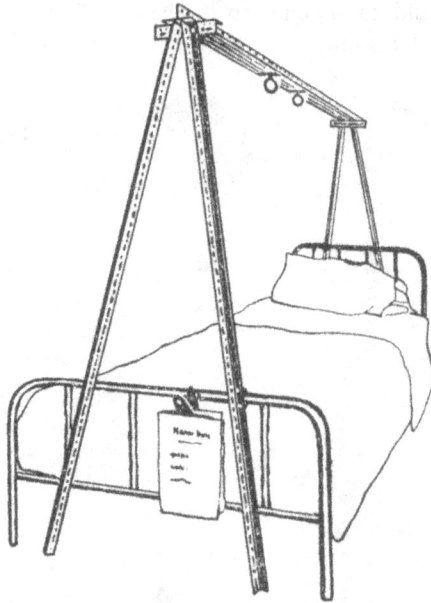

Exercise frame devised by the author

Prognosis of cerebral thrombosis The prognosis depends on many factors. If it is the patient's first stroke, the period of unconsciousness was short, and if the patient was in good mental health before the incident, then the outlook is correspondingly favourable. But so much depends on the cardiovascular system, for which reason particular attention should be paid to the blood pressure, any enlargement of the heart (because of emphysema the patient may have to be screened or X-rayed), the state of the arteries, and in particular the retina arteries, and the condition of renal function. Retinal arteriosclerosis, unless it be accompanied by haemorrhages, may have no particular significance, as also a raised systolic blood pressure; but enlargement of the heart or a rise of diastolic blood pressure above 115 mg of mercury, or a failure of the kidneys to concentrate urine adequately, carries a poor prognosis, not so much as regards the initial attack as to the recurrence of further cerebral thrombosis. If these latter features are not present, then the patient may remain well for many years.

ORGANIC MENTAL SYNDROME

The term organic mental syndrome implies that the patient has mental symptoms which are related to, or caused by, some organic lesion of the central nervous system, or the body, and that they are not basically of psychogenic origin; that is to say, they are not due to Freudian complexes or amenable to psychoanalysis or psychotherapy. The possible organic causes are extremely numerous, whereas the form of the mental symptoms are relatively few and simple in character. The main finding in the organic mental syndrome is some loss of mental capacity, usually some defect in memory or orientation. The symptoms fall into three main groups, namely neurasthenia, delirium or dementia, though symptoms of all groups may be present at one and the same time.

Neurasthenia With this the patient is likely to experience feelings of irritability, lack of mental concentration, lessened control of the emotions, and to be subject to pains and feelings of pressure in the head, and to have some clumsiness and tremor of the muscles of the face, tongue and hands. There may also be obvious lapses of memory and impaired grasp.

Delirium With this the patient may be unduly irritable, restless, suffer from insomnia, from impaired attention and orientation, and even be subject to hallucinations. Consciousness may be clouded with some incoherence of thought, speech and manner. His behaviour may be strange and nonsensical.

Dementia Here the patient is likely to show gross loss of memory, intellectual weakness, lack of concentration, grasp and attention, and to be hopelessly disorientated as to time and place. He may or may not be able to carry on an intelligent conversation. Emotionally, he may be quite out of control, weeping one moment and laughing at another, or flying into petty tempers. Or the patient may show emotional loss with gross apathy and indifference to his surroundings, undue drowsiness and perhaps incontinence.

The elderly patient may present all the above symptoms, but also, in addition, partial blindness or extreme deafness, plus physical debility. He may therefore be only too readily labelled as a senile dement.

The phrase 'senile dement' so often carries with it the implication that the patient's brain is irrevocably damaged by arteriosclerosis and atrophy that no improvement can be expected, no matter what line of treatment is adopted. But this can be shown to be quite wrong in so many instances that the label senile dementia is either meaningless or is used to replace a proper assessment of the most likely cause of the symptoms. The word 'senile' in itself only means that the patient is elderly, and the majority of elderly people are not demented, but quite a number of younger ones are. Consequently, when an elderly person has mental symptoms, the better procedure is to state he has an organic mental syndrome, and this should be followed by the organic cause elicited. It will then be found that many patients have several physical conditions, perhaps remedial by therapy, which are causing the mental symptoms.

Upwards of about 15% of elderly patients referred to a geriatric unit are sent because of 'senile dementia' or mental confusion, but only a few of them are found to be irrevocably demented. One of the first points to ascertain is whether the patient has lucid periods when he is rational and normal. If such periods occur, it follows that the brain is not damaged beyond repair, and that the symptoms are due to temporary factors. It is perhaps worth while re-stating that elderly people react to infection and pain by a phase of mental confusion and that there are also the added factors of malnutrition and avitaminosis to be considered. Renal failure, water depletion, salt depletion and cerebral thrombosis have already been considered and other causes may now be considered in detail.

CONSTIPATION AND FAECAL IMPACTION

Of all the afflictions that affect elderly people, inability to obtain proper action of the bowel seems to be one of the commonest and one which leads to much ill-health, physical discomfort and mental distress. There seem to be many factors which bring about loading of the bowels. A patient may take too little fluid, or only small meals without any rough-age, or the lavatory may be inconveniently placed and the patient has lapsed into habits of very irregular bowel action. For many of the elderly patients the muscles of the abdominal wall and the pelvic floor are so weak and wasted that they are too feeble to evacuate the rectum properly. If they are in bed, this is all the more difficult should they be attempting to use the bed pan. In addition, some patients have large abdominal or inguinal hernias, which again make bowel action more difficult.

The consequences of a loaded bowel are many, the patient is apt to lose his appetite and take less food; this in turn leads to loss of weight, malnutrition, perhaps avitaminosis, to abdominal discomfort, nausea, and if the bowel loading is severe enough to cause faecal impaction the result may be an acute abdomen. During this time, the physical and mental discomfort may result in mental confusion. On the other hand, the patient may take purgatives and run the risk of a bout of vomiting or diarrhoea, both of which are serious illnesses in the elderly. Some patients take drugs that stimulate the action of the colon, but since the patient is too weak for the act of evacuation the drugs are unsuccessful, and larger and larger doses are taken. Constipation in the elderly is better dealt with by a regular regime than by resort to a strong purgative. The regime should be along the following lines:

(1) An elderly person should be up and about and take reasonable exercise.
(2) A chair commode or lavatory should be used rather than the bed pan for easier evacuation.
(3) The patient should take ample fluids and the diet should include moderate amounts of 'bulky substances', i.e. fruit and vegetables.
(4) The patient should open the bowels regularly.
(5) Some kind of lubricant is often advisable to soften the faeces. Liquid paraffin is often used but should not be taken frequently because it interferes with the absorption of calcium phosphates and Vitamins D and K, consequently olive oil or maize oil is more suitable and just as effective.
(6) If there is overloading of the rectum this can be dealt with by giving Dulcolax (Bisacodyl) in a dose of one to two tablets by mouth or by a suppository, or by giving Dioctyl-Medo (two 20 mg tablets) by mouth. Both these drugs have an action on the lower bowel and rectum. If the rectum is loaded with hard faeces then it may be necessary to give an olive oil enema or a Fletcher's Enema (a solution containing Sodium Phosphate and Di-Phosphate) or more rarely a soap enema may be required, but the latter is often too distressing for elderly patients.
(7) When there is good reason to think that the rectum is empty and there is no hard matter in the colon, then a standardised extract of senna, e.g. Senokot, may be used periodically in small doses.
(8) One should bear in mind that drugs which inhibit the parasympathetic action, Methantheline Bromide (Banthine Bromide), Propantheline Bromide, Belladonna, Atropine, Scopolamine Hydrobromide, Artane Hydrochloride, Cogentin, Transentin Pagitane Hydrochloride, etc., and the ganglion blocking agents, impair the action not only of the bladder but also of the bowel. Many patients referred to as senile dements have been found to have loaded bowels and so often the 'dementia' disappears with adequate treatment of the bowel condition.

CYSTITIS

Though the patient may not complain about the passage of urine, if a specimen is examined it may show pus and organisms. An organism sensitivity test should be done, and the patient treated as indicated. The condition is relatively common in old people and apt to recur, but it responds favourably to treatment and many patients are restored to mental clarity.

PROSTATIC ENLARGEMENT

The 1962 Ministry of Health Report 29 estimates the number of men in England and Wales that year aged 65 or over at 2 148 000; it is a matter of conjecture how many had enlargement of the prostate, residual urine and frequency of micturition. Steiglitz[51] states that according to the statistics 70 to 75% of men who reach the age of 55 or over will produce signs or symptoms of prostatic obstruction, so that a figure of half the men over 65, say 1 500 000 in Great Britain, would not seem an unreasonable one for elderly men with prostatic symptoms. That such a large number of men could benefit from prostatectomy is very problematical – certainly as an operation list the number is absurdly impracticable. Selected cases are seen and operated upon, others only come to operation because of the incidence of acute retention of urine. Handy, H. G.[21] states that out of 214 consecutive prostatectomys over 70% were seen with acute retention.

The hazards of operation should be kept in mind and are indicated by Ross, J. M. H.[41] He quotes a mortality of 11% within two months and Bomford, W. B. M.[6] records the mortality in teaching hospitals at 6%, in non-teaching hospitals at 17% and in his own series at 13%. It can be seen, therefore, that prostatectomy should not be lightly undertaken. Further, an immediate prostatectomy carries certain hazards, for Bomford records a case which at operation proved to be carcinomatous, could not be shelled out and the patient died on the fourth postoperative day. He adds: 'A suprapubic tube and oestrogens would have given him a better chance than an attempt at partial removal but it is not easy to know when to stop.'

In geriatric wards rectal examinations are frequent and enlargement of the prostate is commonly observed amongst elderly men. It is usually associated with some frequency of micturition, nocturia and some residual urine, but only in a few does it amount to an illness or disability. Some of these men are found on admission to have raised blood urea, but this can usually be remedied by adequate hydration; essentially the cause seems to be impaired renal plasma flow rather than enlarged prostate. Similar rises in the blood urea level are found in women who also respond to hydration. The enlarged prostate is frequently associated with residual urine and a poor power of bladder contraction. This can be measured with a transparent Portex (Gibbons) catheter; there is sometimes less than 6 inches pressure of urine. It would appear that the prostate, by causing obstruction, leads to distension, dilation and loss of tone of the bladder. However, muscular atony is very common in the elderly and affects not only the bladder but the large bowel and abdominal wall as well; further, a similar atonic bladder with poor contractile power and residual urine is frequently present in females. Indeed, urinary retention in elderly females when in bed readily occurs, fortunately being fairly easily relieved. Study of the *Statistical Review*[39] gives the following figures:

| | 1947 | | 1957 | | 1962 |
	Males	Females	Males	Females	Males
Deaths, all causes	265 739	249 852	266 407	248 463	
Deaths due to disease of the genito-urinary system	10 226	5161	7431	3733	
Deaths due to hyperplasia of the prostrate	4976		3645		2905

Annual Abstract of Statistics 1974, page 41

Hyperplasia of the prostate	*Deaths from in England and Wales in 1973: 1145*

Thus, according to these statistics, the deaths from enlarged prostate are coming down and form only 1·36% of the total number of deaths. This latter figure cannot be directly compared with the prostatic operation mortality rate of perhaps 10%, but even so that comparison is unfavourable for the choice of operation.

As regards malignant neoplasm of the prostate the above *Statistical Review*[39] gives the deaths as follows:

	1947	1957	1962
Malignant prostate	2800	3475	3820
Ref: Statistical Review 1970, Table 17, P. 130.			
Neoplasm of Prostate	Total	3906	

This is not a high figure compared with the total deaths, and yet according to *The Lancet*[27] and to Franks, L. M.[17] more than a third of the men over 50 years of age show prostatic malignancy under the microscope, this evidently being unrelated to any biological malignancy. One can only conclude that microscopic evidence of malignancy, which is likely to be found in one-quarter of the patients aged over 50, is not of itself sufficient indication for operation.

When the patient is younger, nearer 60 years of age, the operation risk should be less and the duration of benefit longer; one is more inclined to operate on such patients than on the very old, where the operation is more hazardous and the benefits may be shortlived.

It often appears that it is not only the enlarged prostate but the weak expulsive power of the bladder which is the root cause of the trouble. The weaker the bladder contraction the more readily acute retention can develop, so perhaps it is worth while to consider what causes further weakness of bladder action and what enhances its function. The act of micturition is partly voluntary, by contraction of the abdominal and pelvic muscles, and partly reflex, but whereas in a young person the voluntary action is of little consequence, in an elderly man it may be decidedly so.

The bladder may not contract properly because of such conditions as interference with full conscious control – as in coma, uraemia and drowsiness due to drugs, or a state of mental confusion arising from such conditions as toxaemia, cerebral anaemia, cerebral thrombosis, myocardial infarction, etc. – and dulling of the bladder muscle stretch reflexes. The latter may be caused by:

(1) repeated over-distension of the bladder
(2) acute distension from an excessive intake of fluids or a massive diuresis
(3) atony of bladder muscles
(4) action of drugs inhibiting the parasympathetic, e.g. Atropine, Artane, Banthane, Probanthane, etc., or ganglion blocking drugs, e.g. Hexa- and Pentamethonium compounds
(5) overloading of the rectum with concomitant loss of the recto-vesical action, together with the mechanical pressure at the base of the bladder and difficulty in relaxing the levati and external urethral sphincter
(6) extreme weakness of the abdominal wall, especially when the patient is in a supine position
(7) lesions of the nervi erigentes, the spinal centre, posterior columns of the spinal cord and other afferent pathways to the cerebral cortex

From these possible causes some impairment of the conscious control of micturition appears to become commoner in the very elderly.

On the other hand, contraction of the bladder is enhanced by:
(a) adopting the standing or sitting position during micturition
(b) rectal evacuation
(c) the use of a parasympathetic stimulating drug, e.g. Carbachol 2 mg by mouth BD

Three groups of patients with enlarged prostates may be considered, namely:

(1) those with a frequency and residual urine
(2) those with a partially distended bladder with overflow
(3) those with acute retention

The first group of patients must be considered to be very numerous and the enlarged prostate almost to be a physiological development of advancing age. Whether such patients should be subjected to operation is a moot point; their very number seems to make this impractical. Many live with such symptoms to an advanced age and then die from another complaint, and there is no great evidence that the bladder condition causes loss of renal function to the same extent as does cardiovascular disease. Unless a decision to operate is taken the patient can be treated medically in the following manner:

(1) Urination should be performed standing or sitting and confinement to bed should be avoided. A commode should be used rather than a bed pan.
(2) Ample fluids should be taken so as to ensure a better action of the kidneys and bring about a constant change of residual urine.
(3) The bowels should be kept well regulated and faecal loading of the rectum particularly avoided. This probably means an out-of-bed regime and an occasional use of laxatives, e.g. olive oil and Dulcolax.
(4) The tone of the abdominal wall should be maintained by a reasonable amount of exercise.
(5) A careful watch should be kept on any drugs which tend to inhibit the parasympathetic and so lead to distension of the bladder.
(6) Avoidance of over-dosage of drugs which interfere with consciousness, e.g. morphine, pethidine, alcohol, paraldehyde, etc.; this also includes the effects of a general anaesthetic.
(7) In the treatment of congestive cardiac failure it is important to avoid promoting a massive diuresis, e.g. by Mersalyl 2 cm^3, which may lead to distension of the bladder.
(8) The elderly man with an enlarged prostate is likely to have residual urine which is already a nidus for infection, and it seems – contrary to many surgical opinions – that cystitis is quite a commonly occurring condition without any question of infection being introduced by catheterisation. It seems most likely that many a retention of urine is due to acute cystitis superimposed on a chronic infection. For this reason any phase of cystitis should be treated promptly. Further, the patient's resistance to infection of the bladder may be

a reflection of his poor general state of health, e.g. anaemia, de-hydration, inanition, etc., so all this requires treatment and that the whole attention should not be focused on the prostate exclusively.

(9) States of mental confusion should be fully investigated and treated early – better, it would appear, with drugs, e.g. Chlorpromazine, than with hypnotics and heavy sedation.

(10) The bladder action may be improved by the use of a parasympathetic stimulating drug, e.g. Carbachol 2 mg BD, from time to time.

(11) Stilboestrol dose 5 mg a day, appears to improve the mucous membrane of the bladder and urethra and facilitates a freer passage of urine, particularly in the male. The dose will, of course, have to be varied according to its therapeutic effects.

While the medical management has been itemised above for the sake of clarity, it should be borne in mind that multiple features of ill-health in the elderly often necessitates a very broad medical approach.

In the second group of patients, where there is partial distension of the bladder with overflow, there is particular risk of the patient developing cystitis or acute retention at any time, or of gradually becoming uraemic. There may be no special urgency in the matter, so the patient's general health should be assessed (especially mental state) and the condition given medical treatment initially. Some may respond favourably enough to medical treatment, but, if not, the risks and the benefits of operation must be weighed against the patient's prognosis under medical treatment. The patient's fitness for operation and the quality of the domiciliary aftercare may be deciding factors.

In the third group, the patient has retention of urine. The opinion has been expressed that one-stage prostatectomy is the counsel of perfection on the basis that the operational site is not infected as it would become after any form of catheterisation. There are many points against the procedure for a very elderly man; for instance, he may be dehydrated, undernourished, anaemic, hypotensive, or have a low blood volume, a pulmonary infection or myocardial degeneration and may be in no fit state for a major operation. Then again the prostate may be malignant, and will then not shell out readily, so that the operation entails great 'shock'. Finally, the assumption that the bladder is not infected (remembering that the retention is often preceded by an atonic bladder with residual urine) is often wrong, since acute cystitis is a common precipitating cause of acute retention.

One is therefore inclined to avoid a major emergency operation in an elderly man unless it is life saving and deal with acute retention first by ensuring evacuation of the bowels and by trying micturition in the upright position. When the bladder is not really tense, and quite commonly this is so in an elderly patient, Carbachol 2 mg by mouth may initiate micturition. Failing this, the bladder must be catheterised or relieved by a suprapubic needle. The risk of introducing infection operates equally for urethral or suprapubic catheterisation. Many surgeons were of the opinion that a suprapubic catheter is preferable because it can be more easily managed at home; but this is rarely true for the very elderly, who so often have to be readmitted to a geriatric ward. The operation is now almost obsolete. Other surgeons have come to think that a Portex (Gibbons) catheter suits equally well and causes less distress to the patient and less necessity for nursing care. The author has had the responsibility of caring for many patients treated with the latter and has found it to be preferable to a suprapubic catheter.

With the application of the medical measure outlined above, and the use of an antibiotic when appropriate, the Portex catheter can be used for months or years without causing cystitis and with an improvement in the tonus of the bladder. Some patients have been found to be able to pass urine normally again as a result of this catheter treatment, or have been brought to a better state for operation.

The important points in the use of the Portex catheter appear to be that ample fluids should be given and that the bladder must drain freely with the patient in an upright position as much as possible. Cook, J. B.[12] has shown that the catheter does not drain the bladder in the supine position. He filled a bladder with a solution of sodium iodide and a small volume of myodil, both of which are opaque to X-rays. The myodil, being heavier, sinks to the bottom of the bladder and he demonstrated by a series of radiographs that the myodil does not drain away through the catheter when the patient is supine but does so when he is erect. When catheter drainage is attempted with the patient in bed, a pocket of pus collects at the base of the bladder and keeps up a cystitis.

The general pre-operative and post-operative medical management of a prostatectomy is similar to that for any other major operation, with the addition of special consideration of bladder action as outlined.

CARCINOMA OF THE PROSTATE

As stated above there is pathological evidence of malignancy in the prostate in about one-third of men over 50 years. Clinically it never occurs to this extent and it seems a small area of malignancy lies quiescent in many prostatic glands. The problem may present itself in two ways. The patient may have a hard prostate and a raised acid phosphatase, say 6 units (normal 0·5 to 2). The patient may well have carcinoma of the prostate and if, on pelvic X-ray, secondaries are found in bone, the diagnosis is certain. It should be stressed that carcinoma of the prostate is the only malignant state which can be diagnosed by a blood test, though at times the acid phosphatase is abnormally high – usually due to a zealous rectal examination – a continual rise of say 10 units almost always means malignancy. If malignancy is diagnosed then the patient should be treated with stilboestrol – a dose of 5 mg thrice daily is usually sufficient to bring the acid phosphatase down to normal or even cause enlargement of the breasts. Larger doses of stilboestrol are liable to cause fluid retention – even an epileptic fit – and bring about cardiac failure in very elderly patients.

If the alkaline phosphatase is raised and it is thought to be due to liver damage rather than a bone disease, the 5 nucleotide test should be done which is raised if the alkaline phosphatase enzyme is coming from the liver.

On the whole, in cases of doubt, it would appear wise to treat the patient with moderate doses of stilboestrol with the hope that no malignancy will develop.

HEART FAILURES

Congestive heart failure has already been touched upon, and this may be a cause of mental confusion. It is occasionally missed, but when adequately treated any associated mental confusion usually disappears. The patient may also be subject to left heart failure; as a result of this he may be subject to cardiac asthma, especially at night, when he may get up to assist his breathing and wander about his bedroom in a confused manner. At other times, the failure may cause not only pulmonary congestion but even basal pleural effusions. Again the clinical features of left heart failure are often overlooked in the elderly as a cause of mental confusion.

MALNUTRITION

Patients with mental confusion are frequently found to be in a very poor state of nutrition. Sometimes this appears to be a consequence of the mental illness, and at others some malignant condition comes to light after careful investigation and accounts for the loss in weight and malnutrition. Some patients on admission have weighed as little as $4\frac{1}{2}$ stone. Many patients put on weight and show a remarkable improvement on an ordinary hospital diet, and at the same time their mental confusion disappears, or materially improves. It may be that they were also in vitamin deficiency which a normal diet has rectified, but for practical purposes the response in hospital implies a very inadequate, or even starvation, diet, while at home.

Nowadays, it seems the general public have the idea that malnutrition, starvation and deficiency diseases are things of the past and belong only to the bad old days. However, if a little thought is given to how the millions of old age pensioners manage on their small income, it would seem not so difficult also to imagine that there could be malnutrition and neglect. There is a good deal of literature about nutrition in the elderly, and many social surveys have been done. The following extracts therefore are worthy of careful attention.

Hobson and Pemberton[24] state:

'In the big cities, the admission to hospital of old people with severe malnutrition, including nutritional anaemia, is fairly common and the old man who has scurvy is no great rarity. The reasons for this are poverty, ignorance and apathy. Those existing on a meagre retirement pension calculated to cover only the necessities of life are the first to suffer when the cost of living rises. Lack of knowledge of what food to buy and how to prepare it is most likely to affect the elderly man who has recently lost his wife. He tends to live on a diet involving little preparation, such as tinned meat, biscuits, jam and tea with condensed milk.'

They also add that the elderly are subject to special risk of deficiency in vitamin C, calcium and the anti-anaemia factors.

Woltereck,[55] regarding the premises for a long and healthy life, states:

'In addition we need a sufficient supplementary amount of the necessary vitamins. In the case of most vitamins, the need for an additional supply of them becomes greater in old age, because then the degree of metabolic activity tends to decline, and the normal foodstuffs no longer supply the body with sufficient vitamins. It is therefore a good thing for older and elderly people regularly to include plenty of foodstuffs rich in vitamins in their diet, such as salads and fruit.'

Chinn[9] carried out a survey on 500 elderly patients, and he states:

'Hospitalisation, with attention to diet and vitamins, resulted in the disappearance of avitaminosis in all patients and in gains of from 7 to 15% of body weight as noted on admission in about one-third of these chronically emaciated persons. Paralleling this was an invariable improvement in attitudes and physical tolerance, resulting in far greater self-sufficiency. About one-third gained only indifferently in weight as well as morale, and the other one-third did not gain or continued to lose weight despite vigorous measures. Though this experience is small, it indicates clearly that older persons are easily subject to inanition and avitaminosis.'

Berk[5] summarised his views in the following way:

'Because old people are often on the borderline of nutritional deficiencies, and because ageing is hastened by degenerative changes, nutrition of the aged becomes a prophylactic and therapeutic project. Fewer calories, an increased intake of protein, a reduced intake of fat, a good supply of vitamins and minerals and a water intake to ensure an adequate urinary output are the essentials'.

The planning of a balanced, adequately nutritious diet is by no means easy, but the Food and Nutrition Board of the National Research Council of the United States have set down recommended dietary allowances for the average man and woman of sixty-five, as follows:

Recommended dietary allowances

	Men	Women
Calories	2600	1800
Protein gm	65	55
Calcium gm	0·8	0·8
Iron mg	12	12
Vitamin A. IU	5000	5000
Thiamine mg	1·2	1·0
Riboflavin mg	1·6	1·4
Niacin mg	12	10
Ascorbic acid mg	75	70

With these basic requirements in mind, it is then necessary to survey the various foodstuffs, having regard to their caloric value and mineral and vitamin content, and advise how much each should be taken. Unfortunately, there are many complicating and variable factors such as the patient's limited economic means, inadequate dentition, physical inability to go out and do the necessary shopping, loss of appetite from various causes, and conditions impairing digestion and absorption of food, for example chronic gastritis or chronic cholecystitis. Then again, the actual value of food varies according to the way it is processed or cooked; as regards the elderly they may feel unable to undertake the preparation and cooking of their meals.

Bransby and Osborne[7] carried out a survey on some 1771 subjects, and in one of their tables give the following data:

Old-age Pensioner

Nutrient	Unit	Men	Women
Calories	Cal	1985	1662
Vegetable protein	gm	29	24
Animal protein	gm	36	30
Fat	gm	78	69
Carbohydrate	gm	235	206
Calcium	gm	0·7	0·7
Iron	mg	13	10
Vitamin A	IU	2084	1898
Thiamine	mg	1·0	0·8
Riboflavin	mg	1·0	0·9
Nicotinic acid	mg	8	6
Vitamin C	mg	19	20

From this table it is apparent that the diet of old age pensioners is deficient both as regards the total calories requirements and its vitamin content, especially that of vitamin A and vitamin C (ascorbic acid), and that they run a grave risk of malnutrition and avitaminosis.

Freeman considers:

'The intake of vitamins should be higher than that which is usually found to be adequate. Two to four times the usual amount of vitamin A in experimental animals has lengthened the reproductive period of females and the length of life of both sexes.'

Stieglitz[52] states that:

'In the older person a deficiency of protein may cause oedema (swelling), poor wound healing, retarded bone healing, and decreased resistance to generalised infection to a greater extent than in younger persons,' and that 'calcium is frequently inadequate in the diet of elderly persons and the older person has difficulty in the absorption and utilisation of calcium. The older individual is frequently deficient in iron also. Low or minor degrees of vitamin deficiency can be assumed to be the rule rather than the exception in the elderly person. It has been shown that liberal additions of the vitamin B group and ascorbic acid to the diets of older persons can make for great improvement in general vitality and vigour.'

Machella[28] summarised his views on vitamin deficiency as:

'Until evidence to the contrary is presented, the vitamin requirements of the elderly should be considered to be the same as for younger adults, and when an inadequate dietary intake is suspected, adequate supplementation of vitamins should be instituted.'

At this stage particular attention should be drawn to the importance of including fresh milk and orange juice in the diet of the elderly, since milk will supply the calcium necessary and orange juice the vitamin C requirements. The value of milk on an 100 gm basis is as follows:[32]

Vitamins and minerals	Per 100 grammes
Vitamin A (international units)	152
Riboflavin mg a	0·156
Thiamine mg	0·043
Vitamin C mg	1·140
Calcium mg	113
Phosphorus mg	90
Iron mg	0·032

and of frozen orange juice, a four-ounce glass contains vitamin C in excess of 30 milligrams.[34]

In the above, malnutrition has been dealt with particularly in relation to the poorly nourished patient, but malnutrition may also take the form of obesity which may occur together with vitamin and other nutritional deficiencies. This is dealt with under the heading of 'Obesity'.

As can be seen on page 116 there has been an increase in deaths due to nutritional disease and avitaminosis. The numbers involved are small but significant – a 95% increase in female deaths in 1956 compared to 1946 – with 52% of these in persons of 65 years and over. This statistical trend has now been halted, there being 238 deaths in 1973.

AVITAMINOSIS

Avitaminosis in the elderly sometimes occurs in an obvious clinical form, for example scurvy, but generally only sub-clinical forms are seen and unless there is an associated research unit, pathological investigation and confirmation is rarely possible. The diagnosis is therefore based on suggestive or significant clinical features, and the rapid response to therapeutic doses of vitamins.

Vitamin A deficiency is suspected when there is exceptional dryness of the skin and follicular hyperkeratosis. Vitamin D insufficiency is considered possible if there is much osteoporosis, lack of calcium in the diet, or the patient has been home-bound for a long time and not been in the sunshine. Many old people bruise exceedingly easily and sometimes have spontaneous bleeding into the skin; this points to the possibility of vitamin K deficiency, and if there is also a more extensive bruising and haemorrhage, and possibly anaemia, a deficiency of vitamin C. Fissuring at the angles of the mouth and circumcorneal injection are frequently seen in the elderly and suggest vitamin B2 deficiency. If there are also symptoms of muscular cramps, tenderness of the calves and diminished reflexes of the knee and ankle joints with paresthesias, then vitamin B12 is deficient in all probability.

Single vitamin deficiency is unlikely and the patient will require to be treated for multiple deficiencies. Vitamin deficiency and malnutrition have been dealt with in association with organic mental disorder, because so many patients with mental confusion have responded dramatically to vitamin therapy, so much so that the possibility of vitamin deficiency should always be considered when dealing with mental confusion in the elderly.

Vitamin K deficiency Vitamin K deficiency in the past has rarely been considered to occur or have any great clinical significance. But vitamin K is important because its presence is essential for the synthesis of Prothrombin and the latter is important for the normal coagulation of the blood. Hazell, K. and Baloch, K. H.[22A] dealt with this matter in the survey of 110 patients. The test used for failure of coagulation was the Thrombotest introduced by Owren (1959), and found there was a low Thrombotest in the majority of patients. They therefore came to the following conclusions: (1) In patients with liver disease, vitamin K is not absorbed or utilised and there is a consistent finding of low Thrombotest. (2) Drugs like salicylates and chlorpromazine, so commonly used in the elderly cause hypoprothrombinaemia and this type does not improve with vitamin K therapy unless these drugs are stopped. (3) Cutaneous ecchymosis so commonly thought to be a normal finding may actually be a presenting symptom of vitamin K deficiency in the elderly. (4) In all cases of malnutrition in the elderly investigations should always be made for evidence of vitamin K deficiency since it is neither expensive nor difficult. (5) A low Thrombotest may be one of the first pointers towards a malabsorption syndrome in the elderly. (6) Antibiotics should not be used for long periods without doing Thrombotest in the elderly. (7) Before using anticoagulant drugs in patients over sixty, careful consideration should be given to all the above mentioned factors. These factors in addition to those already known makes anticoagulant therapy an extremely risky kind of treatment and an extremely unstable one. In the light of this paper the sooner anticoagulant therapy is abandoned in the elderly, the better. (8) Elderly patients presenting with haematuria, melaena, or any form of bleeding disorders should be investigated for vitamin K deficiency. Although this may not be the sole reason for the presenting symptoms, vitamin K replacement may minimise blood loss. (9) When an elderly patient presents an anaemia special care must be taken to exclude vitamin K deficiency. (10) Since a vast majority of patients were found to have low Thrombotest it would be justifiable to do a Thrombotest at least once during the stay of an elderly patient in hospital and if possible to treat with vitamin K.

Treatment Vitamin deficiency should be preventable by ensuring that elderly people have an adequate and properly balanced diet. In particular they require more first-class protein, fresh vegetables, fruit and milk. A good case can be made out for supplying pensioners with milk at a cut price, in the same way as is done for children. Vitamin therapy should not be accepted as a substitute for a proper diet, but where the latter is obviously not being taken, an elderly patient can of course obtain vitamins free from the family doctor.

In patients with mental symptoms, the correction of vitamin deficiency may be a matter of urgency, and in these cases vitamins may be given either intramuscularly or by intravenous injection – several vitamins are included in the injection, such as aneurine, nicotinamide, riboflavin and pyrodoxine. In less urgent instances the patient can be put on a properly balanced diet and given vitamins by mouth. One of the most useful capsules is that provided for expectant mothers, commonly known as the pre-natal capsule. The capsule contains:

Vitamin A	2000 IU
Vitamin D	400 IU
Thiamine Mononitrate (B1)	2 mg
Riboflavin (B2)	2 mg
Niacinamide	7 mg
Vitamin B12	1 microgram
as present in concentrated extractives from streptomyces fermentation	
Vitamin K (menadione)	0·5 mg
Ascorbic acid (C)	35 mg
Folic acid	1 mg
Calcium (in CaHPO$_4$)	250 mg
Phosphorus (in CaHPO$_4$)	190 mg
Dicalcium phosphate anhydrous (CaHPO$_4$)	869 mg
Iron (in FeSO$_4$)	6 mg
Ferrous sulphate exsiccated	20 mg
Manganese (in MnSO$_4$)	0·12 mg

One of these capsules may be given daily for about a fortnight. If the patient has some difficulty in swallowing the capsule, it may be cut into two. There are of course other suitable capsules.

TREATMENT OF MENTAL CONFUSION

The problem of mental confusion often coupled with restlessness or mild delirium presents great difficulties. From what has been said it can be seen that it is most important not to accept senility as a cause and it is necessary to carry out a thorough clinical examination in every case. There are so many causes that an extensive knowledge of medicine is required to come to a reasonable diagnosis. Naturally the main treatment should be directed towards the causal condition, and symptomatic therapy is a secondary line of approach.

Nevertheless, in those patients who are noisy or extremely restless and liable to develop a state of exhaustion, it may be necessary to prescribe sedative drugs. Any drug that is selected should not have untoward side effects and should not cause a serious drop in blood pressure, which is generally undesirable in the elderly; neither should it cause drowsiness to such an extent that the patient is unable to take adequate fluids or nourishment. It has to be borne in mind that there is impairment of renal excretion and the risk of the drug accumulating in the body, such as would not happen in younger patients; there is also the risk that any depression of respiration may lead to anoxia or congestion of the lungs.

Insomnia and restlessness Before considering any drugs in particular, it is perhaps worth while making some general observations on insomnia and restlessness. In the elderly, sleep habits vary from those in the young. There is the habit of taking short naps during the day, and many elderly people get up at night for one reason or another. Usually it is necessary for them to pass urine once or twice during the night, and others have the habit of making a warm drink for themselves, or reading in bed for half an hour or so. All this should be accepted as normal for elderly people and they should not be expected to accommodate themselves to hospital ward routine straight away.

One means of avoiding insomnia is to induce a healthy tiredness during the day, and this may be accomplished by moderate exercise, by physiotherapy or by occupational therapy. Many patients have a bed-time routine which may include a warm drink or a small dose of alcohol, and if possible this routine should be continued in hospital. It goes without saying that patients need a comfortable and warm bed.

Control of movements is mainly a matter of mental control brought about by training, habit, and social need; in young children, frequent restless movements are quite marked, and it may be in the elderly for various reasons there is a loss of higher mental control. This type of patient may require not so much a sedative as a stimulant, and may become calmer after reassurance plus a cup of tea. Similarly, the restless patient with cardiac failure or evidence of anoxia is more likely to become calm on the administration of oxygen than the prescription of a sedative.

Some elderly patients miss the accustomed objects present at home and as the lights are dimmed in the ward are likely to be a little disorientated and have vague imaginings of faces in the shadows. For this reason, some little bedroom knick-knack of the patient should be within sight or reach, and in some instances the patient will become calmer if a light is switched on, or if he is allowed up in a comfortable arm-chair for a while.

Treatment by drugs There are many opinions as to what drugs are suitable out of the vast number available, but it should be borne in mind that all the sedatives come under the heading of narcotics – that is a drug which has a reversible depressant action on cell activity. A small dose of alcohol, for example brandy, whisky or rum, given with all the traditional paraphernalia, may be all that is required to get the patient off to sleep. For a short period of sleep, chloralhydrate 20 gr is very useful. Paraldehyde also has a short but fairly certain action, but if given by mouth the solution should be fresh since the drug tends to decompose and give rise to acetic acid; if given by injection, this must be into a bulky muscle, because any escape of the drug under the skin may lead to infection or even local sloughing. It is not the drug of choice because it is painful and may render the patient comatose and dehydrated. It is usually better to use sparine or chlorpromazine hydrochloride, either of which may be given by mouth or by intramuscular injections in a dose of 50–100 mgs without any risk of local inflammation. The above-mentioned drugs do not cause any serious drop in blood pressure or any unduly prolonged drowsiness, but at times it may be necessary to use morphia, in which case the initial dose should be a small one until the reaction of the patient to this drug is known, or for a short period of action pethidine 50 mg by injection may be considered the drug of choice. Phenobarbitone and sodium amytal do not appear to be well tolerated by elderly patients.

Not all patients react to drugs in the same way and it may take a little time, and frequent visits to the patient, before ascertaining what is the best drug to use, how often, and in what dosage.

PRESSURE SORES

A healthy person normally moves about so that pressure is not sustained at any one point for very long. A 'discomfort response' seems to come into operation at conscious or even sub-conscious levels; even in bed a person turns over frequently up to 20 to 30 times during the night. When this response does not take place pressure on a part of the body occludes the blood supply and the part may die and become gangrenous. A pressure sore may therefore develop when this response is lost or diminished in such conditions as

Coma – Uremic, diabetic or due to cerebral thrombosis or dehydration or head injury, etc.
Semi-coma – due to hypnotic or tranquillising drugs.
Paralysis – as in Parkinsonism or motor neurone disease.
Immobility – as from arthritis or fracture of the femur.
Extreme infirmity.
Sensory loss over a part.

A pressure sore is even more likely to develop if the blood supply is impoverished because of poor cardiac output or local arterial thrombosis; or if the oxygen carrying capacity of the blood is low because of anaemia or hypoxia from lung disease. Further a pressure sore is more likely to occur if there is no pad of fat between the skin and the underlying structures or if infection is introduced by scratching in the presence of urine or faeces or by external trauma. It is even more likely to occur if the part (usually the sacral area or heels) is over a hard mattress or object.

The area of gangrene which is the cause of the pressure sore is likely to occur first deep down in the muscles which are very sensitive to lack of blood; then the gangrene spreads to the sub-cutaneous tissues giving them a blue appearance and finally the skin breaks down. The threat of a pressure sore should be considered long before there is any focal evidence of it at which stage it may be too late to prevent the skin breaking down. It is therefore advisable with most elderly patients on admission to be put into a warm soft bed, perhaps a large cell ripple bed, to have a bedclothes lifter and woollen heel pads applied. If the patient is comatose there will be urinary incontinence. This may be dealt with by incontinence pads, but if the skin over the buttock is constantly wet with urine it may be advisable that the patient should have a catheter and bag in the case of a female or a Paul's tube and bag for a man.

A patient who has one leg amputated puts greater pressure on the good heel which is likely to develop a pressure sore, so particular attention should be paid to this heel. A patient with hemiplegia is apt to develop when sitting up in a chair a pressure sore over the heel of the paralysed leg. Accordingly this heel should be protected by the patient wearing a proper shoe with a heel to it, or the heel should be protected by a heel pad or by a sorbo rubber cushion.

If an elderly person is in bed it is important therefore to ensure that they turn from one side to another from time to time. Even more important is that they should be got up for some period each day into a chair, so that pressure is not applied to the same area of skin all the time. The patient should receive a full nourishing diet which should have a high protein content plus vitamin supplements, especially vitamin c and the vitamin b complex. Some physicians advocate blood transfusions, which can be most effective, but can hardly be advised except in specially selected cases where there is reason to think no other course is likely to be so successful.

Regarding intramuscular or subcutaneous injections, the elderly may be very thin and the usual sites of injection inadvisable: especially is this so for the buttock area, which is also the pressure area, and it may be preferable to give any necessary injections in divided doses elsewhere in the body, for example, triceps or deltoid region, about the shoulder.

Pressure areas should also be attended to frequently. The area should be rubbed with soap and water to improve the circulation, after which the skin should be dried with methylated spirit and dusting powder. If the patient is incontinent, silicone cream should be rubbed well into the skin daily. A break in the skin at a pressure sore area is a very serious complication indeed, for infection now takes place, with all the dangers of increasing toxaemia, often with fatal consequences.

It is therefore essential during any medical or surgical treatment that the patient should not lie in bed and run the risk of developing a pressure sore. Somehow or other, especially in surgical treatment, modifications must be made so as to allow the patient to sit up from time to time. If a pressure sore does develop, it should be swabbed well with dilute eusol solution and then jelonet paraffin gauze dressing should be applied, and the dressing changed frequently. Radiant heat and ultra-violet light therapy is also of considerable value.

Operations in the Elderly

Operations in the elderly carry many attendant risks and complications. General fitness for operation should be carefully assessed. This may involve not only a thorough clinical examination, with special reference to the state of the heart and circulation, to the presence or otherwise of congestion of the lungs, or mental confusion, but also of the functioning of the kidneys. It is commonly necessary to include a chest X-ray, a blood urea and blood examination and an E.C.G. examination. If all these things are done, the attendant risks of anaesthesia operation and possible post-operative complications can be more precisely estimated. Many patients who at first appear unfit for operation will be found to be in better condition than supposed, while others will be found to be in poorer health than was apparent. This pre-operative assessment can be most helpful in deciding the choice of an anaesthetic, and how extensive an operation should be planned. After an operation, an elderly person is likely to develop such complications as circulatory failure, congestion of the lungs, renal failure and dehydration, mental confusion and bed sores. Consequently, careful watch should be kept to note early symptoms of these conditions, with a view to instituting immediate counter-measures.

Maintenance of fluid and electrolyte balance As will already be appreciated, in the elderly person there is often a precarious balance in the nutritional state, the functioning of the cardiovascular system, respiratory system and kidneys, and in addition the elderly patient not only withstands hypotension very poorly, but readily develops a shock-like reaction to trauma or haemorrhage. In particular, post-operative shock is liable to cause fluid and electrolyte imbalance. This subject has been dealt with very neatly by Bell,[4] who advocates the following procedures:

Water requirements Because of a relative oliguria, the fluid intake should be kept at about 1500 cm³ on the day of operation, and 2000 cm³ on the first post-operative day. Subsequently the patient will require, on average, at least 2500 cm³. The oral route is normally used, but if this is inadvisable an intravenous method should be adopted; water may be given as 5% glucose. Subcutaneous infusions are rarely satisfactory and may produce infection or occasionally collapse.

Sodium chloride The urine should be examined frequently for its salt content and an estimation made of the daily salt depletion; in addition plasma sodium chloride estimation should also be taken. It should then be possible to estimate how much salt the patient should receive daily.

Approximately 500 cm³ of normal saline will be about the figure in the average case.

Potassium The average daily requirements of potassium for the person who is not taking fluids or food by mouth is approximately 2 to 3 grammes, but excessive loss of potassium may occur via the kidneys, due to the effect of anaesthesia, surgery, dehydration, shock, etc., on the adrenal cortical activity. Excessive dosage with cortisone may also produce an increase of renal excretion of potassium. Potassium may also be lost if there is diarrhoea. There may also be a fall in the blood level following the use of insulin, dextrose infusions or testosterone therapy, because the potassium passes from an extracellular to an intracellular state. Again, excessive saline infusions may lead to a transfer of sodium into the cells and loss of potassium in the urine.

After an operation, careful watch should be kept for the complication of hypokalaemia, when the patient may be feeling extremely weak with a low urinary output and a paralytic ileus with a distension of the abdomen, and the plasma will show a low potassium concentration. There may be many causes to account for this, as outlined above, but it is important to remember that any further intravenous saline therapy is likely to make matters worse and the proper treatment is the giving of potassium chloride. It is probably a good thing to give potassium to all surgical patients for a short while after the second post-operative day.

Glucose Gamble,[19] has shown glucose to be a protein sparer, a conserver of intracellular water and potassium and also that it reduces the loss of extracellular water and sodium. Accordingly, glucose should be given post-operatively up to about 100 grammes a day, and, of course, glucose can be given intravenously.

In some patients there may be abnormal loss of water and electrolytes other than in the urine, and there may be marked differences in the individual electrolyte loss according to the source. Theoretically, the electrolyte loss should be determined from the actual fluid loss in a particular patient; this is not always practicable, but an approximate estimate may be made on the basis of average figures as outlined by Randall.[37]

Losses from the gastro-intestinal tract			
	Milli-equivalents per litre (average)		
	Sodium	Potassium	Chloride
Gastric (fasting)	59·0	9·3	89·0
Small bowel (Miller-Abbott suction)	104·9	5·1	98·9
Ileum (Miller-Abbott suction)	116·7	5·0	105·8
Ileostomy (recent)	129·5	16·2	109·7
Bile	145·3	5·2	99·9
Pancreas	141·1	4·6	76·6

As regards potassium deficiencies, intravenous therapy is more hazardous than in younger patients, and potassium should be given by mouth whenever possible, and spread out over three or four days. Where there is a need for potassium parenterally, it is usually better to add potassium chloride to another parenteral solution. Volume for volume, replacement of gastro-intestinal losses by saline solutions is not altogether satisfactory. For instance, normal saline provides too much sodium if used to replace loss of gastric juice. It is therefore as well to consider the following list of parenteral fluids and make a suitable choice of one, or a combination of such fluids.

	Milli-equivalents per litre				
	Sodium	Potassium	Chloride	Effective HCO_2	Calcium
Solution					
Sodium Chloride (0·9%)	154		154		
M/6 sodium lactate	167			167	
U.S.P. Ringer's solution	147	4	155·5		4·5
Lactated Ringer's solution	130	4	109	28	3·0
Hartmann's solution	136	5·3	112	33	3·6
Darrow's solution	120	35	105	50	
Electrolyte solution G	63	17	150		
Electrolyte solution I	138	12	100	50	
Potassium chloride (1·49 gm)		20	20		
Ammonium chloride (0·75%)			140		
Sodium bicarbonate (1·2%)	143			143	

Blood The value of whole blood transfusion should never be overlooked since it corrects not only blood loss but also blood volume deficits, counteracts shock, and increases the oxygen-carrying capacity.

CORONER'S INQUEST

Operative surgery is always a great strain. It is not possible for all operations to be successful, and the patient may die during the operation. Too many, or a succession of, fatal terminations have a depressing effect not only on the surgeon but on all concerned. Operations on the elderly have so many hazards that it is almost impossible to avoid fatal termination in a much greater number than in operations performed on the young. Operations in the elderly, therefore, put an especially heavy burden on the surgeon and anaesthetist.

Since it is the custom for a coroner to hold an inquest, or make an inquiry as to the cause of death, when a person dies within a short period of an operation, the surgeon or anaesthetist may be called to account publicly in court, and receive an unfair notoriety in the newspapers. Unfortunately newspaper reporters, and sometimes even the coroner, do not understand the hazards of operations in the elderly, or the heavy burden it imposes on the surgeon. All too often the proceedings imply that the surgeon or anaesthetist is to blame in some way or other, whereas he should receive praise for doing all that he possibly could. A succession of appearances in court can be quite devastating in its effect. The proceedings appear to deter surgeons from undertaking operations on the elderly and there is need for change in the public attitude. It is felt that many conditions in the elderly are amenable to surgery and that more operations should be undertaken than is customarily done at present. It may be well worth while for the geriatric consultant to seek a personal interview with the coroner and explain the various difficulties, surgical and otherwise, relating to the care of the elderly.

Before an operation is carried out, it is advisable to obtain the consent not only of the patient but also of the relatives, to whom the attendant risks should be explained. The following conditions are perhaps worthy of special mention.

ACUTE ABDOMEN

When a patient has the features of an acute abdomen, for example a perforation of the stomach or gall bladder or a strangulated hernia, operation may be the only means of saving his life. The patient may be in very poor condition, but experience so far leads one to the conclusion that expectant treatment and gastric aspiration is hardly ever successful; neither is the patient's condition likely to improve on this regimen and so make him more fit for operation. To this there is at least one exception, namely acute pancreatitis, and for this reason it is well to note the serum amylase or urinary distase in elderly patients with acute abdomen. Another condition that has to be excluded is faecal impaction, which may cause the symptoms of paralytic ileus. However, unfortunately many elderly patients with acute abdomen are *in extremis* and quite unfit for operation.

RECTAL CARCINOMA

A colostomy operation may be considered to relieve obstruction in the case of carcinoma of the rectum, and of course such an operation is successful in this respect, but in many elderly patients the obstruction is more particularly due to faecal impaction, and if this is relieved operation may be unnecessary for a very considerable time, months or even years. A colostomy is undesirable in an elderly patient; not only is it most unpleasant but it so often means that the patient has to have constant personal attention, and this may mean permanent admission to hospital. For the same reason, an excision for carcinoma of the colon is preferable to a colostomy.

CHOLECYSTITIS

Medical treatment with an antibiotic usually gives a successful result, and since many patients do not have a recurrence for some years one usually does not advise operation unless the patient so wishes. After the attack the illness should be fully investigated. If gall-stones are diagnosed a further illness is probable but perhaps not if there is simply a non-functioning gall-bladder. The decision for or against operation should only be arrived at after consultation with the patient and his relatives.

GASTRIC ULCER

Under modern surgical technique, with careful attention to fluid and electrolyte balance, elderly people withstand partial gastrectomy reasonably well, and this may hold out better results than medical treatment.

GANGRENE OF THE FEET

The onset of gangrene may be by coldness of the foot and blueness of the toe. This means the blood supply is impaired and the examination should cover the following possibilities:

(1) Poor arterial supply.
    Feel for adequate pulsation in the femoral popliteal, dorsal tibia, and posterior tibia arteries, remembering that in a state of shock or poor cardiac output the pulsation can be much reduced below normal.
(2) Palpate for an aneurysm of the abdominal aorta and bear in mind the possibility of thrombosis at its bifurcation.
(3) Is there evidence of a poor cardiac output, e.g. valvular disease, enlarged heart, low blood pressure or myocardial infarction. The feet are furthest away from the heart and likely to be affected first from an impoverished circulation.
(4) Examine the lungs for any conditions likely to be causing hypoxia; this includes chronic bronchitis and emphysema and a recent attack of bronchitis or broncho-pneumonia. Hypoxia will logically cause gangrene at the very periphery of the body.
(5) Examine the blood for anaemia, if this is present there is diminished oxygen carrying capacity of the blood.
(6) Test for diabetes mellitus.

If the foot and toes are warm then the blood supply should be adequate; if they are persistently cold and blue the supply of oxygen is probably insufficient. The gangrene is commonly due to obliterative arteriosclerosis and the possibility of embolectomy rarely arises.

It is important that medical treatment should not be continued too long, and the patient's fitness for operation should not be allowed to deteriorate. So often operation becomes eventually necessary, after a period of pain and suffering, that one wonders whether it should be done much sooner than is customary. Needless to say, an extensive gangrene is invariably fatal, and in such a case amputation is the only possible hope of saving the patient's life. It should be added that death from gangrene of a foot is long drawn out and extremely painful. If the patient is fit, one is inclined therefore to advise immediate operation rather than run the risk of a deterioration in health.

In the elderly patient apart from obliterative arteriosclerosis there is commonly a poor cardiac output and features of hypoxia; as a result one has to decide how extensive an amputation should be if deemed necessary. Amputation of the toes will still leave the patient able to walk very well. Amputation of a foot in the very elderly patient causes almost as much disablement as amputation above the knee, and if the impoverished circulation is likely to continue, further gangrene may take place requiring another amputation above the knee at a later stage. The decision as to how much to amputate is a difficult one and varies from patient to patient. As far as the author's experience goes one is inclined towards a 'once for all' amputation above the knee as opposed to amputation above the foot.

FRACTURE OF THE NECK OF THE FEMUR

This condition is extremely common, especially among women. Before the fracture occurs, the patient is often in a very poor state of health and is likely to have widespread osteoporosis and bone atrophy. Cardiac weakness is a commonly associated condition. Many of these patients die, but the cause of death is due not so much to the fracture as to the associated conditions, and finally to the supervention of bed sores. Surgical procedures suitable for young patients are not always suitable for the elderly in poor health. The application of plasters or splints may themselves cause pressure sores, leading to infection and toxaemia. Rest in bed may be contra-indicated, not only because of the risk of bed sores, but because of the danger of pulmonary congestion and bronchopneumonia. Surgical treatment that implies lying in bed should be avoided, and the patient should have a suitable geriatric chair in which she should be nursed as much as possible. Many patients of ninety years and over have been successfully pinned, and age alone is no bar to this procedure. Another type of operation is to excise the head of the femur and replace it by a metal head, i.e. the Austin Moore Prosthesis. This operation has proved very effective and is often advisable in many elderly patients. Naturally it is equally important to deal with the medical aspects of the illness while surgical treatment is being carried out.

MINOR OPERATIONS

Many a patient is referred to hospital because of some simple tumour, such as a lipoma, or for an inguinal hernia, which has been in existence for very many years. Sometimes, the patient has been talked into asking for treatment by over-zealous relatives. But a minor operation can be quite a serious matter in the elderly, and even when successfully performed, other complications may ensue. Sometimes the surgeon will be faced with difficulties over the patient's return home, and the original medical reasons for treatment do not seem so important as originally stated.

It is not the purpose of this book to write a full account of the medical conditions seen in the elderly, but the following appear to be worthy of some brief notes:

MALIGNANT GROWTHS

Malignant conditions are commonly seen in the elderly, but the tumours appear to grow more slowly and the condition may continue for months, or even years. The established facts as regards prognosis in the young may be quite misleading if they are applied to the prognosis in the aged. Before embarking upon a major operation for removal of a tumour, it is as well to examine the patient very thoroughly, consult life expectation figures, and in the light of the patient's general health come to some calculation as to what his life expectation is, regardless of the malignant growth. It has been found on many occasions that a patient dies, not from a malignant tumour, but from such conditions as cardiac failure, cerebral haemorrhage or pneumonia.

CARCINOMA OF THE STOMACH

This is quite common in the elderly and one notes that some 13 956 persons died from this condition in England and Wales in 1962, and 12 191 in 1973 (*Abstract of Statistics* 1974, page 40). It should be kept in mind in all cases of anaemia; diagnosis may require confirmation by barium meal and X-ray, since sometimes the condition is wrongly so diagnosed and the patient has anaemia due to some other cause, which may respond to treatment. A few patients tentatively diagnosed as carcinoma of the stomach, on examination have been found to suffer from pernicious anaemia.

BRONCHIAL CARCINOMA

This is a relatively common condition and caused the death of 24 870 people in England and Wales in 1962 and 32 176 in 1973 (*Abstract of Statistics* 1974, page 40). When a bronchial carcinoma is suspected in an old person, he may not be sufficiently well for the diagnosis to be confirmed by bronchoscopy and the diagnosis may be made on a persistent radiological shadow in the lung. Added pulmonary infection is quite common and may unduly hasten the patient's end. It is often worth doing a sputum organism sensitivity test and then give him a course of treatment with a suitable antibiotic. Often the patient shows considerable improvement and may become ambulant for six months or more. Very occasionally, the shadow in the lung clears up completely and it is evident that the original diagnosis was an error.

CARCINOMA OF THE BREAST

In an elderly person this condition can respond most successfully by treatment with a testosterone hormone namely sustanon. Before considering surgery it is advisable to give the patient sustanon 100 mg intramuscular twice a week for a fortnight and then once a week tapering down to 100 mg a month. If there is a response the lump in the breast and enlarged glands subside very considerably. If there is a risk of a fungating ulcer developing this can be avoided by a local excision. Of course if there are secondaries in the lungs or bones the condition is almost hopeless though there may be a remission for a year or so. Many patients have been treated in this way and quite often, though the growth has not been cured, the condition has been held in check and they have succumbed from another illness, e.g. cerebral infarction.

CARCINOMA OF THE UTERUS

It sometimes happens that carcinoma of the body of the uterus is diagnosed from a purulent and offensive uterine discharge, but because of the patient's poor health she is unfit for operation. Again, it sometimes happens that a thorough course of treatment by a suitable antibiotic either greatly benefits the patient or, in very rare instances, clears up the uterine condition indicating an error in diagnosis.

RODENT ULCERS

Old people are very prone to have rodent ulcers about the nose and eyes, frequently untreated. Since the ulcers respond quite favourably to deep X-ray therapy, the patient should be referred to the radiotherapist.

CARCINOMA OF THE COLON

Some patients with carcinoma of the colon are operated on as a matter of urgency because of bowel obstruction. At the time, they may be in no condition to withstand a major operation, and a simple colostomy may be done. After the operation, the patient may be transferred to the geriatric ward to improve his general health and condition. It is therefore important to refer the patient back to the surgeon in due course, to see whether a more radical operation can be performed and the colostomy closed. Many growths of the colon are slow-growing and may be only locally malignant, and thus possible of local excision.

Blood Conditions

A common finding is an iron-deficiency anaemia. Sometimes the haemoglobin level is as low as 50 %, and the patient has obvious glossitis and koilonychia. The condition usually responds to oral administration of iron, but not always, and then iron may have to be given intramuscularly. Large intramuscular injections are undesirable in thin and wasted muscles, so a dosage at any time should be limited to about 2 cm³, i.e. 2 cm³ of inferon. Pernicious anaemia may be suspected from a blood film which shows a macrocytes and very little polychromasia, and may be confirmed by a low vitamin B12 level in the blood or even more – if necessary – by finding megaloblasts in the bone marrow. Sometimes, though pernicious anaemia appears to be most probable, the anaemia may be very extreme, and a blood transfusion have to be considered.

The generally accepted opinion is that pernicious anaemia patients should not have a blood transfusion because of the risk of overloading the circulation and causing cardiac failure. This risk is clearly a very real one and even more so in a patient over eighty. The risk may be minimised by an exchange blood transfusion, so that a quantity of concentrated red blood corpuscles is transfused into the other arm. A very elderly patient may respond very slowly to even massive doses of cytamen, and still remain in a most critical condition for a period longer than would a younger patient. In a few patients it has been thought advisable, therefore, to give a small transfusion with extreme caution. This has been done quite safely and successfully, so that one cannot accept unreservedly that a patient with pernicious anaemia should not be transfused.

A severe anaemia may be caused by haematemesis. The latter at times occurs in the elderly without any preceding history of peptic ulcer, and barium meal examination after the patient has recovered may not show any evidence of an ulcer. By many it is considered that haemorrhage of this nature is due to the taking of aspirin, but very often there is no such history; other causes come to mind, such as scurvy, but this again is a very dubious possibility, so that in many instances it is impossible to find out the cause of the haematemesis. The condition is treated in the usual manner as for younger patients, but special emphasis is placed on the correction of dehydration and salt depletion. A blood transfusion is given, if indicated. The indications for a blood transfusion are not always precise. A haemoglobin of 35% or below is a fairly clear indication, but if it is above 50% a transfusion may be unnecessary or even inadvisable. Many patients with anaemia do not give a history of either haematemesis or melaenae and are presumed to have had some bleeding from a peptic ulcer from time to time which is not taking place at the time of the examination. This presumption is often correct as proved by a barium meal examination or very positive occult blood test at a later stage. Some form of internal bleeding is quite common in old people so that one cannot be really satisfied with a diagnosis *simply* of iron deficiency and anaemia.

Oral liquid foods, such as milk to which is added some sodium chloride, is given as soon as tolerated – it may be given by milk drip. Starvation is avoided by giving bland food or other foods in puréed form. A distinct advance in ulcer therapy appears to have come from the use of Biogastrone and allied substances – though a complication of hypokalaemia as a result of such treatment has to be avoided.

Careful observation is made of the patient's pulse, respiration and blood pressure, together with frequent blood haemoglobins, blood urea and hematocrit findings. By this means there may be early evidence of a further bleeding, and perhaps the necessity for a further transfusion. The case is discussed with a surgeon early on so that if surgical intervention is considered necessary, this is done before the patient becomes a poor operative risk. It is always advisable also to give 50 mg of vitamin C.

Respiratory Conditions

Emphysema and bronchitis are commonly seen in the elderly, and acute bronchitis is a particularly dangerous infection for them. In such cases treatment should be started as soon as possible. An antibiotic is usually required, and sometimes oxygen. Bronchospasm may be a very dangerous symptom accompanying the lung infection, though it is more characteristically seen in the asthmatic subject. There are various treatments for bronchospasm, and one that has been found most efficacious is a slow intravenous injection of aminophylline 0·25 of a gramme. This may control the attack at once, but if the spasm recurs the drug may be given intramuscularly six-hourly, for several doses. Prednisone 15 mg three times daily for a few days may also reduce spasm and congestion. The standard medical text-book should be consulted for the full treatment of this condition.

Bronchopneumonia and pneumonia should be treated in the usual way, and the elderly respond very favourably. Patients over ninety years have been treated successfully. Basal pleural effusions commonly complicate heart failure and many elderly people are still walking about with unresolved small effusions. Elderly patients, particularly men, also suffer from bronchiectasis and they appear to benefit from periodic treatment with an antibiotic, and more particularly by aureomycin.

PULMONARY TUBERCULOSIS

There is a high incidence of respiratory tuberculosis in the elderly; for instance, for 1956 the peak of male mortality was in the age group 65 to 69, with 67 deaths per 100 000 living, and for females the corresponding age group is 75 to 79, with 17 deaths per 100 000 living. For the respiratory forms, the ratio of male deaths to female was 2·7 to 1. For England and Wales 1969 there were 1092 deaths and in 1973 there were 859 deaths (*Annual Abstract of Statistics*, page 40); the greatest number of men died at 60–64 years and for females 70–74 years.

Stieglitz[52] draws attention to the fact that the elderly people of today are the survivors of that generation of children and young adults in the 1870s and 1890s, when tuberculosis was rife among human beings and cattle, and when mortality rates were of a high order. There is every reason to think that a large number of elderly people were severely affected with tuberculosis in their youth or childhood.

Be that as it may, pulmonary tuberculosis with positive sputum is constantly being found in the geriatric wards. All too often it has been masked by accompanying bronchitis and emphysema, and all too frequently the elderly have never come forward for mass radiography or other such investigation. The condition is, of course, important, because such patients are apt to bring up copious sputum infected with tuberculous bacilli and are somewhat of a menace if undetected. At the same time, their homes are also infected and a danger to visiting children or new tenants. Such cases of pulmonary tuberculosis are usually referred to the chest specialist, and on the whole, although the results are not so dramatic as in younger patients, modern treatment is satisfactory.

LESIONS OF THE CENTRAL NERVOUS SYSTEM

The commonest lesion undoubtedly is that of cerebral infarction often due to thrombosis. But there are more cases of cerebral haemorrhage than clinically apparent. There is usually an old case of tabes dorsalis to be found in a geriatric ward and cases of progressive muscular atrophy, bulbar palsy, and sub-acute combined degeneration of the cord are seen from time to time.

Parkinsonism One of the most troublesome illnesses encountered is that of Parkinsonism. The condition can now be brought about for a temporary period by the use of tranquillising drugs. In the early stages there is difficulty in distinguishing between a state of depression with apathy and immobility and that of the immobility of Parkinsonism not accompanied with tremors. To give tranquillising drugs to a patient with early Parkinsonism would be to worsen the condition; neither would an anti-Parkinsonism drug like artane benefit the depressed patient. One should also bear in mind that the drugs commonly used for Parkinsonism can lead to retention of urine with overflow, obstinate constipation and all too frequently mild delirium. The patient with this disease tends to become more and more rigid, and eventually bedfast. He also experiences greater and greater difficulty in taking nourishment. The end result may be a patient with extensive bed sores. As soon as the patient diminishes his movements and muscular activity, the muscles waste and the joints become stiff.

Apart from drug therapy, treatment is essentially that of physiotherapy, aimed at maintaining ambulation and activities of daily living as long as possible. Failure to do this soon results in a bedfast patient, though of course there are many patients who have the disease in only a mild form, and a form which is only very slowly progressive. After physiotherapy and rehabilitation, these patients may be sent home, but it is more advisable that they should attend for out-patient physiotherapy to avoid a relapse in their condition.

Epileptic Fits Epileptic fits can, of course, occur in old people who have been subject to them during their lives. They can also first be noticed in association with cerebral thrombosis. The specific treatment for epileptic fits is a barbitone drug, usually phenobarbitone. But it is well to remember that if a patient is on phenobarbitone and suddenly stops taking it the serious condition of status epilepticus may result necessitating intramuscular phenobarbitone. For one reason or another older patients on barbiturates often do stop taking the drug. For this reason the author considers there is a case for giving potassium bromide as well as phenobarbitone since the action of the former drug will continue for a longer time even if both drugs are suddenly stopped and may prevent the onset of status epilepticus.

LESIONS OF BONES

A surprisingly large number of elderly people are seen with kyphosis, scoliosis, pigeon chests, genuvalgus and old fractures arising from illness or injury in childhood or youth. One expects that the future generations will not show these deformities. Paget's disease of bone is quite common and is often the cause of deafness. Many patients have been seen with a blood alkaline phosphatase of over 60 units. Old-standing cases of rheumatoid arthritis are constantly coming to light. The acute phase of the arthritis has ceased many years previously but the joints have been allowed to become stiff, the limbs deformed and the muscles wasted. It is clear that many patients have lost heart and resigned themselves to staying in bed. Had active physiotherapy and rehabilitation been continued, the extreme stiffness of the joints and wasting of the muscles need not have occurred. Associated with the arthritis in such patients, there is commonly widespread osteoporosis and a mild iron-deficiency anaemia. A few such patients have been successfully rehabilitated, but in the majority the wasting has become too extreme to bring about any improvement. Severe and crippling osteoarthritis, especially of the knee joints, may defy all treatment and, on account of pain and deformity, the patient is unable to walk.

GENERALISED OSTEOPOROSIS

This is very common, especially in women, and accounts for much invalidism. There may be marked flexural curvature of the spine and the patient's head may be buried in her chest. Fractures, especially fractures of the neck of the femur, may take place with very little trauma. The aetiology of this condition is very puzzling. The bones, apparently, have lost a great deal of calcium, yet blood chemistry is within normal limits and there is nothing to suggest hyperthyroidism or hyperparathyroidism. There may be a deficient intake of calcium, since many patients live on an impoverished diet, with a low milk content. Possibly there is deficient calcium absorption and deposition, but this is almost impossible to ascertain; though recent investigations in research laboratories, using very small quantities of radio-active strontium, may throw some light on this. The urinary output of calcium is generally normal, but in this regard consideration should be given to the high incidence in the elderly of emphysema and of impaired renal function.

Both the lungs and the kidneys serve the function of ridding the body of waste acids. Extensive emphysema carries with it the possibility that carbon dioxide is less readily excreted, and that an extra load is put upon the kidneys. The kidneys deal with acids in two ways. One is by combining the acid with a base, which is usually sodium and the other is by the secretion of ammonia, which is used to neutralise the acids prior to the passage into the urine. But kidneys in a state of failure are unable to secrete adequate amounts of ammonia, so that acids have to be dealt with more and more by combining them with a base.

An important base in the body is calcium. At present it is a plausible theory that the elderly person with emphysema and impaired renal function does in fact utilise calcium in order to excrete acids in the urine. The theory, and it is only a theory, raises interesting research possibilities and makes osteoporosis in the elderly a very interesting subject. If osteoporosis could be successfully treated, then the risk of a fractured femur should be reduced, and any reduction in the incidence of this fracture is of major medical and social importance.

A very informative discussion took place at the Royal Society of Medicine, London, in February 1958, on skeletal manifestations of general disease, and Steiner[53] set out the following classification of conditions giving rise to decreased bone density:

(1) Osteoporosis
    (a) Senile
    (b) Pregnancy
    (c) Disuse
    (d) Hyperthyroidism
    (e) Cushing's syndrome
    (f) Steroid therapy
    (g) Acromegaly
    (h) Malnutrition
    (i) Hypervitaminosis D (soft tissue calcification)
(2) Osteomalacia and rickets
    (a) Vitamin D deficiency
    (b) Steatorrhoea
    (c) Renal tubular defects
    (d) Chronic uraemia (late)
(3) Hyperparathyroidism
    (a) Primary
    (b) Secondary
        (i) Renal tubular defects
        (ii) Chronic uraemia
        (iii) Osteomalacia (late)

To this list may also be added Osteoporosis or Osteomalacia resulting from Partial Gastrectomy (Della, D. J. and Begley, M. D.[15]).

Apart from the question of pregnancy, which of course does not arise in the elderly, each of the points mentioned above is well worth considering when an elderly person is found to have osteoporosis. In addition, all the causes of decreased bone density due to bone replacement by such conditions as neoplastic deposits, myelomatosis, blood diseases, will have to be considered, so that it can be seen that senile osteoporosis is by no means a simple diagnostic problem.

Schechter and Mervine[42] set out an even more elaborate classification of osteoporosis, and deal more fully with the methods of treatment which are along the following lines:

Mobilisation Disuse increases the process of demineralisation and therefore the patient should undergo as much activity and movements as possible. In particular, the elderly should not be kept in bed, plasters should be avoided as also should plaster jackets or corsets; this principle holds good as far as is practicable should there be a fracture consequent upon the osteoporosis. Every effort should be made to bring about early ambulation and development of muscular tone. If the patient has to be confined to bed, there should be an over-head pulley and rope apparatus to give him the maximum mobility.

Diet The proper synthesis of osteoid tissue into bone necessitates the availability of sufficient proteins, and it is most important that the patient receive a high protein diet. This is even more necessary if there is loss of protein in the urine, or if the intake of food is dissipated on account of hyperthyroidism, diabetes, or overdosage with cortisone, the latter of course being antianabolic. In the elderly the danger of hypercalcaemia is not considerable, especially if they are kept ambulant, and moderate amounts of calcium and small amounts of vitamin D may be included in the diet since they aid in the utilisation of protein. Vitamin B12 is reported by Hallahan[20] to cause subjective relief for osteoporotic pains. Vitamin C is also required since it plays a part in matrix formation.

Hormones Both testosterone and oestrogen possess an anabolic action stimulating the growth of all tissues and they diminish the excretion of calcium and phosphorus. Testosterone has a greater action as regards nitrogen retention, while oestrogen has a greater effect on the retention of calcium.

A drug related to testosterone, namely norethandrolone, has become available and can be given by mouth. It has a greater anabolic effect and a lesser androgenic one than testosterone. A study carried out by Woodford-Williams and Webster[56] supports the view that norethandrolone has definite anabolic properties and it may be this drug will become the one of choice for osteoporosis. Even more recently the most effective hormone appears to be sustenon which can be given in doses of 100 mg intra-muscularly, weekly for 4 weeks and a course repeated from time to time. Hormonal treatment frequently relieves pain and since the latter is so often complained of in the back when the patient is sitting up, it does mean very great relief indeed. This effect occurs early, i.e. within two weeks or so. Later on the patient's general well-being appears to improve with increased appetite, better movements of the joints and a gain in weight. Nevertheless, there may be no radiographic improvement, but it should be borne in mind that osteoporosis does not give radiographic changes until there has been about 30 % demineralisation, and it would take an elderly person many years to make up for such a deficiency. In some patients blood transfusions have been advocated as a means of supplying ready protein, and this may have to be considered in selected cases.

In conclusion, osteoporosis has been stressed since in the elderly it is both a common and a serious disease well worthy of the fullest investigation and treatment.

OSTEOMALACIA

In the preceding paragraphs osteoporosis has been dealt with according to the accepted orthodox views. One of these is that in senile osteoporosis the blood chemistry is within normal limits, and that the disorder is one affecting the protein matrix and there is no disorder of mineral metabolism. This view is not supported by experiments carried out by Heaney, R. P. and Whedon, G. D.,[23] who by using isotopic calcium found that a normal adult of 70 kg showed a deposit of 600 mg of calcium going into bone each day and that not by exchange but by actual new bone formation, i.e. there was constant remodelling of bone. The next important finding was that these normal rates of bone formation were found in five patients with senile osteoporosis. The experiment, therefore, suggests that in elderly patients there was no lack of protein matrix on to which calcium could be deposited.

Arising out of this Hazell, K. and Oatway, A. W. N.[22] surveyed the alkaline phosphatase levels in a random selection of 23 patients with osteoporosis and very surprisingly seven showed abnormally high levels. Further after a course of calcium and vitamin D, i.e. tabs. calcium and vitamin D (BPC) two tablets t.d.s. for two to three weeks, the raised alkaline phosphate levels returned to normal. These findings suggested that the seven patients actually suffered from osteomalacia and so responded to vitamin D and calcium.

Hodkinson, H. M. and Exton-Smith, A. N. and Crowley, M. F.[25] also made a study of skeletal rarefaction in 80 elderly subjects. They correlated the densitometry of a hand bone objective measurement of skeletal density, blood calcium, blood phosphorus and blood alkaline phosphatase levels, and came to the conclusion that osteomalacia may be present to some extent in many cases. In the *British Medical Journal*[8] bone rarefaction in the elderly was considered and attention drawn to the possibility of osteomalacia as a cause of senile osteoporosis. The present position appears to be that when an elderly patient has senile osteoporosis it cannot be accepted that the blood chemistry is normal. An investigation of the blood, alkaline phosphatase, blood calcium and blood phosphorus should be done to exclude the possibility that the patient has osteomalacia.

Treatment Apart from general measures treatment would appear to necessitate giving tabs. calcium (BPC) as mentioned above. Each tablet contains calcium sodium lactate 7·5 g, calcium phosphate 2·5 g, vitamin D 500 units. More recently one capsule only of calciferol containing 50 000 units of vitamin D has been given to patients with a high alkaline phosphatase suspected of having osteomalacia, and it has been found that when the latter is present the alkaline phosphatase returns to normal in about one week. No further capsule is then necessary for over one month.

Abdominal Conditions

The anatomy of the abdomen as regards the position of organs in the elderly may be different from that in the young. There is often visceroptosis, and the kidneys may be palpable and mistakenly considered to be tumours. The liver is commonly ptosed and may give the impression of being enlarged; the presence of Riedel's lobe may be particularly misleading. There may be gross visceroptosis of the stomach. In the female a lax abdomen may in addition have a large umbilical hernia, and in the male there may be a gross inguinal hernia extending into the scrotum. At times the hernia contain loops of bowel which may become strangulated. In a lax abdomen also, a pulsating abdominal aorta is more readily felt and wrongly considered to be an aneurysm. Many elderly people have palpable lymphatic glands in the axillae and the groins, which have no special significance. Where there is obstinate constipation, the sigmoid colon may be felt to be full of faeces which can be indented by pressure from the fingers.

There are of course innumerable abdominal conditions to be considered, but mention will be made only of two, namely appendicitis and acute pancreatitis.

APPENDICITIS

Christensen[10] analysed some 1254 cases and found that 7% occurred in patients 60 years and over. By making a comparison between 90 patients in the older age group with 142 in the group aged 30 to 39, he found that in the former 53·8% showed appendicitis with perforation and peritonitis, compared with 12·1% in the latter. This is a high degree of perforation and draws attention to the need for early operation in the aged. In the elderly acute appendicitis is not marked by the same amount of muscular guarding and tenderness in the right iliac fossa as in younger people, and since in the elderly severe constipation is so often present and there may be no great rise in temperature, or the steady increase in pulse rate so characteristic in the young, the correct diagnosis may be missed in favour of obstinate constipation.

There is, I believe, a view rather prevalent that appendicitis is rare in the elderly, but my own experience in the wards, and Christensen's observations, do not support this and perhaps operation should be performed rather more frequently than at present.

ACUTE PANCREATITIS

Acute pancreatitis seems to be more common in the elderly than in the young. The condition is marked by the sudden onset of abdominal pain accompanied by abdominal rigidity, vomiting and usually abdominal distension. There may be a past history of dyspepsia, ulcer or gall bladder disease. In suspected cases, a serum amylase test should always be done. The normal serum amylase level is between 80 and 150 units. A figure of 200 units is almost diagnostic of acute pancreatitis.

Treatment Operative treatment is not very successful, but may be considered if there are signs of increasing peritoneal irritation, or a rise in serum amylase. Otherwise the treatment is along the following lines:

The patient should be in bed in shock position. Morphine sulphate grains 0·25, or pethidine, should be given, as also atropine sulphate grains one-hundredth, as an anti-spasmodic. Fluids and food should be withheld by mouth and the stomach aspirated continuously. Fluid should be given intravenously; plasma 250–500 cm^3 immediately, then repeated if necessary. If this is not available, then normal saline or 5% glucose should be used. The patient's condition should be checked every half-hour, as well as haematocrit and serum amylase records being repeated from time to time. After the acute phase, no fluids or food should be given by mouth for about two days, when small quantities of bland fluids may be started. The subsequent course of the illness should be followed by further blood examinations. At a later stage, further consideration should be given regarding elective surgical treatment.

The condition has been specially mentioned because, in the differential diagnosis of an acute abdomen, its possibility can be so readily overlooked especially so because it requires a serum amylase investigation, whereas the diagnosis of most causes of acute abdomen can be made solely on the clinical features.

Cardiovascular Conditions

Almost all elderly persons have some lesion of the cardiovascular system. Usually this is a matter of arteriosclerosis, but arising out of this, or associated with it, are the innumerable conditions fully described in a text-book on cardiology. Much of the work of a geriatric physician is taken up with the diagnosis and treatment of these conditions, and assessing their importance in relation to other illnesses from which the patient may suffer, fitness of operation, and extent of rehabilitation that should be attempted. It is important to make a proper assessment of a patient's cardiac function and cardiac reserve before further physical effort is encouraged.

In the elderly, there are some changes in the ordinary physical signs elicited on clinical examinations. Emphysema is very common, which makes it difficult, or even impossible, to ascertain the size of the heart. Associated breathlessness and the adventitious sounds of emphysema and bronchitis make auscultation of the heart a little more difficult. Unfolding and rigidity of the aorta may be associated with an aortic systolic murmur, which is quite commonly heard in the elderly, rarely has much significance. A rough mitral systolic murmur is also relatively common, but rarely implies serious mitral valvular disease.

Under such conditions, screening of the chest is frequently indicated, when the size of the heart can be more accurately estimated and evidence of an enlarged pulmonary conus more readily seen. The pulse is frequently irregular. Sometimes this is due to ventricular presystole, which, however, instead of being of an innocent nature as in the young, is of more significant importance. Auricular fibrillation is commonly diagnosed but not all cases are as simple as they would appear sometimes. ECG examination reveals, in some instances, that the irregularity is due to such conditions as partial part block complicated by numerous auricular and ventricular extra-systole. Cardiac arrhythmias of all types are quite common. Occasionally, the diagnosis of heart block and Stokes-Adams attacks is missed by the general practitioner, and the patient considered by him to have had a stroke from a cerebral attack, or to be subject to epilepsy, and consequently not treated correctly.

The geriatric unit so often receives the 'failures' from other doctors and has the opportunity of observing the patient in the later stages of his illness, and for a long period of time, that it is little wonder errors of an original diagnosis sometimes need correction. But these occasional errors should not be considered as a reflection on the doctors concerned, who have to practise under very trying conditions.

CORONARY THROMBOSIS

Statistically, there is a considerable incidence of this disease in younger age groups, especially in men round about fifty years old, in whom it is an important cause of death. Coronary thrombosis is also very common in the elderly, but they seem to be more subject to minor attacks. They are also less able to give a clear account of their symptoms. During an attack they take to bed for a few weeks and the true nature of their illness is only diagnosed later on by electrocardiography. A few patients have been admitted because of mental confusion (one patient was sent in on a Magistrate's Order) and have been found to have recent coronary thrombosis. There is considerable doubt as to the value of anti-coagulant treatment and a great deal of evidence as to its dangers – especially in causing an intra-cranial haemorrhage. For these reasons many physicians do not advise anti-coagulant treatment for elderly patients.

BLOOD PRESSURE

High blood pressure is quite common, but its importance and treatment requirements differ from those applied in the younger age groups. A long-continued high blood pressure is likely to lead to arterial disease, and eventually to cardiac failure, cerebral thrombosis, or renal failure. In the elderly, the high blood pressure is unlikely to be of recent origin, and much of the damage to the arterial system has already been done, so that a lowering of the blood pressure may have no beneficial effects. Lowering of the blood pressure may also have a disastrous effect in lessening the circulation to the brain and to the kidneys.

Before considering any line of treatment, it is important to have a record of the blood pressure over as long a time as possible. It is the diastolic pressure that is the more important, because the systolic pressure can vary from week to week. If a series of records are observed, it may be found that the diastolic pressure has been coming down over a period of time. Whereas in the young this might be considered as a favourable sign, in the elderly it so often implies that hypertensive cardiac failure is beginning. It has been found in the geriatric unit that it is at this stage, i.e. when the heart is failing, that the patient is likely to suffer from cerebral thrombosis or renal failure. Such a patient may have a relatively normal blood pressure, but marked retinal arteriosclerosis, poor renal function and an enlarged heart points to a pre-existing history of high blood pressure. There are evident dangers in lowering the blood pressure too rapidly, and treatment towards this end should be given with caution.

The patient may benefit from a little rest in bed, or a more sedentary life. If there is obesity, this should be treated by strict dieting. A tranquilliser may have a sufficiently beneficial effect. Or serpasil may bring about a sufficient lowering of the blood pressure without producing untoward symptoms. If the patient does not respond to simple hypertensive procedures, and the clinical features are sufficiently serious, then ganglionic blocking agents, for example the methonium compounds, may have to be used, but with extreme caution.

The treatment of hypertension is a very complex one and for fuller details a text-book on medical treatment should be consulted. In those patients well over seventy, one has been impressed rather more by the untoward side effects of drastic treatment than by the benefits. Many elderly patients have relatively low blood pressures, and if there has been no previous history of hypertension, it is usually a healthy sign. But this is not invariably so, since quite a number are found to have myocardial degeneration, and this is especially true of the very elderly. Low blood pressure is also met with in patients with malnutrition, or with low-grade toxaemia, anaemia, old coronary disease, hypothyroidism, etc.

TEMPORAL ARTERITIS

Elderly people often have prominent and sometimes thickened arteries in the temporal region. But occasionally the arteries have nodes on them which are painful on palpation. The patient may be suffering from temporal arteritis, i.e. giant cell arteritis. If so the presenting symptoms are likely to be: severe headaches, malaise and perhaps low-grade fever. Out of the various complications a most serious one is that of blindness in one or both eyes. For this reason in a suspected case it may be necessary to take a biopsy of a piece of the artery for histological confirmation of fibroblasts in the intina and giant cells in the media of the vessels. If the diagnosis is confirmed the patient should receive cortisone therapy which will relieve many of the symptoms and lessen the danger of blindness.

TOXIC EFFECTS OF DIGITALIS

Diseases of the circulatory system form a major cause of death, and elderly people very commonly show some cardiac weakness. Though digitalis can be very effective in controlling disorders of rhythm it cannot, of course, make a myocardium stronger than it actually is. The first logical step to take when there are signs of cardiac failure is to so order the person's life as to lessen the load on the heart. Better a Home Help thrice weekly, than digoxin twice daily. The indications for the use of digitalis in an elderly person are not always clear. Auricular fibrillation is quite common in the elderly and if the heart rate is slow it is not of itself an indication for digitalis. Some puffiness or slight oedema of the feet later in the day is also fairly common in elderly persons. It usually indicates that the activity during the day has been a little too much for the heart, though sometimes it is simply dependent oedema and at other times the cause lies with a measure of anaemia or low blood protein. Considering the very large number of elderly persons, and that so many of them have slight signs of cardiac failure, there may well be hundreds of thousands of persons on digitalis. Though digitalis has many beneficial effects it also has many disadvantages and, as indicated below, toxic effects. It is difficult to lay down hard and fast rules about the use of digitalis for elderly persons but generally if a patient is put on the drug there should be some clear evidence that it is doing him good, and if this is not so, a continuation of the drug may cause an unnecessary loss of appetite, which can be a very important matter if the elderly patient is not well nourished.

The elderly appear to be more susceptible to the toxic effects of digitalis; even digoxin 0·25 mg daily can produce toxic results.

The usual symptoms of over-dosage are anorexia, nausea, vomiting, headache, blurred vision and diarrhoea. But in the elderly there is also a risk of mental confusion or even a frank psychosis. Anorexia can be quite important if the patient is malnourished and one is hoping he will eat more and build up his strength. Again many elderly patients can be apathetic and not make much mention of nausea or an occasional vomiting.

As regards the toxic effects of digitalis on the heart itself one should bear in mind that in the elderly patient the heart is more likely to be severely damaged and further, the patient is probably on a diuretic and subject to the risk of potassium deficiency. It is this latter complication which seems so important in the elderly for so often the general toxic effects are minimal or clouded by the patient's lack of alertness and the toxic effects on the heart predominate.

Usually digitalis slows the heart rate, especially the ventricular rate if the patient has atrial fibrillation. This slowing is considered to be due to vagal inhibition of the impulses from the atrial to the ventricule. Greater dosage of digitalis can further slow the heart, causing bradycardia or heart-block. But digitalis also increases the excitability of the cardiac muscle and may bring about ventricular presystolies.

In the early stages these presystolies occur after each normal ventricular beat, giving the effect of coupling of the pulse, this being a sign of some over-dosage of the drug. If the drug is now given in excess the number of presystolies may increase and the pulse rate will go up but still be very irregular, and yet the patient may not show the general toxic manifestations. Thus at this stage it may be wrongly thought that the patient has uncontrolled atrial fibrillation and that further digitalisation is indicated.

Since further digitalis treatment could then lead to almost any form of arrhythmia – e.g. paroxysmal atrial tachycardia – or even ventricular fibrillation – it is clearly important to know what dosage of digitalis the patient is receiving and for how long it has been continued. In cases of doubt it will be necessary to have an electrocardiograph. Over-dosage with digitalis usually causes sagging of the S–T segment in leads 7 and 8, together with ectopic atrial or ventricular beats. At the same time one should consider the possibility of excessive potassium loss. If there is evidence of over-dosage it would probably be advisable to give potassium chloride 2–3 g by mouth daily for a few days, and stop digitalis treatment.

In conclusion one should perhaps re-emphasise that digitalis intoxication is one of the causes of mental confusion in the elderly.

Skin Conditions

Skin affections are commonly seen among the elderly and, fortunately, the advice of a dermatologist can generally be obtained and acted upon.

ULCERATED LEGS

Elderly patients with ulcerated legs can be a special problem in the geriatric ward. The patients tend to remain in the ward for a very long period, the ulcers heal very slowly, and after discharge ulceration so often tends to recur. A procedure outlined by a discussion on ulceration and varicose veins by Rivlin 40 has been found to be of particular value. Rest in bed is not advocated and the rationale of the treatment is to encourage the patient to use his legs in a normal manner. The muscular movements press on the deep veins and enhance the return of blood to the heart, and in this way lessen oedema of the part due to stagnation. The patient does not require admission to carry out the treatment. Briefly, the procedure is as follows:

A strip of non-adhesive elastic bandage is applied to the affected leg from the dorsum of the foot extending upwards over the front of the tibia. An elastic adhesive bandage is now applied from the base of the toes to well above the ulcerated part. A 'Dalgo' bandage is very suitable. A non-adhesive elastic bandage, such as Poroplast, is now applied on top of the adhesive bandage. The patient wears these two bandages for a period of a week, or more at first, and the bandages are then replaced. The interval of replacement is gradually lengthened; the bandages are readily removed with a pair of scissors down the front of the leg where the strip of non-adhesive bandage has been placed.

While under bandage treatment, the patient is instructed to move his legs normally, avoid standing still, wear shoes, not slippers, not sit with the legs crossed, or sit close to a fire, and when sitting normally to carry out a foot exercise, namely flexion and extension of the foot by tapping the floor. The elderly need careful instruction and encouragement, since they have in the past so often been advised to sit down more, not to use the leg too much, and so on.

Even when the patient's ulcer has healed up, it may be necessary for him to continue with a non-adhesive bandage, and at times have a further treatment with the adhesive bandage. The procedure appears to be admirably suited to the geriatric patient.

Metabolic Disturbances

OBESITY

Many obese patients are seen and the condition is more common among women than men patients. Obesity, apart from being undesirable in

Diet for Obesity
Approximately 1000 Calories

Breakfast	Tea *or* coffee with milk, no sugar 1 egg *or* portion fish 3 Ryvita *or* Vitaweat biscuits Butter thinly spread Fresh fruit *or* tomatoes
Mid-morning	Bovril 1 plain biscuit *or* fresh fruit
Dinner	Lean meat, chicken, rabbit *or* steamed fish (moderate helping) Greens, cauliflower, marrow, spinach, fresh beans *or* green salad Carrots, turnips, onion, leeks *or* tomatoes Fruit raw *or* stewed without sugar
Tea	Tea with milk—no sugar 3 Ryvita or Vitaweat biscuits Butter thinly spread Green salad, Marmite, meat *or* fish paste
Supper	Cheese *or* lean ham *or* eggs *or* fish *or* lean meat (moderate helping) Greens (as at dinner) *or* salad 2 Ryvita *or* Vitaweat biscuits Fruit raw *or* stewed without sugar
Daily allowance	Butter ½ oz Milk ½ pint

Note – The foods in the diet may be rearranged to suit taste provided the quantities are kept approximately the same. Instead of 8 Ryvita biscuits, 3 oz bread may be taken during the day. A 'moderate' helping of various foods is indicated below:

Meat	2 oz
Fish	3–4 oz
Cheese	1–1½ oz
Greens	6 oz
Root vegetables	4 oz

¼ pint of milk allowance may be taken as junket, milk jelly, or egg custard sweetened with saccharine, once during the day.

(A) ALLOWED: *These foods are not fattening:*
(1) Salads (without oil or dressing)
(2) Cooked vegetables
(3) Fresh fruit and fruit stewed without sugar
(4) Clear soup, Bovril, Oxo, Marmite, lemon and water (no sugar) Meat and fish pastes
(5) Saccharine for sweetening, vanilla and other flavouring essences

(B) FORBIDDEN: *Do* not *eat:*
(1) The following sugary foods: sugar, sweets, chocolates, jams, marmalade, honey.
(2) The following starchy foods: cakes, pastry, puddings, sweet biscuits. (Bread and unsweetened biscuits only as shown on your diet sheet).

general, also throws an extra burden on the heart and it is frequently associated with, and a casual factor in, hypertension. It may be also very essential to reduce obesity if an operation is being planned, especially if it is one on the abdomen.

There is no particular difficulty in drawing up an obesity diet, and an example is attached. The great difficulty is to get the patient to follow out instructions. In the elderly, these instructions must be very simple, and in practice it seems important to instruct them in what articles of diet they can have without any anxiety. The patient is allowed to eat as much as she likes of vegetables provided fat is not used, salads and tomatoes without oil or mayonnaise, beetroot, radishes, watercress, parsley, fresh fruit of any kind, clear soup, broth, Bovril, Oxo, Marmite, salt, pepper, mustard, vinegar, Worcester sauce, potatoes provided they are not fried, roasted, sauted or chipped, fish only if boiled or steamed, lean meat, poultry, liver and kidney, provided there are no additions of bread or thick sauces.

Only small pieces of bread should be allowed, and the following articles of diet should not be eaten: butter, margarine, fats, sugar, jam, marmalade, honey, sweets, chocolates, cocoa, puddings, ices, dried fruits, biscuits, toast, oatmeal, cereals, rice, macaroni, spaghetti, etc. Restriction of fluid should be avoided.

If the patient has adopted a stagnant way of living, she should be encouraged to take all reasonable exercise. The patient should be weighed weekly. A drastic reduction in diet is usually far too disagreeable and further, it takes some time to alter dietetic habits. The treatment, therefore, should aim at a steady reduction in weight. Usually the patient will have to continue weekly weighing and restrict her diet as required.

Successful dieting may be all that is required in mild cases of diabetes mellitus, and in the hypertensives it often causes a fall in blood pressure and relief of symptoms. Though at first the patient may feel a little queer, eventually there is likely to be a great improvement in general well-being.

HYPERTHYROIDISM

If a patient has obvious hyperthyroidism, it is hardly likely to be overlooked, but there are many elderly patients who have symptoms suggestive of, but not sufficiently diagnostic of, hyperthyroidism. There may be a slight exophthalmos or tachycardia, undue sweating, loss of weight, nervousness, anxiety or brisk reflexes. Sometimes there is a cardiac irregularity without an apparent accountable cause. Undoubtedly, when hyperthyroidism is suspected, the patient should be referred to the radiotherapist for an assessment of thyroid action. Dependent on the strength of radio-iodine 'take-up', the radiotherapist is then in a position to advise on the extent of any hyperthyroidism and to give an estimated dose of radio-active iodine by mouth if indicated. Many elderly patients have been treated in this way with excellent results, and it is worth while stressing that the assessment and treatment is quite painless, and of course devoid of all risks of operation.

When it is impossible to confirm the diagnosis by the above method, one may have to rely on the therapeutic effect of an anti-thyroid compound to point to the true state of affairs. A therapeutic trial in this way, using carbimazole (neo-mercazole) 5 mg three times daily, has been found to be very beneficial in quite a number of patients, there being an increase in weight, a lessening of exophthalmos, sweating, tachycardia, etc. It would appear that there are a number of elderly patients with mild hyperthyroidism who would benefit from investigation and treatment.

MYXOEDEMA

A few patients with gross myxoedema are admitted to the wards every now and then. The difficulty in diagnosis seems to be that the patient's myxoedematous change comes on so gradually over months, or years, that this change is not noticed by a doctor constantly attending the patient, though it is all too apparent to some other physician. Minor hypothyroid features can even more readily escape diagnosis. The usual points to look for are – myxoedema affecting the nose and face; large flabby tongue; falling out of the hair with absence of the outer half of the eyebrows, and a deposition of fat about the nape of the neck, backs of the hands and abdomen. The patient is also likely to complain of constantly feeling cold and of obstinate constipation. The blood may show a microcytic, a normocytic or a macrocytic type of anaemia. A significant finding is considered to be a blood cholesterol above 350, but in practice the elderly often have high cholesterole, without any particular symptoms. Sometimes the most outstanding symptoms may be mental and there is likely to be slowing of thought processes, which may be accompanied by mental confusion. There may, or may not, be an enlarged thyroid gland. Hypothyroidism may be suspected in an obese patient, or if some of the clinical features mentioned above are present.

PITUITARY MYXOEDEMA

If hypothyroidism is present, though it is usually simple hypo function of the thyroid, this cannot be assumed always to be so. The hypofunction of the thyroid may be secondary to failure of the pituitary. Under these circumstances there may be an accompanying lack of suprarenal function. It requires fairly exhaustive tests to ascertain any failure of the pituitary or suprarenal functions and the fact that the patient does not show Addisonian pigmentation does not necessarily mean a normal suprarenal. Since it is dangerous to give thyroid extract in the presence of suprarenal failure it is generally safer to prescribe a small dose of prednisone, e.g. 5 mg daily at the start of thyroid treatment indicated below.

A therapeutic trial with thyroid extract may be the best method of establishing a diagnosis. L-thyroxine sodium 0·05 mg may be given once a day. It is unwise to start with a large dose because the treatment may quicken the pulse and throw an extra strain on the heart. At the end of a week, the dose may be increased to L-thyroxine sodium 0·05 mg b.d., and this should be sufficient to bring about a therapeutic response, marked by a clinical improvement in the patient and a lowering of the blood cholesterol. If the diagnosis is established, the thyroid dose may be increased gradually, but should be limited to the minimal dose which will keep the patient clinically free of symptoms. Any associated hypochromic anaemia or hyperchromic anaemia is likely to respond to iron and thyroid respectively, but if there is an Addisonian anaemia, vitamin B12 may become necessary.

HYPERGLYCAEMIA AND DIABETES MELLITUS

A very important survey of some 25 700 persons at Bedford has been carried out by Sharp, C. L. et al[43] as to the incidence of glycosurea and hyperglycaemia. They found that urine testing for glucose was often too insensitive for the diagnoses of hyperglycaemia or diabetes. Further, though sensitivity was improved, by testing urine after a loading dose of 50 g glucose, this gave many false positive results amongst the younger age groups. Their criteria for the diagnoses of hyperglycaemia or diabetes or pre-diabetes was a blood sugar above 120 mg/100 cm³ two hours after taking 50 g of liquid glucose. Their conclusion on the incidence of diabetes was as follows:

| | Treated Cases | | | Untreated Cases | | |
Dectection	Severe	Symptoms Mild	None	With symptoms up to	Without symptoms up to	Total incidence up to
Clinical biochemistry glucose tolerance	0·1%	0·5%	0·11%	3%	9%	12%

Year 1962

That 12% of persons should have a measure of diabetes or hyperglycaemia is of course an indication of a metabolic disorder on a considerable scale. Since this figure applied to persons of all ages and since diabetes is more common in the elderly, the incidence of hyperglycaemia in the elderly is likely to be much above 12 %. The authors laid emphasis on the particularly high proportion of random non-diabetic elderly persons showing hyperglycaemia. They further correlated the incidence of hyperglycaemia with vascular disease; with the following results:

	Blood sugar below 120 mg/100cm³	Blood sugar above 120 mg/100 cm³	Total
Number in sample	480	90	570
With symptoms or signs of arterial disease	134 (27·9%)	39 (43·3%)	173 (30·35%)

The importance of the survey is far-reaching, not only as to the number of undetected and untreated persons for diabetes but also because it reveals there are a large number of people with hyperglycaemia. In the light of the above findings a random sample (excluding known diabetics) of some fifty elderly patients on admission to a geriatric ward were selected by Hazell, K. and Ortiz, S. The patients were each given 50 gm of glucose and a blood sugar estimation was done two hours later. The results obtained were correlated with the incidence of eye-lens opacity, the pulsation of the popliteal arteries and the extent of cerebro-vascular accidents. They were as follows:

	Blood sugar below 120 mg/100 cm³	Blood sugar above 120 mg/100 cm³	Total
Number in sample	16 (32%)	34 (68%)	50
Number with Glycosurea	Nil	12 (24%)	
Number with Lens Opacities	1	10	
Number with Impaired flow in Popliteal arteries	2	10	
Number with Cerebral Thrombosis	5	14	
Number with Blood Sugar over 200 mg/100 cm³	Nil	9 (18%)	

Again in this survey it should be noted that in practice random urine testing for glucose is not detecting hyperglycaemia and is unlikely to do so because of high renal thresholds. The question naturally arises whether old people should have their blood sugars done more routinely. Recently a strip reagent has become available, i.e. Dextrostix. If a drop of blood is put on the Dextrostix a colour reaction will indicate the level of the blood sugar. Should this procedure prove to be sufficiently accurate it should then be possible to diagnose many diabetics at present escaping detection. It is intolerable that with a free National Health Service tens of thousands of diabetics remain unknown and untreated. Incidentally it is clearly wise that reagents for detecting diabetes should be made freely available to doctors, so that they are commonly in use. Sometimes the general practitioner has to meet the cost of the various reagent strips.

It may well be considered that the hyperglycaemia causes athero-sclerosis as suggested by the authors' correlation with arterial disease, and if they have hyperglycaemia (even without the symptoms) whether they should be treated as mild diabetics with the object of preventing the complications of diabetes and the onset of atherosclerosis. The hyperglycaemia may be an innocent association with ageing though this is hard to believe; or it may, perhaps, be a major cause of the arterial changes and other manifestations of degenerations that occur in so many elderly people.

From what has been said it will, therefore, be no great surprise that despite the various diabetic clinics throughout the country, patients are admitted to the wards without previous diagnosis of diabetes having been made. Usually the patient has been admitted for some other reason and the condition is discovered by a routine urinary examination, but in a few instances an undiagnosed diabetic is first seen in coma. There appears to be a fairly large number of elderly people with mild diabetes, that is to say, they only suffer from glycosuria occasionally. The diag-nosis is therefore easily missed unless previous to urinary examination the patient is given a loading dose of glucose, or submits to a glucose tolerance test. Sometimes the patient has been declared controlled on a restricted carbohydrate diet and returned home. Elderly patients, how-ever, often do not keep to a prescribed diet, and as a result continue to suffer from symptoms of diabetes.

The symptoms may not be severe, as would result from acidosis or coma, but are sufficient to cause poor health, polyurea, mild dehydration and perhaps dermatitis. There are again a number of diabetics with a high renal threshold, and they do not show glycosuria even on repeated urinary examination. A few patients have been seen with all the features of a diabetic dermatitis, which has continued for well over a year, while the general practitioner has dismissed the idea of diabetes because no sugar was found in the urine. These patients have been proved by sugar tolerance test to be diabetics but to have a high renal threshold. The dermatitis has responded satisfactorily to insulin therapy.

ORAL HYPOGLYCAEMIC AGENTS

The very elderly living alone, or in poor home conditions, are often unable to administer insulin to themselves. Even when it is possible, they often fail to do so. In many instances, a relative or a district nurse cannot manage to call in daily to give insulin. Even if a small dose of insulin were considered advisable for the large number of elderly mild diabetics, it would be practically impossible to have it administered. Until recently, such cases were better controlled by dietary restriction.

The drugs that can be used are the sulphonylureas group, i.e. Tolbutamide (Rastinon) and Chlorpropamide (Diabinese) and the Diguanides Group, i.e. Phenformin (Dibotin) and Metformin (Glucophage), the latter group acting in a quite different manner to the former. For the use of those drugs the reader should refer to a text-book of medical treatment. However, as regards tolbutamide this drug, which may be given by mouth, has now been tried out extensively throughout the world and found to be satisfactory in properly selected cases. The drug would appear to be eminently suitable for elderly mild diabetics, who can then treat themselves. The effects of long-term treatment can hardly be assessed until the lapse of several years but so far the drug does not appear to cause any serious complications or untoward symptoms. A number of cases have been treated in the geriatric unit along the lines outlined by Conn.[11]

Briefly, the therapeutic procedure is as follows:

Patients taking up to 40 units of insulin a day may be controlled by tolbutamide alone, though many patients do not show a satisfactory response if on such a high dosage. The therapy is not suitable for patients who have had diabetic coma, or for those in which the diabetes is complicated by infection, trauma, gangrene or kidney or liver impairment. Hypoglycaemic reactions may occur, as with insulin and should be treated in the usual manner. The tolbutamide may also cause mild indigestion or nausea and skin eruptions such as urticaria or dermatitis Such symptoms subside quickly if the tolbutamide is stopped, or may even disappear though the drug is continued. If a patient is on tolbutamide and becomes subject to another illness, such as pneumonia, nephritis or coronary thrombosis, the tolbutamide may be ineffective in controlling the diabetes. Should ketonuria appear, then it is important either to supplement with insulin or change completely to insulin therapy. In very elderly people a maintenance dose is likely to be one tablet three times a day, but in most instances it is less than this. Those requiring a greater dose than this do not seem to be satisfactorily controlled by tolbutamide. The results have been very encouraging, and there is every reason to think that elderly diabetics who would otherwise require small doses of insulin daily can be more effectively controlled by the use of tolbutamide or other oral hypoglycaemic drugs.

Response of the Elderly to Drugs

DRUG POISONING

Nowadays massive amounts of drugs are prescribed to patients. In former times bottles of medicine mainly consisted of Galenicals, i.e. extracts of plants, and were relatively harmless with very rare possibilities of overdose. Today most drugs are special chemical substances made in a laboratory. This change came about with the introduction of sulphonamides. These modern drugs have a very effective therapeutic action but usually also important toxic side effects. The dangers of drug poisoning are now very real, especially amongst the elderly. The latter may have poor eyesight and poor memories and they can be taking even up to 15 various types of tablets – can get into quite a muddle. The difficulties become even more as new drugs come on the market almost weekly. Many patients admitted to hospital show signs of drug overdosing, example digoxin, artane, phenformin, diabenase, barbiturates and so on. The hazards of drug overdosage can perhaps be lessened if all bottles of tablets are clearly marked; if drugs with known possibility of toxic overdosage are avoided as much as possible and if there is more medical supervision or supervision by a responsible relative, home nurse or health visitor.

It can be understood that many elderly persons have loss of reserve functional capacity and may indeed be living with a very small margin of safety, especially as regards pulmonary function, renal function, cardiac action, etc. It is obvious, therefore, that this margin of safety should not be further reduced – as it well could be – by the use of a drug which is unsuitable for them either because of an accompanying small toxic effect (of no importance to a younger person) or because the established dose is, for them, too high.

The actual pharmacological action of any drug is likely to be the same in both an elderly and a young person but by and large the established dose of any drug has been arrived at not only by biological assay and other methods but from what has been found to be safe and effective in ordinary medical therapeutics. In this regard the customary dosage of a drug in the past has been built up on experience with what are now relatively younger age groups in the country. It is only of recent years that the very elderly have been numbered in millions. For instance, the British Pharmacopoeia gives the dose of Morphine Hydrochloridum as one-eighth to one-half of a grain, which may be increased. One has little hesitation in stating that for an elderly person of, say, 80 or for one with impaired pulmonary function a dose of half a grain of morphine could be fatal and that any greater dose is out of the question. Dosages of drugs as at present established in the Pharmacopoeia cannot altogether be accepted for the very elderly without the confirmation of further and more extensive experience as to the effects on the very elderly in whom there are very many individual physiological variations and a lesser margin of safety.

In all patients the response to a drug is to a certain extent an individual matter but whereas in the young, as stated above, there is almost invariably a large physiological functional reserve capacity, in the elderly there is a general diminution of this capacity and perhaps a very serious one in some particular aspect, e.g. pulmonary function or renal function. The carrying out of a routine of pre-operative and post-operative administration of drugs which may be suitable for the young can precipitate dangerous complications in the elderly patient.

The effects of a drug are influenced not only by the dosage but by its rapidity of absorption, its diffusion through the body, action, detoxication and excretion, and in all these aspects the elderly show variations from what is normal in the young, and many individual variations in their own age group. For instance, the fate of barbiturates after absorption is that they are partly destroyed in the body and partly excreted into the urine. Gaddam[18] states: 'After a dose of barbitone the drug can be detected in the urine for as long as 14 days, but 45% is excreted in the first 24 hours.' If, therefore, the secretory power of the kidney is impaired – as it often is in the elderly – it is clear that an untoward accumulation of the drug will take place and the usual prescribed dosages and repetitions of the drug would be inappropriate for that patient.

There can be so many variations in the 'fate' of drugs administered to the elderly that to establish the correct dose one has to feel one's way at first by prescribing small doses and return to the patient from time to time to ascertain the clinical effects. Rarely can any effective drug, new to the patient, be prescribed in such and such a dosage for a long period of time without the advisability of repeated clinical assessment. It may be understood that the correct assessment of any particular drug can be a little difficult, but the matter is often made more complicated still by the drug firms, which frequently put two or three drugs, sometimes with opposing action, together in one tablet.

A patient treated with a tablet or injection in which there is a combination of drugs, *A*, *B* and *C*, might require relatively more of *B* and less of *A*, another more of *A* than of *B*, and so on. Though this compounding of drugs is moderately satisfactory it appears basically wrong in principle and its very convenience often masks its disadvantages. In the case of the elderly these disadvantages are of increased importance, and for them it is generally advisable to use single drugs rather than combinations in the same tablet or injection.

Many textbooks lay down a regime, sometimes in tabulated form, for this or that illness or emergency. No drug should be given in accordance with this without a clinical examination and a clear indication of its need. For instance, one patient suffering from haemorrhage from a peptic ulcer may be unduly anxious and restless without any impairment of pulmonary function. In such a patient morphine might well be indicated. Another, perhaps elderly, patient with the same haemorrhage may be quite calm but noted to have an impaired pulmonary action; for him morphine could be unnecessary and possibly dangerous because of its side effects of depressing the respiration. Younger patients can usually be fitted into some therapeutic regime according to types of illness or operation, but the elderly require a more individualised approach.

The various drugs commonly used in the treatment of elderly patients may now be considered in more detail.

HYPOTENSIVE DRUGS

There are various drugs which bring about a fall in blood pressure but hypotension in an elderly patient is generally undesirable. This is because the arteries are generally more rigid in the elderly and the heart responds unfavourably to changes in blood volume even of a transient nature, and so often any fall in blood pressure means an insufficiency of supply to vital organs, such as the brain, the heart itself or the kidneys. It is important, therefore, to enquire whether the patient is on any drug likely to cause a severe drop in blood pressure and to use with caution any drug which may have this effect. The drugs in common use which have a hypotensive effect are Rauwolfia (Serpasil) and the Chlorpromazine and Promazine groups (Largactil, Sparine, etc.), both of which have a relatively mild hypotensive action and a greater tranquillising action. The more effective hypotensives are usually ganglion blocking agents of the Pentolinium Tartrate variety (Ansolysen, Ecolid, Inversine, Bretylium, Tosylate, Guanethidine, etc.). The latter group of drugs have the added disadvantage of causing paralysis of the parasympathetic ganglia and lowering the tone of smooth muscle, and in an elderly person may bring on paralytic ileus or, in elderly men with enlarged prostate, retention of urine. Most narcotics or hypnotics, including the barbiturates, in effective doses are also liable to lower the blood pressure and depress respiration.

NARCOTICS

All narcotics interfere temporarily with the cell metabolism of the neurones, usually causing imperfect oxygenation and, if given in large doses, they will cause excessive drowsiness or even coma. Apart from the particular effect of any one narcotic an excessive state of drowsiness or sleep has many disadvantages to the elderly patient. It means that he will be lying in bed in a supine position for a long time during which some impairment of respiration may be going on and if there is a weak control of bladder action he may be incontinent. The patient is unlikely to turn about in bed as during natural sleep and can the more readily develop a pressure sore. If the drowsiness is very prolonged there will be no opportunity to give fluids and the patient can go into dehydration. The drugs in common use are:

Morphine This is usually given by injection but its rate of absorption can be variable. A patient with a very impoverished circulation or in a slight state of 'shock' may absorb the drug very slowly and there may be no clinical effect during the time usually expected. The physician may now be tempted to give a further injection and then, as both injections become absorbed, the effect may be that of an overdose. This matter of delayed absorption is, of course, true for all injections. The great disadvantage of morphine is that it depresses respiration, particularly the cough reflex, the latter being a most serious matter if there is any mucus within the lungs that should be coughed up. It is rarely advisable to give a dose of morphine above gr one-sixth until the patient's response to this drug has been ascertained. Morphine at times causes nausea and vomiting and is not always suitable for a patient with gastric haemorrhage.

Pethidine Hydrochloride (*Demerol*) This is, in action, rather similar to morphine but in a dose of 50 or 100 mg by injection is less potent. Like morphine, it closes the sphincter of Oddi and is, therefore, not indicated for bilary colic.

Chlorpromazine Hydrochloride This drug produces calmness and some drowsiness but in therapeutic doses does not cause deep sleep or coma or depress the respiration or cough reflex. Whilst the patient is under its influence he can still receive food and fluids, move about in bed and co-operate in his nursing care. The drug, therefore, has great advantages over morphine in many instances. It can be given by mouth, e.g. in dosage of 25 mg TDS ranging up to 100 mg TDS. By mouth it may take a day or so to have its full effect. It can also be given by injection in dose 50 mg or even 100 mg in a very agitated patient but then acts fairly quickly. The drug seems to be the one of choice for the patient who is confused, restless and agitated rather than in great pain. There are, however, accompanying features of a moderate lowering of the blood pressure and temperature and at times a toxic feature of jaundice, and, very rarely, the more serious condition of agranulocytosis. There are many other drugs allied to Chlorpromazine Hydrochloride which do not cause these toxic features and can therefore be used with greater safety.

Barbiturates There are various barbitones in use, e.g. Veronal, Soneryl and, for an action of short duration, Amytal. They have a hypnotic

action but also depress the hypothalamic centres with control of auto-
nomic activities. Amytal, for instance, may lower the blood pressure
unduly. Barbiturates in general do not appear to be very suitable for
the elderly because of their probable accumulative effects. All too
commonly they cause some mental confusion or even mild delirium.

Chloral Hydrate BP (0·3–2 gm) This has an effect in about half an
hour and enhances sleep for six to eight hours. The drug is detoxicated
by the liver – so the function of the kidneys is not so important. It has
very little cumulative action and because of this is often the drug of
choice for an elderly person. It is usually given in solution but can also
be administered as a tablet, e.g. Welldorm.

Hyoscine Hydrobromide BP (0·3–0·6 mg) This drug is sometimes used
for a very restless patient and its effect lasts for about six hours. Its
peripheral effect is like that of atropine, paralysing the action of most
of the cholingergic nerves and thus depressing the vagus nerve to the
heart and dilating the bronchi. It may also paralyse the action of the
bladder. The latter action, like the ganglion blocking drugs, may bring
on retention of urine in an elderly man.

Paraldehyde Ampoules of 2 ml, 5 ml, 10 ml are available. This hypnotic can be given by mouth but is usually given intra-muscularly in a
dose of 5 or 10 cm³. The drug should be fresh and not exposed to sun-
light, which can cause it to give rise to acetic acid. If injected it must be
into a bulky muscle because it is likely to cause sloughing if it escapes
under the skin. It is quite a painful injection. This local irritant action
and its tendency to cause coma makes its use rather hazardous in the
elderly. One, therefore, advises *against* the use of Paraldehyde – even for
Status Epilepticus since a barbiturate injection is preferable.

Alcohol The taking of alcohol is a widespread social habit. Alcohol
can be rightly classified as a drug; it is a useful and not very expensive
tranquilliser; it tends to cheer people up, it also stimulates the appetite,
causes vasodilation and diuresis. Properly used it therefore has a place
in therapeutics. But it is habit forming and also has toxic effects on the
brain, the liver and various organs throughout the body. Some old
people – like young people – drink to excess though the number is small
probably because of the expense. Nevertheless some elderly patients do
get drunk and can fall about, have a phase of incontinence or phases of
restlessness and bad temper. If they are in the habit of taking alcohol it
is also important to consider more carefully the prescription of drugs,
since alcohol can accentuate the action of many drugs in common use.
A large intake of alcohol in an elderly man can and often does precipitate retention of urine, this resulting in a medical emergency. At intervals
patients are admitted to hospital in a confused and restless state. If a
careful history is taken sometimes their condition can rightly be ascribed

to alcoholism; perhaps with some added infection, e.g. bronchitis. At other times the confusion and mild delirium is found to be due to the 'withdrawal' of their customary intake of alcohol whilst in hospital. There are many instances therefore when the patient should be given some alcohol, example a bottle of beer or sips of sherry, according to the patient's custom – to prevent withdrawal symptoms.

DIURETICS

The usual indication for a diuretic is congestive heart failure with oedema. Commonly the oedema is obvious with swelling of the legs and pitting oedema where the swelling has taken place. There may also be ascites or pleural effusion present and an obvious right heart failure. At other times the diagnosis of oedema may be difficult. Puffiness and slight swelling of the ankles is not uncommon in elderly people but may be due to a dependent position of the legs and will clear up if they walk about. Again, oedema is not always solely due to heart failure, but sometimes more to an accompanying anaemia, under-nutrition or hypoproteinaemia. When the patient is lying in bed oedema in the legs may, of course, clear up and as a routine one customarily looks for its presence in the sacral region. In many patients evidence of some cardiac failure may be missed unless the sacral region is examined and also the base of the lungs for persistent moist crepitations. When an operation is under consideration it is probably advisable to try the effects of a diuretic on the latter type of patient, who might respond very favourably to it. The usual diuretics cause an excessive excretion of both salt and water and it is important not to overtreat the elderly patient who can more readily go into both dehydration and salt depletion, particularly if the patient is thin and under-nourished.

Mercurial Diuretics Preparations in common use are Novasurol or Mersalyl. They act by inhibiting the re-absorption of chloride ions and in this way increase the excretion of chlorides and water. The effect may be enhanced by also giving ammonium chloride by mouth. Novasurol and Mersalyl act with exceptional speed and can promote a massive diuresis. In an elderly patient there is a danger from the speed of action since the need to pass urine frequently may wear him out or, alternatively, the bladder may become over-distended, leading to retention of urine; the latter is a very serious hazard for elderly men in bed. The usual dose for Mersalyl is 1–2 cm³ by injection but if given it is probably advisable to start with ½ cm³ and repeat it according to the effect.

Saluric (Chlorothiazide tablets 0·5 gm) This drug, which can be given by mouth, has a similar action to that of Mersalyl in causing diuresis but it also causes an excessive excretion of potassium. It does not produce as massive a diuresis as Mersalyl and therefore a more gentle and continuous action can be sustained with its use. The depletion of potassium can be made good by giving potassium chloride tablets BP 500 mg. Some drug firms already have combined potassium and chloralthiazide in one tablet, e.g. Hydrosaluric K. However, the use of the combined tablet has one disadvantage, namely, that potassium may be given in excess, and this could be important if there is any renal failure.

The above-mentioned diuretics can bring about such considerable loss of sodium chloride that for practical purposes it is unnecessary to place a patient on a salt-free diet, and in fact it may be advisable, where there is considerable loss of sodium chloride in the urine (as estimated by the Fantus test), to give the patient sodium chloride by mouth, e.g. sodium chloride 0·5 g gelatin-coated capsule. Usually digitalis is given in association with the above diuretics and, of course, it also causes diuresis.

ANTIBIOTICS

There are now a multitude of antibiotics in use, many of which have important side or toxic effects. The side effects take on an added importance in the elderly because they are often on the verge of vitamin deficiency and respond very poorly indeed to a phase of diarrhoea.

There is particular danger in giving antibiotics by mouth. The mixture of organisms constituting a normal healthy bacterial flora in the nose, mouth and alimentary tract can be very deranged by oral antibiotics in any patient. There are variations in the amount of antibiotic absorbed from the bowel and it appears that the absorption process is somewhat slower and less effective in the elderly than in the young, with a consequent over-concentration of the antibiotic in the bowel and a lesser one in the blood stream. There is, therefore, a greater possibility of a patient developing glossitis or ulcerative stomatitis or diarrhoea, and in this respect aureomycin, chloramphenicol terramycin and the newer antibiotics may do more harm than good. Then again there is the possibility of a resistant organism developing and being conveyed about the ward. Penicillin-resistant staphylococcal infections seem to have been causing more trouble recently. One is inclined, therefore, to give antibiotics by injection rather than by mouth and to give full treatment over a short period, i.e. not more than five days, and to give the patient vitamin B complex to avoid vitamin deficiency.

Before commencing any antibiotic therapy it is advisable, of course, to isolate the organism and to apply sensitivity tests to the various antibiotics. Unfortunately, especially with acute chest infections, this is not always possible. At the same time it is most important to curb the infection quickly in, say, a debilitated elderly patient. The efficacy of the antibiotic in a young patient is usually shown by a rapid return of the temperature to normal, but the elderly patient often shows very little fever, so one may have to judge the effect of the antibiotic by an improvement in the clinical condition. Where no sensitivity test has been performed it may become apparent, but only after a few days, that the infecting organism is resistant to the antibiotic chosen. To avoid this possibility it may be considered advisable to give a combination of two antibiotics initially until the result of the sensitivity test is known. If the organisms are resistant to penicillin they are very likely to be sensitive to streptomycin or aureomycin. Unfortunately streptomycin tends to give rise to resistant organisms and more particularly to resistant strains of tubercle bacilli if used in a tuberculous patient, unless it is combined with other anti-tuberculous drugs, e.g. isoniazid 200 mg or sodium aminosalicylate 20 gm daily. The risk of producing a resistant strain of tubercle bacilli is, however, not of any great importance. A combination of antibiotics such as penicillin and streptomycin (conveniently combined in one ampoule – Seclomycin) may, therefore, be given initially if considered advisable.

The Importance of Drugs

The importance of drugs, their usage and poisonous effects can hardly be over emphasised for in 1969[59] The *Journal of Medicine 4* 'Poisoning and drug induced disease' page 274 there were 283 million prescriptions costing £163 million. In the same journal (page 273) an article by Henry Matthew states concerning all age groups that 'in Britain at least 10% of acute adult medical admissions to hospital have taken an overdose'. Again in Scotland a campaign to bring in unwanted medicines in the home resulted in a total of 4½ million tablets and capsules handed in for destruction; almost half were hypnotics or tranquillisers[60] Wilson, G. M. *Prescribers Journal* June 1972 (page 63).

One would have to be extremely foolish to think all the drugs issued are beneficial to the health of the people, more likely to be otherwise and a saving in this direction might well pay for a new hospital each year or pay for a liberal attendance allowance or twice the number of home helps.

Clearly completely free medicine is not always the boom some politicians think it is. The giving of drugs is not the key to good health. A new form of illness namely that due to the treatments has required a new label viz. Iatrogenic disease. Because there are now so many drugs and so many have poisonous effects it is all the more important to assess the significance of the data on which indication for their usage is based so as to avoid dangerous medication.

CHI-SQUARE SIGNIFICANCE TEST

Quite often figures are quoted intended to support a particular drug or line of treatment and are so presented as to appear to be highly significant but one can be misled by an impression and really at least one test for significance should be used. The Chi-Square test is based on the hypothesis that there is no difference in result beyond that caused by chance.

The formula is:

$$\chi^2 = \sum \frac{(|O - E| - \frac{1}{2})^2}{E}$$

Ref. Statistical Analysis, Edward C. Bryant, McGraw–Hill Book Company (page 113).

Here O = observed frequency
E = expected frequency

For example:

Carcinoma of the Breast

Treatment	O	E	$|O-E|-\frac{1}{2}$	$(|O-E|-\frac{1}{2})^2/E$
X Survival after 5 years	10	7·5	2	0·533
Died	40	42·5	2	0·094
Y Survival after 5 years	5	7·5	2	0·533
Died	45	42·5	2	0·094
Total	100	100·0		$\chi^2 = 1·254$

If treatments X and Y were of equal value the number surviving in each group would be proportional to the numbers surviving in the whole sample. Thus out of 100 persons 15 survived so that out of 50 persons 7·5 are expected to survive and 42·5 to have died. Reference is now made to the Chi-Square table for $\chi^2 = 1·254$ and the tables indicate that the above result could have risen by chance 20 times in a hundred. This gives the significance of the treatments provided each group was equivalent that all were of the same age, sex, state of health, the same extent of the cancer and no one died in a road accident, from heart failure, a stroke and so on. Such conditions can rarely be met in medical trials so comparisons are rarely truly significant unless thousands of persons are tested. Then again the national mortality rate should be referred to. There are many treatments for carcinoma of the breast but for England and Wales the deaths among females in 1960 were 9042 and in 1973 11 495, so the treatments do not appear to be very effective.

On the contrary tuberculosis in men the deaths in 1960 were 2463 but in 1973 tuberculosis of the respiratory system for both sexes in England and Wales were 859. This is a great reduction, so that the treatments are undoubtedly effective. (Ref. *Annual Abstract of Statistics* 1974, page 40.)

One has turned away from the mumbo and jumbo and ritual in medicine prevailing a century ago but there is always the risk of succumbing to doctrinaire and pseudo scientific outpourings still with us today.

Summary

This chapter has dealt with some of the medical problems in the elderly, and points of interest have been briefly dealt with. The object in this has not been to give a full account of geriatric medicine, because this would encompass practically the whole of general medicine, but to draw attention to the fact that there are numerous clinical features and conditions peculiar and almost limited to the elderly, and that the medical study of these, and related social conditions, constitutes a speciality in its own right.

It is also hoped that the brief discussions and information of these conditions in the elderly will arouse further interest in those who have their medical care.

REFERENCES

1 ADAMS R D 'Recent Developments in Cerebrovascular Diseases' *British Medical Journal* 5 April 1958 page 785

2 *Ibid* page 786

3 ADAMS G F McQUITTY F M and FLINT M Y *Rehabilitation of the Elderly Invalid at Home* fig 2 page 45 The Nuffield Provincial Hospitals Trust

4 BELL G O *The Surgical Clinics of North America* **34**, 3 page 578

5 BERK Nathanial G 'The Principles of Sound Nutrition in the Aged' *Geriatrics* May 1958 **13**, 5 page 334

6 BOMFORD W B M 'Prostatectomy for Retention of Urine' *The Lancet* 5 September 1959 page 262

7 BRANSBY E R and OSBORNE B 'A Social Food Survey of the Elderly, Living Alone or as Married Couples' *The British Journal of Nutrition* 1953 **7**, 1 and 2 page 160

8 *British Medical Journal* 14 March 1964 page 650

9 CHINN Austin B 'Some Problems of Nutrition in the Aged' *The Journal of the American Medical Association* 22 December 1956 **162**, 17 page 1912

10 CHRISTENSEN E 'Appendicitis in the Aged' *British Medical Journal* 4 October 1958 page 832

11 CONN Howard F *Current Therapy* 1958 page 307

12 COOK J B 'The Residual Urine in Bladder Rehabilitation' *Proceedings of the Royal Society of Medicine* April 1960 page 265

13 COWDRY Edmund V   *Problems of the Ageing*   1952   page 629

14 DAVIES Dean F and SHOCK N W   'The Variability of Measurement of Insulin and Diodrast Tests of Kidney Function'   *The Journal of Clinical Investigations*   1950   page 505

15 DELLER D J and BEGLEY M D   'Bone Changes after Partial Gastrectomy'   *Modern Medicine of Great Britain*   **9**,   7,   July 1964   page 497

16 DUNLOP D M   *Text-book of Medical Treatment*   1955   page 102

17 FRANKS L M   *The Lancet*   1956   pages 11 and 1037

18 GADDAM J H   *Pharmacology, 5th edition*, page 137

19 GAMBLE J L   *Companionship of Water and Electrolytes in the Organization of Body Fluids*   1951   Lane Medical Lectures

20 HALLAHAN J K   'Symptomatic Relief of Osteoarthritis and Osteoporosis with Vitamin B12'   *American Practical and Digital Treatment*   1952   3: 27

21 HANDY H G   'Discussion on Prostatectomy – Early or Late'   *Proceedings of the Royal Society of Medicine*   July 1960   page 538

22 HAZELL K and OATWAY A W N   'Senile Osteoporosis and Osteomalacia'   *Geront. clin.*   5 : 203–208   1963

22A HAZELL K and BALOCH K H   'Vitamin K Deficiency in the Elderly'   *Geront. clin.* 12 : 10–17   (1970)

23 HEANEY R P and WHEDON G D   Calcium – 45 Dinamics in human metabolic bone disease   Presented to Endocrine Society   New York   1 June 1957

24 HOBSON W and PEMBERTON J   *The Health of the Elderly at Home*   (a study in Sheffield)   page 196

25 HODKINSON H M   EXTON-SMITH A N and CROWLEY M F   'Diagnosis and Assessment of Osteoporosis'   *Post-graduate Medical Journal*   1963   **39**   433–7

26 HOUGHTON B J and PEARS M A   'Chronic Potassium Depletion due to Purgation with Cascara'   *British Medical Journal*   7 June 1958   page 1328

27 *The Lancet*   21 February 1959   page 398

28 MACHELLA Thomas E   'Masked and Obvious Vitamin Deficiency States in Older Age'   *Pennsylvania Medical Journal*   1955   **59**   page 589

29 MINISTRY OF HEALTH   *Report*   1957   part II   page 257

30 *Report*   part II   table 1   page 23

31 *Report* on the State of Public Health   1962   page 13

32 *Nutrition Sourcebook*   1955   page 100

33 page 202

34 page 222

35 OLBRICH O   FERGUSON M H   ROBSON J S and STEWART C P   'Renal Functions in the Elderly'   *Edinburgh Medical Journal*   1950   page 127

36 PRICE *Textbook of the Practice of Medicine* page 1624

37 RANDALL H T 'Water and Electrolyte Balance in Surgery' *S Clin. North America* April 1952 **32** 445 469

38 REGISTRAR GENERAL *Statistical Review of England and Wales* 1956 part I Tables Medical Table 17 page 134

39 *Statistical Review of England and Wales* 1959 pages 11 and 30

40 RIVLIN Stanley 'Ulceration and Varicose Veins' *Proceedings of the Royal Society of Medicine* October 1956 volume 49 pages 785–8

41 ROSS J M H 1959 *Geront. clin.* **I** 2 page 174 'Prostatectomy in the Octogenarian'

42 SCHECHTER D C and MERVINE C K 'Current Concepts in the Management of Osteoporosis' *Journal of the American Geriatrics Society* August 1958 **V1** 8 page 592

43 SHARP *et al* *Proceedings of the Royal Society of Medicine*

44 SHOCK N W 'Kidney Function Tests in Aged Males' *Geriatrics* 1946 page 223

45 SORSBY Arnold Blindness in England 1951–4 Ministry of Health

46 *Ibid* page 7 table 6

47 *Ibid* page 32

48 *Ibid* page 42

49 *Ibid* page 44

50 STEIGLITZ E J 'The Nephritides' Geriatric Medicine 1954 pages 579–80

51 *Ibid Nutrition Sourcebook* pages 225–6

52 *Ibid Geriatric Medicine* page 336

53 STEINER R E *Proceedings of the Royal Society of Medicine* **51** 7 page 480

54 THOMPSON R K and SMITH G W 1951 'Experimental Occlusion of Middle Cerebral Artery during Arterial Hypotension' *Trans. Amer. Neurol. Ass.* 76 203

55 WOLTERECK H *A New Life in Old Age* page 139

56 WOODFORD-WILLIAMS E and WEBSTER D 'An Anabolic Study with Norethandrolone in Four Elderly Underweight Males' *British Medical Journal* 13 December 1958 page 1447

57 WRIGHT Samson 'Consequences of Excess Salt and Deficient Salt in Renal Function' *Applied Physiology* 1953 pages 63–64

58 YATES P O and HUTCHINSON E C 'Cerebral Infarction: The Role of Stenosis of the Extracranial Cerebral Arteries' *Privy Council Medical Research Council Special Report Series* *300*

59 *The Journal Medicine 4* 'Poisoning and drug induced disease' page 274

60 WILSON G M *Prescribers Journal* June 1972 page 63

6

MENTAL DISORDERS IN THE ELDERLY

K. L. G. NOBBS, GM, MB, BS, FRCPE

Consultant Physician (Geriatrics)
South and East Birmingham Groups of Hospitals
University Clinical Lecturer
University of Birmingham

Mental illness in old age falls into two main categories:

(1) Primarily psychiatric illness
(2) Mental disturbance due to other causes

The first category is the province of the psychiatrist. The second category covers all other forms of mental disturbance including 'organic mental syndrome'. If the family doctor is in doubt as to whether a patient is primarily suffering from purely mental illness or whether mental symptoms are secondary to toxic confusional state, it is advisable, initially, to consult a physician. The most difficult cases are those which cannot clearly be placed in either category, and the term 'psychogeriatric' is usually applied to this type of patient.

If a geriatric physician is in charge of such patients in designated mental beds, i.e. in a mental hospital or department, it is advisable to have sufficient experience in psychiatry to enable him to apply to the Local Authority for powers under the Mental Health Act 1959 by virtue of special experience in the diagnosis and treatment of mental illness. This recommendation covers the whole of the United Kingdom and is renewable every 5 years.

Misplacement of physically ill patients in mental hospitals produces mortality nearly three times that of correctly placed psychiatric cases. The mortality of misplaced psychiatric cases in geriatric units is more than twice that of the correctly placed medical cases. Among survivors, misplaced patients were less often discharged than properly placed patients.[1]

A large proportion of mental disorders in the senium can be treated successfully.[2] As the number of people in this country aged over 65 is about $7\frac{1}{2}$ million and rising the problem is one of magnitude.

The ageing process is described in another part of this book and is, in considerable part, due to failure of replacement of cells which wear out by equally efficient cells. In the case of the central nervous system it is generally accepted that when such cells die they are not replaced at all and so continued function can only be maintained by introducing previously inactive cells to take over the functions concerned. This is one reason why cerebral damage, e.g. cerebral thrombosis, can be treated by rehabilitation probably by opening up new pathways in the central nervous system. The effect of diminished circulation on the central nervous system is often compensated for by an increased stroke volume in the cardiac output, which may be attained by a rise in the blood pressure or in the heart rate. It is, therefore, manifestly dangerous to attempt reduction of what might be described as compensatory hypertension by the use of ganglion blocking or equally powerful drugs. The result may well be catastrophic, not only in the brain but also in other vital organs such as kidneys, liver, supra renals, etc. Hypertension in the elderly should only be treated when causing symptoms directly attributable to it or by signs such as exudates or other signs in the optic fundus. A blood pressure of 200/110 at age 70, provided there are no attributable signs or symptoms, can be considered quite acceptable. At least part of the reason for this decline in circulatory efficiency is due to the degeneration of the muscular and elastic layers of the arteries and arterioles and their replacement by fibrous tissue. This constitutes arteriosclerosis, not to be confused with atheroma, and means that the elastic and muscular recoil of the peripheral circulation on the closure of the valves at the end of systole does not take place and has to be compensated for in some way as described above.

It can be accepted that the ageing brain is as it were on a knife edge of hypoxia. Any reduction in the supply of oxygen to the brain is therefore much more critical than in younger age groups. The same applies to the supply of glucose (the brain's main source of energy) and the clearance of waste products. Thus in the ageing brain compared with the younger and middle-age groups we have relative hypoxia, starvation and autointoxication even in health.

SPECIFIC MENTAL ILLNESS

Any patient with an endogenous mental illness who lives until over 60 will carry his condition with him and until the so-called degenerative diseases of old age have either an aggravating or depressing effect upon them, they will present as at any other age and in the appropriate manner.[2]

    a. Affective psychosis
    b. Senile psychosis
    c. Arteriosclerotic psychosis
    d. Organic mental syndrome
    e. Late Schizoid (paraphrenia)
    f. Miscellaneous: e.g.
        G.P.I.
        Epilepsy
        Secondary to heart failure
        Cerebral tumour
        Head injury (including chronic subdural haematoma)
        Secondary dementias (syphilis, demyelinating disease in the brain, similar to subacute combined degeneration of the cord and due to the same aetiology, i.e. lack of Vitamin B12).
        Cerebral Buergers disease
        Migraine
        Polyarteritis
        Endocrine
        (Myxoedema thyrotoxicosis)

(a) AFFECTIVE PSYCHOSIS

The majority of these patients can be improved by psychiatric treatment and can be discharged, relieved and treated as out-patients. On the other hand the majority of senile psychotics die within 2 years. Psychosis due to arteriosclerosis falls between these two (affective disorder and senile psychosis) for chronicity, mortality and prognosis. Senile and arteriosclerotic psychoses together form the majority of admissions to mental hospitals of the geriatric group. Of the delirious states (toxic confusion, organic mental syndrome) approximately half die and the other half are discharged relieved. Organic degeneration due to senescence or other causes, e.g. toxic, tends to bring out endogenous psychotic tendencies but in an unrelated manner, i.e. these are two separate disease processes. On the other hand specific pathology such as Huntington's Chorea, Alzheimer's disease, Pick and Jacob-Kreutzfelt syndrome advance to dementia as a part of their natural progress. The last mentioned is sometimes misdiagnosed in its early stages as progressive muscular atrophy or motor neurone syndrome, as the most noticeable symptoms are weakness in the leg and arm muscles with fasiculation. Psychometric tests may show up a dementing process which is not overt in such cases.

Dealing in some more detail with affective psychosis, this presents largely as a mood change. It frequently occurs in old people and the end result may well be a depressed or apathetic state in a previously hale and hearty old person. Industrialisation has led to disruption of families, the young active members following their occupation as it moves, leaving the old folk in their backwater. Old people are compulsorily retired at age 65 usually without proper preparation for retirement. The psychological shock of being 'surplus to requirement' causes a rapid vegetating affect in some people. This effect is not only mental but physical, e.g. coronary thrombosis and strokes within one year of retirement occur far too frequently. If such people are kept active in some other way either in part time employment or hobbies, sports, clubs, etc., such catastrophic effects can be avoided.

The rise in numbers of mental disorders in the elderly is greater than can be accounted for by the mere increase in numbers. There are schemes in some firms and industries and professions where an elderly person can be usefully employed but at slower speeds. It is no good for instance expecting old people to keep up with the modern production line as apart from causing them mental distress there is the back lash effect on the younger individual who wants to get on with the job. Without such stimulus introspection occurs leading to hypochondriasis, depression, apathy and sometimes suicide. In some cases depression may not be overt, but may present as constipation, listlessness, insomnia, slowness, loss of efficiency, sexual deviation, loneliness, inability to adapt to new situation, e.g. admission to hospital, and finally carelessness, slovenliness and gradual dissolution. This is especially likely to occur where there is a neurotic tendency earlier in life. Loss of spouse is a frequent immediate cause for depression. Old people have low reserves and what would be a slight stress in a younger person may cause complete breakdown in the elderly.[3] Hypomaniacal episodes may lead to erotic excitement (sexual assaults, exhibitionism, etc.). This condition carries a poor prognosis due to exhaustion, etc. Such cases are best treated by the psychiatrist as powerful drugs and ECT and psychotropic treatments including surgery can bring about dramatic improvement.

(b) SENILE PSYCHOSIS
The majority of these patients die within 2 years. It used to be thought that their prognosis was 6 months but in fact it is now 2 years or more and this is partly due to earlier admission to mental hospitals which in turn is partly due to the overcoming of the stigma of 'putting Mum away'. This diagnosis has been the 'dustbin' of failed diagnosis, as referred to elsewhere in this book and reference 3.

Senile dementia is one form of senile psychosis and can more often than not be actually diagnosed clinically, certainly with a cortical biopsy showing more than 7–12 amyloid plaques per high powered field of the optical microscope.[6]

Clinical diagnosis is aided by negative findings such as the absence of cerebrovascular episodes and the absence of remissions and the progressive mental deterioration with early loss of personality, pride in appearance and continual incontinence with no distress to the patient. Localised forms such as Alzheimer's disease may retain personality considerably longer. An electroencephalogram may also be of assistance as may examination of the fundi and CSF.

(c) ARTERIOSCLEROTIC PSYCHOSIS

This is characterised by episodic psychiatric and neurological disorders with personality retained to a late stage. It need not necessarily be associated with systemic arteriosclerosis. Each episode leaves residual deterioration. Senile psychosis and arteriosclerotic psychosis together carry a 70% mortality within two years as against a 10–20% mortality over the same period in affective psychosis. There are various methods of differential diagnosis. Some are purely psychiatric but assistance can be obtained from examination of the fundus oculi, CSF and cortical biopsy and EEG.

Many other clues may be present such as peripheral arteriosclerosis, X-ray evidence of calcification in aorta or arteries, moderately elevated blood pressure which in such cases is compensatory, as described in my own general remarks above and should *never* be lowered by the use of hypotensive drugs as the only result will be to say the least of it deleterious and could produce disastrous results such as coronary thrombosis, uraemia and further aggravated mental confusion and possibly strokes as well which might present as 'little strokes' (these usually present as mild transient dysphasia, diplopia and clouding of consciousness without actual loss), to a major stroke and hemiplegia. The induction of such tragic episodes would not justify the end and would come into the category of iatrogenic disease. It is necessary to treat pathological hypertension (i.e. a level of say 300/140 BP) which is causing symptoms such as tinnitus, vertigo, headaches, etc. In such cases examination of the fundus will often show evidence of exudates or haemorrhages and possibly papilloedema thereby confirming the pathological nature of the hypertension. Another aid to differential diagnosis from senile psychosis is that the prognosis is considerably longer even up to 5 or 10 years or more.

(d) ORGANIC MENTAL SYNDROME

This group of mental disorders includes a wide variety of causes, in fact any disturbance of the endogenous or surrounding status quo. It is perhaps helpful to bear in mind the differential causes of actual coma, which could be considered in a conscious patient as the cause of mental confusion without or with incontinence, such as trauma, infection, new growth, diabetes, uraemia, haemorrhage, drugs and so on, the list being almost endless.

To this list should be added the commoner infections such as otitis media, pneumonia, meningitis, cystitis, pyelonephritis and even perhaps going so far as septic corns and acute paronychia. Other common causes are dehydration, vitamin deficiency (particularly Pellagra), senile phthisis, cachexia from any cause including cancer and general malnutrition, the latter of which is quite often in its turn due to loneliness and self neglect. The main points in differential diagnosis between this condition and arterioscolerosis or senile psychosis are that the patients concerned are confused but attempts at rationalisation are made. This may occur in arteriosclerotic psychosis but other points of differential diagnosis made above should be helpful in separating them.

In senile dementia particularly rationalisation is not attempted. On the other hand this is a feature of the Korsakow syndrome due to alcoholism which comes in the drug and toxic category. It is important to make this differential diagnosis as an organic mental syndrome is eminently susceptible to treatment and the prognosis relatively good. Perhaps a good way to define organic mental syndrome is that it is a condition in which mental symptoms are related to or caused by some physical disturbance in the body not basically of psychogenic origin. It may be present in three main groups which can be described as:

(1) *Neurasthenia* This presents itself in many ways familiar to the family doctor, e.g. irritability, poor concentration, emotional lability, 'aches and pain' (including headaches), clumsiness, tremors.

(2) *Delirium* As in neurasthenia but with the addition of hallucinations, delusions, disorientation, confabulation (especially in Korsakow syndrome due to alcohol (vitamin B1)), Marchiafava due to damage to corpus callosum, Pellagra (vitamin B7). Obviously treatment of this condition has to be related to the cause, i.e. withdrawal of alcohol, replacement of vitamin deficiency, as indicated.

Having mentioned the Marchiafava syndrome due to disturbance of the corpus callosum a rare case in my experience occurred where a patient was admitted in a state of confusion and delirium associated with hemiballismus which proved to be due to syphilis. Treatment with penicillin cured the hemiballismus and when the patient came to post mortem some years later a healed gumma in the corpus luysii was found.

(3) *Dementia* This is a more severe form of 1 and 2 found together with incontinence of urine and or faeces without distress to the patient, loss of personality and self respect with general deterioration both physical and mental.

Basically the reason why the above states occur more commonly in old age is that the circulation is less efficient and the replacement of broken down cells is slower. The net result of this in the brain is reduced available nourishment (mainly glucose) and oxygen together with inefficiently cleared waste products. The elderly brain is relatively hypoxic and any condition which tends to aggravate this may bring about a state of confusion. This can be anything from cardiac and pulmonary inadequacy or intoxication from the bowel or by ingestion (barbiturates, digitalis, etc.). Drug intoxication is quite common and it must be borne in mind that with reduced renal efficiency, drugs normally excreted by the kidneys are retained in the body longer than is the case in younger patients. This applies particularly to digoxin. Sometimes mental confusion is the only sign of serious illness in the elderly, e.g. penumonia, uraemia, cardiac infarction.[3]

(e) LATE SCHIZOID (PARAPHRENIA)[2]

The late schizoid type of mental disorder, often called paraphrenia, is commoner in women. There are hearing and visual defects in 25%. The main features are delusions with regard to property, money, neighbours, sexual desires of others, systematised hallucinations (visual, auditory and olfactory).

These patients often have a history of schizoid episodes in the past which may not be brought out unless sought for. The onset *de novo* of schizoid states, which may be labelled paraphrenia after the age of 60, is not all that unusual and carries on the whole a poor prognosis for mental recovery. Physically such patients appear to be in good health and they form a large section of the in-patient community of a mental hospital for the rest of their lives. It is similar to schizophrenia in younger patients but the elderly can be more difficult to rehabilitate to the community.

(f) MISCELLANEOUS

The last group can be classified as above and includes various non-specific cortical atrophies which may cause anything from mild confusion to grand mal or dementia. Loss of tendon reflexes and diminished vibration sense are not uncommon in the elderly and may not be of any significance though they should not be disregarded especially when associated with extensor plantar responses which also in their turn occur without obvious CNS lesions in some old people.

Section 29 of the Mental Health Act 1959 is sometimes misused to bypass the geriatric waiting list. Cases can be admitted under section 25 of the Act or informally when admission to a geriatric unit or general hospital would have been more appropriate.[4]

TREATMENT

Elderly patients are best treated out of bed because the erect posture eases the load on their myocardium and also helps to keep bowels and bladder in better tone and prevents decubitus ulcers. This is why a geriatric chair is of such value in the treatment of the elderly. Supply of oral fluids is essential, together with salt. Old people can be dehydrated but not thirsty due often to salt deficiency as in 'heat stroke'. Antibiotics are very effective, sub-cutaneous perfusion is very useful but intravenous medication is only given in selected cases as the risk of pulmonary oedema is considerable.

Occupational therapy and physiotherapy should not be regarded merely as a method of rehabilitation but should be extended to the, as it were, non-rehabilitatable patients as it does maintain them at the peak of their condition, poor though it may be. Physical and psychological therapy of this kind may not appear to the uninitiated as being of any use but anything which increases the circulation of the blood and makes the patient more comfortable and helps prevent or ease pressure areas, urinary infections, pneumonias, etc., is clearly of the greatest value.

Unfortunately, due to staff shortages and too low rates of pay, this ideal is not at present attainable in our hospitals and we have to content ourselves with limiting occupational and physiotherapy to patients who are likely to be rehabilitatable. Even this is at present inadequate and recruiting desperately needed in both professions. In the case of cerebro-vascular accidents it is of the essence that treatment in this direction, i.e. Occupational Therapy and Physiotherapy, should be instituted as soon as possible even though a certain amount of confusion is quite usual even after the 5 days period from the stroke has been completed. Only after these 5 days have passed is it possible to give any prognosis in a case of CVA, conscious, unconscious, confused or otherwise.

When using drugs it is advisable to avoid those which increase cortical hypoxia such as barbiturates though even these may be used with large doses of ascorbic acid (500 mg daily). Continuous oxygen may be given by Tudor Edwards spectacles or the Venturi mask provided that carbon dioxide narcosis is combated by respiratory centre stimulants such as Coramine at 2 hourly intervals, reduced if twitching occurs.

Cerebral arteriolar dilators may be useful and small doses of nicotin-amide will give a clue as to whether they are likely to be effective. Some authorities feel that such medication is never effective and a waste of time and money. While it is agreed that sclerosed vessels cannot be dilated by such drugs my own experience is such that I am convinced they do work. It may be that the mechanism is by opening up collateral circulations which have not become sclerosed. In any case such drugs as

Cyclospasmol and Duvadilan have been shown by thermocouples and red cells labelled with radio active isotopes to increase the flow in the internal carotid artery. It is sometimes necessary to discontinue the use of such drugs as the degree of insight into his condition by the patient is increased and causes distress in a number of cases. Discontinuance of the drug results in the reversion of such patients to their previous comparatively calm and unemotional state.

Heart block can be treated by sustained action Isoprenaline (Saventrine). Care must be exercised with patients on anti-depressives – (side effects of mono amine oxidase inhibitors with amines (ephedrine, adrenaline, amphetamine) and intake of cheese, bananas, marmite, etc.). Personally I do not send out mentally ill patients who are still requiring MAOI type drugs but wean them from these onto the tricyclics or one of the other anti-depressive drugs. The reason for this is that they cannot really be relied upon to avoid these articles of diet mentioned above. The elderly, like children in many ways as far as their response to drugs is concerned, are particularly susceptible to the opiates. Side effects of the MAOI group when combined with amines is rapid, and severe hypertension with subarachnoid haemorrhage is a commonly presenting fatal sign. This group potentiates pethidine about ten times.

Anti-depressives which lower blood pressure must be used with caution otherwise catastrophic results mentioned above can be brought about by such treatment and may then correctly be labelled iatrogenic hypotension. Imipramine (Tofranil) is one of the most notorious of these and if used at all should be used with extreme caution, using the geriatric 10 mg tablet. It is probably best given at night so that the orthostatic affect is not added to the drug affect in producing hypotension.

I have found that 8 hourly medication with the phenothiazine type of drugs results in a smoother affect with a smaller dose than the t.d.s. regime. The reason for this, particularly in psychotics, is that overnight there may be 12 hours between doses during which time the drug is diluted and the patient becomes aggressive or disturbed as previously.

Digitalis should be used in roughly half the maintenance dose as for an adult. It is not at all uncommon for patients on digitalis to present with mental confusion. Particular care is also required when using oral diuretics. Everybody knows that special care is taken to replace potassium when using oral diuretics but sometimes sodium loss is such that the patient becomes salt deficient and dehydrated. Correction of the electrolyte imbalance alone may correct the confusional state and the concomitant physical disorder due to disturbance of homoeostasis.

There is a critical period of 12 weeks up to which patients are ready and prepared for discharge when fit. The relatives having been advised on the patient's admission that we hoped to improve his condition sufficiently for return home are also prepared during this period. After a 3 month period however the patient tends to become 'institutionalised' and this has been described by some authorities as 'institutional neurosis'.[5]

MENTAL HEALTH ACT 1959

Mention has already been made of the advisability of obtaining powers under this Act when in charge of mentally designated beds. This will enable the consultant concerned to act as a second signatory for section 25 of the Act (28 days detention in hospital) and may well save time involved in calling in a consultant psychiatrist. Section 29 of the Act, the old 3 day order, can be put into effect by a general practitioner and the mental welfare officer. It is necessary on such occasions to ensure that there is a bed to receive the patient in the mental hospital chosen. Under the Act hospital does not necessarily mean a mental hospital but follows the definition of a hospital laid down in 1946. Section 30 of the Act enables a 'responsible medical officer' to detain a patient in hospital for three days. This usually means the consultant but could be an SHMO with special responsibility as a responsible medical officer is defined as a doctor in ultimate clinical charge. Section 26 of the Act enables patients to be held for longer periods subject to appeal to the respective authority, i.e. the Area Health Authority.

NATIONAL ASSISTANCE ACT 1948

Powers exist under this Act for the forcible removal and detention in hospital on the order of a magistrate after application by the community physician in conjunction with the general practitioner concerned. This action is taken when a person is in obvious need of care and protection and a danger to himself or others. This need not necessarily be a mental hospital. These powers are not widely used. Indeed in the city of Birmingham I believe it has only been used about ten times in as many years.

COURT OF PROTECTION

This is a branch of the high court of London to which application can be made for an order placing the affairs of a patient who is incapable of running them himself in the hands of a receiver who may be a relative or a solicitor. Application for such an order would be made by the physician in charge of a patient who felt that advantage might be taken of him by relatives or others.

CONCLUSION

I would like to emphasise that the best place to tackle the problem of the elderly sick, mentally and physically, is in the home particularly ensuring that any lonely people are reintegrated into the community with a proper diet which for old people means a high protein diet and supplementary vitamins.

REFERENCES

1 KIDD C B B.M.J. December 1962 *A study of patients admitted to Geriatric and Mental Hospitals Misplacement of the elderly in hospital*

2 MAYER-CROSS W SLATER E and ROTH M *Clinical Psychiatry* Cassell & Company (1960)

3 NOBBS K L G 'Confusion in the Elderly' *The Lancet* 22 October 1960

4 PATTERSON and DOBBS *British Journal Psychiatry* March 1963 'Section 29 of the Mental Health Act 1959'

5 BARTON R *Institutional Neurosis* published John Wright & Sons Bristol 1959

6 SIM M TURNER E and THOMAS SMITH W 'Cerebral Biopsy in the Investigation of Pre-Senile Dementia' *British Journal Psychiatry* February 1966

7

THE NURSING CARE OF PATIENTS IN A LONG STAY HOSPITAL

W. A. HURR, SRN, SCM, RMN

TYPE OF PATIENTS

Amongst the patients in the long stay ward it is common to find those suffering from such conditions as:

loss of power of a lower limb, chronic osteoarthritis, rheumatoid arthritis with gross disablement, hemiplegia, Parkinson's disease, multiple sclerosis, diabetes mellitus, Paget's disease, chronic bronchitis and emphysema, bronchial asthma, chronic heart failure, malnutrition, advanced carcinoma, mental confusion or patients with blindness, deafness or aphasia.

They have usually been under treatment for some time before, in assessment wards of other hospitals. There they have been X-rayed, medically examined and undergone blood tests, electrocardiograms and so on and have been under treatment before they come to the long stay hospital. All those admitted generally require a good deal of nursing. They have come to the stage in their lives when they are too incapacitated, ill or confused to look after themselves. A man may have been cared for by his wife for many years; she dies and he is left alone. Or a woman may have been looked after by her husband and he dies and again there is an emergency situation. All too often the strain of looking after an aged relative by a single daughter or a sister or a housekeeper leads to a complete breakdown of the latter. One finds that the long stay patient may have been in hospital several times and she seems to know all about her own symptoms and what treatment she should have. This adds to the difficulty of nursing them because what the patient thinks should be done may be quite out of date.

SOCIAL PROBLEMS

Very few old people live in the right accommodation. Many of them live in blocks of flats with too many stairs to climb. Some are cared for by a busy mother looking after her own small children, probably also doing some part time work and she really has insufficient time to look after an elderly relative. Usually the task is left to a single daughter who after months or years can suffer a complete mental or physical break-down. Patients have been admitted to a long stay hospital direct from nursing homes or rest homes because they, or their relatives, have run out of money. They may also be admitted because they have become too dirty in their habits, too difficult to manage or too mentally confused to stay in a home. Occasionally a patient living like a recluse, alone and perhaps in appalling conditions, is admitted on a magistrate's order.

FINANCIAL PROBLEMS

A man and his wife both receiving an old age pension do manage to scrape along on the money they receive from the state, but if one of them dies there is a real hardship for the one left behind. Many will not apply for social security as they feel it is like asking for charity. As a consequence they may get behind with payment of rent, or live on poor, unsuitable food and suffer from malnutrition. The winter is a great hazard for the aged because apparently they can't afford enough money for sufficient heating and lighting, neither are they able to prevent the rooms being draughty, with a result they more readily become subject to bronchial pneumonia and hypothermia.

There is a completely opposite state of affairs between those who are in financial difficulties and those patients who have money, but hoard it up and are not willing to spend it on matters necessary for their health and welfare. Such an instance was a gipsy who came into hospital with a necklace of gold sovereigns as her personal property who nevertheless was in a state of considerable self-neglect.

The Long Stay Hospital

The hospitals in which long stay patients are usually nursed were not purpose built; most of them are old public institutional type of buildings; not designed to house sick, elderly people. These buildings have been taken over by the National Health Service. Outside some look depressing and forbidding, but a great deal can be done to improve the inside where there is the will and the energy to turn them into bright homely places. It is important to gain the support of the members of the building works committee and to be asked to see the plans of any structural changes, so that the point of view of those actually nursing the patients can be properly considered. The wards should be at ground level because of the risk of fire; floors should also be on one level with a minimum of steps and stairs into other rooms or corridors; doors should be wide enough, especially those of lavatories and bathrooms, to allow wheel chairs and sani-chairs to go through easily. There should be, adjacent to the ward, a day space to receive patients who are up and about or able to use their wheel chairs and overcrowding should certainly be avoided. The ward should be well lit and well ventilated and it is important that the windows can be adjusted to avoid draughts – nothing is more uncomfortable than having to sit near a window or a door that is wide open. Where there are large windows through which the sun can shine too fiercely, venetian blinds or sun blinds should be provided for patients are very unhappy in the hot sun and often cannot move themselves and are unable to or will not ask to be moved to another position.

FURNITURE

Beds should not be too high, otherwise patients will not be able to get into them or too low as this may cause the staff to develop backache. The mattresses should be made of rubber or foam rubber and covered with a waterproof cover. Blankets should be of the aertex variety as this makes frequent laundering possible. Pillows should have disposable covers. Polythene disposable macintoshes now replace the previous heavy rubber ones. Chairs should be of the right height; the winged arm-chair with padded arm rests can now be bought in pleasing colours and they can easily be wiped clean. Disposable chair seats are very useful for the worse type of incontinent patient. Day rooms should be decorated in light pastel shades and a few nice pictures are an attraction and should be changed occasionally. Dining-room space is important so that the ambulant patient can be helped to carry out little exercises and to walk short distances. Patients seem to enjoy their meals more if it is served at a table rather than if a plate of food is placed on the tray of their geriatric chair – in which they have been sitting all day. Cantilever tables are much appreciated by patients and especially those who are able to write their own letters. Lockers should be light with formica tops which can be easily cleaned, and they should be placed so that a patient can pick up their belongings easily; otherwise a patient may fall out of bed stretching for something beyond their reach. There is a special kind of unit furniture which combines a wardrobe, dressing table and chest of drawers and also adds more privacy to the patient as it divides one bed from another. Some day rooms can be carpeted with 'Heyga-Lux' carpet squares which withstand the wear and tear of wheel-chair traffic and does not stain if fluids get spilt.

BATHING PATIENTS

Patients should be encouraged to have a weekly bath as it adds considerably to their comfort and wellbeing. In the bathroom nurses are able to inspect the conditions of the patients and their skin more closely. Thus they can readily notice any scars or slight bruises and look for excoriation of the skin, under the breasts, or in the groin and observe for any discharges. Some patients have dry hard skin which easily cracks, others have fragile thin skin and this has to be dealt with carefully to avoid causing any bruising. Men, especially those who have some incontinence of urine, are apt to have excoriation of the skin about the groins and scrotal area. There are many trains of thought and contradictions in treating these affected areas. The application of greasy ointment sometimes makes the areas worse and they are difficult to wash off. Frequent washing and drying followed by the application of Sterzac dusting powder or a similar powder seems to be successful. Patients should bathe with as much privacy as possible as no one really likes to be naked in front of others. The bathroom should be warm and the water already at the right temperature before the patient comes in and towels and toilet requisites should be ready at hand. Finger nails and toenails are easier to cut after the patient has been immersed in a warm bath. To assist in the bathing there are available various bathing aids. A bath hoist is a great help because then patients do not have the fear of falling into the bath. A suitable aid for bathing is most necessary for the staff who may have to bath 20 to 30 infirm and elderly patients weekly. Elderly patients do not seem to like showers, nor to be undressed before the water in the bath is ready. The Capecraft bath hoist and system has been found to be most helpful and sparing on nursing time. To avoid fatigue patients can be bathed late in the afternoon or early evening and then put straight to bed. After a bath patients should be put into their clean clothing. Of course ill patients should have a blanket bath.

HAIRDRESSING SALON

This is a great asset to a long stay hospital as a visit to the hairdresser does a great deal to uplift the old ladies' morale and incidentally it gets them out of the ward for a reasonable time. Most women patients like to keep their hair cut short and many have a permanent wave, but if an old lady requests her hair to be left long no pressure should be brought on her to change her mind. Many elderly patients do not like bows of ribbon. The nursing staff can do a great deal to encourage the patient to take pride in their personal appearance and although it is hard work to have patients up and dressed in their own clothes it has a good psychological affect on their wellbeing and is preferable to leaving them sitting in a nightgown and dressing gown. Helping the patient to be up and about also prevents bed sores. As regards the men a barber should be employed to shave them daily and cut their hair as required.

CLOTHING

Women's day dresses should be made of materials which will stand many washings, i.e. Crimplene and orlon, these wash well and do not crease. Dresses can be adapted for the disabled and incontinent patient by opening the back or side seam and sewing in pieces of Velcro at intervals – this being better than using one long piece. Women's cardigans should be made of nylon or orlon as they will then survive the strain of perhaps being washed in a group laundry. A fortnightly dry cleaning service deals with a lot of the problems of keeping clothes clean especially men's jackets and trousers as well as articles of women's clothing. The storing of long stay patients' clothing presents a problem which can be met by employing local labour to fit suitable linen cupboards in each ward which will take dresses, coats and other clothing. Coloured wincyette open backed gowns can be bought from a women's dress shop. Men's nightshirts and pyjamas designed for sitting or bedfast patients can also be obtained as well as shawls for the shoulders, bed jackets and knee blankets.

SHOES

Patients who are ambulant like to go for a walk in the grounds when the weather permits, especially the men who so often have spent most of their lives working outdoors, e.g. gardeners, farm workers and fishermen. The importance of properly fitting shoes has to be seen to be believed. Many accidents are caused by patients attempting to walk in unsuitable footwear or sloppy ill-fitting slippers. Those patients who require special surgical shoes will have to be referred to a surgical appliance fitter. Slippers are only comfortable for the patient who sits in a chair for most of the day.

Chiropody is often necessary to attend to corns, overgrown toenails and foot deformities.

STAFF SELECTION

One of the chief hazards of running a long stay hospital is that whatever one does there is often a shortage of nursing staff and an even greater shortage of domestic and ancillary staff. Advertising in the local press, *Nursing Times* or *Nursing Mirror* often gives a better response if the word 'geriatric' is included in the advertisement. The staff who wish to do long stay work usually write to the matron and also ask to see the hospital. Bearing in mind that one cannot exceed more than the allowed nursing establishment the hospital is at a great disadvantage when staff go on holidays or on courses or absent because of sickness. The greater number of the staff when first employed are often untrained and unskilled. Nursing auxiliaries may come and go; some of them stay only one or two days, some only a few hours, presumably because it does take a great effort to get used to working and caring for the aged. The best type of nursing auxiliaries for this kind of work are those who are more mature. It is important that they have a sense of humour and also the desire to be kind and to look after the aged and chronically ill patients. Some in-service training is essential but one finds it useless to give high powered technical information; their need is more for basic practical lectures on how to lift a patient, how to dress and undress a patient and especially those who have had a stroke or are paralysed in an arm or leg. They should also be taught the taking of temperatures, pulse and respiration, how to feed a patient with difficulty in swallowing, the giving of a disposable enema, the carrying out of an immersion bath or blanket bath and how to observe the patients and be able to give a short verbal report to the sister. They should also be taught how to approach patients and their visitors, be instructed in the care of the patient at night, the reading of the patient's treatment card and instructions in the case notes. They should be gently instructed in dealing with the death of a patient, how to care for the dying and how to lay out a patient after death. It can take a very long time to build up an efficient staff and a happy hospital atmosphere. Long stay hospitals are the patients' home and probably where they will spend their last days, but one must be prepared to listen to and be sympathetic, not only with the patients, but also the staff.

RECEIVING PATIENTS

Old age is no respecter of persons; people from all walks of life come into the long stay wards. Many come in full of resentment and this is not surprising since they may have lost their homes and possessions. They find themselves amongst twenty to thirty old people who are absolute strangers to them; they have lost the privacy of their own homes and most of all have lost their freedom and independence. Change is a strange matter to old people and they are often tearful and unhappy feeling they are a nuisance and cannot accept the service of the staff looking after them. No two patients are alike and one may resent being ordered about by a young slip of a girl no older than one of their grandchildren or in some cases their great grandchildren. Many of these old people have worked hard all their lives, have gone through the experience of two world wars and must find it difficult to be so dependent on the young people around them. The staff should address them by their proper names, treat them as individuals, win their confidence by their kindness and their assurance that the patient's welfare is their concern. They should do all they can to make the patient comfortable which is really rewarding; take time to listen and converse with patients. This is very necessary for patients who have active minds and are still lucid, but even those who are confused and disorientated can sense the atmosphere around them and should not be treated as if they were very foolish or had lost their sanity. With a proper diet, a kindly atmosphere, good nursing care and correct treatment, most patients settle down in a ward very well. But those patients whose behaviour is confused, wandering, noisy or violent may require the prescription of a sedative from the doctor.

PATIENT RELATIONSHIPS

Patients can be jealous of each other and at times quarrel. Having to live in the same ward day in and day out with the same people must be hard to bear, especially with those with irritating habits like constant coughing, spitting, snoring loudly, talking in their sleep or soiling the floor. Patients should be encouraged to look at television, read the daily papers and local newspapers; books with large print can be obtained from the libraries. Where necessary those with defective vision should be referred for eye examination and perhaps prescription of new glasses. Patients should be taken out of the ward from time to time since it is one of their greatest pleasures. Relatives should be encouraged to take the patients out in the grounds for a walk or in their wheel chairs or when they can take them for a ride in their car. Daily visiting should be allowed and whenever possible patients should also be able to see their grandchildren. All the above measures help to relieve the boredom of sleeping and living in a ward. Men and women can be nursed in adjacent wards with some women attendants and nursing auxiliaries working on men's wards and vice versa. Husband and wife patients should be allowed to visit each other every day and take a meal together. Church services and Holy communion normally takes place in the wards and patients are visited by Church of England and Free Church clergymen and Roman Catholic priests. Some patients can be taken to the services in the hospital chapel.

OCCUPATIONAL THERAPY

This particularly helps to relieve boredom which is one of the patients' most tedious problems. Everything should be done to avoid 'institutional neurosis'. Apart from the usual occupational therapy patients appear to like entering competitions in some form of handicraft. Many competitions are run by local welfare authorities and the patients seem to enjoy competing to win a prize, a silver cup or a certificate just as do other age groups. Diversional therapy is also helpful, e.g. bingo sessions, games of dominoes and cards, tea parties, singing old time songs, etc. Birthdays are also worthy of a special mark by providing a birthday cake, glass of sherry, bottle of beer and such like – all of which helps to make life more natural and happier.

PHYSIOTHERAPY

Every long stay hospital needs a physiotherapy department which the patients can attend and sufficient physiotherapists to go around the wards and maintain the patients in as physically fit a condition as possible. Much of the simpler kind of physiotherapy can be done by nursing, but it does require the overall supervision and instruction from a qualified physiotherapist. It is often difficult to obtain a physiotherapy department and the services of a physiotherapist, but the benefit from them both is very soon felt both by the patients and the staff.

It is usual for a medical social worker to visit the hospital every week and attend to the personal problems of the patient, e.g. money, rent, clothes, property, etc.

VOLUNTARY ORGANISATIONS

One of the vital helps for long stay hospitals is to have an active League of Friends. There are some 600 members in our league and there is no limit to the generosity in their efforts to raise money. The league helps in such ways as: running an annual hospital fête to raise money, paying the rent for television in every ward, supplying furniture, carpets, sunblinds, bath hoists, the hairdressing salon, a recreational hall and sun lounge for patients and visitors. Running a canteen service; in part paying for a new ward and a physiotherapy department, managing a trolley shop so that patients can purchase fruit, sweets, cigarettes, writing paper, envelopes, etc., in the wards; keeping a register of lonely patients and arranging for visits to be made to them; helping with Christmas decorations and giving a present to the value of £1 to every patient, sending out birthday cards, providing easter eggs, providing flowers for the chapel and wards in the winter when there are none in the hospital gardens, providing private transport for relatives and friends who cannot afford to visit the patients and at Christmas time setting up shopping stalls in the recreational hall where patients can buy presents for each other or their relatives.

PATIENT – STAFF RELATIONSHIP

A happy atmosphere in a ward depends on the sisters and charge nurses working together as a team. One should ensure that there is careful instruction and communication between staff though this may require constant attention and patience. It is important to select staff who are likely to get on well with their patients and will encourage them to take an interest in what is going on around, and to take a pride in their personal appearance, particularly as regards making an effort to be up and dressed each day. Working for long periods on the ward can cause a lot of petty irritation between staff or between staff and patients. If there is a bad breakdown of relationship with patients it is recommended that an effort be made to find out what has brought about this state of affairs, because if it is allowed to continue it will only get more serious. Usually it is necessary to move that member of the staff or patient who is at fault to another ward.

PATIENTS' PROPERTY

On admission all patients' property should be listed. Money and valuables like jewellery should be put into the hospital safe and a signature obtained by the ward sister or charge nurse that the articles have been received. Aged patients develop strange ideas about their belongings and it is a good policy to see everything they bring in with them is carefully noted. If a solicitor wishes to see a patient they should be taken to a private room. Despite the fact that large notices are put up in hospitals to the effect that the hospital management committee is not responsible for the loss of patients' property, there are many complaints from the patients themselves that some article has been lost or possibly stolen. It is hard to convince the relatives that the patient has in fact put the article like, e.g. false teeth or a gold watch down the lavatory. All the patients' personal clothing should be plainly marked with their own name and the name of the hospital.

PATIENTS' DIET

Elderly patients prefer food that is easily chewed and digested such as: minced meat, minced chicken, steak and kidney pudding, eggs, cheese, fish (filleted), sausages, ham, fresh vegetables, bread and butter, jam, home made cakes, scones or buns, milk puddings, jelly, ice cream, mousse, fruit, etc. Salad and uncooked food is not a favourite with old people though they may like pickles, beetroot or tomatoes. Special diets will be prescribed by the doctor when the patient suffers from a condition like diabetes or extreme obesity, etc. Patients who sit about all day getting very little exercise soon put on weight. Relatives tend to bring them lots of chocolates, sweets and cake. Whilst no one would like to deprive the patients of anything it is a good plan to watch what they are eating and weigh them regularly; a portable weighing machine is a must for all wards. Seriously ill patients usually require a nourishing fluid diet, e.g. complan, bovril, egg nog, milk jelly, casilan, Ovaltine, Horlicks and adequate vitamins should be included in the diet.

WARD MANAGEMENT

Trained staff should already have had experience in geriatric nursing, but they should also be given the chance to attend middle management courses, study day courses, visits to other long stay hospitals, or to exhibitions of hospital equipment or of clothing, mechanical aids and so on, suitable for the elderly. Long stay hospitals cannot be run just like a teaching hospital. There should be a general rota of duties worked out and written instructions should be issued in the wards for the nursing auxiliaries. The latter need constant help and perhaps their greatest need is to be told plainly what to do and how best to help their patients. Charge nurses and sisters have to be very careful and patient, since there is no easy formula for the delegation of duties to junior staff. The trained staff are especially responsible for the patients' welfare, very often over a period of years, during which they have to hear complaints, not only from the patients but also from their relatives. The staff should try to understand the ward problems by periodically having sisters' meetings, discussing each point of view and seeking always for new methods which will improve the patients' welfare. The staff should bear in mind that long stay patients can get well, and can go back to their own homes or to hostels or welfare homes. There should be a good liaison with the consultant physician. He has seen most of the patients either in the assessment unit or in their own homes and the sister or charge nurse should acquaint herself with any useful information as the patient is admitted. The nursing officer in charge of the ward should be responsible for seeing the patients have the treatment prescribed by the doctor at the correct times and that all dangerous drugs in her charge are checked and doses given accurately and properly recorded. Seriously ill patients should not be left entirely to the unskilled staff but the sister herself should observe for any important changes and as necessary report to the doctor. Patients' meals should be served under a trained nurse's supervision with special attention paid to those patients who are unable to feed themselves properly. Bathing should also be adequately supervised. The nurse in charge should arrange a rota of duties for her nursing staff well in advance and since very few long stay hospitals have a domestic supervisor she may be responsible also for arranging the work of the domestic staff.

PRESSURE SORES

Patients who are chairfast or bedfast, incontinent or paralysed are hard to keep free from bed sores, pressure sores, ulceration of the legs, etc., but every effort should be made to prevent these complications as it is always preferable to the long drawn out task of actually treating established pressure sores. There is something to be said for what is now considered to be old fashioned and rather out of date, namely, rubbing the part with the palm of the hand with soap and water then drying it with spirit or eau de Cologne and applying Sterzac powder. If the patient is incontinent do not allow her to remain long in a pool of urine; keep a urine rash at bay by frequent changing, washing and application of a barrier cream, e.g. silicone cream coupled with an ample supply of bed linen, night clothes, etc. One main factor which helps to prevent pressure sores is two hourly turning of the patient from side to side. Large cell ripple beds are also helpful in this matter and can now be rented. Heels and elbows should be protected by specially designed woollen pads. When a bed sore has occurred all dressings should be sterile; swabs may have to be taken for sensitivity tests for an appropriate antibiotic. Amongst the dressings commonly used are, fucidin tulle gras, sofra tulle gras, thovalin gauze, thovalin spray, cicitrin spray, powder or cream, aserbine cream or lotion, eusol and paraffin, or lotio rubra. It is possible to use sheepskin or nylon fleece skins under patients, but with these there is a laundry problem.

INCONTINENCE

Many long stay hospitals in which so many patients have frequency or incontinence have insufficient lavatories, e.g. one or two to 30 patients. Constant reminders for more lavatories when necessary should be sent to the authorities with precise requests – this is likely to be successful but perhaps only after years. Patients with incontinence should be placed near the lavatory and in general they should be encouraged to walk to and from there. Sometimes there is a risk of them falling so that supervision from the nurse may be required, but this is preferable to allowing patients to sit all day in chairs, having no exercise and becoming more confused. Many patients with urinary incontinence will require an indwelling catheter. Either the Portex or disposable Foley type can be used, with a tube and drainage bag. There should be a fixture to hold the bag attached to the bed or chair and it should not be in full view of the patients. Patients' catheters should be introduced with a sterile non-touch technique, but some patients despite all precautions do develop urinary infection, in which case mid-stream and catheter specimens may have to be sent to the laboratory for sensitivity tests. The importance of changing catheters and giving bladder washouts with chlorhexidine and distilled water every week or two is worth mentioning, but there is a lot of controversy about this procedure. It has however given good results in hospital. Elderly patients tend to drink insufficient quantities of fluid but those with an indwelling catheter should take copious amounts. Sometimes it is reported that a patient has not passed urine and on examination one finds that the bladder is distended. Nurses should be taught how to recognise this, how to palpate and percuss for a distended bladder and how to catheterise the patient. Quite often the patient with retention of urine also has a loaded bowel and the nurse should know how to recognise and deal with this also.

CONSTIPATION

Women seem to suffer from constipation more than men, probably because their pelvic floor has been weakened by childbirth or gynoecological operations. Often they have suffered considerably from constipation before their admission and it is likely to continue unless treated. In the 'bowel' book on the ward one may find an entrance that a patient has had a daily bowel action; whereas in reality the patient has been incontinent past a hard mass of faeces in the rectum. Because of this occurrence a sister should be taught how to do a simple rectal examination to establish the true state of affairs. Many patients can have normal bowel actions if given Normax capsules, or 5 ml of Dorbanex periodically. When the rectum is loaded the condition may respond to dulcolax suppositories or a 'disposable' enema; though these will only clear the lower rectum leaving perhaps impacted masses higher up. Such a situation may require repeated suppositories or enemas or even manual removal. Patients who become obstinately constipated are also apt to become irritable and confused and sedatives may make matters worse rather than better. Some elderly patients have a bowel complex; they forget when they have had a motion, imagine they are constipated and secretly take laxatives. Boxes of laxative pills or of Epsom salts may be found in their lockers; though this may not be suspected until the patient has diarrhoea for no apparent reason. A diet including 'All Bran', porridge, fruits, etc., can be helpful in preventing constipation but constant observation and regular bed pan and commode rounds are also needed.

PATIENTS AT NIGHT

Many patients are remarkably different at night. They may be wakeful for such reasons as:
finding it too hot, or too cold, for which more bedclothes can be put on or taken off; finding themselves hungry or thirsty, a drink of Ovaltine may help this; blinds or windows may be rattling; lights are not sufficiently shaded; they are disturbed by other patients talking, snoring or coughing; they wish to use the commode or require a bed pan or their bed is wet, or a urinary catheter has become blocked or they need a change of position or of a dressing.

Patients who become markedly confused at night can be very restless and if on the ground floor wander out of the ward in their nightclothes into the grounds. Things of this nature can happen if there is a shortage of nurses on duty. A patient kept awake by another patient may shout at the offender and wake up everyone in the ward. Some nights can be chaotic and the night staff do sometimes have to deal with patients who are wildly excited and perhaps violent. The doctor should be informed of the patient's behaviour at night so that where indicated a sedative can be prescribed.

SICK NOTICES

One can never be sure what may happen to aged patients; they can become seriously ill in a short space of time and staff should be prepared for any emergency. If the patient has become very ill the doctor should be informed and a sick notice should be issued to the patient's next of kin well in time and not left until the patient is almost dying. Usually this task is the responsibility of the sister and she should know the name and address of the person to be informed and perhaps the telephone number and of any wishes which a relative may have expressed. Where there is difficulty in establishing a relative's address a message may have to be sent to the police. If the patient is in a dying condition the priest of the patient's faith, e.g. Church of England, Free Church, Roman Catholic or Jewish, should be informed. If there is a death the sister may also have the duty of interviewing a depressed relative when she should give what comfort and assurance she can and probably also some guidance as to death certificates, funeral arrangements, etc. As regards a patient of the Jewish faith there is a laid down procedure for attending to the body. The patient's property should be given to the next of kin and a signature obtained. Even after death a nurse's duty may not be quite finished, because if there is no porter on duty it may be her lot to escort the relative to view the body in the chapel mortuary.

DYING PATIENTS

Many of the untrained staff will not have seen the death of a patient and so they should be gently prepared for this. They will also require instruction on how to care for the dying and should learn something of the 'last offices'. A death in a ward is always distressing. The dying patient should be nursed in a single room, or failing this, in the utmost privacy behind drawn curtains – away from the vision of other patients so that they will not see a patient die or a body being taken out of bed. If cut flowers are sent to the ward after a funeral, they can be enjoyed by the patients without mention being made of how the flowers came to be sent.

CONCLUSION

An account has been given of the nursing of elderly patients in a long stay hospital, dealing with most of the difficulties which can arise. Where the standard of care is good the patients can spend many months or years quite happily in the hospital atmosphere. But if the buildings are badly sited or wards are ill suited for the elderly and if there is a lack of day space or too few lavatories or lack of proper beds, equipment and aids, the patients may not be really comfortable. Further, if there is also a shortage both of skilled and unskilled staff the whole atmosphere can be very dreary. The consequences of all this can lead to a situation where there are the possibilities of patient neglect. If this should happen the fault rarely lies with just one nurse and some unfortunate incident, but more with the whole hospital 'set up' and all those in authority who make the decisions and should shoulder the responsibility.

Aids and Equipment

Whenever some equipment is required it is always useful to have at hand the name and address of the makers, otherwise a request may never be made. The following is a list of equipment which has been used, though no doubt similar products can be obtained from other firms.

Name	*Obtained from*
Foley's Disposable Catheters	Warne Surgical Products Ltd., South Way, Andover, Hampshire, England.
Sterilin Disposable Urine Bags	Sterilin, Hill Rise, Richmond, Surrey.
Bardic Dispoz-A-Bag Thigh Bags Code 1509 With M.T. Valve Supplied by:	Davol International Ltd., Valley Bridge Road, Clacton-on-Sea, Essex. CO15 4AF
Disposable Male Incontinence pouches	Portland Plastics, Hythe, Kent. Tel: Hythe 66863
Disposable Enemas	W. B. Pharmaceuticals Ltd., Southern Industrial Estate, Bracknell, Berks. RG12 4YS
Heel and Elbow Pads Decubitus Anti Pressure Pads	Brinmark, Nether Street, London, N.3.
Capecraft Bath Hoist size 30/24	Capecraft, Cape Road, Warwick. Tel: Warwick 41321/6

Name	*Obtained from*
Zimmer Light Weight Walking Frames Zimmer Heavy Duty Hoist	Zimmer Orthopaedic, Bridge End, Glamorgan.
Feeder Beakers 113/PP narrow spout	Home Nursing Supplies Ltd., P.O. Box W.4, Westbury, Wiltshire.
Manoy Range of Table Ware	Melaware Limited, Commerce Road, Brentford, Middlesex.
Disposable Bibs	Molnycke Hospital Division, 32–36 Great Portland Street, London, W.1.
Vinyl Winged Armchairs	G. E. Curtis & Co., 339–344 Sheridan Road, London E7 9EF
Charcoal Pads for offensive pressure sores and leg ulcers	Deindor, Jeffreys, Miller & Co. Ltd., Leyland Mills, Wigan, Lancs.
Plastic Flexi Straws Kleenex Disposable Towels in Rolls and Holders	Kimberly Clark, Kimberly Lark Field, Maidstone, Kent.
Disposable Bed Pan Covers and Urinal Covers Tubegauze Micropore Surgical Tape Micropore Skin Closures	
Eldo Disinfectant used in lavatories, commodes to remove offensive smells	Mirfield Agricultural Chemicals Ltd., P.O. Box No. 1, Mirfield, Yorkshire.
Paper Handkerchiefs Plastic Sputum Mugs Disposable Kleenex Tissues 15/15 3 ply instead of diet cloths.	
Invalid Reacher With Magnet	Homecraft Supplies Limited, 27 Trinity Road, London, S.W.17.
Plastic Flex Straws	Hygienic Drinking Straws Co., Bristol.
Disposable Bed Pan Covers and Urinal Covers	DRG Hospital Supplies, Redcliffe Street, Bristol B99 7QY

Name	*Obtained from*
Micropore Surgical Tape Micropore Skin Closures	Macarthys Lyon Road, South Street, Romford, RM1 4JX.
Disposable Macintoshes	Henleys Medical Supplies, Alexandra Works, Clarendon Road, Hornsey, London, N.8.
Ster-Zac Powder	Macarthys, Lyon Road, South Street, Romford, RM1 4JX.

8

THE ELDERLY AT HOME

The information given here is also intended to help anyone having the care of an elderly person at home. It aims to supplement the advice given by the family doctor, but in no way to supplant it, and indeed no nursing procedure should be attempted without full consultation with, and approval of, the family doctor.

PROLONGED BED-REST

The relative should bear in mind the dangers of prolonged bed-rest in the elderly and should encourage an up-in-a-chair regime if so advised by the doctor. The patient's bed should be of a height as will allow placing of the feet on the floor when sitting on the bed – this will lessen the risk of injury whenever the patient has to get in or out of bed. Near to the bed should be a suitable arm-chair or geriatric chair, and as indicated a chair commode and walking aid should be provided.

Pressure sores The great thing to remember is that bed, or pressure, sores are caused basically by pressure; there may be additional causes but unless pressure on the affected part is relieved, other treatments will prove of little avail. To prevent pressure sores, the patient should have a soft warm bed, preferably with an overhanging bed-arm, which she can use to help herself turn over in bed. If at all possible the patient should be got up into a soft geriatric chair for part of the day. In bed, the sacral region can be protected by an air ring, and the weight of the bedclothes on the feet lightened by using a combined bed cradle and foot-rest, or even a suitcase if the latter is not to hand. A very suitable foot cradle can be made out of a length of metal by welding the ends together and fashioning it as described by Russell Barton.[2] The heels should be protected by a small cushion wrapped round each ankle so as to keep the heels from touching the bed; this seems to be a somewhat better method than heel rings of cotton wool. The hip areas, particularly if there is some incontinence, may be protected by hospital underpads – each pad is about 24 inches by 16 inches and consists of wads of paper and Marsiline pulp, the whole backed with polythene or water repellent paper. These pads should be placed over a plastic sheet but under a drawsheet. When the patient is up in a chair it is most important to protect the heels by properly heeled shoes, or heeled slippers. The skin over pressure areas should be kept clean with soap and water, massaged at times with the use of silicone cream, and Drapoline may be found useful to neutralise the effect of any irritative urine. The general health of the patient should be maintained by a good, nourishing, balanced diet and by medical attention to any associated anaemia, infection, circulatory failure, etc. Should the skin break down and an open bed sore develop, the patient should be considered as being very seriously ill and in need of more expert nursing care and attention than can be expected from a relative.

URINARY INCONTINENCE

First it should be remembered that the elderly often pass urine more frequently than young people, and also that they frequently get up at night to do so. If they are confined to bed, or on account of weakness cannot go to the toilet themselves, bedwetting is inevitable unless they are attended to promptly. Secondly, it is easier to pass urine in an upright position and relatively more difficult when lying down. There are many and varied causes of urinary incontinence which may operate at one and the same time, which may now be considered. Normally, evacuation of the bladder is initiated by conscious control, i.e. by relaxation of the sphincter muscles at the base of the bladder coupled with voluntary contraction of the muscles of the abdominal wall and pelvic floor. This is followed by a series of subconscious reflexes, bringing about contraction of the bladder and evacuation of urine.

Incontinence of urine may result when there is loss of conscious control in such states as:

Coma – e.g. Cerebro-vascular accidents, diabetic coma, uraemia, coma due to alcohol, drugs, head injury, meningitis, etc.
Mental confusion – from whatever cause, but in the elderly pain or toxaemia should always be under consideration.
Mental indifference – Some patients in a state of depression, or if being confined to bed and not attended to promptly, become indifferent to bedwetting. It may become a habit with them, though in fact complete conscious control of urination has not been lost.

Loss of conscious control is likely to result in irregular automatic evacuation of the bladder, or to partial retention of urine with dribbling overflow, or even to complete retention.

Local causes Apart from the loss of conscious control, there are many possible local conditions which can interfere with proper action of the bladder, such as:

ATONY OF THE BLADDER

In elderly people of either sex, there may be weakness and loss of tone not only of voluntary muscles but also of the bladder muscle itself. The power of the bladder to evacuate urine is lessened. The lack of tone may allow it to hold a large quantity of urine without causing much discomfort and as time goes on the bladder becomes more and more toneless. Further, such a bladder may not evacuate its contents completely, whether there be prostatic or other obstruction present or not, and the supervention of cystitis, frequency of micturition, loss of control or overflow incontinence may complete the picture.

Cystitis After a loss of conscious control, this is perhaps the commonest cause of incontinence. It should be suspected if the urine is cloudy or offensive, even though there may be no fever or complaint of pain on passing urine. Cystitis is often associated with and sometimes the cause of mental confusion. To confirm the diagnosis, a specimen of urine will have to be examined microscopically for pus and organisms, and the latter again for sensitivity to the various urinary antiseptic drugs. Incontinence may also result when the action of the sphincters at the base of the bladder and urethra is lost on account of such conditions as: cancer of the bladder, prostagic growths, prolapse of the bladder, trauma, instrumentation, prostatectomy, spinal cord tumours, spinabifida, tabesdorsalis, disseminated sclerosis, etc.

CONSTIPATION AND LOADED RECTUM

A loaded rectum may mechanically interfere with the action of the bladder, particularly so if there is an enlarged prostate, but it can also cause local irritation and frequency of micturition. If an elderly person cannot get to the toilet readily, frequency will amount to urinary incontinence. It is important, therefore, in the treatment of incontinence, to ensure a proper action of the bowels.

COLOSTOMY

Many thousands of people have had a colostomy operation, that is a false opening into the bowel through the abdominal wall. The operation is usually done for an obstruction of the bowel lower down, so that the bowel contents can be evacuated through the false opening into an attached bag. The care of a colostomy at home needs experience, but is not as formidable a task as some relatives imagine. If cared for properly, there need be no smell in the house, and indeed the patient's condition may be quite unknown to friends and acquaintances. The aim in the care of a colostomy is to have the bowel action occur at known intervals and for the contents to be semi-solid, so that on the one hand they do not soil all around the opening, and on the other that the contents are not so firm as to block the passageway. The drinking of fluids soon causes an action of the colostomy, as also will laxatives or irritating particles in the food like pips and shreds. The patient will learn by experiment what foods and fluids are suitable and how meals should be spaced but it is always an advantage for a relative to acquaint herself with the procedure. A regime of care will probably have been outlined by the surgeon and put into practice by the home nurse. Commonly it is somewhat as follows, *viz*:

The morning is started by taking a copious drink of water, tea, coffee, cocoa, etc. This should cause an action of the colostomy; after which the colostomy bag should be emptied, the skin around cleaned and a clean bag replaced with a fresh colostomy dressing. A teaspoonful or two of methyl-cellulose ('Celevac Granules') should now be taken since it will aid in the formation of a semi-solid motion later on in the day. One hour after the copious drink, a normal breakfast can be eaten. During the course of the day, fluid intake should be restricted until evening, when further fluids should be taken to bring about an action of the colostomy before going to bed. After the colostomy has acted, another small dose of methyl-cellulose may be taken to settle the colostomy for the night. Bland foods like meat, milk, eggs, bread and butter, etc., are usually found to be suitable for a colostomy patient. The colostomy bag can be made of polythene – which is disposable – or rubber which can be washed out as required. A suitable dressing around the colostomy is cellulose wadding, which is absorbent and can be disposed of in a lavatory; this is an important detail for a patient going out shopping or to work. If the colostomy is over-active, fluids will have to be reduced, and if it becomes obstructed its action should be restored by gentle expression and cleaning. Incidentally, there are various booklets on the care of a colostomy at home available through the medical profession.

ARTHRITIS

A great number of elderly people suffer from arthritis. As regards rheumatoid-arthritis, the early stage may have started many years previously and have been marked by fever and pain and swelling of the joints. At this stage, because of pain and toxaemia, a patient may have been immobilised and confined to bed. As time goes on, the inflammatory stage of rheumatoid-arthritis usually 'burns out', and as soon as the acute pain is over a continuous struggle has to be kept up to prevent muscular wasting and fixation of joints; otherwise the patient will be crippled with stiff hands, elbows, shoulders, back, ankles, knees, hips, etc., to the extent that he may be unable to walk, to feed himself and may even be completely bedridden. The treatment of rheumatoid-arthritis is long drawn out and usually involves the application of heat, of wax baths, massage, passive and active movements and other forms of physiotherapy. All too often, after a long illness a patient loses heart, resigns himself to being dependent on others for his meals, making his bed, dressing, undressing, etc., just at a time when continuation with active treatment would prevent his becoming crippled. It is in such a situation that a relative can be so helpful. She should be sympathetic but nevertheless encourage the patient to carry out for himself muscular and limb movements and the activities of daily living such as getting in and out of bed, going to the toilet, dressing and undressing, so that the patient will retain as large a measure of physical and mental independence as possible. In short a relative's role is not so much in doing things for the patient as helping the patient to help himself. If the joints are still becoming fixed, it is important to prevent their doing so in crippling positions. In bed, a bedclothes lifter with attached footrest should be used, to prevent fixation in the footdrop position; the knees should be kept straight rather than flexed, and the elbow and wrist joints should be kept in a position of flexion, as will allow the patient to eat. Plastic splints are often used to maintain the joints in a desired position at night, and removed during the course of the day for passive and active movements. During the illness, considerable medical supervision is necessary, but success or failure so often depends not so much on intricate medical treatment as sustaining the patient's will to master his disability. If outpatient physiotherapy has been advised, the relative should do all she can to see that the patient attends regularly, and in all other ways should encourage the patient to carry out the treatment prescribed.

CERVICAL ARTHRITIS

Special mention should perhaps be made of arthritis affecting the neck. The patient may merely complain about pains and aches about the neck, or they may be gross kyphosis with an unnatural extension of the head. Radiology in the necks of older people frequently shows some disorder of the spinal vertebrae and joints. It is only in a small number however that there is actual pressure on nerves and even a smaller number again where there is pressure on the spinal cord. Many elderly patients show wasting of the small muscles of the hands and commonly it is an accompaniment of general muscular wasting. At other times the wasting is due to pressure on cervical nerves and if the spinal cord is also affected there is likely to be brisk reflexes in the legs with some spasticity and paralysis. It is well to keep the possibility of cervical arthritis in mind and to differentiate it from a minor stroke. Chronic motor neurone disease, i.e. PMA, will give the picture of wasted small muscles of the hands and spasticity in the legs, but in this condition one would look for muscular fasiculation.

COMMON ILLNESSES

Since so many elderly patients cannot give a clear account of their illness, the more a relative knows about the common illnesses in the elderly and is acquainted with the patient's medical history, habits, diet and mode of life, the more she is able to help when illness occurs. An account has been given of the more common medical conditions in the elderly, for example, anaemia, malnutrition, dehydration, constipation, lack of vitamins, mental confusion, heart failure, diabetes, etc., which should enable the relative to observe early symptoms and take note of departures from normal. In particular she should note such things as gain or loss of weight, changes in appetite, the action of the bowels and the bladder, whether the patient has developed a cough, has had a slight stroke, a fall, a phase of mental restlessness or confusion and she should acquaint herself with the patient's past history of illness or operations. A relative must guard against making the patient completely dependent upon her; she should encourage the patient to take reasonable exercise and a healthy diet. A relative cannot always be present with the patient so consequently she should instruct him in the carrying out of the activities of daily living, so that he can at times look after himself.

ACCIDENTS IN THE HOME

From the above description of home conditions, one can anticipate that home accidents are likely to occur amongst the elderly. Some statistics for fatal home accidents are as follows (as supplied by Boucher):[3]

Statistics for Fatal Home Accidents in the Elderly

(1) The General Registry Office statistics for fatal home accidents include those which occur in the house and those which occur in its equivalent, e.g. hospital, hostel, school, prison, etc.

(2) 57% of fatal home accidents in England and Wales in 1955 affected old people aged 75 years and over. A further 16% affected those aged 65–74 years. Females to males were affected in the proportion 2·4 to 1.

(3) Falls accounted for 63% of the fatal home accidents. Females were affected more than males.

(4) 74% of the fatal falls affected old people over 75 years of age.

(5) During the last few years there has been an increase in the number of fatal domestic accidents and a corresponding increase in the number of fatalities in people aged 65 years and over. The increase in fatalities in old people is largely accounted for by an increase in fatal falls.

(6) The average death rate per million living 1952–3 from falls diminished in both sexes in the two age groups 65–74 years and 75 years and over from a high level in Scotland to a comparatively low level in the South of England.

(7) Local surveys in Sheffield and Wolverhampton showed that 39% and 36% of the samples were liable to falls and that 10% and 12% respectively had sustained fractures.

(8) Surveys of accidents in hospitals, both teaching and non-teaching, suggest that the majority of victims are aged over 60 years and that a fall is the most frequent accident.

Accidents in the home and residential institutions: Deaths by sex and ages, 1955 England and Wales

Deaths all Causes					
All Ages		65–74 years		75 years and over	
Males	Females	Males	Females	Males	Females
266 976	251 888	74 874	63 457	93 758	123 217
Gas Poisoning					
All Ages		65–74 years		75 years and over	
Males	Females	Males	Females	Males	Females
290	452	62	108	100	235
Burns and Scalds					
All Ages		65–74 years		75 years and over	
Males	Females	Males	Females	Males	Females
258	472	48	81	105	194
Falls from stairs, from ladder or from one level to another					
All Ages		65–74 years		75 years and over	
Males	Females	Males	Females	Males	Females
560	732	102	167	286	467
Falls on same level					
All Ages		65–74 years		75 years and over	
Males	Females	Males	Females	Males	Females
271	787	49	112	210	650
Unspecified falls					
All Ages		65–74 years		75 years and over	
Males	Females	Males	Females	Males	Females
447	1340	77	177	334	1105
Other accidents					
All Ages		65–74 years		75 years and over	
Males	Females	Males	Females	Males	Females
598	444	34	42	35	48

For the year 1970 there were deaths due to Accidental Falls:
Males 1818   Females 3815

(Ref. Registrar General's Quarterly Return England and Wales 1970 page 27)

A study of the foregoing statistics may be rather bewildering since so many figures are given, but what is quite apparent is that home accidents are a very serious matter to the elderly. They are causing an increasing number of deaths, and constitute a major hazard to the very old. The figures, of course, relate solely to accidents leading to death, but there must be an even greater number of accidents which have not proved fatal, but have caused much suffering and perhaps disablement. It is impossible to assess the number of non-fatal accidents, but perhaps it is ten times the figure for fatal accidents. In 1955, by adding up the deaths due to accidents, in the 65 years and over age group, there were 4930 fatal accidents, so there could be perhaps 49 000 home accidents among the elderly every year. The incidence of fractures in the elderly is also of considerable importance to the hospitals, since, for instance, duration of stay in hospital of a patient with a fractured femur may be as long as four months, and in many instances much longer. As the numbers of elderly and very elderly in the population continue to increase, the hospitals are likely to be faced with a serious demand for long-term treatment and accommodation, unless some means can be found of lessening accidents in the home.

Accidents in the home are therefore assuming the importance of an acute social and medical problem, and even now are perhaps of more importance than the problems caused by infectious fevers.

CAUSES OF FALLS IN THE ELDERLY

It will be seen from the accompanying statistics that falls in the elderly constitute a serious hazard; from a medical point of view the failure in balance may be considered under the following headings:

(1) Loss of consciousness
There are many causes of loss of consciousness but in particular there are two groups, those due to cardiac disorders such as cardiac failure, arythmias, syncope, etc., and those which are *cerebral* such as strokes, thrombosis, haemorrhage, etc.

(2) Transient imbalance
Under this heading are included all the causes of giddiness, ranging from acute vertigo, as in Menieres syndrome, to such conditions as undue sensitivity to barbiturates, alcohol, etc. Then there are numerous neurological conditions and perhaps mention should be made of senile cerebellar atrophy as a rather rare cause.

(3) 'Drop' seizure
In this kind of attack the patient does not feel dizzy, neither is there any loss of consciousness, but he is subject to sudden loss of maintenance of posture. The condition is receiving more attention than

formerly; aetiology is uncertain but it has been suggested it is due to a sudden drop in blood pressure in the basilary artery circulation.

(4) Defective power of co-ordination

This may be due to various tract lesions, for example:

    (a) the pyramidals which are commonly affected by strokes so that hemiplegics particularly have a tendency to fall

    (b) the extra-pyramidal tracts so commonly affected in Parkinson's disease

    (c) lesions of the cerebellum or cerebellar tracts. In some patients such lesions do not appear to cause loss of normal movement when the patient is recumbent and the lack of balance only becomes apparent on walking

    (d) lesions of the cerebral cortex from whatever cause, though there may be no focal paralysis, are apt to interfere with the proper co-ordination of bodily movements and such patients frequently attempt sudden movements and acts of balancing beyond their powers.

(5) Polyneuritis

Quite a number of elderly people have diabetes mellitus with an accompanying neuritis and an unknown number suffer from a mild polyneuritis from various vitamin deficiencies, and other causes.

(6) Muscular weakness

Elderly people often have weak and wasted muscles together with stiffness of the joints and slowing of their reflex actions. As a consequence, when they feel themselves about to fall, neither their muscle power nor quickness of reaction prevents them from doing so. As a result, any unevenness of the floor, slipperiness of surface may be disastrous to them.

(7) Poor eyesight

A good deal of correct balance depends on good vision and elderly people are particularly prone to suffer from defective vision, cataracts, partial blindness, etc. Many have to wear strong reading glasses or other spectacles, and if for some reason they are without these their eyesight may be too poor to avoid obvious obstructions in their path. Particular mention should be perhaps made of the difficulties of focusing objects correctly, especially when going up or down stairs, after cataract operation.

Considering all the medical defects from which the elderly can suffer, it is really remarkable how so many of them, even over the age of 75, get about as well as they do. Even so, many of them should not be getting about by themselves, either indoors or out, without the friendly assistance of some younger person.

SOCIAL ASPECTS OF FALLS IN THE ELDERLY

Apart from medical reasons leading to falls in the elderly, there are many aspects of their home life and mode of living which should receive attention, such as:

(1) Personal assistance in the home
    Many elderly persons come under the heading of frail ambulants, who should not move about to any extent without some personal help or guidance. It is for this reason, in the care of the elderly, that great emphasis should be put on housing them in close relationship to, or as part of, a family.
(2) Ground floor accommodation
    In particular the elderly require ground floor accommodation so as to avoid the hazards of going up and down stairs, either to the bedroom or the toilet.
(3) All open fires should be suitably guarded.
(4) Elderly people should avoid stooping, standing on chairs, reaching up to clean windows or light the gas and so on.
(5) Many houses require better lighting in the rooms, passageways and staircase.
(6) In many houses, handrails and supports could with advantage be put in the kitchen, bathroom, lavatory, stairs, etc., and many old people would benefit from walking aids.
(7) Some old people injure themselves by falling off a chair and it would appear that many homes would benefit by having a proper geriatric arm-chair.
(8) Floors should not be uneven or slippery, and rugs on a smooth surface should be particularly avoided.
(9) Many elderly people do not avail themselves of the ophthalmic services and continue to grope about at home with impaired vision. Even those who have been fitted with glasses all too often have broken them and have not requested repairs.

Outside the home, many elderly people cannot get about, cross streets, go shopping, or get on and off buses, without considerable danger to themselves. Possibly for this reason, the elderly people tend to keep to a restricted diet instead of going to the grocer's or butcher's to buy their few necessities.

It will be seen from the above that a great deal can be done to prevent falls in the elderly by help from relatives, neighbours, health visitors and voluntary workers.

One is not unduly surprised to note that 50% of fatal home accidents affected persons aged 75 years and over, or that 74% of the fatal falls also affected this age group. The stairs are a particular hazard, because of steepness, bad lighting and the absence of a handrail. One of the most common conditions resulting from a fall is a fractured femur, and most local newspapers record death by misadventure on this account almost weekly. Gas is another hazard for the elderly, both because their sense of smell may be impaired and because of their forgetfulness.

Here is a sample cutting from a newspaper:

'The police, acting upon information received, broke into the house during the late afternoon and found Mrs X, aged 79, in an unconscious condition. The gas tap on the wash boiler was found to be on, and the kitchen was full of coal gas. A few feet away lay her dog also in a collapsed condition.'

Some old people living alone sustain fatal accidents or illnesses which may not be discovered until the police break in. Sometimes elderly people, though mentally confused, still continue to live at home, and there are innumerable harrowing stories of what the police found when they broke in. Here is another quotation from a coroner's statement, regarding a man who had been dead for several weeks:

'This old man had been dead for a long time, and with him all the while had been his wife who was mentally deranged and probably did not appreciate that he was dead.'

Sometimes the illness of an elderly person is first noted by a neighbour who happens to observe that no milk has been taken in for the last few days.

HOME SAFETY

The importance of accidents in the home has already been dealt with. A survey of reports shows that deaths from home accidents during the second quarter of 1959 were 1525 – out of which 1126 persons were 65 years or over. Further, the deaths from home accidents exceeded in number the total deaths from transport accidents. A relative, therefore, should pay considerable attention to home safety, with special reference to the prevention of falls, gas poisoning and burns. In addition to the points given mention should perhaps be made of:

Gas Poisoning A large number of elderly people have impaired sense of smell and are unable to smell gas. They are consequently in danger if there should be a gas leak or a gas tap inadvertently left turned on. If, in addition, an elderly person is forgetful, mildly confused and depressed, he may wander away forgetting to light the gas as he intended. A relative should note if there is impairment of smell and should check the safety of gas taps, pipes, fittings, etc., or in cases of doubt, the Gas Board may be asked to do this. It is important that the gas meter and taps be so sited that the patient can readily see what is going on. When needed, safety devices can be fitted by the gas authorities, but should the patient have loss of smell, be alone much and a little forgetful, then alternative lighting and heating by electricity may be advisable.

Burns A fireguard is essential, not only for an open coal fire but also for any open bar type of electric fire. The bed and bedclothes, or inflammable material, should not be too near the fire lest they catch alight. If the patient smokes there is a danger from unstubbed cigarettes, or paper spills used to light a pipe – so ash trays should be plentiful and especially so for the patient who smokes in bed.

Oil Stoves seem to be particularly dangerous for elderly people and they are fond of using them. There is the danger of over-filling and spilling paraffin on the floor, or over part of the clothes, or of tipping them up if the stoves are carried when lit. Again, if the wick is not properly attended to the oil may flare up, catch clothing, curtains, etc., alight; or the stove may be placed under a shelf containing clothes, or too near curtains which can blow across the top. A relative should therefore take particular care of any oil stove in the house.

Dangerous drugs Many elderly persons are on dangerous drugs or using liniments which could be poisonous if taken internally. Consequently it is wise to keep these dangerous drugs in a manner separate from the supplies of simple tablets like aspirin, throat tablets, gargles, etc., with which they may be confused.

HYPOTHERMIA

Until a few years ago the thermometer was mainly used to find out whether the patient was feverish (i.e. with a reading above 98·4° F). It has now become important to consider a low body temperature. The ordinary thermometer is not suitable for this and it is only since the introduction of a special low temperature thermometer that the matter of low body temperature has really come to light. When the temperature falls to 95°F or below the patient is considered to have hypothermia. Hypothermia may be considered to come on in two main ways:

(1) There is a spell of cold weather during which the elderly person's house becomes cold, the bedroom cold, the lavatory cold and also perhaps the living room. At the same time there may be insufficient heating by shortage of coal, oil or other fuel. The patient may also be unable to go out to buy food. If such conditions continue for several days the patient is gradually unable to maintain a normal temperature. Or associated with this there could be an attack of influenza, bronchitis and perhaps a fall. The patient is then apt to take to her bed, but is still unable to maintain a normal body

temperature and gradually she lapses into hypothermia, dehydration and semi-coma.

(2) There may be an intensive period of cold with ice and snow and within a matter of hours the patient's temperature falls and she becomes hypothermic.

PREVENTION

Individually a patient can bear in mind the possibility of hypothermia and take precautions such as having sufficient heating in the house, lack of draughts, sufficient food and drink, warm clothing, sufficient bed-clothes with the support of an electric blanket.

From the point of view of the community a winter weather care plan can be evolved. This is brought about by establishing an 'at risk' register of old people likely to require help in cold weather. The names can be collected by the health visitors, doctors and from various voluntary organisations. The next thing is to establish a list of volunteers who will help in time of cold weather. This may perhaps be done through youth clubs, girl guides, Red Cross and senior schools. The services required from the volunteers would be such things as snow clearing, bringing in fuel, laying and lighting a fire, preparing a hot drink, shopping, supply of blankets, collection of pensions, attention to freeze-up of water supplies and matters of this sort. The scheme should probably go into action at least with the onset of snow and icy conditions.

TREATMENT

The first important thing is to have a low temperature recording thermo-meter, otherwise the condition of hypothermia is overlooked, and the temperature is best taken in the rectum. Any temperature approaching 90°F is very serious. One should also bear in mind that a patient at the same time can be ill with a lung infection, dehydration or suffers from an injury. The whole presentation may be complicated by mental con-fusion. At home the simple things to do are to warm the room, give the patient warm drinks and a warm bed. In cases of doubt the patient should be admitted to hospital though this may be difficult because so often in the winter hundreds of elderly people become ill at the same time.

In hospital many elderly patients are admitted during the winter and it is always important to use a low temperature thermometer since quite a number of them have hypothermia as well as another illness. It is not considered good practice to heap bedclothes on top of the patient because this diverts the body heat from the deep seated vital organs to the skin and it is very important they be placed in a really warm atmos-phere. It will be usually found necessary to treat infection or dehydra-tion as well as deal with conditions like strokes or heart failure. Those patients with really low temperatures unfortunately are apt to die a few days later from pancreatitis or thrombosis within an artery.

LONELINESS

There is little doubt that one of the most serious hardships for the elderly is loneliness. Out of the millions, there are some who do not object to it, but this should not mislead anyone into thinking it is not a dreadful hardship to the great majority. The affliction is of a negative kind – just being left alone, of no interest to anyone, just waiting to die, or as if they never existed or their lives had any meaning. For those without relatives it is a hard thing to bear, and for those with relatives who never visit them it leads to cynical despair. Continued loneliness brings about not only mental illness in the way of apathy, indifference, depression or even dementia, but also physical illness resulting from lack of reasonable exercise, inattention to diet with poor nutrition, and failure to obtain treatment for any accompanying illness. The physical ill-health worsens the mental state, and vice versa, so setting up a vicious circle of poor general health. Needless to say, every effort should be made to make an elderly person feel he or she has a significance in society. 'Loneliness', as stated by a former Minister of Housing and Local Government, 'is the biggest problem from the human and psychological point of view, and there is no service which people can give more truly Christian than to help to save the old people from feeling forgotten and neglected.'

USING THE SOCIAL SERVICES

An outline has been given of the social services, but it is important to an elderly person, and to a relative, to know what services are available locally and in some detail. To begin with, the services provided at a national level, such as pensions, family doctor, hospital services, etc., or locally through the Local Authority, e.g. housing, home nurses, home helps, health visitors, etc., are for all age groups and not specifically designed to meet the needs of the elderly. Though most Authorities and people are aware of the large number of elderly persons, so far the care of the elderly has not been accepted as a specific problem requiring a special kind of service, with the possible exceptions of hospital geriatric units and such organisations as Age Concern and the National Council of Social Old People's Welfare Committee and the National Council of Social Service. A 1958 survey of some 2000 persons aged 80 years and over, at Stockport,[1] shows the services are used only scantily by the elderly. For instance, the Survey showed that:

6·4% had no knowledge of any Local Authority or welfare service.
25·3% with defective eyesight had either no spectacles, or inadequate spectacles, and could not read on this account.

16% of men and 9·5% of women were without teeth or dentures.
1116 persons had impaired hearing, but very few had any hearing aids.
6·5% of the men and 9·25% of the women had no hot meal during the course of a week.
92 old people had nobody to nurse them during their last illness.
5·2% of the men and 3·3% of the women were never visited by anyone.
10% were never visited by any relatives.
Apart from health visitors, no agency had concentrated on old people living alone.
Almost half of the over-80 population occupied houses of 5 rooms or more.
Health visitors visited 34 133 houses in 1956, but less than one-tenth were classified as visits to old persons. But in Great Britain 1973, case visits to persons 65 and over came to 1 028 100. (Ref. Health and Personal Social Service Statistics for England 1974, page 107).

It would appear that it is the infirmities of old age, physical weakness, defective vision, defective hearing, etc., which make it difficult for the elderly to know about, make contact with, or seek help from the social services. Many indeed are house-bound and unable, either from defective sight or hearing, to write or to phone to the appropriate organisation. A relative, therefore, should act on behalf of the patient. First it will be necessary for the former to ascertain what services are available and the names and addresses of the persons in charge. The following services are in operation in most areas.

Pensions The local office of the Department of Health and Social Security now deal with all matters relating to pensions and what was formerly supplementary pensions. There are various leaflets dealing with pensions and benefits such as leaflets NI 15 on Retirement Pensions, NI 9 on Hospital Patients – Reduction of certain benefits during a prolonged stay in hospital, NI 3 on Industrial Injuries – Pneumoconiosis and Byssinosis, NI 4 on Industrial Injuries – Hospital Treatment Allowance, NI 7 on Industrial Injuries – Unemployability Supplement, constant attendance allowance and exceptionally severe disablement allowance, NI 15A on National Insurance – Retirement Pensions for Widows, NI 16 on Sickness Benefit, NI 49 on Death Grant and other National Insurance matters arising on a death, NI 50 on War Pensioners in National Insurance. It would be impossible to expect an elderly person to clarify in her mind all the kind of information given and since the amounts of pension and supplementary pension are constantly changing the best thing for a relative to do is to obtain the appropriate claim form and help the patient fill it up. The authorities concerned are always anxious to help but can hardly do so until the elderly person comes to their notice. At the time of writing (1975) the basic retirement pension is £11·60 a week or £18·50 for a married couple.

ATTENDANCE ALLOWANCE FOR ADULTS. (Ref. Leaflet NI 205. For all benefit rates see Leaflet NI 196, April 1975.)

A brilliant innovation is the making available of a special allowance for 'a person who is severely disabled physically or mentally and who needs a lot of looking after day and night'.

Undoubtedly there are a vast number of elderly people who fall into this category. Those relations who can, usually do, though there is a minority who do not, care for the elderly person. Many such disabled persons have no relative, or no relative near, and an even greater number have a relative who has to be gainfully employed and cannot afford the time looking after the disabled person. One such example comes to mind of a single daughter trying to look after a very infirm father. But his pension was not sufficient for them both to live on and pay the rent and so on. The suggestion was made that she should give up her job. Her answer to this was that she could not afford to do it, and anyway she was a Home Help, looking after some ten other old people. There are vast numbers of disabled persons suffering loneliness and neglect in need of personal care – which might be helped by an Attendance Allowance. By such means old people could be cared for at home. Further the method should be less expensive than calls from the Home Nurse, Health Visitor, Social Services, Hospital Day Centre, drugs from the doctor and periodic admission to hospital for food and nursing at £50, or more a week.

Of course claims for the allowance could be abused – as with most aspects of welfare – nevertheless if done on a large enough scale and liberally, it should reduce the cost of the hospital service (now doing so much social work for the elderly) by millions.

At present the attendance allowance is tax free at £9·20 a week.

As time goes by one expects this aspect of care to be the most significant, the most beneficial and the most pleasing of all measures designed to help the elderly.

Health The patient should always be registered with a family doctor and when he calls, a relative should attempt to be present so that she can more clearly understand the situation and see that the medical advice is carried out. The relative should also encourage the patient to undergo a periodic medical examination, and if a visit to hospital is advised she should attend with the patient and generally act on his behalf. Through the general practitioner, further advice can be obtained if necessary from a consultant physician or surgeon, either at hospital or at home if unfit to travel. The hospital can supply such things as hearing aids, artificial limbs, trusses, belts, splints, wheel chairs, etc., or make arrangements for these to be provided for the patient; most of the above are supplied free. The family doctor can also, through the local Health Department, arrange for transport by ambulance and the attendance of home helps, home nurses or health visitors, or the provision on loan of home aids such as chair commodes, bed pans, beds, walking aids, etc. The function of the home nurses is to provide professional attention and to instruct others in the house on the care of the patient, but she should not be expected to undertake duties normally the responsibility of a relative. At present there seems to be no agency responsible for cleaning a house in a dirty condition, and usually this can only be done by private arrangement.

Dental service An appointment may be made directly with a dental surgeon, but there are certain charges, which are recoverable in the case of a person on a supplementary pension.

Welfare Through the Chief Welfare Officer (or in some areas through the Medical Officer of Health), for certain elderly persons admission can be arranged to a Welfare Home. A Welfare Officer, on request, will also protect a patient's property while she is in a Home or in hospital. Apart from Homes run by the Local Authority, in most districts there are also Homes for the elderly run privately or by voluntary organisations.

Housing The matter of housing is very important to the elderly and the view should be taken that they should live near a relative or friends, who can give assistance during an illness, and that they should have ground floor accommodation with modern conveniences, preferably centrally heated and situated near to shops without having to cross busy roads, etc. A relative should keep this in mind and if in the future the patient's house is likely to be unsuitable, for instance too many rooms, only outside sanitation, a dangerous staircase, too far away from friends or relatives, etc., then she should advise the patient to put her name on the waiting list for rehousing some time in the future. Should the house be Council property, and the condition unsatisfactory or unsafe, she should refer this matter to the Housing Manager.

Laundry service Many local authorities have a large institution, equipped with a laundry department. They are thus able, with a little additional cost, to undertake free laundry or a low-price laundry service for the elderly in their locality. Several authorities provide this service. Considering the very small amount of money on which a pensioner may have to live, the cost of laundry can be a very serious item. The very elderly are unlikely to be able to do their own washing, or to be able to pay for the heating of the water and the detergent used. Unfortunately, the elderly are often bedridden and also subject to incontinence, so their clothes may require much more washing than younger people's do. Very often this burden of washing clothes is too much for a relative, who may herself be elderly, to undertake. And it may be solely on this account that admission to hospital may be sought. A laundry service is therefore a valuable social service, not only because it is a comfort to the pensioner but also because it can often do away with the need for institutional care. It seems a service that could be developed much more widely than it is at present.

Voluntary organisations In almost all areas there is a branch of the National Old People's Welfare Committee, or one of the National Council of Social Service. The local committee has usually organised services available to the elderly, such as:

Home Visiting.

Meals on Wheels – WVS often provide this service by taking hot meals directly to old people at home.

Chiropody (Note: the Local Authority is now permitted to run such a service).

Holiday Scheme for the Elderly.

Night Sitting Service.

In addition, there are usually many clubs for old folks, and a relative might find it worth while to introduce the patient to one of them. Information about these services and clubs should be obtained from the local secretary, who can often supply much needed information and guidance on the care of an elderly person.

Those who are looking after an elderly person at home no doubt already realise that it is quite an onerous task, but it is hoped that this chapter will provide useful information and emphasise the importance of making greater use of the social services available.

REFERENCES

1   Report on the Survey of the Aged in Stockport   1958
2   BARTON Russell   *The Lancet*   2 April 1960   page 736
3   BOUCHER C A   Address to the Medical Society for the care of the elderly at the Royal Society of Medicine   1957   London

9

PREVENTIVE MEDICINE IN THE ELDERLY

SIR WILLIAM FERGUSON ANDERSON

Cargill Professor of Geriatric Medicine
University of Glasgow
Regional Adviser in Diseases of Old Age
and Chronic Sickness
Western Regional Hospital Board, Scotland

As knowledge of illness in older people has advanced it is now generally accepted that old people are ill not because they are old but because there is some disease process at work and this teaching if spread widely enough would help to prevent many an illness in the elderly.

Many older people living at home are not in a sound state of health and this was shown first by Sheldon[19] who, in an investigation in Wolverhampton of a random sample of old people, found much physical and psychiatric disability. This finding was confirmed by Hobson and Pemberton[11] who, in a study in Sheffield of men aged 67 or more and women aged 62 or more, discovered many pathological conditions, including diabetes, myxoedema, scurvy, rodent ulcer, hernia, visual defects, dental conditions and hypochromic anaemia. In the Netherlands, Van Zonneveld[20] in a survey of patients over 65 years noted many previously undetected conditions, e.g. hypertension and heart disease. In general practice Miller[14] examined women 60 or over and men aged 65 or over and discovered much disability, and in the same year Roth and Kay[16] studied the psychiatric state of a random sample of old people and concluded that 30 % had psychiatric abnormalities. In more recent investigations Richardson[15] in North East Scotland and Williamson[22] and his colleagues in Edinburgh reported much morbidity. In the latter survey the outstanding feature was that much of the disability detected was unknown to the general practitioner. Williamson[21] showed clearly that elderly people tend on occasion not to report illness to their own doctor. Where the older person was convinced that there was some disease present, for example, he had noted breathlessness, swollen ankles or loss of power of an arm or leg, he was likely to inform his general practitioner. Whereas with disabilities involving the urinary system, for example incontinence, painful feet, anaemia or dementia, the patient did not consult his own doctor. The thesis was evolved therefore that many old people require some form of ascertainment so that their problems may be detected at an early stage when simple and timely measures and continued surveillance will prevent or slow down further deterioration. It is generally agreed that multiple lesions affect the elderly (Wilson et al[23]) and that anaemia must always be excluded.

Sharp[18] in his diabetic survey in Bedford showed an incidence of diabetes mellitus of 1·4% and found that the occurrence of glycosuria rose with age until in men in the 70–80 year age group 8% had glycosuria. There must therefore be a not inconsiderable number of undetected elderly diabetics. It is interesting to record that in 1961 in the U.S.A. it was estimated that 77% of persons 65 years and over had one or more chronic complaints and that 42% had some degree of chronic activity limitations (Baumgartner[6]).

This introduction demonstrates that the elderly living at home are not in a sound state of physical and mental health and as it is generally recognised that old age is associated with unsatisfactory social conditions it seems reasonable to make a combined attack to assess the physical, mental and social needs of the elderly. Unless efforts are made to improve the health of elderly people, the present situation whereby the active geriatric unit can produce a great many frail ambulant people often too unwell to live an independent life, and yet not ill enough to need hospital, will continue.

There are three ways in which an attempt at prevention of disease in old people can be made.

(1) THE PREVENTION OF PHYSICAL ILLNESS

An attempt has been made at a Consultative Health Centre in Rutherglen, Scotland, to devise means for the prevention of disease in old people and for the continuance of healthy living. This Centre, which was started in 1952, represents integration of effort by the three divisions of the Health Service and voluntary action, that is, by Dr Nairn Cowan, Medical Officer of Health, Rutherglen, myself representing the hospital service, the general practitioners of the area and the Rutherglen Old People's Welfare Committee. The Centre is advisory in character; deals only with patients referred by their general practitioners; is concerned with people aged 55 years and more who feel unwell or have minor ailments or are emotionally disturbed, and provides chiropody and physiotherapy. The Centre is not intended to be a substitute for the recognised out-patient departments of a general hospital (Anderson and Cowan[2]).

Since 1952 many old people have used the Centre and this analysis is concerned with 1300 people seen consecutively who were within the age range 55 to 93 years, and of whom 663 were men and 637 women, with 373 of these people being more than 74 years of age.

The commonest condition found was high blood pressure with symptoms of vertigo and headache, but against this almost 50% of the individuals in this study had arterial pressures over 140/80 with no symptoms of headache, vertigo or any upset whatsoever. The use of 140/80 mm as an upper limit of normal arterial pressure in older years is, of course, quite illogical. This becomes clear when statistical analysis of the data which relate to the wealthy people in this series who are not more than 24% over ideal height as estimated from Anderson's nomogram (Greene[10]) is studied. Systolic and diastolic blood pressure means increase with age and the increase is greater for the systolic. The range of blood pressure in healthy old people is wide and in the highest age range 80 years and over systolic blood pressure readings may reach a figure of 220 mm while irrespective of age diastolic blood pressure of up to 108 mm may be found (Anderson and Cowan[2]).

Hypertension with symptoms was followed in frequency of occurrence by osteoarthritis, microcytic hypochromic anaemia, chronic bronchitis, fibrositis and coronary artery disease. Intermittent claudication came next and was succeeded by valvular heart disease and malignant tumour. Lastly came a group composed of angina pectoris, diabetes mellitus and pernicious anaemia. There were 18 cases of diabetes mellitus found and 9 of pernicious anaemia.

Twenty-two women were referred to the gynaecologist and 19 people to the general surgeon. The psychiatrist, dermatologist, ENT consultant and opthalmologist each received less than one per cent of the patients in this series.

Thirty-one people were referred to hospital for in-patient investigation or treatment and this hospital group included 11 with incipient cardiac failure, 7 with carcinoma at various sites and 5 with diabetes mellitus for stabilisation. The admission of the incipient cardiac failure cases was very worth while. They only required a short period of hospitalisation and came out much improved. They were all admitted at a very early stage in their illness, much earlier than is customary in such cases.

In an endeavour to keep people fit the most satisfactory example is the reduction of obese patients. Obesity was common particularly among women and in the accompanying table the percentage over ideal weight calculated from Anderson's nomogram (Greene[10]) is shown. When figures for 25% overweight and above are examined, a much smaller number of men can be seen at all age ranges over 55, and when the age range over 80 is taken there are no men or women 50% overweight or more. Fat men seldom live to a ripe old age and fat men over 60 are usually unhealthy and are prone to disease of the cerebral or coronary arteries. Only 5 men 25% or more over weight were considered to be healthy out of 663 men examined.

Percentage overweight calculated by Anderson's nomogram (Greene[10])
1300 patients

Age Group years	Under 10%		0–24%		25–40%		50%+		Total	
	Men	Women	Men	Women	Men	Women	Men	Women	Men	Women
55–69	132	87	143	118	14	83	2	28	291	316
70–79	147	96	125	112	11	37	1	9	284	254
80+	53	30	31	29	4	8	—	—	88	67
Total	332	213	299	259	29	128	3	37	663	637

One more point must be stressed here. Elderly people are very prone to accidents and it is often necessary to go over the whole routine activity of the older person with a view to giving advice on improving their habits of daily living. Rowe[17] has shown how frequently spinal fractures in elderly people were due to a fall, loss of balance or a mis-step and he feels that many older folk have accidents because they cannot break the habit of hurrying. Anand[1] has demonstrated that many elderly people have no sense of smell and there is no doubt in my mind that household gas is a great danger to those over 60 and if it must be used, safety taps should be installed.

In assessing the elderly person for fitness experience suggests that as well as a complete physical examination including a rectal, the blood pressure should be taken, and the urine tested for albumin and sugar. A rectal examination is stressed not only because it is possible that some abnormality will be discovered but also if the patient knows that such a part of his anatomy is to be looked at then he will often give a story of a rupture or, if a woman, of gynaecological trouble previously undisclosed. Estimation of the haemoglobin content of the blood should be undertaken and the chest X-rayed. Such a simple routine would reveal the hernia or the haemorrhoid, the abnormally elevated diastolic pressure, the diabetic state, the anaemia or the chest condition which may otherwise be so readily missed.

Chiropody and physiotherapy have been most useful services and have now come to be regarded as essential in keeping elderly people fit.

(2) THE PREVENTION OF MENTAL ILLNESS

The next important principle in the prevention of disease in the elderly is to try and keep them in a good state of mental health.

Of the 663 men and 637 women, 21% of men and 25% of women

were emotionally disturbed, that is, such people had anxieties and depressions, which, because of their severity, merited our attention. Hobson and Pemberton[11] found abnormal degrees of anxiety or depression in 24% of men, which is comparable to the incidence in this study, and in 50% of women, which is greater than the proportion observed in Rutherglen.

While emotional disturbance was often due to many unfavourable factors acting on the individual, the commonest primary cause was an adverse home environment including the state of living alone. This was followed by bereavement, personal ill-health, ill-health of a relative, neglectful children, enforced retirement and financial difficulty. Women were more prone than men to be emotionally disturbed over the ill-health of a relative, while enforced retirement as a cause of mental illness was a problem of men. The occurrence of parental neglect by all the children in one family was uncommon and this study supported Sheldon[19] in his finding that financial difficulty by itself was rarely a cause of anxiety or depression, though it often co-existed with other more important causes of emotional disturbance.

The means by which attempts were made to enhance mental health generally and delay emotional stress were as follows:

(i) Reassurance on physical health

It was found that reassurance based on a complete and thorough physical examination with a sound history taking was of the greatest help. Many elderly people fear disease and time given to eliciting their worry followed by a careful survey of their health form a solid basis from which such apprehension can be banished. Advice was given at the same time on the scope of living within the physical capacity of the individual. This process was continued and reinforced by recalling the patient for frequent encouragement and continued guidance.

(ii) Unhappiness at home

Suggestions were made by which stress situations within the home might be alleviated or eradicated. Hostility between parent and daughter or son may be revealed on questioning and a clear statement of advice on future policy by the physician may help to overcome the constant strain which may be present in the household. A conference between relatives and their children to formulate a proper course of family action was often needed as well. It is felt that assessment by an individual outside the family with experience in such situations can be of the greatest help.

(iii) Home visiting

The health visitors were asked on occasion to carry out frequent home visiting in order to try and improve the patient's mental health or the patient was introduced to the Old People's Welfare Committee and voluntary visitors were arranged to keep the old person under surveillance. Admission to the residential home of the Local Authority was sometimes essential in order to provide the old person with company and friendship when living alone at home had failed.

(iv) Psychiatric help

The patient, where necessary, was referred for psychiatric opinion and treatment.

(v) Interests

When it was thought that people attending the Centre needed guidance on the development of hobbies and interests this was given, and there was active liaison with a Unit where diversional therapy could be supplied.

SPECIAL ASPECTS OF MENTAL HEALTH IN THE ELDERLY

(a) *Depression*

There is a great deal of undetected depression among the elderly and this is one factor which seems to me remediable. Incidentally, bereavement is perhaps the commonest cause of severe and lasting depression and here it is felt that a religious background is of great help. It was found at Rutherglen that some 50% of the men and 20% of the women seen had no religious connections and, if what they said was correct, had not opened a Bible for the last 10 years. They showed little intention of rejoining their Church.

(b) *Retirement*

It is very difficult for us to understand the impact which retirement has on the life of the working man. One day he is busy all day long, meeting his friends and associates and doing a sound constructive job in the community – the next day he is retired with no interests and perhaps no hobbies and nothing to get up for or to interest himself in. This subject is now of great importance when it is recalled that some 1000 men and women are retiring each day in the United Kingdom.*

Of 530 men seen at the Rutherglen Consultative Health Centre aged 65 years and more, 382 were retired and 142 were still in employment. Of the 382 retired men, 82 stopped work in a voluntary manner to enjoy their leisure; 61 did so because of their increasing difficulty in meeting the physical or mental demands of their employment; 21 because of adverse home circumstances; 77 because of personal ill-health; 14 as the

*The number of new pensioners in the 12 months preceding the middle of July 1975 is approximately 657 656. (Ref. Department of Health and Social Security—personal communication.)

result of accidents, while 127 were compulsorily retired by their employers. Thus only a minority of men – 21 % – enjoyed the privilege of retiring voluntarily in the full sense of the word. Furthermore, 469, or 88 %, of the 530 men regarded compulsory retirement as harmful to the continuance of healthful living. The small minority remaining either considered such a method of retirement was a good thing or offered no opinion.

(c) Pre-retirement training

It is reasonable to believe that the judgement of these men fairly reflects the thoughts of the older men in the population, consequently it is probable that compulsory retirement from whatever cause is injurious to the mental health of man. This conclusion played a part in the formation of the Glasgow Retirement Council (Atkinson and Anderson[5]). This is a Council which is concerned with studying the problems of the older worker in industry, of seeking ways and means by which men and women can be prepared not only for the time of retirement, but also for a new life in retirement, and to promote for retired persons crafts, hobbies and the best use of leisure time. In order to promote these objectives, courses have recently been arranged for employees who are within 3 to 5 years of their probable retirement, and employers have been prepared to release them from normal duties without loss of earnings for one full day each week for seven weeks. The idea behind these courses is to persuade men and women, while still at work, to think about and plan for their years of retirement, to guide them as to how best to adjust themselves successfully to life in retirement and to instruct them in the interests and opportunities for social enjoyment among themselves, which will help them to find personal satisfaction, contentment and fulfilment in their years of enforced leisure.

Since October 1959, 2614 men and 780 women of varied occupations have attended 150 courses for men and 55 courses for women. They have expressed appreciation of the courses and have declared themselves as feeling better equipped to confront and plan for their own retirement. They have strongly recommended the course both to their employers and to those working beside them at the same stage in their career. For the last few years the Retirement Council has also had in being Centres for crafts and hobbies for retired people. The activities of these Centres are recreational – no payment is offered for the work done, but this is given a sense of purpose in that apart from making household articles for their own use, the members are making aids for disabled persons. These aids are supplied to the Red Cross Society, and to hospitals, while an important link has been established between the Centre and Geriatric Units in Glasgow.

(d) The place of the elderly in society

Preparation for retirement has been discussed as it seems to be that in youth we are prepared for our employment by some form of apprenticeship or university training. Then in our middle age work is our main interest. As old age advances we should turn our mind to some form of voluntary activity or some interest outside our work. During the days of our active working life we are protected by a trade union or some similar organisation, but in old age this is not so. Work has now ceased, often there is no outside interest and there is no one to look to for help. Since 1967 a re-employment bureau has been organised by the Glasgow Retirement Council and this office, staffed by volunteers (expert employment counsellors) is open every afternoon. Here retired people who wish part-time employment come and state how many hours they wish to work and what type of work they desire. In the last five years over 500 positions have been found for such people. Some industrial organisations have introduced re-employment schemes of varying types and this is often combined with a retired employees association. Such an association maintains contact through the personnel officer with the former employees and arranges for club activities, sick visiting and many other social activities. This type of association is a good remedy for depression. By such schemes, re-employment or retired employees associations, the older person can be made to feel he still has a place in our society. Old people must know that they are needed.

Dunn[8] describes this in a different way. He details two types of longevity, type I and type II, and means by this that type I is that part of survival due to supportive measures of medical care and health, while type II is the years which might be added to the life of the individual if his inner world is strengthened by purpose, effective living and self fulfilment. He believes, and I agree, that the body's available physical energy must be employed for useful purposes or the tissues of the body will be subjected to a variety of psychosomatic illnesses.

(3) SOCIAL SURROUNDINGS

The final way in which I think old people can be protected from ill health is by an improvement in their social conditions. Ideally older people at the age of 55, 65 and 75 should be assessed physically and a detailed story taken of how they are living. As a practical proposal for action now, the age of 70 is an appropriate starting point for examination due to the increased morbidity which occurs at that age. It is thus possible to try to secure the gradual building up of a poor social set-up. Frequently, when a doctor is called to see an ill, old person he finds not only difficulty in making a clinical diagnosis but surroundings in which he can no longer adequately care for his patient. I am sure that foresight can help us here and looking ahead may well prevent deterioration of the social circumstances of the old person. The help of the Local Authority can be obtained at a much earlier stage. Rehousing can be asked for long before it is urgently needed, and time given to a well-intentioned Housing Department to rehouse the old people without this being done as an emergency.

In recent years the use of sheltered housing (i.e. small purposely designed houses for the elderly giving each person or each couple their own home with 24 hour on call cover) has provided the opportunity to give older people a continued life in the community. Small groups of such houses enable elderly amazingly frail people to continue living in their own well known social surroundings. The value of this step in social progress in preventing mental ill-health may well be very great.

Other measures which would seem to me necessary to benefit old people are – the real need for public propaganda, so that people should not expect to be ill when they are old; the fact that old people are ill not because they are old but because there is something wrong with them should be publicly and repeatedly stressed. I should like to see posters with sayings such as 'Have you attended to your feet today?' because care of the feet is one of the very important factors in keeping old folk active and out of bed. The public generally have not realised that people are not old now until they are over 80 years of age. The importance of health education by the use of radio and television has not been realised and these media would be an excellent way of conveying information to older people.

Medical authorities in America and Russia stress the importance of graded exercise in the elderly as a method of improving health. Exercise appropriate to the age and physical condition of the old person are agreed to be of great value in preserving mobility and preventing illness and such should be encouraged.

The working of a consultative health centre as described above is directed towards co-ordination of the present differing agencies trying to help older people. As Baumgartner[6] says, 'Fragmented unco-ordinated medical care is wasteful of money, of professional manpower which is in short supply and above all is poor care for patients.'

Other Centres (Maddison[13]) have been established but the essential feature of the Rutherglen Centre, which I feel is all important, is that every patient seen has been referred by his own general practitioner who continues to be responsible for his therapy and remains the patient's personal doctor. The basic principle advocated here is integration and co-ordination of the three divisions of the Health Service, namely, general medical service represented by the general practitioners, local health authority in the person of the Medical Officer of Health, and hospital service by the consultant with the local voluntary effort.

FUTURE DEVELOPMENTS

The establishment of health centres in which general practitioners work has encouraged the use of health visitors in the ascertainment of unknown illness among the elderly. Burns carried out a medico-social survey by health visitors of 391 patients of 65 years of age and over who were living alone or who were old couples alone, and discovered illness in the form of anaemia, hearing defects, difficulty in vision; people who needed dental attention and chiropody were found and necessary action was taken in all cases. Burns[7] felt that such a plan of geriatric care was successful. Andrews, Cowan and Anderson[4] investigating a random sample of 200 people of 65 years and over, found much undetected need and postulated that health visitors, based on a health centre, were of great value in seeking out illness. An attempt to validate the use of the health visitor at the Kilsyth Health Centre, has shown a high correlation between the findings of the health visitor and a general practitioner checking her findings. A simple and accurate proforma can be constructed which can be satisfactorily completed by the health visitor and the results reported back to the general practitioner. It is suggested that people 70 years and over should be visited in the first instance. Preventive measures based on the health centre with the general practitioner as the key person, will be greatly aided by a visit from the physician in geriatric medicine, coming from the hospital once per week in company with other specialists, such as a psychiatrist. The physician in geriatric medicine will fulfil two main functions, (a) an out-patient service for old people referred by the general practitioner at the health centre and, (b) an ascertainment service organised to detect early disease and functioning through the trained health visitor. At the health centre there should be co-ordination between health centre, the hospital domiciliary and voluntary services. It is clear that special training is needed before health visitors uninvited can visit older people in their own homes who have not sought advice. The health visitor must not change a healthy person into a patient and the whole attitude by the health visitor towards the interview must be completely different from that of a normal patient/doctor relationship.

It is hoped, in the future, that an elderly person or a relative will be able to obtain advice on any subject concerned with the elderly or indeed the appropriate service by calling at the Health Centre. Lowther et al[12] examined critically early diagnostic services for the elderly; medical examination was offered to a group of high risk old people, those living alone or recently bereaved or recently discharged from hospital who were not necessarily known to their family doctors but were seen with their agreement. Clear evidence of improvement was found in one-half of the patients who carried out the recommendations and this was attributed to earlier diagnosis than would have been achieved without the examination at the clinic in 42% of cases. Including all the patients examined the proportion helped by early diagnosis at 18–30 months follow up was 23%. These authors concluded that the offer of a routine examination to a high risk group was of benefit and was a form of medical practice which should be widely adopted. Only 3% of those seen were recommended for geriatric admission.

Elliott,[9] in drawing attention to the need for co-ordination, admits that the general practitioner has the major part to play in the harmonising of the domiciliary services and in assuming leadership of the term. He doubts however that the training of the medical student is attuned to the present needs of the aged in the community. My conclusion is that in order to provide a first rate service for old people, active steps must be taken to train medical students in the practice of geriatric medicine, particularly with regard to the use of the domiciliary services and the need for decision in assessment of the individual case.

Prevention of illness is the most important aspect of future work in geriatric medicine. Unless active steps are taken now to learn more about prevention of disability and disease in the elderly and to implement that knowledge the ever growing numbers of ill and frail older people will throw an impossible load on the shoulders of the health services of the country.

REFERENCES

1 ANAND P *Accidents in the Home Current Achievements in Geriatrics* edited by W F Anderson O B Isaacs Baillière, Tindall & Cassell Ltd. 1965

2 ANDERSON W F and COWAN N R 'A Consultative Health Centre for Older People' *The Lancet* 1955 **2**, page 239

3 'Arterial Pressure in Healthy Older People' *Clinical Science* 1959 **18**. page 103

4 ANDREWS G R COWAN N R and ANDERSON W F 'The Practice of Geriatric Medicine in the Community'. In McLachlan G. (Editor): *Problems and Progress in Medical Care* Oxford University Press London 1971

5 ATKINSON A and ANDERSON W F 'The Glasgow Retirement Council' *British Medical Journal* 1962 **2**, pages 1743–4

6 BAUMGARTNER L 'Public Health and Ageing' editorial *The Gerontologist* 1961 **1**, page 160

7   BURNS C   'Geriatric Care in General Practice. A Medico-social Survey of 391 patients undertaken by Health Visitors.'   J R Coll Gen. Pract. **18**   287

8   DUNN H L   'Physiological Adequacy and Longevity type 11'   *The Gerontologist*   1962   **2**, 1   pages 18–22

9   ELLIOTT A   'Home Care of the Elderly'   *The Practitioner*   1962   **188**, 1128   pages 765–72

10 GREENE R   *The Practice of Endocrinology*   1951   2nd edition edited by Raymond Green   page 337

11 HOBSON W and PEMBERTON J   *The Health of the Elderly at Home*   1955   Butterworth & Co.   London

12 LOWTHER C P   MACLEOD R D M and WILLIAMSON J   'Evaluation of Early Diagnostic Services for the Elderly'   *British Medical Journal* **3**   275

13 MADDISON J   'Setting up a Clinic for Preventive Medicine for Older People'   *Public Health*   1960   **74**, 10   page 362

14 MILLER H C   *The Ageing Countryman*   1963   The National Corporation for the Care of Old People   London

15 RICHARDON I M   *Age and Need – A Study of Older People in North-East Scotland*   1964   E & S Livingstone   Edinburgh & London

16 ROTH M and KAY D W K   Social, Medical and Personality Factors associated with vulnerability to psychiatric breakdown in Old Age   1962   *Geront. Clin.*   **4**,   page 147

17 ROWE C R   'Prevention of Accidents to the Aged'   *Post Grad Med*   1963   **33**, 1   page 96–8

18 SHARP C L   'Diabetic Survey in Bedford'   1962   *Proceedings of the Royal Society of Medicine*   1964   **57**,   page 193

19 SHELDON J H   *The Social Medicine of Old Age*   1948   Oxford University Press   London

20 VAN ZONNEVELD R J   *The Health of the Aged*   1961   Van Gorcum-Assen

21 WILLIAMSON J   'Ageing in Modern Society'   Paper presented before the Royal Society of Health   Edinburgh   9 November 1966

22 WILLIAMSON et al   'Old People at Home'   *The Lancet*   1964   **1**,   page 1117

23 WILSON L A   LAWSON I R and BRASS W   'Multiple Disorders in the Elderly'   *The Lancet*   1962   **2**,   page 841

10

STATISTICS

To obtain an overall view of the problems of the elderly it is necessary to study the national statistics. First the total population as given by the *Statistical Review* for 1962[14] is as follows:

Population (in thousands) 1962
Note: The acreages shown comprise land and inland water

	Great Britain and Ireland			England and Wales		
	Area 78 280 350 acres			Area 37 342 463 acres		
Year	Persons	Males	Females	Persons	Males	Females
1962	56 125	27 266	28 860	46 669	22 651	24 018
	Scotland			Northern Ireland		
	Area 20 075 023 acres			Area 3 495 617 acres		
Year	Persons	Males	Females	Persons	Males	Females
1962	5197	2496	2701	1435	700	736

United Kingdom 1973 – Total population 56 021 000

Excess of births over deaths – 76,000 (lowest ever) (Ref. Annual Abstract of Statistics 1974, page 8)

Numbers receiving retirement pensions (1973) – 7 936 000 (Ref. Dept. Health & Social Security Annual Report 1973, page 72)

Life Expectation England and Wales

Age	1948–1950		1971–1972	
	Male	Female	Male	Female
60	15·3	18·3	15·4	20
65	12·2	14·6	12·2	16·1
			(no improvement)	

The Elderly

Health and Welfare – The Development of Community Care

During the twenty years from 1963 the numbers of people aged 65 and over, and 75 and over, will, according to the projections of population published by the Registrar General, increase as shown in the table below.[13]

England and Wales

Age Group		*Mid-year figures*			
		1962	1967	1972	1982
65 to 74	Males	4457	1612	1839	2019
	Females	2136	2296	2473	2584
	Total	6593	3908	4312	4603
75 and over	Males	691	709	756	982
	Females	1318	1426	1546	1840
	Total	2009	2135	2302	2822
65 and over	Males	2148	2321	2595	3001
	Females	3454	3722	4091	4424
	Total	5602	6043	6686	7425

Thus the numbers aged 65 and over will increase by 1 823 000, or 32·5%. Within this total, the proportionate increase of the group aged 75 and over will substantially exceed that of the group aged 65 to 74, the numbers aged 75 and over will increase by 813 000 or 40·5%, while the numbers aged 65 to 74 will increase by 1 010 000 or 28·1%.[8]

A further breakdown of these figures (opposite) shows that the proportionate increase from 1962 to 1982 in the numbers of the very old will be greater still: 41·2% for the group aged 80 and over and 44·1% for the group aged 85 and over. There is a significant difference, however, between the first and second decades. The numbers aged 65 to 74 will increase by 20% in the first decade but by only 6·7% in the second, whereas the corresponding figures for the group aged 75 and over are 14·6% and 22·6% respectively. Thus, the numbers aged 65 to 74 will be increasing more slowly in the second decade than in the first, and it is in this second decade that the great acceleration will occur in the increase of the groups aged 75 and over.

During the next two decades, a substantial proportion of the elderly will be without children. It was estimated in 1954 that roughly one-quarter of the elderly in Great Britain were without children either because they had never married or because their marriages were childless. This estimate did not include those whose children had died or emigrated.

Since the very old and the elderly unsupported by children are the groups likely to make the heaviest demands on the health and welfare services both domiciliary and residential, the figures in the preceding

Age Group		Mid-year figures			
		1962	1967	1972	1982
65 to 69	Males	851	958	1096	1118
	Females	1185	1271	1369	1356
	Total	2036	2229	2465	2474
70 to 74	Males	606	654	743	901
	Females	951	1025	1104	1228
	Total	1557	1679	1847	2129
75 to 79	Males	398	404	440	589
	Females	699	736	798	945
	Total	1097	1140	1238	1534
80 to 84	Males	201	210	216	277
	Females	407	449	477	573
	Total	608	659	693	850
85 and over	Males	92	95	100	116
	Females	212	241	271	322
	Total	304	336	371	438

paragraphs are significant for the planning of the services for the care of the elderly in the next decade and beyond. In general they show that throughout this period the services must be prepared to meet a large increase in demand. It is therefore quite clear that there is to be a great increase of very elderly persons, many of whom are unsupported by any children. It may be thought that for present day society this task is much greater and almost overwhelming. But this view is not entirely correct for the *Statistical Review*[15] draws a comparison between the year 1911 and 1961 in the following way:

'In 1911 children and old people together amounted to nearly 36% of the entire population (30·6% under 15 years of age and 5·2% aged 65 and over). In 1931 they were 31% (23·8 %children and 7·4% old people). By mid-1961 the proportion had risen to nearly 35% (22·9% children: 11·9% old people). It is thought the proportion may reach its maximum before 1980 – with about 25% children and perhaps some 14% old people and that decline in the total proportion and in the ratio of children to old people may be very slight over the following twenty years or so. Measured in these terms, the economic pressure of dependency has not varied much and is not substantially greater now than in 1911.'

Since the country is now affluent and conditions of work so much improved it should be reasonably possible to care for both those under 15 years and those over 65 years.

LIFE EXPECTATION

It is very difficult but of considerable importance to assess the likely elderly population in ten or twenty years' time, so that proper planning can be started now. The expectation of life for 1950–2, for 1962 and for 1881–90 is given as follows:[12]

Expectation of Life in Years

	Males			Females		
Age	*1881–90*	*1950–2*	*1962*	*1881–90*	*1950–2*	*1962*
0	43·66	66·42	68·0	47·18	71·54	73·9
25	40·27	49·64	50·5	42·42	54·17	55·8
40	25·42	30·98	31·5	27·60	35·32	36·6
50	18·82	22·23	22·6	20·56	26·34	27·5
60	12·88	14·79	14·9	14·10	18·07	19·0
65	10·31	11·69	11·9	11·26	14·33	15·2
70	8·04	9·00	9·2	8·77	10·97	11·7
75	6·10	6·70	7·0	6·68	8·10	8·7
80	4·52	4·86	5·1	5·00	5·83	6·3
85	3·29	3·48	3·7	3·71	4·20	4·4

There has, therefore, been some improvement in life expectancy but nothing very considerable for those aged 65 and over. An interesting figure is given by the Metropolitan Life Insurance Company:

Life Expectancy

	1900	1955	Increase of
	Life expectancy of Males		
At birth	48·2	67·3	19·1 years
At 65	11·5	12·9	1·4 years
	Life expectancy of Females		
At birth	51·1	73·6	22·1 years
At 65	12·8	15·5	2·7 years

It should, however, be remembered that life expectancy is based on mortality rates and is in no way suitable 'for predicting the size and age structure of the future population'. For instance, according to the Metropolitan Life Insurance Company, the bulk of people born in 1900 should have died several years ago; this has obviously not happened. Too much should therefore not be made of life expectation. Nevertheless it is disappointing to find so little improvement in life expectations of the 65 years and over as compared to the 1900s. From a medical point of view many elderly people are saved from dying of bronchial pneumonia, pneumonia, winter infections, diabetes, acute abdomen, fractured femurs, etc., and one would think there would be an appropriate improvement in life expectation; even though death continued from neoplasma, vascular lesions of the central nervous system and diseases of the circulatory system. Could it be that the social and especially the domestic conditions of the elderly today are not as good as in 1900? In 1900 there were often many members in the household able to look after the grandmother or grandfather; this does not pertain today, and the place of the relatives is not being adequately filled by domestic helps. Do the adverse social conditions of the elderly cancel out the advantages they derive from modern medicine?

RATES – EXPENDITURE ON THE ELDERLY

There is a considerable amount of conversation and talk about doing things for the elderly. Whilst the Ministry of Health attempts to look after the elderly sick, the great mass of elderly people, and there were some 2 427 000 over 75 in England and Wales in 1971, have either to care for themselves or look for help in the matter to the local authorities. How seriously the local authorities take this responsibility may be gathered by seeing what proportion of the rates in the pound are spent on the care of the elderly. Below are given two such statements, one from a Labour borough and one from a Tory borough:

County Council 1–1964	*s*	*d*
Education	9	4·93
Public Health (including health services under the National Health Services Act 1946)		11·41
Services for aged, infirm and handicapped persons		3·36
Care of deprived children		1·78
Fire Service		4·26

County Council 2 – 1975	*p.* (*pence*)
Education	52·6
Fire Brigade	1·95
Library	1·24
Social Services	5·97
Other Services	1·87

Could it be that 3d for old people and thirty-six times as much for education is somewhat out of proportion? Education is obviously very important, but is it becoming a 'sacred cow' to which all must make sacrifices, especially the elderly?

Despite the National Health Service and the National Welfare State, the welfare of the elderly, totalling 7 591 000 over 65 in 1973, has been left to the local authorities.

So far their efforts have not been very impressive and, surely, the care of so many millions is a national problem and should be dealt with directly or indirectly and accepted as the responsibility of National Government.

ADMISSION TO HOSPITAL AND DOMICILIARY CARE

Despite the low expenditure on the elderly out of the rates many people may still think this is of no great importance since the needs of the elderly will be met by the Health Service. Regarding this matter it is perhaps as well to consider the advice given by the Ministry of Health in a memorandum of July 1962.[11]

(1) The aim should be to care in the community for all patients who do not require treatment of a kind which can only be given in hospital.

(2) Admission to hospital may be unnecessary for some patients, particularly the elderly or those with certain types of chronic illness or mental disorder, if the domiciliary services of the local authority are effectively mobilised. The support of these services will often also be needed while a patient is on a hospital waiting list. The services concerned include the home nurse, health visitor, social worker or welfare officer and home help. For elderly people who are infirm rather than sick, admission to an old persons' home is preferable to admission to hospital.

(3) A patient should not be put on the waiting list (just as he should not be admitted to hospital) without a clear-cut decision that he needs, at that time, such treatment, investigation or nursing care as only admission to hospital can provide.

Without reading between the lines it would appear that the major responsibility for the care of the elderly should be undertaken by the local authority – how can they do this with such a small expenditure on welfare homes and local public health?

FINANCE OF HEALTH, WELFARE AND SOCIAL SECURITY

According to the Annual Report of the Department of Health and Social Security for the year 1968[1] the cost was set out as follows:

The accounts of the National Insurance and Industrial Injuries Funds for the year ending 31 March 1968 were published on 20 February 1969.

At the end of 1968, flat rate contributions were being paid by employers and insured persons at the rate of about £3340 million a year. Of this sum about £183 million represented National Health Service contributions, about £52 million employers' Redundancy Fund contributions, and about £1610 million SET. The remainder, about £1490 million, was being paid into the National Insurance and

Industrial Injuries Funds. In addition, contributions to these Funds at the rate of a little under £360 million a year were being made out of the Consolidated Fund. Of these flat-rate contributions being paid by employers and insured persons, about £1340 million was collected by adhesive stamps obtained from post offices and affixed to contribution cards, about £1450 million under the Direct Payment Scheme and a little over £380 million by impressed stamping of contribution cards. In addition to flat-rate contributions, graduated contributions from employees and employers were running at about £440 million a year.

Expenditure on the administration of Social Security schemes by the Department was £95 million in 1967–8.

Note: £3340 million plus another £360.

Scale of operations

Numbers Receiving Benefits[2]

On average the number of benefits and allowances (including supplementary benefits) being paid in any week was about £16·5 million. At the end of 1968 the following pensions and allowances were in payment. Corresponding figures for the previous year are given for comparison overleaf.

All these statistics are rather bewildering, but at least it can be seen that the total cost of health, welfare and social security is over £5000 million; that each week about £16·5 million are paid out in the form of benefits and allowances. This latter procedure obviously involves much bureaucracy, unproductive work and no doubt explains the enormous queues so often found at the post office. It will also be seen that the National Health Service contributions amount to £152 million out of a total of £1651 million and the former procedure also involves much bureaucracy and tiresome attention to forms and possibly at the same time misleading the ordinary person to think that their contribution is actually paying for the health service. For England, the estimated cost of Health and Personal Social Services 1973/74 showed a rise from £1919 million in 1970/71 to a figure of £2992 million. (Ref. Dept. of Health and Social Security Annual Report 1973, page 17), or according to *The Daily Telegraph*, May 12th, 1975, was £3143 million for 1974.

The key question is, does the cost of the welfare state cause inflation? If the answer is that it does then it is worth giving some thought as to how it will affect those on fixed incomes, particularly the elderly pensioner who is unemployed. The pensioner is at the mercy of disputes between the trade unions and their employers. The former are always trying for higher wages and the latter for better profits and it is the pensioner who is the casualty in this struggle. There are many countries considering bringing in compulsory health and welfare services and for

	1968	1967
War Pensions		
Disablement	409 000	423 000
Widows and other dependents	148 000	154 000
Retirement Pensions	6 973 000	6 769 000
Widows' Benefits	600 000	609 000
Guardian's Allowance	5000	5000
Industrial Injuries		
Disablement Pensions	203 000	201 000
Widows' Pensions	28 000	27 000
Supplementary Benefits		
Pensions	1 847 000	1 796 000
Allowances	790 000	763 000

Health and Welfare Services – England and Wales – Ref. Department of Health and Social Security Annual Report 1970 page 211.[2]

Cost of Service	1970/71 Estimated £ million	Sources of Finance	1970/71 Estimated £ million
Central Administration ($\frac{1}{2}$%) (£9 million)	11		
Hospitals Current* (51%) (£843 million)	998	Consolidated Fund (73$\frac{3}{4}$%) (£1200 million) (Excluding Consolidated	1401
Hospitals Capital* (6$\frac{1}{2}$%) (£107 million)	113	Fund grants to local authorities)	
Executive Council Services Administration ($\frac{3}{4}$%) (£11 million)	12		
General Medical (7$\frac{1}{4}$%) (£121 million)	151		
Pharmaceutical (9$\frac{3}{4}$%) (£163 million)	177		
General Dental (4$\frac{3}{4}$%) (£78 million)	95	National Health Service Contributions (9$\frac{1}{4}$%) (£152 million)	185
General Ophthalmic (1$\frac{1}{2}$%) (£23 million)	27	Payments by persons using the service (5%) (£83 million)	89
Welfare Foods (2%) (£33 million)	38		
Local Health Authority (9$\frac{1}{4}$%) (£152 million)	170	Rates & Consolidated Fund Grants to local authorities	239
Local Welfare (5$\frac{1}{2}$%) (£92 million)	104	(12$\frac{3}{4}$%) (£212 million) Other income ($\frac{1}{4}$%)	5
Others (1$\frac{1}{4}$%) (£19 million)	23	(£4 million)	
Cost 1969/70 £1651 million	£1919	Source of Finance 1969/70 £1651 million	£1919

*Includes hospitals, etc., directly administered by the Department of Health and Social Security.

Note: Total cost of Health and Welfare and Social Security would appear to be over £5190 million.

this reason it has been thought fit to point to some of the dangers outlined above. The financial provision for the aged is so vital for their health and welfare that unless this provision is adequate – and it may not be with repeated inflation – no health service is really likely to be of much benefit to them.

The elderly can be helped by a greater pension, which will allow them to purchase what they require, or by provision of social and health services designed to meet their requirements, or by a combination of the two. The provision of services possesses several advantages over the mere raising of the pension. First, there are the number of elderly people who could afford to pay for such services, if they were in existence, who otherwise are unable to look after themselves and have to be admitted into institutions. There are quite a number of elderly people living in large houses, with a fair income, who have become very aged and frail and require personal help which they are unable to obtain. Second, it is to be noted that there are almost $2\frac{1}{2}$ million people in England and Wales aged 75 years and over, and it is clear that most of these require some help with the housework, cooking, assistance at dressing and undressing, and almost full-time attention for periods when they are ill. The responsibility of looking after these people at present falls upon the relatives and neighbours, but it has already been pointed out in the earlier chapters of this book that many have no relatives. The present picture is that about a million and a quarter old people are living alone. A great number have relatives, but many of the latter cannot, or do not, take on this responsibility. The provision of health and social services has an additional advantage; they can operate to a large extent regardless of the problems of inflation and deflation.

SOCIAL SERVICES

Pensions, National Health and Social Security have already been dealt with, and it is now necessary to consider Welfare Services. In general, the Welfare Services come under the Local Authority, and this is a very important point because they are paid locally, whereas the previous services are paid for by national taxation. Since there is no clear distinction in the elderly between social care and health care, as already pointed out, when the social problems of the elderly are not adequately dealt with by the Local Authority, the Health Service is burdened with social problems. Conversely, when the Health Service is inadequate, the burden of health problems fall upon the Local Authority. It can be well appreciated that according to the outlook of the Local Authority, the provision of Welfare Services varies from one part of the country to another. It is perhaps now worth considering the Local Authority's Welfare Service in detail.

HOME HELP SERVICE

The provision of home helps now comes under the control of the Social Services Department.

Home helps were originally planned for maternity cases, and many of them were trained and recruited especially for this work. As a consequence, such home helps had to meet certain requirements, and some idea of these requirements can be gained from the following list of home help duties:

(i) Full-time helps attend between the hours of 8.0 a.m. and 5.0 p.m. Monday to Friday, and 8.0 a.m. and 12 noon Saturday. Part-time helps attend 8.0 a.m. to 12 noon Monday to Saturday inclusive, or less frequently by arrangement. Neither part-time nor full-time workers attend on Sundays or Bank Holidays.

(ii) The full-time home helps will do the ordinary current household washing for the family but will not undertake any arrears of washing. She will also cook for the family and be responsible for the general supervision of the children. She will be responsible for keeping the house clean but will expect to find it clean when she arrives. Part-time home helps will do some of the above in accordance with arrangements previously made between the householder and the organiser.

(iii) The home help will bring her own food. No money should be given to her, nor must she accept beer or spirits. Householders are requested to give home helps facilities for cooking and consuming their midday meal – one hour is allowed for this purpose.

(iv) The home help must not interfere in any way with the instructions of the doctor or midwife. She will not wash the patient or make her bed, or undertake any of the duties of a nurse.

(v) In confinement cases all applicants for the services of a home help will be notified in advance as to the amount of fee payable. The fee should be paid at least one month before her services are requested. No home help will be sent unless the fee is paid.

(vi) The home help takes up her duties after the birth of the baby and not before. All requests for home helps must be received by 10.30 if required for the following day.

It is I believe pretty obvious that this kind of home help is not suited for geriatric patients, and further the number of do's and don'ts are unlikely to encourage people to take up this kind of work. It can also be seen that the care of the elderly is linked with that of the care of the maternity case, and in practice it so often happens that a home help is withdrawn from looking after an elderly person, perhaps when she is very ill, and put on a maternity case.

In 1966 to 1968 the Home Help Service was set up as shown:

Home Help Service – 1966–68
Number of Staff (whole-time equivalents in brackets)[1]

	1966	1967	1968
Organisers, whole-time	823	861	908
Organisers, part-time	145 (55)	129 (47)	137 (50)
Total	968 (878)	990 (908)	1045 (958)
Home Helps, whole-time	2981	2981	2966
Home Helps, part-time	61 395 (27 263)	64 767 (29 008)	65 129 (28 984)
Total	64 376 (30 244)	67 748 (31 989)	68 095 (31 950)
Total staff	65 344 (31 122)	68 738 (32 897)	69 140 (32 908)

For 1973 the number of equivalent whole-time home helps came to 3067 and 86% of all recipients were 65 years or over with a further 7% for the chronically ill. (Ref. Dept. Health & Social Security Annual Report 1975, p. 63–64.)

It can be seen that the bulk of the work of home helps is concerned with old age and chronic sickness, and perhaps the duties of a home help for the aged should be specifically slanted to meet their needs and should not involve attending maternity cases.

There are variations from one local authority to another, from less than 0·1 to more than 1·2 whole-time equivalents per 1000 population, and in their plans for 1972 variations from 0·26 to 1·53. It seemed that a ratio of 0·73 was likely to be too low for 1972.

Comment As it is stated in the Health and Welfare Memorandum: 'The right division between hospital and community care, and, in the case of the elderly, between residential care and care in the home, can never be achieved where the home help service is deficient', thus it would appear obvious that in those areas where there are too few home helps, e.g. 0·26 per 1000, this 'right division' is not taking place and is unlikely to do so in the future, unless their numbers are trebled, and there is a greater expenditure on all of them.

The number of home helps varies from town to town; in one town there may be a couple of dozen to a population of 150 000, whereas in another town of comparable size, the home helps are numbered in hundreds. The cost of a home help varies, but is approximately (60p) an hour, and this is quite beyond the means of the average old age pensioner. A home help from the Social Department may have to travel a considerable distance to a patient's home, and since the geriatric patient usually requires a little help for about half an hour at breakfast, midday and in the evening, the home help from the Social Service Department cannot meet this need.

Elderly persons do receive help in the homes in another kind of way; usually the Social Security Department gives the pensioner an allowance to pay for the services of a neighbour. This latter kind of 'home help' is admirably suited to the work, since she is able to pop in two or three times a day to help the patient dress, or get a little meal, etc. This kind of home help need not be of any particular official standard, because she is actually employed by the pensioner, though indirectly the money comes from the Social Security Department. There is every reason to think that it is this kind of home help that should be organised on a large scale. In this regard it should be noted there are a large number of females receiving a pension at the age of 60 who perhaps could be encouraged to do this work. Until recently they were discouraged from this kind of work, because they were penalised if they earned money. The inadequate organisation is also discouraging. There appear to be a large number of people who would do home help duties in their own locality, but who are unable to travel around and therefore cannot be recruited into the Social Department Many thousands of pounds are spent on building Welfare Homes and maintaining a few elderly persons in this kind of way.

HOME HELP SERVICE ON A NATIONAL SCALE

Such a service should be less costly than the building of further Welfare Homes and maintenance of old people in Institutions, or alternatively using the hospitals for social admissions. If this service could be accepted as designated employment, that is to say, pensioners employed in the service could earn money without any corresponding deduction in their pension, then it is probable that a sufficient number could be recruited. At present, there is approximately three-quarters of a million persons unemployed in Britain, and $4\frac{1}{2}$ million unemployed in America, so that the organisation of such a service would give a measure of employment.

MORAL PRINCIPLE

There appear to be two different kinds of interpretation of the responsibility of relatives. In the first, the law does not place any legal responsibility on a relative for the care of the parents, whereas the Department of Social Security, in practice, takes the view that people have a moral responsibility to look after their parents as regards personal care. Thus it is that an elderly person in very poor health may receive no assistance for a home help if there are relatives in the neighbourhood. This places many elderly pensioners in a most invidious position, since so many of them are unable to obtain any assistance, either from their relatives or from social security. There seems a need to define clearly the responsibility of the relatives and that of the State, capable of only one interpretation, so that the patient does not fall between two stools. It is contrary to human nature, and to family life, to expect the State to undertake full responsibility and it is unlikely that it will ever do so.

Apart from the question of home helps, the whole relationship of a family to their parents seems to require much more careful consideration. The welfare of the elderly was evidently a matter of considerable concern to the Israelites in the time of Moses and was written into the Ten Commandments, and these have been accepted as a moral code of behaviour throughout our civilisation. Yet today, despite the numerous churches in the country and the large numbers of clergy of all denominations, no special emphasis has been made by them on the duties of the family towards each other. It also seems particularly unfortunate that whatever influence they may have does not bear directly on the making of laws in Britain. To many it seems there is no moral foundation to a number of the Acts of Parliament, and that these confuse, misinterpret and at times undermine the Christian way of life. Though it may seem vague and unrealistic to touch upon theology and religion, it is by no means unimportant, since a proper sense of family ties and responsibilities can do more for the elderly than all the pension rights, rules and regulations.

HEALTH VISITING SERVICE

Local Authorities operate a Health Visiting Service, so that the health needs of people in their homes can be brought to the attention of the Community Physician. It should be remembered that every patient has the free services of a general practitioner, and that he is pretty well acquainted with the patient's health and home conditions. Now as regards the elderly, there is little difficulty in ascertaining how unsatisfactory the home conditions are and the problem is what is to be done when the health visitor's report has been read. It may be obvious that the patient has insufficient money to live on, but this is a matter for the Department of Social Security, or the house may be in a bad state and this has to be referred to the Housing Authority, or that there should be home improvements to lessen the risk of a home accident. (Note: 74%

of the fatal falls at home affect old people over 75 years of age.) The weakness of health visiting as regards the elderly is that the recommendations of the report can rarely be implemented, and it so often leads to an impossible number of requests for admission to hospital or a welfare home. There seems to be a need for a special fund to be set aside to carry out necessary improvements in the homes of the elderly.

In 1968[5] the personnel employed in health visiting were as follows:

Health Visiting	1968
Whole-time	992
Part-time	6749 (4417) (Whole-time equivalents)
Persons 65 and over visited =	357 997
(but note there are 2 100 000 persons 75 and over)	

In 1973 there were the whole-time equivalent of 6212 health visitors and a total of 8172 such personnel, and they dealt with 531 721 visits to those 65 years and over, out of a total of 4 196 214 visits. (Ref. Dept. Health and Social Security Annual Report 1973, page 26.) There is a great shortage of nurses and whether such a number who have the nursing skill to deal with ill people will be used to the best advantage is a moot point. Considering the vast number of elderly people the number visited by health visitors is not really very great and there does seem a need to concentrate more health visiting on the elderly.

HOME NURSING

The Home Nursing service is run mainly by the Local Authorities and partly by voluntary bodies. In 1968 the number of home nurses were given as in the table opposite.[6]

One notes there is a considerable increase of nurses.

It is clear that home nursing is a very valuable and vital service for the elderly.

However, the nursing demands of the elderly are very considerable indeed, and the home nurses are too few in number. The consequence of this is that many elderly patients have to be removed to hospital, who could otherwise be nursed at home. But even if there were, as there should be, more home nurses, they would not be effective unless there was also help in the home or provision of home helps. Neither the services of the family doctor nor the visiting nurse can be properly made use of, unless there is someone in the home who could keep the bedroom warm, and see that the patient has enough to eat and drink.

There is considerable difficulty in the recruitment of both home helps and home nurses, but all too often the trouble is not so much difficulty

Home Nursing – 1968	
Home nurses, whole-time	6470
Home nurses, part-time	4492 (2333) (whole-time equivalents)
Patients aged 65 or over at time of first visit	502 611
All patients (including those 65 or over)	908 447
The figures for 1973 (Ref. Dept. Health & Social Security Annual Report 1973, page 26) are given as –	
Whole-time equivalents	10 217
Number of home nurses	11 970
Patients aged 65 or over at time of first visit	877 679

over recruitment as the low establishment for home helps and home nurses. There is every reason to think a great emphasis should be made on the Home Nursing Service, especially for the care of the elderly.

AMBULANCE SERVICE

The Ambulance Service is usually provided by the Local Authority under the responsibility of the Community Physician. The provision of an efficient ambulance service is most important for the elderly. This is particularly so when a geriatric unit is established, and an out-patient department for geriatric patients is opened. In fact an out-patient department can hardly function without an adequate ambulance service. A five-year survey of the ambulance services was carried out, and the following figures may be of interest:[7]

Number of Ambulances, Sitting-case Cars and Drivers		
	5 July	31 March
	1948	*1952*
Ambulances	3228	3380
Sitting-case cars (excluding the hospital car service)	583	1031
Drivers and attendants (whole-time paid)	5846	9436

The figures show an increase in drivers and attendants, but no great increase in the number of ambulances. The advent of the National Health Service meant the whole population became a health responsibility, so that the increase in the ambulances does not appear to be very considerable. The Ministry of Health is placing greater emphasis on the development of geriatric units throughout the country, and this in its turn must mean an increased load on the ambulance service; this load having to be borne by the local authorities. Clearly, the development of the National Health Service involves the local authorities in many extra commitments, for instance:

	Period	Estimated Cost
Net expenditure of Local Health Authority 5 July 1948 to Services	31 March 1949 £18 960 551	1953–4 £41 593 000

Projected Ambulance Service is as follows:

	31/3/1962	31/3/1967	31/3/1972
Stations	965	953	964
Ambulances	5275	5853	6285
Staff (whole-time equivalent)	12 855	14 611	15 634

For 1972/73 the cost of the ambulance service for England rose to £48 842 000. (Ref. Health and Personal Social Services Statistics for England 1974, page 25.)

Residential Care

WELFARE

At March 31st, 1973, accommodation in England was provided for 106 361 persons 65 years and over. In the future, it is planned that there should be 25 places in Residential Homes and 50 places in sheltered housing for every 1000 persons 65 years and over. But nowadays a person at home receives a pension, free medical care, nursing care, health visiting, care at a day-hospital, home help, meals on wheels, etc. If their needs are greater than this, they are often unfit for residential accommodation. At the same time, many in such accommodation could be cared for in sheltered housing. There is also an element of unfairness in accommodating a very few in Star 2 homes for life whilst the great majority of elderly persons in need continue to live in slum-like conditions. One notes there has been an increase of admissions for short stay from 26 033 at March 31st, 1972, to 29 096 at March 31st, 1973. A good argument can be made for using Residential accommodation mainly for short stay for social emergencies. At present there are about 15 places in residential homes per thousand elderly persons but it would appear more necessary to make the building of sheltered housing a greater priority and to rethink the role of the Residential Accommodation.

Some 600 small Homes for old people have also been provided by voluntary bodies since the war. It is becoming evident that the persons in the Institutions and Homes are much older and more infirm than in former times. The welfare accommodation provided by the Local Authority often consists of two types, i.e. the older type of Institution, and the smaller Home. In all areas the responsibility comes under the Department of Social Security. This arrangement is convenient since they are also responsible for the provision of home helps.

OLD-TYPE INSTITUTION

Many of these Institutions were originally work-houses, and were built many years ago. They were not intended for the very aged and frail, so much as the destitute person who was ambulant. The historical background often still clings to the Institution and an attitude of caring for the down and outs, the poverty-stricken and the socially undesirable. The Institution has commonly one or more floors, various stairways, long draughty corridors, and a huge assembly and dining hall. The ground-floor accommodation is often limited because of the presence of the kitchens, linen rooms, administrative offices, etc. The whole atmosphere is hardly in keeping with the care of elderly persons who have been nicely brought up and used to more homely surroundings; neither is the physical accommodation suitable to the care of the aged and infirm. The maintenance, repair and renovation of these buildings can be very expensive.

THE SMALLER HOME

Many Local Authorities set up smaller Homes for groups of about thirty residents. Some of these have been properly planned and newly built, but most of these Homes have been obtained by purchasing large houses which, being old fashioned and out-of-date, have been bought cheaply. Such houses often have two flights of stairs, large spacious rooms and a large garden. At present, for every bed in a small Home, there are slightly less than two beds in an Institution, whereas previously, for every bed in a small Home there were eleven beds in an Institution. The small Home has many advantages, but one very big disadvantage, namely the presence of stairs and insufficiency of ground-floor accommodation.

The control of the admission and discharge of the people to the Homes rests with the Local Authority. In all areas the responsibility comes under the Dept. of Social Security. This arrangement is convenient since they are also responsible for the provision of home helps.

Welfare Homes for the elderly require careful consideration. The author is indebted to the late Dr S. Cieman for the following observations:

SICK BAY

A sick bay for both sexes is essential and in view of the numbers of those requiring two or three days in bed with some nursing attention it should be possible to use the ordinary bed units which are close to a small treatment room, itself adjoining the office of the Warden of the Home.

EXAMINATION AND TREATMENT ROOM

This room should be fitted up as a minor dressing room with an examination-treatment couch, a dressing trolley, a surgeon's handbasin, a small sink and drainer, a small electric steriliser, a medicine cabinet incorporating a small double lock, DDA and poison compartments, dressing and nursing cupboard with a top and some wall shelving.

A shelf or two is required near, or adjacent, to the sink for urine specimens, and lavatory containers together with a gas bunsen burner would also be required. If the warden is not a trained nurse, the visiting nurse would use this treatment room as her work centre.

A SMALL UTILITY ROOM

A small utility room should be provided as part of the sick bay, and if possible, the urine testing alcove and treatment room should be put in there instead of in the examination or treatment room.

The question of providing a combined office and consulting room for the *visiting doctor* preferably adjoining or communicating with the treatment room should be considered. An ambulant resident could be seen here in privacy and examined in the treatment room if necessary. Of course, a doctor's desk, etc., could be incorporated in the examination and treatment room, but a separate room is preferable.

BATHROOMS

In my view a bathroom should have shower arrangements, preferably in the form of a shower stall, a stainless steel basket seat which is ringed to the wall, and shower nozzle adjustable both as a spray or jet and for height. The hot water temperature should be thermostatically controlled. Both the bathroom and shower floor should have a slight gradient towards a galley.

A bathtub designed for the infirm has some special features. The head end should be continued as a flat top upon which a person can sit, rotating his or her buttocks so that the legs dangle over the head of the bath and with the aid of a wall handrail lever himself or herself into the bath. The head end constructed stepwise is an advantage. A hand rail mounted above the taps is also useful for levering oneself into or out of the bath.

Alternatively a special bath may be purchased whose height can be varied by means of adjustable legs and which is fitted with hand-grips and a fibre-glass seat.

There are many types of bathing procedures and one which has been found very safe and acceptable to the patient is known as the Droitwich

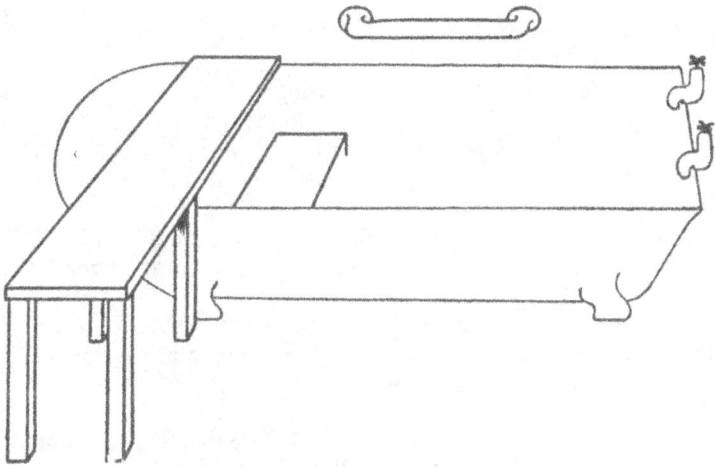

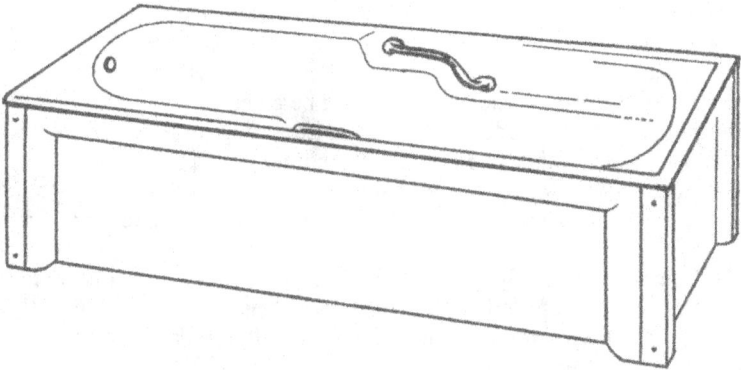

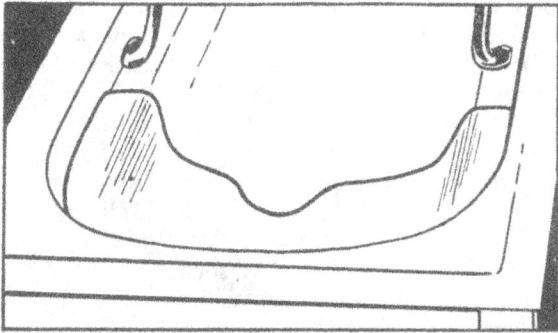

bathing system. Essentially the patient comes to the bathroom in a wheel chair and then is gently lifted up by the nurse using a hand motivated hydraulic pump; the patient is swung round over the bath water and very gently lowered. For the patient to get out of the bath the procedure is reversed. The great point about this system is that no lifting is required – one nurse can bath a patient and there is no fear of the latter being suddenly immersed in hot or cold water.

I would remind you that some, if not all, bathroom lavatory doors should be wide enough for the passage of a wheel chair without the risk of damaging the furniture.

A blanket warming cupboard is required on the ground floor.

There should be an *emergency bell* in each bedroom and bed-sitting room as well as in each bathroom.

Planning should allow for a light room large enough to accommodate wheel chair, stretcher trolley and walking-sticks, etc.

I assume lounges and dining room will be shared by both sexes. In some homes it has been found necessary to assign a small sitting room for each sex, so that the men and women could sit apart if they wish.

If the local authority has not provided chiropody and hairdressing facilities elsewhere, consideration should be given to provide a comprehensive service to include chiropody, hairdressing and barbering.

May I list a number of items which require careful planning.

(1) Accommodation for general stores, groceries, provisions, together with refrigeration readily accessible to the rear entrance for tradesmen.

(2) Kitchen larder adjacent to the grocery store and leading directly to the wash-up and dining room which is to be designed with a self-service counter communicating with the kitchen and with doors leading on into a verandah.

(3) The stores and kitchen should be readily accessible to refuse and swill bins and the latter area should easily hose down.

(4) The lounges should be so designed as to provide (a) a quiet section for reading and writing (?Red Cross or an extension of the Municipal Library) (b) A recreation room for indoor games (c) A television room (d) A handicrafts room. All the sub-divisions should be inter-communicating so that they can be merged into one hall for concerts, movies, sing songs, whist drives, dances, lectures, discussions, etc., if possible the lounge and dining room should communicate direct with a verandah or terrace to the garden area.

(5) Room equipped as a residents' personal laundry with automatic washing and drying machine and facilities for ironing, etc., preferably located in a light and airy basement (if any).

(6) A flower arranging room with the appropriate cupboard, shelving, sink and refuse bin on each floor.

(7) Storing space for mattresses, blankets, pillows, etc., on each floor.

(8) Linen room on each floor, or, if a daily exchange of clean or soiled linen is to be organised, large linen cupboards in recesses strategically placed would suffice.

(9) Soiled linen. This can be sent via a chute to a small hosable enclosure on the ground floor, or at basement level close to the rear entrance accessible to the laundry van.

(10) Cleaner's closet with a slop sink on each floor.

(11) Workshop in the basement for the general handyman.

(12) Box room to be located in the basement provided a lift service is available.

(13) Sink slab can easily be placed on each floor for filling and emptying hot water bottles.

(14) A warden's accommodation – self-contained flat or non-resident.

(15) Staff accommodation. Resident staff may be housed in a partitioned-off section of the Home, with a separate entrance, or in an adjacent house, the staff lounge and dining room should be large enough and changing rooms and lavatories adequate for use by the non-resident staff also.

(16) Night accommodation for a resident night attendant and her relief.

(17) Male and female cloakrooms to be provided near the entrance hall for outdoor clothes, umbrellas, etc.

(18) The flooring space, lighting, night lighting and individual bedside and chairside lighting to be in common rooms and bedrooms will require careful and special consideration. The heating arrangements may call for discussion.

Additional Amenities

(1) Garden allotments to interest male and female residents with the usual storage space.

(2) A bar. One of the more recent additions in Old Folks amenities is the provision of a small bar open during certain hours of the day and managed by a committee of residents.

(3) A bowling green. If space permits the construction of a bowling green may be outlined at a later date.

(4) GPO telephone. Facilities should be provided on each floor.

(5) Bicycle shelter for motorised cycles and a garage for staff will also be required.

(6) Space in the grounds or in the house itself might be provided as a workshop for interested residents.

The requirements outlined may seem to be extensive but it should be kept in mind that as time goes on the residents will be very aged.

HOSPITAL

Whilst of course many elderly persons are treated in the acute wards, in fact, usually 25% of the patients are elderly; they are only, or (in view of the cost and lack of special facilities appropriate to their care) should be there, only for short periods. The total geriatric beds show a slight and quite unrealistic rise by 1975. As regards beds for mental illness, if one remembers that about one-third of the patients in mental hospitals are elderly, a proposed reduction of about 60 000 beds could mean a reduction of 20 000 beds to the elderly confused, just when the assessed number of very elderly people is rising steeply.

Hospital Beds (Ref. Health and Personal Social Services Statistics for England 1974, p. 62–63)

	Great Britain thousands	
	1959	1973
Total	548	502
Average daily available:		
Medical	89	69
Surgical	89	98
Geriatric and units for younger disabled	62	70
Mental Illness	178	135

MEMORANDA ON GERIATRIC CARE

A recent official survey of services for old people and the chronic sick has been made, and the principal general conclusions have been set out in the Guillebaud Committee's Report. As a result, the Ministry of Health have issued two memoranda, one to the hospital authorities entitled *Geriatric Services and the Care of the Chronic Sick* (HM (57) 86),[11] and one to the local authorities entitled *Local Authority Services for the Chronic Sick and Infirm* (Circular 14/75). In a very elderly person, it is often a matter of difficulty to decide how much of the care is welfare and the responsibility of the local authority, and how much is ill-health and the responsibility of the Health Service. The relative responsibility is defined in paragraphs 11 and 12 of the Memorandum HM (57) 86, and reads as follows:

11 Apart from the active elderly person who is in need of residential care, and who is clearly the responsibility of the welfare authority, the latter's responsibility also extends to the following:

(a) Care of the otherwise active resident in a welfare home during minor illnesses which may involve a short period in bed.

(b) Care of the infirm (including the senile) who may need help in dressing, toilet, etc., may need to live on the ground floor because they cannot manage stairs and may spend part of the day in bed (or longer periods in bad weather).

(c) Care of those elderly persons in a welfare home who have to take to bed and are not expected to live more than a few weeks (or exceptionally months) and who would, if in their own homes, stay there because they cannot benefit from treatment or nursing care beyond what can be given at home, and whose removal to hospital away from their familiar surroundings and attendants would be felt to be inhumane.

All these are people for whom any necessary nursing care would be given by relatives, etc., with the help or advice of the home nurse if they were living in their own homes. In welfare homes that care should be given by attendants, assisted or advised by the visiting home nurse in the small welfare home, or by a small staff with nursing qualifications or experience in the large homes.

It is not regarded as the responsibility of the welfare authority to give prolonged nursing care to the bedfast (except in those in (c) above) nor is it a good thing to make separate 'infirmary wards' in large homes, in which patients from other homes are concentrated.

12 Apart from the acute sick and others needing active treatment, who are clearly the responsibility of the hospital authority, the latter's responsibility also extends to the following:

(a) Care of the chronic bedfast who may need little or no medical treatment but do require prolonged nursing care over months or years.

(b) Convalescent care of the elderly sick who have completed active treatment but are not yet ready for discharge to their own homes or to welfare homes.

(c) Care of senile, confused or disturbed patients who are unfit to live a normal community life in a welfare home.

It is not the responsibility of the hospital authority to give all medical or nursing care needed by an old person, however minor the illness or however short the stay in bed; nor to admit all those who need nursing care because they are entering upon the last stage of their lives.

It is clearly most desirable that the respective responsibility should be defined in this way, as in fact should perhaps each factor relating to the care of the elderly, but the definition does imply that the Local Authority accept a much greater responsibility than hitherto. Up to the present, the Authority has in many instances declined to accept a person who could not manage stairs, or who needed some assistance in dressing, or going to the toilet. The Memorandum now is clearly asking the local authority to look after this kind of case. This raises many difficulties. Their Homes, whether of the old type institution or the smaller Home, have very little ground-floor accommodation, and it may be physically impossible to look after such infirm people unless they make alterations such as putting in lifts, replacing steps by ramps, widening doors for wheel chair cases, etc. They are also expected to undertake simple nursing care as would be given by relatives, and frequently they have not the staff to do this work. If the local authority are able to accept this new responsibility, it means a completely new idea of who should be in a Welfare Home. If a patient can go upstairs, and needs no help in dressing or going to the toilet, far from being suitable for a Welfare Home he is far too able-bodied and should be accommodated in some other way. The Welfare Homes would in this way gradually take on the function of looking after the very infirm, who up to now have been considered as suitable only for a 'Halfway House' kind of home. This change in function will bring with it an increase in running cost.

If this change is brought about in the Welfare Homes, it should greatly assist the hospitals who so often have many frail ambulants unfit to return home. It will also imply that the fully ambulant person should be accommodated in an old person's bungalow, flat, etc. Groups of bungalows or flats could be set aside, and a warden with home help duties accommodated nearby.

The present position, therefore, is that the responsibilities of the local authority have been defined, but it is a far cry from this to its translation into action. First, the change in the type of accommodation has to be properly explained, together with all its implications, and then the Authority has to consider the cost and the question of increasing local taxation. Finally, if this is approved, there will be the problem of architectural alterations or new Homes, or the taking on of additional staff, if they can be obtained. Clearly, all this will take time; how long will depend on the enthusiasm with which the matter is taken up, and the amount of vision put into any forward planning.

Looking back over the matter of care for the elderly, one gets the impression that the government is becoming concerned about the enormous cost of the Health Service as at present, and even more so when the hundreds of millions for new district hospitals are taken into account. As a result, the government plans seem to put a limitation to the hospital service – perhaps quite rightly. This may still give a good service for the younger age groups, but the number of very elderly are increasing rapidly, and surely there should be not a limitation but an increase of geriatric beds. After all, there are over $7\frac{1}{2}$ million elderly persons, and the hospital geriatric and welfare beds put together only amount to 176 361.

To define what is a hospital responsibility and leave elderly people who are outside the definition to the care of the local authority may have the attraction of being administratively neat. But since it is quite obvious that the expenditure and personnel for domiciliary care is too little, in effect it means putting the care of the elderly in a kind of bureaucratic no-man's land. The local authorities' 10-year plan has now been published; is it likely to meet the needs of the elderly?

The Ministry of Health Report makes some criticism, couched in very mild phrases such as: 'Regarding Home Helps. A ratio of 0·73 is likely to be too low for 1972.' Or 'Regarding Home Visitors. A ratio of 0·17 per 1000 for 1972 is necessary.' And so on. The attitude of the government towards the local authorities seems almost reverential as if they were sacrosanct. Where the matter is purely of local concern, for example, the Fire Service, this can be understood, but in the eyes of most people, including councillors themselves, the care of the elderly is still national responsibility. True the local authorities are democratically elected, but so often the number of voters actually taking part surely does not give the councillors the right to resent criticism. The local authorities appear to have tried hard to provide a local health service – their expenditure in this direction since 1948 has gone up over four times. But the problem seems so vast that it cannot be met out of local rates. One must always stress co-ordination but this does not of itself provide personnel and facilities. Yet without adequate domiciliary care the elderly, not only the sick but the infirm, become a hospital responsibility. This entails great expense, for a vast number of elderly persons are admitted to acute wards. Further, is this hospital care proving to be successful?

For men the expectation of life at 65 today is only a little better than it was in 1890. This fact must not be lightly glossed over. Does it mean that all this surgery, medicine, pathology, radiology and treatment of elderly persons is rather futile, and that the hospital expense is wasteful? One cannot think this is true. But probably as regards the acute wards there is some truth in it. The causes of death amongst the elderly include those due to degenerative conditions and neoplasms. In 1890 elderly people died from these conditions in much the same way but they also died of smallpox, scarlet fever, diphtheria, whooping cough, typhus fever, enteric fever, diarrhoea and dysentery, cholera, phthisis and many other infectious diseases as listed in the Registrar General's Report.[17] Today elderly people do not die of all these latter conditions and one would, therefore, have expected a much greater expectation of life for older people. One can only conclude that hospital care and much of the medical care is not proving successful. The reasons for this are difficult to give. Perhaps the elderly in 1890 were the privileged few and belonged to the better off section of the community, but from looking at the causes of death at that time this seems rather unlikely. There seems an idea about that times then were very dreadful and vast numbers of people died in the work-house. A study of the statistics shows this to be untrue. Only a minority of people died in any institutions then as compared to a large number who do today. On questioning some elderly people and inquiring how things were for their parents when the former were very young, they often say that times were hard and their parents worked, even though very aged. Also that there were usually sons or daughters living with the parents or close by and frequently visiting them and caring for them. Again there is a common impression that all was misery for old people in 1890, as if spring never came, the flowers never bloomed or the birds sang, and that it was continual winter. This again seems to be wrong. The answers to the questions are often that, despite all their hardships, their mothers and fathers were quite happy and certainly more contented. As far as one can conclude from personal experience, the reason why the expectation of life hasn't improved for the elderly is that for them there is not the same amount of companionship and home care as there was with previous generations. It would also appear that if better home care could be arranged a great amount of hospital admissions would be unnecessary. This matter is taken up again when considering home helps.

The usual explanation given for the poor improvement of life expectation in the male is that in them there is an increasing incidence of lung cancer and of bronchitis. True, there is an increase in lung cancer, but comparatively not greater than the increase in females of hypertensive heart disease, pneumonia, accidents, etc. Further, bronchitis is a winter disease related to *cold* – cold houses, cold draughts, damp bedrooms, bad housing conditions and other *sociological* rather than medical factors. Thus social conditions, including housing, have to be considered when considering life expectancy.

HOUSING

A large number of houses are under the control of the Local Authority and the co-operation of the housing department is very important in any programme for the care of the elderly. The housing department should be knowledgeable about the needs of the elderly, but this is not always so. Very expensive houses, flats and bungalows are put up, without any discussion with the Local Health Authority on the geriatric position, or others who have to look after the elderly in their homes. The allocation of bungalows and flats also does not seem to take into account the various welfare problems in the area. One knows of instances where the Housing Department has taken over a house because the tenant was in a welfare home or hospital temporarily, and the rent was in default. The cost to the Local Authority of keeping someone in a welfare home is likely to be over £20 a week until another home is provided, whereas the rent the elderly person was paying may have been only a few pounds a week, so that the lack of co-operation between the housing department and the welfare department is a costly one to the taxpayer. At other times, the pensioner enters hospital and it is clear he will not be fit to return home, yet he continues to pay his rent and hence keeps empty much needed housing accommodation. At the same time, in the same ward, there may be an ambulant elderly person fit for discharge, but without any home available. There is also the question of bungalow accommodation. Some tenants in bungalows are very old and infirm and would be better accommodated in a welfare home, and, conversely, many pensioners in a welfare home are quite ambulant and could be better accommodated in a bungalow. If the situation is thoroughly surveyed, the problem may be not so much of building new homes, but the more correct placing of old people according to their physical and mental fitness, in bungalows, flats, ground-floor accommodation, welfare homes or in the hospital. Much of this can only be brought about by closer co-operation between the various departments of the local authority.

Housing is important in planning Home Care. At present, for the most part, elderly people are living in ones and twos scattered throughout a town or rural area. Thus, if a number of elderly persons require help it may mean the doctor, home nurse, health visitor or home help having to spend a good deal of time travelling hither and thither from one place to another. It thus often becomes impossible with the staff available to sustain the very elderly at home, especially in the winter. On the other hand if they could be housed in small groups, e.g. 20–30 persons in specially constructed 'Granny Flats', more elderly people could be attended to with much greater efficiency. It has been advised by the Ministry of Housing that when providing new housing accommodation, about 30% of it should be for elderly persons. Remembering that there are about 12% elderly people in the population, in round numbers a rough estimate for the housing of 100 persons might be:

Home units for	4	Single elderly persons (1 bed)	4
Home units for	4	Couples, elderly persons (1 bed)	4
Home units for	22	Families of mother, father and two children (3 beds)	22
Total persons	100	Home units	30

Unless elderly persons are housed in something like the above proportions, it would mean a measure of over-crowding for young families and a continuation of under-occupation by older people in 2, 3 or more bedroomed houses. The design of the 'Granny Flats' mentioned above has been set out with considerable detail in the appendix to Ministry of Housing and Local Government circular No. 18/57 and the Ministry of Housing and Local Government's handbook *More Flatlets for Old People*.

Terminal Care

Much has been said about the situation of old people at home and the difficulties of home care. It is, therefore, not surprising to see that the majority of deaths are now taking place in hospitals and institutions rather than at home.

Many patients are unhappy at being taken away from their own homes to die in a hospital amongst strangers, however kindly they may be. At the same time neither the expensive hospital facilities nor the wards are really suitable for this type of case. To die at home seems a more natural process. The moving of elderly people by ambulance when seriously ill can be more detrimental to their recovery than any possible gain from hospital care. The matter becomes all the more serious because the deaths are concentrated into a few winter months (see below) which usually disorganise the hospital service every year.

Deaths at different ages by month of occurrence, 1962

Age		January	August
All Ages	M	35 592	19 088
	F	35 668	17 806
1	M	57	32
	F	44	33
30	M	175	145
	F	138	110
60	M	3879	2135
	F	2229	1288
65	M	4590	2526
	F	3245	1764
70	M	5335	2846
	F	4841	2449
75	M	5458	2644
	F	6479	3086
80	M	4704	1985
	F	6938	2932
85	M	3641	1404
and over	F	7165	2872

The total deaths for the UK in 1973 were given as follows. (Ref. Annual Abstract of Statistics 1974, p. 35.)

Male	Female	Total
338 788	330 904	669 692

Other statistics of perhaps some interest are also set out in Table 14 of the Statistical Review 1967 as follows:

Age last birthday	Persons	Males Total	Females Total
50–54	21 158	13 075	8083
55–59	35 278	22 902	12 376
100 & over	419	72	347

Registrar General's Quarterly Return for England and Wales – March 1969					
Year	Persons all ages	Males 65–74	Males 75 and over	Females 60–74	Females 75 and over
	(In thousands)				
1968	48 593	1622	707	3798	1493
1971	49 485	1756	715	3921	1558
1981	52 550	1934	889	3973	1831
1991	56 144	1929	999	3804	2038

Total over 75 – Males and Females
                1968 – 2 200 000
                1971 – 2 273 000
                1981 – 2 720 000

It is also of some interest to see the number of deaths from common conditions. (Ref. Annual Abstract of Statistics 1974, p. 39.)

Death by Cause	1969	1973
Malignant neoplasm of lung and bronchus	33 590	36 416
Neoplasm of breast	12 069	12 911
Ischaemic heart disease	161 671	175 544
Influenza	5 066	3 609
Bronchitis and emphysema	36 260	29 585
All accidents	20 069	19 704
Diseases of the circulatory system	337 199	347 251
All neoplasms	131 571	137 300

Apart from the variability of death from influenza, it is remarkable how relatively constant the causes of death remain despite all kinds of treatments and claims of 'break-throughs' and advances in the treatment of cancer and other conditions. It is also worth noting that deaths from accidents are greater than those from neoplasm of the breast, and more than half those from neoplasm of the lung.

Glyn Hughes[9] has surveyed terminal care and his findings make distressing reading. Many elderly people die at home, often without adequate attention and sometimes in conditions that are a disgrace to our society. No plea is entered for special terminal care units, since these would become 'death centres' and the idea is an affront to all sense of humanity, but there is an urgent need, first for an adequate provision of home helps and home nurses and secondly for more geriatric beds.

Since this book was first written it has been possible to see various changes. The pensions for older people have gone up. More are living in council houses, and there has been some increase of welfare beds and domiciliary facilities. But neither the improvements nor those envisaged in the hospital and local authorities' ten year plan would seem likely to meet the needs of the ever-increasing elderly persons. Pensions can be raised quickly, but it will take a long time for sufficient 'Granny Flats' and Welfare Homes to be built, though these are of the utmost importance. Even then, there will always be an increasing number of extremely frail elderly people commensurate with those in the older age groups, who will require hospital long-stay care. Thus there should be provision for many more long-term hospital beds with facilities for rehabilitation and also an increase of beds to meet the demand for terminal care. The author thinks the domiciliary care is inadequate and will not be successful until there is a tremendous increase in home helps. This is unlikely to happen if left to local authorities and the rates, and direct government intervention seems appropriate. Home helps are not an essential part of the medical or nursing discipline or necessarily better organised through the Health Department. Though home helps for maternity care should, as at present, be part of the health service, yet the majority of work by home helps is for old people. It is therefore suggested that geriatric and maternity home helps should be separate services. Now in 1975 the health service has been reorganised and the home help service is part of the Social Service Department. But, the department of social security officers visit six to seven hundred people a week in a given area and are well acquainted with the needs of the elderly. It is for these reasons that a geriatric home help service could be based, organised and paid for through the department of social security. The home helps should be made available as considered necessary by the department for their own pensioners and on request by doctors to other persons in need. The Department of Social Security by direct government action could make an immediate improvement in home care and very possibly at the same time, relieve the strain on both acute and long-stay hospital beds.

REFERENCES

1 DEPARTMENT OF HEALTH AND SOCIAL SECURITY *Annual Report* 1968
2 HEALTH WELFARE SERVICES – England and Wales *Annual Report* 1970
3 Health and Welfare Services England and Wales Diagram 1
4 Table 43
5 Table 41
6 Table 42
7 HEALTH AND WELFARE The Development of Community Care – Plans for the Health and Welfare Services of the Local Authorities in England and Wales 1963 page 13
8 page 14
9 HUGHES G 'Peace at Last' A survey of Terminal Care in the United Kingdom 1960 The Calouste Gulbenkian Foundation
10 *The Lancet* 27 January 1962 page 202
11 NATIONAL HEALTH SERVICE Memorandum H.M. (57) 86 *Geriatric Services and the Care of the Chronic Sick*
12 REGISTRAR GENERAL *Decennial Supplement for England and Wales* 1951 Life Tables G page 12
13 REGISTRAR GENERAL *Quarterly Return for England and Wales* March 1960 Appendix K page 48
14 REGISTRAR GENERAL *Statistical Review of England and Wales* 1962 part II Tables Population pages 2 and 3
15 part I

11

NATIONAL HEALTH SERVICE
HOSPITAL ADVISORY SERVICE

E. WOODFORD-WILLIAMS, Bsc, MD, FRCP
Director, Hospital Advisory Service

Most organisations which give a public service have found it necessary to develop means for assessment of the standards achieved and to improve the general level of performance. The National Health Service Hospital Advisory Service for England and Wales is an independent body, first set up in November 1969 by the then Secretary of State for Health and Social Services in response to public concern about conditions in certain hospitals[1]. Factors leading up to this decision are described in the Annual Report of the Department of Health and Social Security for 1969[2]. Details of its initial plan of operation were published in the first of the five Annual Reports of the Hospital Advisory Service.[3-7]

Among its main functions are:

(1) by constructive criticism and by propagating good practices and new ideas, to help to improve the management of patient care in individual hospitals (excluding matters of individual clinical judgement) and in the hospital service as a whole

(2) to advise the Secretary of State for Social Services about conditions in hospitals in England, and the Secretary of State for Wales about conditions in hospitals in Wales.

Although the Hospital Advisory Service operates independently of the Department of Health and Social Security and the Welsh Office, nevertheless it can draw on information available to these Departments about the hospital and associated community services with which it is involved. Furthermore, the Director co-ordinates the work of the Hospital Advisory Service with that of the Regional Health Authorities, who continue to discharge their responsibilities for promoting the improvement of hospital standards in their own regions. In relation to England the Director reports to the Secretary of State for Social Services, and in relation to Wales to the Secretary of State for Wales.

As an Advisory Service the Hospital Advisory Service does not investigate individual complaints or allegations against individuals as it is not equipped to investigate or settle these matters but refers complaints to the channels established for dealing with them. The Advisory Service may, however, contribute in two ways to the solution of some of the problems in this field:

(1) It may examine the services of a hospital that are the subject of serious allegations or an unusual volume of complaints; and advise of deficiencies of management, organisation, physical resources etc. that may give rise to complaints.

(2) Its interest in matters that are the subject of complaints affords the staff who complain some assurance of protection against victimisation.

Concentration at first was on the most vulnerable services, i.e. those for longstay patients in hospitals for mentally handicapped, mentally ill and geriatrics and chronic sick. However, in her foreword to the HAS Annual Report for 1973[6] the Secretary of State for Health and Social Services commented on an announcement she had made in Parliament[8] (Hansard) in which it was said that consideration was being given to extending the role of the Hospital Advisory Service to cover children receiving longstay care in hospitals other than hospitals for the mentally handicapped. And in view of the need to look in a more comprehensive way at services for those groups of patients the Hospital Advisory Service covers at present – the mentally ill and some of the elderly – it was hoped it would be possible to agree that the remit of the Hospital Advisory Service should in future extend to advise on the links between hospital and community health care for these groups of patients, and that it would operate in close association with the Department's Social Work Services who already have a close working relationship with the Local Authority personal social services. Arrangements such as these would bring the Hospital Advisory Service more in line with the reorganised National Health Service enacted in 1973 which came into operation in April 1974[9].

The Director is responsible for planning and direction of the Service and is assisted by a staff of professional advisers who visit hospitals in teams. Teams usually consist of five to six people drawn from the following professional groups:

1. A Consultant.
2. A Senior Nurse of Chief or Principal Nursing Officer or equivalent grade.
3. A Ward Nurse or Charge Nurse.

4. A Hospital Administrator.
5. A Social Worker.
6. A Remedial Therapist.

Psychologists and General Practitioners and representatives of other professional disciplines have been recruited at times for special assignments. The teams are on secondment for periods of from three months to two years and are drawn from people who are relatively senior in their grades and rising in their professions.

Four teams may be operating at any one time but each in a different region of the country. Teams spend approximately one to two weeks in the larger hospitals and lesser periods in smaller units, some of which may contain as few as 20 beds. By the end of 1974, 538 hospitals for geriatrics, containing a total of 41,988 beds, had been visited by the Geriatric Teams, and the number of return visits made by a full team in addition to these were to 8 units containing 1,439 beds.

Hospitals visited are assessed in relation to the total hospital service provided for that specialty for the population served. Therefore when visiting large hospitals serving a considerable catchment area, visits are also made to satellite units run by the main hospital and the individual wards or departments serving the same population sited in general hospitals.

When visiting hospitals, Advisory Teams look at the full range of services provided and consider how far these conform to the norms or minimum standards and other policies as set regionally or nationally. In particular, information is sought and advice given upon:

(1) The service the hospital affords the community and the links it has with the community within the hospital, including relations between the Hospital Management Team and staff, and relations between doctors, nurses, administrators and other professions.
(2) Relations between staff and patients, and
(3) The physical conditions and staff ratios within the hospital.

Prior to undertaking a visit the Department's Regional and the Local Authority Area Offices are asked to supply relevant information concerning hospital statistics, difficulties in the area or in staffing in the hospitals being visited, and invited to make comments. District Management Teams and senior medical and nursing staff and others at the hospital are also notified of the proposed visit and asked to supply information about the hospital's services and invited to submit observations. Arrangements are also made for a meeting with general practititioners and the Directors of Social Services and their staff. Voluntary organisations are notified of the visit and invited to meet the teams.

Prior to the visit notices are posted in the hospital asking for comments, and letters are sent to a group of discharged patients of their relatives. The response to these letters is most satisfactory. A study of the comments made by patients discharged from geriatric hospitals over a period of two years has recently been published[10]. Some of the comments are highly critical while others, by far the majority, are appreciative of the services given, at the same time pointing out deficiencies which, by and large, they attribute to staff shortages.

At the beginning of a visit the Team meets representatives of the Hospital Management Teams and senior staff, primarily for introduction and clarification of the purpose of the visit. After this the Team usually visits some parts of the hospital together, this being important to indicate that the Advisory Service relies on a multidisciplinary approach. Later the Team members begin to form relationships with their opposite numbers to understand the hospital as seen by those who work within it, and staff then may be seen singly or in groups. At the end of a visit the Team members meet again with those who had assembled at the first meeting, often inviting other members of the hospital staff as well. At this meeting the Team presents its observations about the hospital to find out if the staff accepts the portrait as reasonable and accurate, and if not to identify areas of disagreement. Any discussion which follows gives the Team the opportunity of assessing whether the hospital welcomes and supports the proposed changes, which may lead to significant modification of previous conclusions.

It is significant that many of the problems are already resolved prior to the final meeting, as the advice of the Teams is practical so that a great deal of it can be acted upon immediately. The Reports, which are confidential, are sent direct to the Secretaries of State for England, and for Wales and to the Department of Health who are responsible for the follow-up. Feedback is requested by the Department from Regions six months after the visit, but in cases of urgency this time limit is much shorter.

The effective use of available resources on patient care is dependent upon sound operational policies, not only for the individual patient but also for the ward, the day hospital or the hospital as a whole. Regrettably doctors are trained mainly to consider the treatment of the individual patient and it is therefore often only late in their careers that they realise the importance of planning in relating hospital resources to the needs of the population concerned. This helps to explain some of the gross discrepancies that have been found in visiting hospitals.

In general, hospital staff welcome the opportunity of discussing their services with fellow professionals – to many it is more important than physical change, additional finance or material improvement. It does not come as a surprise that the vast majority of staff in the hospital service are deeply concerned about whether or not they are providing the best care for their patients, and welcome the opportunity of discussing critically the various alternatives available. Frank comment is welcomed and is more likely to be productive than counter productive. Hospitals often labour under difficulties and frequently are reluctant to face unpleasant situations, particularly those created by faulty organisation, lack of resources and by personality problems. Hospitals with high morale and well organised can often accept and make good use of constructive criticism; on the other hand hospitals with low morale and major problems may find criticisms difficult to accept and be reluctant to consider change.

Over the years it has become apparent that the Hospital Advisory Service has an important function in the facilitation of change, and in particular of the value of multidisciplinary teamwork, ensuring that a group of different professionals can discuss problems, disagree significantly, and yet can come to a final concensus opinion which will allow decision and action and what is more, following disagreement, can retain good inter-personal relationships. All evidence suggests that multidisciplinary teamwork forms a better basis for patient care than systems which rely on the doctor alone to make the significant decisions and attempt to provide the major treatment resources.

It has been pleasing to note during the past two years the general acceptance of most staff of the need for change and the need for teamwork in the interests of better patient care, and the accumulated evidence suggests that the quality of a department depends very much on the quality of the multidisciplinary team, in particular on its leadership. The leader must be able to weld the skills of all the professionals within the group (doctors, nurses, therapists and social workers) and motivate them towards a common purpose – to improve the quality of life of the individual patient. It is of significance that this does not necessarily involve money but does require a great deal of teamwork and imaginative thinking.

REFERENCES

1 ROBB, B 'Sans Everything – A Case to Answer' Thomas Nelson (1967)
2 Department of Health and Social Security *Annual Report* 1969 pages 43–44 HMSO (Cmnd. 4462) (1970)

3 National Health Service Annual Report* of the Hospital Advisory Service to the Secretary of State for Social Services and Secretary of State for Wales for the years 1969–70 HMSO (1971)

4 *Ibid* for the year 1971* HMSO (1972)

5 *Ibid* for the year 1972* HMSO (1973)

6 *Ibid* for the year 1973* HMSO (1974)

7 *Ibid* for the year 1974* HMSO (1975)

8 HANSARD Vol. 878 Cols. 414–16 Secretary of State's Statement on the future of the Hospital Advisory Service (31 July 1974)

9 National Health Service Reorganisation Act, Chapter 32 HMSO (1973)

10 BALDOCK, P– 'Geriatric Services' – The Patients' Views' *Gerontologia Clinica* 17: 13–22 (1975)

*References in the text of the HAS Annual Reports to 'Department of Health and Social Security' should be assumed to refer also to the Welsh Office where appropriate.

12

HOME HELP SERVICES

K. P. O'CALLAGHAN
Assistant Principal
Home Help Services
Essex County Council

The Home Help Service really began to gain momentum when the National Health Service Act 1946 came into force in 1948 giving local health authorities extended power to provide help in the following circumstances:

'for households where such help is required owing to the presence of any person who is ill, lying in, an expectant mother, aged, or a child not over compulsory school age within the meaning of the Education Act 1944'.

It was not, however, until the Health Service and Public Health Act 1968 that it became a statutory duty for local authorities to provide such a service.

Responsibility for the provision of the Home Help Service passed from the Health Service in 1971 to the newly formed Social Services. The interpretation of need and the means of meeting that need varies with different authorities, some of whom will be providing all or some of the following services.

A weekly or daily allocation of hours or short-term residential help in the home, night sitting service, good neighbour service, home warden service, laundry service, specialised help for families with multiple problems, mobile emergency helpers, provision and loan of household equipment, meals-on-wheels.

Part of the cost of these services may, if appropriate, be recovered from the client. The scale of charges varies considerably between different authorities, some having a free service for pensioners or at some fixed age limit, others providing a free service for those receiving a supplementary pension. The constant factor in terms of the Home Help Service is the elderly receive the greatest part of the available resources; approximately 80% of the budget is spent helping to maintain the elderly in their own homes.

Requests for help come from many sources – hospitals, doctors, district nurses, health visitors, social workers, Department of Health and Social Security, voluntary organisers, i.e. meals-on-wheels, ministers of religion, colleagues within social services and self referrals, the latter being particularly encouraging in that it can be seen as an awareness of the potential preventive quality of the service.

The quality of the referrals is important and as much care as is possible should be taken to ensure the information given is accurate. A responsible attitude by the referrer to the appropriateness and degree of urgency of the request can save a lot of valuable time and quickly build up a mutual trust between the agencies to the eventual benefit of the client. Good two-way communication is of inestimable value to all concerned. Each request for help is followed by a visit from the home help organiser to the prospective clients in their own home, or, if necessary, in hospital prior to their discharge home.

To enable an allocation of hours help to be made, the Home Help organiser will need to observe mobility, alertness and the degree of dependence or, more hopefully, of independence demonstrated by the client, the type of accommodation, i.e. small overcrowded rooms, large cold rooms, how many rooms in use, means of heating rooms, ability and means of cooking a meal, how the water is heated, and sanitation. The toilet may be outside and in some country areas is still an earth closet at the bottom of the garden. Environment is also very important, the distance of nearest neighbour, how far from shops and buses, any pets or livestock to be considered.

Quite a comprehensive picture is built up from this information and the Organiser will have formed an idea of the sort of Helper most likely to fit into the household. It is also then possible to brief the Home Help in advance, if necessary, of any difficulty she may encounter, i.e. blindness necessitating extra care in replacing things as found, deafness, dietary problems, lack of amenities, eccentric behaviour, depression and, in case of difficulty, the means of entry. A simple record should be made of the information gathered at this first interview to aid continuity and communication. The reverse of the record could be divided to record impressions and information on subsequent visits and home help attendances.

Recruitment and selection of helpers is a vital part of the Home Help organiser's job, for it is on her ability to recognise the essential stability and compassion inherent in a good home help that the quality of service available in her area will rest. A personal recommendation from an established helper is a welcome but insufficient means of recruitment; competition from local industry affects, to a considerable extent, the potential help available. Recruits tend to be aged between 28–50 and to have children of school age or older and come from a variety of work experience backgrounds, i.e. hospitals, nursing, clerical, shops, catering, voluntary work, or they may be returning to work after an absence of some years bringing up their families. They are attracted by the flexible hours, variety of work and the job satisfaction gained from 'helping others'. The male home help is frequently recruited from the newly retired. It is often difficult to keep him sufficiently employed because the anti-social male client for whom he is frequently recruited refuses to have a male helper! Female clients are often embarrassed when asked to accept a male helper for anything other than the most routine of household tasks.

Home Helps are in a position of great trust working as they do in isolation. This isolation also calls for considerable resourcefulness on their part, as they do not enjoy the comfort, taken for granted by most people, of turning to a colleague for help, support or guidance when faced with a sudden emergency. It is frequently the home help who finds the elderly client has fallen out of bed and possibly spent many hours on the floor, or may have spent the night wandering around in a confused state, perhaps from accidents with fire, gas taps or pills. Whatever help and support is ultimately provided in any situation, it is the initial shock of coping alone that calls for that extra strength of character.

Good induction and training, seen as an aid to reduce staff turnover, provide a sound basis for the home help to develop her skills and extend her practical experience and to achieve a preparedness for the emotional and physical difficulty of the elderly living alone and for the unhygienic conditions and lack of equipment of some households in which she will be expected to work. 'In Service Training' is invaluable in giving an added awareness of the potential of the Social Services as a whole and the Home Help Services in particular and also other social and medical support services. Speakers from as many disciplines as possible are invited and also included in the programme are visits to a residential home and a geriatric hospital – other subjects frequently include home safety, first aid, nutrition, diets, invalid cookery, hygiene, problems of ageing, stress and personal relationships, giving an understanding of need to attend sensitively with distressed and difficult clients without becoming over involved.

Happy arrangements in the home would not be needlessly changed but physical help is only of minimal use if there is a constant personality difficulty between the client and helper. If the difficulty is mutual, help can be rearranged to the advantage of both sides. If the client complains of a number of helpers, or a succession of helpers ask to be removed from a client, it is sometimes necessary to devise a rota system for helpers to attend for a few weeks at a time. It is not unknown for a client to have had every helper 'on the books' and still not be satisfied or still be so difficult to help that having come to the end of the list the organiser will have to persuade the original helpers to return. If a home help is constantly finding fault with a variety of households she is asked to attend, she would obviously be advised that she is not suitable for this very personal one to one service. It is sometimes difficult for persons with very high standards to accept that people are at liberty to live as they wish in their own home and if, despite the best endeavours of all concerned, help is refused, it has to be accepted that there is no 'right of entry'.

Confusion in the elderly and incontinence, particularly if the latter is suspected to be the result of laziness, are the most difficult problems to overcome.

The confusion that leads the client, particularly if she is living alone and unsupported by relatives, constantly to mislay things such as her pension book or purse, constantly to lose valued possessions or having asked the helper to take some ancient piece of household equipment to be repaired then accuse her when the repair is completed of substituting some inferior article keeping the original for herself, even accusing her of eating the food in the pantry and replacing the empty tins on the shelf, these things are distressing enough for the helper. But, if added to these difficulties there is that of incontinence, the problems increase considerably.

The initial handling of soiled linen is particularly difficult in country districts where households have no flush toilet or running water. It is in these areas that there is less likely to be a laundry service or an accessible launderette. Even in areas with the basic essentials, i.e. running water, there is frequently no adequate means of heating it.

The Home Help, working alone in a household day after day facing these difficulties, can become very demoralised and disheartened. It is then sometimes essential in the interest of maintaining help to the client to relieve the home help for a time of the case and substitute another helper, even acknowledging that the change can sometimes add to the confusion of the client.

Time properly used is the tool of the Home Help Services, not only the amount of time allocated but the time of day for which it is allocated. Every effort is made to arrange the times of attendance to suit the client and by far the greatest number of requests in coal burning areas is for help 'first thing' to light the fire and possibly in areas of modern centrally heated accommodation the requests would be for help to cook a mid-day meal. This is not, however, a practical possibility in every case as each helper has a programme of work and may be attending several households a day; it therefore becomes a matter of priority as to who should receive the early or mid-day visit.

Houses that are sub-standard by modern living standards have repercussions within the Home Help Service because it is so wasteful of time; time taken to bring in water from an outside stand pipe, endless time spent trying to heat sufficient water on the stove to do a little washing, time to empty commodes because the lavatory is down the garden, interminable buckets and boxes to be filled with coal. Kitchen and wash-house across the yard and no electricity means no appliances to get the job done more speedily. These conditions frequently undermine the client's ability to remain in their own home for as long as otherwise would be possible.

It is frequently the case that a home help is the sole regular support for an 80-year-old living alone and she will provide the vital link with daily living, encouraging the client to shop and eat wisely, giving reminders to order coal and guarding against the risk of hypothermia.

It is increasingly being recognised that in these circumstances the helper becomes the 'eyes and ears' of the social services, alerting the social work team to the need for any further action. It is not surprising in this role of caring that bonds of real affection are frequently formed between helper and client and that they come to regard each other as 'family'.

Earlier discharge from hospital means patient/clients are arriving home in a most noticeably more incapacitated condition than previously. The discharge from hospital at short notice or without prior warning to the domiciliary services makes it difficult to plan help to the best advantage. The inclusion since April 1974 of the Medical Social worker to the social work team is seen as a welcome addition to the communication link.

It is unlikely in the present national financial climate that additional money will be forthcoming greatly to increase the support services. It therefore becomes even more essential to use all available resources to the best possible advantage of the client. To this end, it is imperative that good communications are established and maintained to ensure maximum utilisation of available resources.

13

GENERAL CONCLUSIONS

The care of the elderly, covering over seven million people, is a major social problem. Subject to certain improvements the expectation of life will be maintained and there is every evidence to show that the number of old people is likely to increase. This problem must therefore continue into the foreseeable future and it will not solve itself; only a combined effort by a great number of people can bring about a solution.

From what has been said it can be seen that, apart from the pensioners themselves, who are personally concerned, an immense number of people holding executive positions should have a clear understanding of the problem and its various implications and ramifications. These people include politicians, members of parliament, newspaper journalists, administrative officers in the Ministry of Health and throughout the regions, hospital management committees, Department of Health and Social Security, the planners in the Ministry of Social Security, and, among the local authorities, those in administrative positions dealing with health, welfare and housing. Then there are also the large number of people doing voluntary work as well as the nurses, doctors, home helps, health visitors, social workers and so on, who deal with the elderly more personally. On the fringe of the problem there are trade union leaders and employers, who should have some understanding of how their struggle for higher wages and higher profits affects elderly people on fixed incomes.

Above all, it is the doctor who is at close quarters with the situation who is better able to understand the urgency of the matter and the extensive distress among the elderly. He in particular knows that the benefits of modern medicine are denied to the elderly because of the adverse home conditions, whereas those operating at a distance in offices and committees, and dealing only with reports, minutes, books and figures, are unlikely to feel the urgency of the situation. For the above reasons, it may well be that the impetus for improvement and social reform must come from the doctors, and if this is lacking, changes will only take place at a snail's pace.

This book takes a bird's-eye view of the problem and outlines the relationship of various factors concerned. For this reason, mention has been made of pensions, social security, health service, geriatric units, old-age clubs, domestic helps, welfare homes, ambulances and so on. Particular mention has been made of the medical problems of the elderly, since it is felt that the medical profession should be alerted to the need for a special medical approach to their care. In the first instance, the book aims to enlighten doctors, not only on these special medical problems, but also on the wider aspects of the care of the elderly in general. The medical section has been written in simple, non-technical language, so that the lay public, who perhaps are more interested and more involved in the social aspects of the problem, may nevertheless appreciate the close link between social conditions and illness in the elderly.

It should be remembered that for every thousand elderly persons the national government supplies ten geriatric beds and perhaps five beds in a mental hospital whilst the local government provides twenty beds in a welfare home. Thus the total institutional care only amounts to thirty-five places per thousand people. Though this is a vital and valuable provision it really does little for the 965 persons living in the community and thus cannot be considered other than a very minor part in the care of the elderly. Even if this provision were doubled it would not make all that much of an impact. Those working in the institutional care of the aged are fairly well aware of its limitations. Yet they are exhorted to make a greater effort by a series of memoranda giving all kinds of advice, much of which is impracticable from the very beginning. Usually the 'planners'' advice contains recurrent platitudinous remarks about greater co-ordination, integration, liaison, participation, forward planning and the like and apparently over the last twenty years to little avail.

The phrase that 'the best place for old people to live and be cared for is in their own homes' is also frequently repeated from time to time without any actual enlightenment as to what homes – there being thousands of almost uninhabitable houses for the elderly – or what type of care which in thousands of instances is actually none at all. It is very nice to return a patient from hospital to 'community care' but of a truth so often this is a meaningless phrase since the patient returns to a dilapidated house with insufficient heating; no home help is available and the patient has to fend for herself.

EUTHANASIA

There is much talk about euthanasia nowadays, the idea being that a person could die comfortably and not suffer from a terminal illness, or that a person could opt to be put peacefully to death if he or she so wished it. The boon of euthanasia apparently is something on offer to old people, not really for children or young people. If an old person had proper regard for the welfare of society and state the jolly decent thing to do would be to put in for euthanasia when he began to draw his old-age pension; undoubtedly this would practically solve all the problems of old age. Elderly people suffer from many tribulations, poverty, ill health, bereavement, loneliness and so on and it is not uncommon that they have periods of depression when they make such statements as 'I wish I could go to sleep and not wake up' or 'there is nothing more in life for me' or 'can't I be put to sleep'. If one took these remarks too seriously euthanasia could be going full blast, but the truth is that most of these people given comfort, attention and company come out of their depression and are just as keen to go on living as anyone else. Unfortunately there are a small number of elderly people who when they become ill or abandoned by their relatives make no effort to go on living and refuse food and drink, become withdrawn and virtually bring about their own death. Of course if death is seen to be inevitable in a short period of time from an incurable illness there is certainly no point in prolonging any suffering, so that the doctor must keep in mind the welfare of his patient and relieve unnecessary suffering. Some patients have an illness where there is a faint chance of recovery but only if he submits to hazardous medical or surgical treatment which can also cause a good deal of pain. The faint chance is at times successful, though it is always in a minority of cases – persons well over 90 have undergone serious operations with success. On the other hand numerous old people submit to hazardous medical or surgical treatment with no real success and often their lives are shortened in the process. Should this be considered as some form of euthanasia and how far should it go? The author feels there is a great need to alleviate suffering in old age but does not think legalised euthanasia is in any way appropriate.

Since the vast number of old people still live at home though helped by a pension and provision of a general practitioner, a home help or home nurse, the latter does not satisfy the claim by the state that people will be looked after from 'the cradle to the grave' or 'womb to tomb', and the idea that the state could ever look after millions of old people is really a vain ideological boast. For past centuries old people have had to care for themselves as best they could with such help as was given by relatives and neighbours. The position is very much the same today, except they now form an easily identifiable class of impoverished people of a previous generation.

Where the state does take on some responsibility there is naturally a need to work to some plan and planners are present in abundance. Yet after some twenty years of planning and promoting various schemes for caring for old people in a very rich and enlightened country, old people to the extent of almost a million are still in a state of poverty and near neglect. Anyone who thinks he has a blueprint which if followed precisely will solve the problem of caring for seven million elderly people must be foolish, conceited, arrogant or all of these things. One does not exactly blame the plans, it's rather that the planners have a wrong assessment of human needs. For instance the number of elderly women outnumber the men two or three to one because men die at an earlier age. Can this be corrected? Otherwise there is a great need to combat loneliness for elderly women. Further laying down of national criteria for the provision of institutional beds and services for the population if rigidly adhered to will not take account of local differences. Thus an inland town may have only 11% elderly people and a coastal town 25% and the same national plan is applied as if the problems were similar.

Since most old people are going to live at home the author is of the opinion that in the first instance they should try to make themselves as independent as possible. This they can do with an adequate pension, suitable housing and moderate health. It is therefore most important to maintain good health in old age, and prevent the onset of infirmity. Much more can be done in this respect by attention to a proper well balanced diet, reasonable exercise, keeping up interests, avoiding withdrawal from society into a state of loneliness, with all its accompanying physical ailments. This maintenance of health can be encouraged by the general practitioner (the health visitor who up to the present has not given full attention to the elderly person), by the home nurse and by voluntary bodies with their numerous clubs. An even more helpful measure to maintain the health of old people is the provision of hospital geriatric day centres, and clinics where they can have health check-ups, meet friends and have courses of physiotherapy, occupational therapy, and proper attention to their diet and general health.

Finally there is the general attitude of society towards the elderly and the responsibility of relatives and neighbours to be considered. Present day society as in so many western countries is generally focused on the young, their upbringing, education, further education, employment opportunities and recreational needs. The culture is practically geared to the needs of the young. Each generation spends a good deal of its time and energy in preparing the way for the next generation, not concerning itself overmuch with the previous generation. This appears to be the natural law of nature and is likely to continue for the maintenance of any nation. However, in turn the young generation in time becomes the previous generation and it is only sensible that life should be viewed as a whole. Religion at one time kept things in proper balance and perspective and it does seem necessary to develop a more wholesome way of life suitable for citizens of all ages and without a generation gap.

INDEX

For Product Safety Concerns and Information please contact our EU
representative GPSR@taylorandfrancis.com
Taylor & Francis Verlag GmbH, Kaufingerstraße 24, 80331 München, Germany

www.ingramcontent.com/pod-product-compliance
Lightning Source LLC
Chambersburg PA
CBHW070554270326
41926CB00013B/2311